教育部财政部首批特色专业建设项目资助
热带园艺专业特色教材系列

热带园艺专业英语

李绍鹏　陈艳丽　主编

中国建筑工业出版社

图书在版编目（CIP）数据

热带园艺专业英语/李绍鹏等主编. —北京：中国建筑工业出版社，2012.12
（热带园艺专业特色教材系列）
ISBN 978-7-112-15002-1

Ⅰ.①热… Ⅱ.①李… Ⅲ.①热带-园艺-英语-高等学校-教材 Ⅳ.①H31

中国版本图书馆 CIP 数据核字（2012）第 299849 号

责任编辑：郑淮兵 杜一鸣
责任设计：董建平
责任校对：姜小莲 王雪竹

热带园艺专业特色教材系列
热带园艺专业英语
李绍鹏 陈艳丽 主编

*

中国建筑工业出版社出版、发行（北京西郊百万庄）
各地新华书店、建筑书店经销
北京科地亚盟排版公司制版
北京同文印刷有限责任公司印刷

*

开本：787×1092 毫米 1/16 印张：18½ 字数：450 千字
2013 年 3 月第一版 2013 年 3 月第一次印刷
定价：39.00 元
ISBN 978-7-112-15002-1
（23072）

版权所有 翻印必究
如有印装质量问题，可寄本社退换
（邮政编码 100037）

本书编委会

主编：李绍鹏　陈艳丽
参编：李绍鹏（海南大学）
　　　陈艳丽（海南大学）
　　　姜成东（海南大学）
　　　冯素萍（琼州学院）
　　　李茂富（海南大学）
　　　王　旭（海南大学）
　　　刘　建（海南大学）

前 言
Foreword

"园艺专业英语"课程是很多高校园艺专业本科生和硕士生的必修课程。一般是在学生经过两年的基础英语学习，掌握一定程度英语语言知识和专业技能的基础上，再进行专业英语方面的训练，目的在于让学生深入了解专业英语文体特征和专业英语文献阅读方法，培养学生专业英语学习能力和英文科研论文的写作能力。国内目前有关园艺专业英语的正式教材较少，而且主要是针对温带园艺而编，有关热带亚热带特色的园艺专业英语教程，目前国内尚无这方面的教材出版。为此我们特组织主讲专业英语课程的老师编写了这本《热带园艺专业英语》，以期为热带园艺专业英语教学提供适宜教材。

本教材分三部分组成：正文、阅读材料和练习题。正文及阅读材料主要摘选自园艺专业的原版欧美教材、书籍、杂志、国际会议论文以及从网站下载的材料等，内容涵盖了园艺学的基础知识（总论），以及热带果树、热带蔬菜、热带花卉及设施园艺、无土栽培等方面的技术和研究动态（各论），并在最后一篇课文里详细介绍了如何撰写英文科研论文。每课正文为精读内容，阅读材料为泛读内容，用于扩大学生的专业词汇和知识面。教材内容按照从基础到应用，从总论到各论的递进式安排，使学生在掌握园艺专业英语词汇、语言特点的同时，系统地了解和学习热带园艺的一些发展和研究动向，并能够熟悉科研论文的写作方法。部分课文配有插图和表格，力求将知识性和趣味性相结合，便于学生理解，提高其学习兴趣。为巩固学习，我们在每篇课文后面都根据该课学习内容设计了一定的练习题，便于学生对课文理解和掌握。此外，在本教材的附录部分里，我们将本教材的词汇整理成总词汇表，并制作了热带园艺作物名录，以便师生查阅。

本书的编写分工：第1、5、14、15、18课由李绍鹏编写；第2、3、4、6、11、24、26、29课由陈艳丽编写；第9、12、16、22、23课由李茂富编写，第10、13、19、20、25课由王旭编写；第7、8、17、21课由姜成东编写；第27、28课由刘建编写；第30课由冯素萍编写，全书的附录部分（热带亚热带园艺作物名录与专业英语词汇表）由冯素萍和陈艳丽整理编校，全书由李绍鹏、陈艳丽统稿。

本书承蒙宋希强教授审稿，在此谨表谢意。由于编者水平有限，书中难免有疏漏不妥之处，希望读者多提宝贵意见，以便再版时修订。

李绍鹏　陈艳丽
2010.12

Contents

Lesson 1 1
    Part A   Introduction and Commercial Branches of Horticulture 1
    Part B   Basic Botanical Background of Horticulture Crop 7

Lesson 2 13
    Part A   Horticulture Plant Classification 13
    Part B   How plants are named 18

Lesson 3 23
    Part A   Environments of the Tropics 23
    Part B   Cultural Requirements of Plants 28

Lesson 4 32
    Part A   The Tropics Soils and Fields Management 32
    Part B   Plant-growing Media and Soil Properties 37

Lesson 5 41
    Part A   Physical Control of Growth 41
    Part B   Chemical Control of Growth 45

Lesson 6 48
    Part A   Mechanisms of Plant Sexual Propagation 48
    Part B   Asexual Propagation 52

Lesson 7 57
    Part A   Plant Tissue Culture 57
    Part B   Tissue Culture in the Banana Industry 60

Lesson 8 64
    Part A   Genetic Engineering and Tropical Horticultural Industry 64
    Part B   Mango Cultivar Improvement and Genetic Engineering 69

Lesson 9 73
    Part A   Seed Production for Horticulture Crops 73
    Part B   Seed Treatment for Disease Control 78

Lesson 10 81
    Part A   Plant Pathogens in Horticulture Crops 81
    Part B   A Greenhouse Without Pesticides: Fact or Fantasy? 85

Lesson 11 89
    Part A   Handling and Storage before Marketing 89

Part B	Marketing of Fruits and Vegetables	94
Lesson 12		97
Part A	Horticulture and the Home	97
Part B	House Plants	101
Lesson 13		106
Part A	Organic Farming——Agriculture with a Future	106
Part B	Organic Gardening	110
Lesson 14		112
Part A	Subtropical and Tropical Fruits	112
Part B	Constraints of Lychee Development in China	117
Lesson 15		121
Part A	Flowers and Fruit Setting of Evergreen Fruits	121
Part B	Fruits of Evergreen Tree	126
Lesson 16		130
Part A	Physiology in Evergreen Fruit Tree——Building Materials, Photosynthesis and Respiration	130
Part B	Freezing Injury in Evergreen Orchard	136
Lesson 17		141
Part A	Postharvest Physiology of Tropical Fruit	141
Part B	Harvesting and Postharvest Handling of Tropical and Subtropical Fruits	144
Lesson 18		150
Part A	Getting the Orchard Established for Macadamia	150
Part B	Managing Young Trees of Macadamia	156
Lesson 19		159
Part A	Olericulture	159
Part B	Tomato	162
Lesson 20		165
Part A	Cucurbits or Vine Crops	165
Part B	Muskmelon	168
Lesson 21		171
Part A	The Type of Tropical Flowers	171
Part B	Tropical Orchids and its Adaption to Tropical Climate	174
Lesson 22		178
Part A	Foliage Plants and Bedding Plants	178
Part B	Cut Flowers	181
Lesson 23		186
Part A	Floral Arrangement	186

  Part B Bonsai ··· 190
Lesson 24 ·· 194
  Part A Elements of Landscape Design ······································· 194
  Part B Goals and Principles of Landscaping ······························· 198
Lesson 25 ·· 203
  Part A Establish New Lawns ·· 203
  Part B Maintaining the Lawn ··· 206
Lesson 26 ·· 209
  Part A Types of Greenhouses and Characteristics of Greenhouse-Related
      Equipment and Covering Materials ································ 209
  Part B Innovative Plant Factories ··· 214
Lesson 27 ·· 217
  Part A Greenhouse Construction ·· 217
  Part B Greenhouse Design ··· 221
Lesson 28 ·· 225
  Part A Environmental Control of Protected Cultivation ················· 225
  Part B Cooling Greenhouse ·· 229
Lesson 29 ·· 234
  Part A Hydroponics ·· 234
  Part B Type and Management of Nutrient Solution ······················ 239
Lesson 30 ·· 245
  Part A Writing a Research Paper ·· 245
  Part B Common Errors in Student Research Papers ······················ 250
References ·· 255
Appendix Ⅰ List of Subtropical and Tropical Fruit Tree Species in Chinese,
       Latin and English ··· 258
Appendix Ⅱ List of Subtropical and Tropical Vegetable Species in Chinese,
       Latin and English ··· 263
Appendix Ⅲ List of Subtropical and Tropical Flower Species in Chinese,
       Latin and English ··· 268
Appendix Ⅳ **Glossary** ·· 272

Lesson 1

Part A Introduction and Commercial Branches of Horticulture

Selected and rewritten from *Horticulture*, by R. Gordon Halface & John A. Barden Mcgraw.

Horticulture is the intensive cultivation of plants. The term *horticulture* in English to refer to the science and art of growing fruits, vegetables, flowers, and ornamental plants.

Horticulture encompasses all life—especially humanity—and bridges the gap between science, art, and human beings. A horticulturist cannot simply deal with plants as a science or as an art but must study plants as food for people and as an aesthetic and functional part of the environment. Human beings survive through horticultural foods and through the landscape. In a sense a horticulturist touches the beauty, perfection, and serenity of nature and all its boundless moods and temperaments. All this is accomplished with the final and total effect of helping mankind survive in a beautiful world.

Agriculture and Horticulture in the New World

Agriculture always has played and always will play a great role in the history and development of any given country. Early civilizations referred to agriculture as the cultivation of field crops. *Agri* is Latin for "field", the word "agriculture" in its earliest connotations was used exclusively for the cultivation of a field. The present view of agriculture includes the production of both plants and animals. Horticulture is only one part of the broad field of agriculture.

For thousands of years vegetable gardens and fruit trees have been planted and cultivated to provide the family with its horticultural needs. Commercial horticulture, on the other hand, is a more recent innovation. Horticulture departments in all landgrant universities have provided programs in teaching, research, and extension services to supply the needed information for the growing horticultural industry. Through scientific research the horticultural industry has expanded to meet the ever-increasing demand for its products.

Horticulture in Relation to Other Disciplines

Horticulture is related to many other disciplines. Horticulture includes landscaping and the production, storage, and marketing of fruits, vegetables, floricultural products and nursery crops. Agronomy encompasses the production of grains, fibers and other field crops as well as soil science. Forestry includes forest management and wood production and utilization. All are applied sciences in the field of agriculture, and all are interrelated. Botany and its various branches, including plant physiology, are pure sciences dealing with the fundamental principles of plant life. Horticulturists, agronomists, and foresters generally apply these fundamental principles to the production and utilization of plants. They generate, assimilate, and disseminate information about solutions to the problems encountered in the industry. The field of horticulture relies on many other disciplines including chemistry, physics, botany, engineering, architecture, plant pathology, bacteriology, geology, meteorology, economics, entomology, genetics, and ecology. It is the incorporation of various aspects of each which makes horticulture such a diverse and exciting career. A complete understanding of horticultural problems involves research in several of the basic and applied sciences.

Commercial Branches of Horticulture

There are five basic branches of horticulture today. Probably the oldest of these is *pomology*, fruit production. Other areas are *olericulture*, vegetable production; *floriculture*, flower production; *nursery culture*, nursery crop production; and *landscape design*, landscaping. These divisions can be broken down into different commercial branches such as the production and marketing of seed, nursery stocks, specialty and greenhouse crops, and pharmaceutical crops; market gardening; private gardening; operation of trial grounds; arboriculture; education; turf production and management; landscape design; advertising; photography; special promotions; processing and storage; and operation of support industries, such as the manufacture, sale, and service of equipment, machinery, growing structures, and pesticides and other chemicals.

Pomology The study of fruit production is called *pomology*, workers in the field are called *pomologists*. The horticulturist defines a fruit as expanded and ripened ovary with attached and subtending reproductive structures. Generally a fruit is considered to be the edible fleshy portion of a woody herbaceous or perennial plant whose development is closely associated with the flower. In some cases the ovary may be only a small portion of the fruits.

Fruit crops include the deciduous tree fruits which are divided into pome fruits (pear, apple, and quince) and drupe or stone fruits (peach, cherry, plum, apricot, and almond); the small fruits (blueberry, blackberry, raspberry, grape, strawberry currant, gooseberry, and cranberry); the nut tree fruits (pecan, filbert, walnut, chestnut, and macadamia nut); and the evergreen or tropical fruits (lemon, orange, tangerine, lime, and grapefruit as well as banana, mango, date, avocado, pineapples, and papaya).

Olericulture The study of vegetable production is called *olericulture*, workers in the field are called *olericulturists*. A vegetable is the edible portion of an herbaceous garden plant. There is no clear-cut delination between fruits and vegetables, however, some crops such as tomatoes and melons, are classed as vegetable crops but are valued horticulturally for their production of fruits. Other vegetable crops—such as lettuce, celery, potatoes, and carrots—are valued for their edible leaf, stem or root organs instead of their fruits.

Vegetables are used either fresh or processed. Onions, tomatoes and potatoes enter world trade in the unprocessed form, but most vegetables must be processed before shipment because of their bulk or perishable nature. Fresh vegetables therefore, do not enter world trade as extensively as some of the fruit crops. Vegetable production is classified as either market garden or truck crop. *Market gardening* refers to the growing of an assortment of vegetables for local or roadside markets and *truck crop* production refers to large-scale production of a limited number of crops for wholesale markets and shipping.

Floriculture The study of growing, marketing and arranging flowers and foliage plants is called *floriculture*, workers in the field are called *floriculturists*. Flowers and other ornamental plants have always played an important part in our lives. They have been used for generations to express joy or sympathy. Today flowers encompass every social function, being extensively used in arrangements, in corsages, and as pot plants.

Floricultural plants are classified as cut flowers, flowering pot plants, foliage plants, and bedding plants. Cut-flower production has dominated the floral industry. Roses, carnations, chrysanthemums, snapdragons, and orchids are grown for cut flowers predominantly in the greenhouse, whereas most gladioli, chrysanthemums, and straw flowers are grown outdoors during the summer or in suitable mild climates.

Flowering pot plants are sold as whole plants in bloom. These include the Easter lilies, poinsettias, cyclamens, geraniums, begonias, and hydrangeas. Foliage plants are no flowering plants grown in greenhouses or produced outside. Examples are philodendrons, ferns, and palms.

Nursery culture In the United States the production of fruit crops led to the development of the nursery industry. Although many nurseries do produce fruit trees, the great majority of the nursery business today is developed to production of perennial ornamentals. A person who produces or distributes ornamental plants is called a *nursery grower*. A person who does research, teaching, or extension in this area is called an *ornamental horticulturist*.

The nursery trade involves the propagation, growing, and maintenance of young trees and shrubs and herbaceous annuals, biennials, and perennials other than bedding plants. The production of young fruit trees, some perennial vegetables (asparagus, rhubarb, and chives) and small fruit plants is an important part of this industry. Another important area in the production of young ornamental plants is turf for landscaping public and private buildings and residences, roadsides, and parks. The nursery industry also produces evergreen trees for use as Christmas trees.

Landscape design Landscape design is the profession concerned with the planning and planting of outdoor space to secure the most desirable relationship between land forms, structures, and plants to best meet man's needs for function and beauty. It is part of horticulture because the essence of the landscape is living plant material. A person who is a landscape designer sells landscape design plans—which include general plans, construction plans, planting plans and specifications—but does not sell plants.

Landscape is not decorating the environment by planting trees and shrubs, it is the aesthetic and functional development of space. Plants and construction materials are used to enhance the site not to detract from it. Landscape maintenance should be considered with the design or the end result will be a breakdown in the desired environmental impact.

A landscape design encompasses the entire area, not only the garden area, the house, the utility, the comfort, and the aesthetic effect should all be considered in landscape design. The desires and space needs of the homeowner and family, coupled with their likes and dislikes, must be analyzed before a design is begun.

The landscape designer is educated in art and science related to landscaping. He or she must be competent in many engineering and architectural process and techniques, and needs sensitivity in order to analyze the environment so that a work of art rather than a hodgepodge is created. Some landscapers try to decorate with their design, this detracts from the natural environment. The landscape designer should try to blend structures and personalities into the existing environment through good site planning and planting.

Glossary

1. horticulture   *n.* 园艺，园艺学
2. ornamental plant   观赏植物
3. landscape   *n.* 园林，景观
4. connotation   *n.* 内涵，含义
5. commercial horticulture   *n.* 商品园艺学，市场化园艺
6. floricultural product   *n.* 花卉园艺产品
7. nursery crop   *n.* 苗圃作物
8. agronomy   *n.* 农艺学，农学
9. forestry   *n.* 林业，林学，森林学
10. plant physiology   植物生理学
11. architecture   *n.* 建筑学，体系结构
12. plant pathology   植物病理学
13. bacteriology   *n.* 细菌学
14. meteorology   *n.* 气象学，气象
15. entomology   *n.* 昆虫学
16. genetic   *adj.* 遗传的，起源的
17. ecology   *n.* 生态学
18. olericulture   *n.* 蔬菜栽培学
19. floriculture   *n.* 花卉；花卉栽培
20. landscape design   景观设计，园林设计
21. pharmaceutical crop   药用植物

22. arboriculture *n.* 树木栽培学，树艺学
23. pesticide *n.* 农药，杀虫剂
24. pomology *n.* 果树学，果树栽培学
25. woody plant 木本植物；herbaceous plant 草本植物
26. perennial plant 多年生植物，宿根植物
27. deciduous tree 落叶树，落叶树种
28. pome fruit 仁果类水果，仁果，梨果
29. quince *n.* 榅桲，榅桲属
30. drupe *n.* 核果
31. stone fruit 核果类果树，核果类
32. cherry *n.* 樱桃
33. plum *n.* 李子
34. apricot *n.* 杏，杏树
35. almond *n.* 杏仁，扁桃树，巴旦杏树
36. blueberry *n.* 越橘，蓝莓
37. blackberry *n.* 黑莓
38. raspberry *n.* 树莓
39. grape *n.* 葡萄
40. strawberry *n.* 草莓
41. gooseberry *n.* 醋栗，醋栗树
42. cranberry *n.* 蔓越橘
43. pecan *n.* 美洲山核桃
44. filbert *n.* 榛，榛属
45. walnut *n.* 胡桃
46. chestnut *n.* 栗子
47. macadamia nut 澳洲坚果
48. evergreen plant 常绿植物
49. lemon *n.* 柠檬
50. tangerine *n.* 柑橘，橘子
51. lime *n.* 来檬
52. grapefruit *n.* 葡萄柚
53. date *n.* 椰枣，枣椰子
54. avocado *n.* 油梨
55. pineapple *n.* 菠萝
56. papaya *n.* 番木瓜
57. lettuce *n.* 生菜
58. celery *n.* 芹菜
59. carrot *n.* 胡萝卜
60. onion *n.* 洋葱

61. perishable *adj.* 易腐的
62. flower arrangement 插花
63. corsage *n.* 装饰的花束
64. cut flower 切花，鲜切花
65. flowering pot plant 盆栽观花植物
66. foliage plant 观叶植物
67. bedding plant 花坛植物
68. carnation *n.* 康乃馨，香石竹
69. chrysanthemum *n.* 菊花，菊
70. snapdragon *n.* 金鱼草，金鱼草属
71. gladioli *n.* 唐菖蒲，唐菖蒲属
72. straw flowers 麦秆菊，蜡菊，贝细工
73. Easter lily 复活节百合
74. poinsettia *n.* 一品红，猩猩木
75. cyclamen *n.* 仙客来，仙客来属
76. geranium *n.* 天竺葵，老鹳草属
77. begonia *n.* 秋海棠，秋海棠属
78. hydrangea *n.* 绣球花，绣球花属
79. philodendron *n.* 喜林芋，喜林芋属
80. ferns *n.* 蕨类植物，蕨类，真蕨纲
81. palm *n.* 棕榈树，棕榈科植物
82. perennial ornamental 多年生的观赏植物
83. propagation *n.* 繁殖；[物]传播
84. asparagus *n.* 芦笋，石刁柏
85. rhubarb *n.* 大黄，食用大黄
86. chive *n.* 细香葱

Exercises

A. Please answer the following questions in English.

1. Please define the ***horticulture***.
2. What is the relationship between agriculture and horticulture?
3. What are the relationships between horticulture and other disciplines?
4. How many commercial branches of horticulture are there in this text?
5. How to define ***pomology***, ***olericulture*** and ***floriculture***?

B. Please translate the following paragraph into Chinese.

All animals including human beings are dependent upon the process of photosynthesis, which takes place only in green plants. Photosynthesis transforms light energy into chemical energy which is necessary for life process in green plants. Since each progressive step in the food chain results in a reduction of energy available for transfer, much energy must be converted to satisfy the physiological needs and comfort desires of human population. To meet these demands, the farmers and gardeners of the world must understand the principles of crop growth in order to apply the most productive cultural practices to produce the highest possible yields of high-quality crops.

C. Please translate the following sentences into English.

1. 园艺业，即园艺生产产业，它包括蔬菜生产、果树生产、西瓜和甜瓜类生产、花卉和观赏树木生产、芳香与药用植物生产等。

2. 未来的中国大农业——农作业（粮棉油）、园艺业、畜牧业——是三个产业平分天下，园艺业的前景令人鼓舞。

Part B Basic Botanical Background of Horticulture Crop

Selected and rewritten from *Horticulture: A Basic Awareness*, by Robert F. Baudendistel.

All plant enthusiasts should have knowledge of the plant kingdom and the various terminologies associated with it. In this chapter, the parts of the plant will be covered, with special attention being paid to the functions of each.

The plant kingdom is separated into four major divisions:

1. *Thallophytes*. The simplest plant types are found in this division. They include the algae, bacteria, fungi, and lichens. Most lichens consist of an alga and a fungus living in harmony with each other.

2. *Bryophytes*. This division contains all the mosses and their relatives, the liverworts.

3. *Pteridophytes*. The ferns and their allies, the horsetails and club mosses, comprise this division.

4. *Spermatophytes*. This division comprises the largest number and the most complex of all the plants. They are referred to as the seed-bearing plants. The spermatophytes are further subdivided into the gymnosperms and the angiosperms.

The gymnosperms are characterized by being evergreen, cone-bearing plants. These include the pines, spruces, junipers, and firs. The angiosperms are known as the flowering plants. They, too, are further subdivided into monocotyledons and dicotyledons. Monocots have leaves that are narrow with parallel veins, and their flower parts occur in sets of three or multiples of three. Dicots are characterized by having two embryonic leaves, called cotyledons, and leaves that are broad with veins running at angles to the leaf's midrib. Their flower parts are arranged in sets of four or five.

Parts of the Plants

The Root There are five major functions associated with most plant roots. They are:

1. *Water and nutrient absorption*. This function is almost solely the responsibility of the minute root hairs. Without them, the uptake of water and nutrients would not be pos-

sible and plant death would result. This process is known as *osmosis*, or diffusion through a semi-permeable membrane. This occurs whenever there is a larger concentration of water and soluble nutrients in the soil than within the plant.

2. *Water conduction.* Once the water and nutrients enter the root hair, they are transported through the conducting tissues of the root and carried upwards through similar conducting tissues in the stem (xylem), eventually reaching their desired destination, the cells with the leaf or stem.

3. *Anchorage.* The larger roots are distributed throughout the soil area and serve to support the top growth and prevent the plant from being lifted out of the soil during periods of high winds.

4. *Storage of reserve food.* Any excess food produced by the cells in the leaves is conducted from the plant stem and may be stored in the roots for future growth.

5. *Propagation.* The roots of a few plants are used to produce new plants.

The Stem Plant stems are characterized by the production of buds, which give rise to new branches, leaves, and flowers. There are four major functions of plant stems. They are:

1. *Support.* Stems are necessary as support for branches, buds, and leaves.

2. *Conduction.* Plant stems are used to conduct the water and nutrients from the roots to the leaves and back again to the roots.

3. *Storage.* The stems, like the roots, are capable of storing the excess food produced by the process of photosynthesis.

4. *Propagation.* Both herbaceous (soft, nonwoody) and ligneous (woody) plant stems can be used to obtain new plants from stem cuttings.

A typical plant stem has a terminal bud and many lateral buds. These buds may be either flowering buds (large and fat) or vegetative buds (narrow and thin). All buds arise from a node, and the space between individual buds is knows as the internodes. Buds may be found opposite each other on the stem or alternate on the stem, giving rise to only one leaf or stem.

Certain plants have modified stems that may be found above ground, such as thorns, tendrils, and stolons or runners. Modified storage stems found below ground include bulbs, corms, rhizomes, and tubers.

The Leaf Plant leaves have three distinct parts, the main body is known as the *blade*, which is either *simple*—in one piece—or *compound*, where the leaf is divided into segments or divisions called leaflets. The petiole, or leaf stalk, is attached to the blade and to the leaf base at the other end. The base is that portion of the leaf which is attached to the plant stem.

The four primary functions of plant leaves are:

1. *Photosynthesis.* This is the unique process of leaves whereby they convert water and carbon dioxide in the presence of sunlight to food in the form of carbohydrates.

2. *Respiration*. This process involves the oxidation of the manufactured food to perform the vital life functions within the plant. This process is not unique only to leaves, since it is carried on by all living cells.

3. *Transpiration*. It is carried out and regulated by the openings in the leaves, known as *stomata*. Transpiration involves the release of excess water from the leaf's surface to the surrounding air.

4. *Propagation*. Plants having thick, fleshy leaves are usually propagated from leaf cuttings or from leaf petiole cuttings.

Plant leaves are most commonly used for identification and determination of an unknown plant. It is important for all horticulturalists to be familiar with the terminology used to separate one plant species from another.

Certain plants have modified leaves for specific purposes. They are used for:

1. *Protection*. Leaves become bud scales and are used to protect the tissue within the bud, like the willow.

2. *Food storage*. An example is the scale leaves of the onion.

3. *Water storage*. The fleshy leaves of the cacti and most succulents are able to store water.

4. *Trapping insects*. The Venus flytrap and other insectivorous plants have leaves capable of trapping insects.

The Flower The flower is divided into two separate types of organs, referred to as *accessory* and *essential*.

Accessory organs These are commonly called the *perianth*, and consist of:

1. The *calyx*, which is usually green in color and is composed of *sepals*, it is used to protect the interior flower parts.

2. The *corolla*, which is composed of *petals*. Their bright colors are used to attract the bees and insects needed for pollination and eventual seed formation. Terminology associated with the corolla includes the following:

1) *Regular*. All the petals are similar in size and shape, as in the rose.

2) *Irregular*. Some of the petals differ in size and appearance, as in the snapdragon.

3) *Apopetalous*. Each petal is separate from the other.

4) *Sympetalous*. All the petals of the flower are fused together.

Essential organs These are the flower parts necessary for the all-important pollination, and consist of:

1. The *stamens* or male parts. Each stamen consists of a filament or slender stalk which is topped by an *anther* or pollen sac. Within each anther are the *pollen grains*, which are liberated at just the right moment of time.

2. The *pistil* (carpel) or female parts. Each pistil consists of a *stigma* or tip, which receives the pollen grains. The *style* is that area of the pistil between the stigma and the ovary and consists of a slender stalk down which the pollen passes. The *ovary* is the basal

part of the pistil and may contain from one to many ovules or eggs, which after pollination develop into seeds.

The following terminology is used to describe and classify flowers:

1. *Perfect.* Flowers are designated as perfect when they contain both male and female organs.

2. *Imperfect.* Flowers in which either of the organs is missing are labeled as imperfect. When both the organs are found on the same plant, but in separate male and female flowers, as in the birch, they are called *monoecious*. Plants having male and female flowers on separate plants, like the Ginkgo, are labeled *dioecious*.

3. An *inferior ovary* is identified as one that appears to be united with the calyx.

4. A *superior ovary* appears above and free of the calyx.

Types of Flower Inflorescences The term *inflorescence* is used only to describe a cluster of flowers and is related to how the flowers are arranged on the stalk. Inflorescences are of two main kinds: In the *indeterminate* inflorescence, flower buds continue to form and open as the stem grows in length, and the outer or lower flowers are older than the inner or higher ones on the stalk. The *determinate* inflorescence is characterized by having the terminal bud form a flower and halting the growth of the flower stalk. Additional flowers that do develop would be found only on side branches below the terminal flower.

After fertilization or pollination, all the essential flower parts dry up except the ovary. It matures into a fruit or seed pod and the ovules (egg cells) become seeds. Fruits are separated into two types, *fleshy* and dry.

Fruits

Fleshy types

1. Pome: apple, pear
2. Drupe or stone fruit: cherry, plum, peach
3. Berry: grape, tomato
4. Gourd: cucumber, gourd
5. Aggregate (cluster of drupes): raspberry, blackberry
6. Multiple: fig

Dry types

These are divided into two types:

1. those that split open
    1) Legume: pea, bean
    2) Follicle: milkweed, larkspur
    3) Capsule or pod: poppy
2. Those that do not split open
    1) Achene: buttercup
    2) Grain: grasses, cereals

3) Samara: maple
4) Nut: oak, hickory

Glossary

1. terminology *n.* 术语，专用术语，术语学
2. thallophyte *n.* 原植体植物，叶状体植物，菌藻植物
3. algae *n.* 藻，藻类植物，水藻，海藻
4. bacteria *n.* 细菌
5. lichen *n.* 地衣，苔藓，青苔
6. fungus *n.* 真菌，霉菌
7. pteridophyte *n.* 蕨类植物，羊齿植物
8. gymnosperm *n.* 裸子植物，裸子植物门
9. angiosperm *n.* 被子植物
10. pine *n.* 松树，松属
11. spruce *n.* 云杉，云杉属植物
12. juniper *n.* 刺柏，刺柏属，杜松，杜松属
13. fir *n.* 枞，冷杉
14. monocotyledon 单子叶植物，单子叶；monocot crops 单子叶植物
15. dicotyledon 双子叶植物，双子叶
16. embryonic leaf 胚芽，胚叶
17. cotyledon *n.* 子叶，绒毛叶
18. midrib *n.* 中脉，中脊
19. osmosis *n.* 渗透，渗透性；osmosis pressure 渗透压
20. semi-permeable membrane 半透膜
21. water conduction 水分传导，水分输导，导水
22. xylem *n.* 木质部
23. anchorage *n.* 锚位，锚地，（砧木）固着土地，扎根，固定
24. ligneous *adj.* 木质的，木头的
25. thorn *n.* 带刺小灌木，荆棘
26. tendril *n.* 卷须，蔓，卷须状之物
27. stolon *n.* 生殖根，葡匐茎，葡匐菌丝，葡匐枝
28. bulb *n.* 鳞茎，球茎，种球；corm *n.* 球茎，球鳞盘；rhizome *n.* 根茎，根状茎，地下茎；tuber *n.* 块茎，块根
29. blade *n.* 叶片；leaflet *n.* 小叶；petiole *n.* 叶柄
30. photosynthesis *n.* 光合作用，光合速率
31. carbohydrate *n.* 碳水化合物，糖
32. respiration *n.* 呼吸，呼吸作用，呼吸强度
33. transpiration *n.* 蒸腾，蒸腾速率
34. stomata *n.* 气孔

35. insectivorous plant 食虫植物
36. perianth *n.* 花被；calyx *n.* 花萼；corolla *n.* 花冠；petal *n.* 花瓣
37. stamen *n.* 雄蕊；pistil *n.* 雌蕊
38. pollen grain 花粉粒
39. carpel *n.* [植]心皮
40. stigma *n.* 柱头
41. dioecious *adj.* 雌雄异株的；dioecism *n.* 雌雄异株
42. inflorescence *n.* 花序
43. pome *n.* 仁果，梨果；drupe *n.* 核果，核果类；berry *n.* 浆果
44. gourd *n.* 葫芦，瓜类
45. aggregate fruit 聚合果，聚心皮果，聚心皮果
46. multiple *adj.* 多数的，多重的，倍数的，倍的
47. legume *n.* 豆科，豆科植物
48. follicle *n.* 小囊，滤泡，卵泡
49. capsule *n.* 蒴果，孢蒴；achene *n.* 瘦果；samara *n.* 翅果，翼果

Questions

1. What are the main functions of the root and stem of the plant?
2. How many essential organs are there in the perfect flower?
3. How many types of fruits are there in this text?

Lesson 2

Part A Horticulture Plant Classification

Selected and rewritten from *Horticulture*, by R. Gordon Halface & John A. Barden Mcgraw.

The plant kingdom includes a wide diversity of plant types ranging in complexity from one-celled algae to large trees that often exceed 30 meters in height. Within this diverse plant kingdom, no two species are ever exactly alike. Some are very similar, and it is quite obvious from superficial observation that they are closely related. Others are so different from one another that few, if any, apparent bonds of relationship exist. Furthermore, these currently observed relationships among plants are not in a static condition because each of these plant groups is changing progressively with time through the process of evolution.

To understand and utilize the various plants, it is essential to arrange them in an orderly system of classification and give each of them a name, a name that refers to this one and only this one group of plants. As scientists, human beings need unity, shape, and direction in order to learn a subject. The science that includes classification, nomenclature, and identification of plants is plant *taxonomy*, the oldest branch of botany. Botanists have worked for centuries on the classification of plants; and while much has been accomplished, much remains to be done.

Classification Systems

Over the centuries, many different systems have been devised for classifying plants. They generally fall into one of three categories: artificial, natural, or phylogenetic. *Artificial systems* have been devised for convenience and are often based on arbitrary, variable, and superficial characteristics. The artificial system is based on the ultimate use of the plant being described. Agricultural plants are classified as to grain, fruit, or medicinal plants and ornamentals are classified into such groupings as herbs, greenhouse plants, foliage plants, garden perennials, shrubs, and trees. Since the artificial classifications serve chiefly for convenience in communication, they are used primarily as a nonscientific, practical system of identification rather than a system designed to indicate relationships among plants. This system uses convenient and readily observable characteristics of plants regardless of anatomic, morphologic, physiologic, genetic, or evolutionary relationships. But this classification system has so much overlap that other systems must be used for more ex-

13

acting descriptions. For instance, azalea plants are used as flowering shrubs in landscaping, but they are also considered as flowering pot plants under the classification of a greenhouse crop.

The *natural system* of classification attempts to show relationships among plants through the use of selected morphological structures. The thesis underlying this system is that morphologically similar plants are closely related. The system represents an effort to reflect the order that exists in nature by utilizing all available knowledge.

By classifying plants according to their evolution pedigree, a *phylogenetic system* reflects genetic relationships between and among plants and establishes their progenitors. The chief limitation of this system is the limited knowledge of earlier plant forms. Through the use of cytogenesis, paleobotany, anatomy, and biochemistry, along with other sciences, taxonomists increase their knowledge and understanding of plants. In so doing, taxonomists can better determine the intricate relationships and interactions that exist within the plant kingdom as it exists for the living plants of today.

As plants evolve, taxonomy must follow. Plants cross-breed and mutate to create new forms, and existing species become extinct because their niche in the environment disappears. Plants also change as their environment changes or as they are moved from one area to another.

The systems of organized classifications have gradually shifted from purely artificial systems to natural or phylogenetic systems. Early systems were artificial and were based on the growth habits of plants, these systems were supplemented by a broadly adopted system based on the numerical aspects and sexual parts of the plant. This was later replaced by systems which established the natural morphological relationships as the focal point. The most recent systems use phylogenetic relationships to establish classification.

Plant Classification Today

The system of plant classification used today blends features of the natural and artificial systems. The family and specific categories are generally classified largely by natural and phylogenetic methods. This results in a genus in which the species are similar in morphological features and are closely related genetically. Flowers and fruits are usually the basis for classification; but roots, leaves, and stems may also be used. Environmental variations do not affect the flower or fruit characteristics as much as they affect other parts. In addition, flowers have many distinct and discernible units. Phylogenetic studies establish the origins of each group of plants and its relationships to both its present-day relatives and also to those of long ago, including those that may now be very distantly related. In theory it should be possible to relate all present-day plants to that very first plant precursor which first began to photosynthesize.

Researchers continue to try establishing an even more exacting system of plant classification. Taxonomists use many methods to establish a logical classification system. Scientists realize that the ultimate classification system will never be devised because too many of the key pieces to the puzzles have become extinct. However, taxonomists continue to perfect the present system by delving into data on the relationships of individual plant groups. Studies of vascular and floral anatomy, embryology, and plant geography contribute precise knowledge needed for better classification. The more botanists learn about plants and the more they discover about natural relationships, the more changes will need to be made. All bases will be used in the future to develop as much as possible a classification system that will reflect the exact and true genetic-historical relationship among all plants within the plant kingdom. Among the area taxonomists use for containing data for studying these possibilities and classifying plants are:

1. *Morphological* Traditional taxonomists used morphological characteristics to classify plants into defined groups. They feel that the more similar two plants are in form and structure, the more closely related they are. In most cases, this is the only type of information available.

2. *Anatomical* The anatomical taxonomists study cell types of the vascular system to establish evolutionary patterns. For example, a plant that has long fiber cells is believed to be more advanced in evolution than one with short fiber cells. Much work is also now being done on pollen anatomy.

3. *Embryological* Embryological taxonomists use the morphology and anatomy of embryonic development to support classifications. Such characteristics as number and position of cells in embryo sacs or the placement of the micropyle are used as bases of comparison.

4. *Biochemical* Biochemical taxonomists use biological compounds such as sugars, amino acids, fats, oils, alkaloids, alcohols, terpenes, or phenols as additional characters to establish in which category a plant belongs. The basis for classification is that more complex compounds are believed to have evolved at only one time and in only one group of plants. Hybrids are classified by the presence of intermediate levels of the compounds which are present from both parental groups.

5. *Ecological* Ecosystematics in botany isolates the natural biotic units resulting from natural barriers such as oceans or high mountain range. These are used to establish classification on the basis of divergent evolution, chiefly below the special level. Present-day researchers look at small units of plants within the species level, theorize and prove theories of evolution at these levels, and then extrapolate to larger and larger units.

6. *Numerical* Numerical taxonomists take statistical data from divergent pieces of evidence, instead of only one or a few criteria, analyze them, and then classify the plants. They use the findings from all methods and present a composite analysis. Careful analysis has revealed that classification schemes arrived at numerically often correlate very closely with those arrived at by traditional means.

Common Classifications

Some horticultural groupings are based on length and season of growth (annual, biennial and perennial), form (tree or shrub), and use (fruits, vegetables, or ornamentals). Horticulturists use the botanical classification in conjunction with an artificial but convenient system they have developed. This system often groups plants that are vastly different, its chief justification is the convenience of classification based on actual usage in gardening.

As the name indicates, *annuals* complete their life cycle in one year or less. These plants germinate from seeds, produce vegetative growth, flowers, fruits, and seeds, and die within one growing season. Examples of annuals are marigold, pea, bean, corn, squash, pumpkin, ageratum, and garden cress.

Biennial plants ordinarily required two years or at least part of two growing seasons with a dormant period between growth stages to complete their life cycle. The first year is used for building up reserves to allow the plant to flower and produce seeds in the second year. Only vegetative growth is produced the first year, and the following spring or summer the plant produces flowers, fruits, and seeds, after which it dies. Examples of biennials are celery, sweet William, cabbage, carrot, and beet.

Perennials are plants which do not die after flowering but live from year to year. Perennials are further divided into herbaceous and woody perennials.

Herbaceous perennials have soft, succulent stems whose tops are killed back by frost in many temperate and colder climates, but the roots and crowns remain alive and send out top growth when favorable growing conditions return. Examples are rhubarb, asparagus, oriental poppy, chrysanthemum, and many cultivars of phlox.

Woody perennials contain woody fibers and are longer-lived and more durable. These perennials are classified according to form and habit of growth as trees, shrubs, or vines, although not all of them can be clearly classed in this manner. Trees are upright in growth, with stems or trunks forming the central axis or the main part of the framework. Shrubs do not have a central axis or predominant trunk but have a number of stems radiating from the root crown. The basic difference between shrubs and trees is form, not size. Vines have stems that are too slender and flexible to support their branches and leaves in an erect position. Therefore, vines must grow on the ground or climb support object, such as trees. Woody perennial plants are also classified into zones for hardiness.

Glossary

1. algae   *n.* 藻类，藻，藻类植物
2. taxonomy   *n.* 分类，分类学，分类法
3. botany   *n.* 植物学
4. botanist   *n.* 植物学家，植物工作者
5. phylogenetic system   亲缘系统，系统分类
6. herb   *n.* 草本，草本植物，药草
7. greenhouse plant   温室植物
8. foliage plant   观叶植物

9. garden perennial 多年生园艺植物
10. shrub *n.* 灌木，灌丛，灌木林，灌木丛
11. azalea plant 杜鹃花属植物
12. morphological *adj.* 形态学的
13. progenitor *n.* 祖，祖先
14. cytogenesis *n.* 细胞发生
15. paleobotany *n.* 古植物学
16. anatomy *n.* 解剖学，解剖
17. biochemistry *n.* 生物化学
18. taxonomist *n.* 分类学家
19. cross-breed 杂种，杂种的；hybrid *n. adj.* 杂交种，杂种的
20. precursor *n.* 前体，先质
21. vascular *n.* 导管
22. floral anatomy 花部解剖
23. embryology *n.* 胚胎学；embryological *adj.* 胚胎学的
24. anatomical *adj.* 结构上的，解剖学的，解剖的
25. vascular system 维管系统，维管系
26. pollen anatomy 花粉解剖学
27. embryo sac 胚囊
28. micropyle *n.* 珠孔
29. amino acid *n.* 氨基酸
30. alkaloid *n.* 生物碱
31. alcohols *n.* 醇类
32. terpene *n.* 萜烯，萜(烃)，松烯
33. phenol *n.* 苯酚，石碳酸
34. ecosystematic *adj.* 生态系统的；ecosystem *n.* 生态系统，生态区
35. divergent evolution 趋异进化，分裂演进
36. extrapolate *v.* 推断，推知，预测，推测
37. annual *adj.* 一年生的；*n.* 一年生植物
38. biennial *adj.* 二年生的；*n.* 二年生植物
39. perennial *adj.* 多年生的；*n.* 多年生植物
40. marigold *n.* 金盏花，万寿菊属
41. squash *n.* 南瓜
42. pumpkin *n.* 南瓜，西葫芦
43. ageratum *n.* 胜红蓟属(菊科)，藿香蓟
44. garden cress *n.* 葶菜属(十字花科)，独行菜，水芹
45. celery *n.* 芹属(伞形科)，芹菜，旱芹；西洋芹菜
46. sweet william ［植］美洲石竹，美人草，须苞石竹
47. cabbage *n.* 结球甘蓝，卷心菜；甘蓝

48. carrot   *n.* 胡萝卜，胡萝卜属
49. beet   *n.* 甜菜，甜菜属
50. woody perennials   木本多年生植物
51. herbaceous perennials   多年生草本植物
52. rhubarb   *n.* 大黄属(蓼科)，食用大黄
53. asparagus   天门冬属(百合科)，石刁柏，芦笋，龙须菜
54. oriental poppy   东方罂粟(庭院宿根花卉)
55. chrysanthemum   *n.* 菊花、菊、菊属
56. phlox   *n.* 草夹竹桃属植物，夹竹桃植物

Exercises

A. Please answer the following questions in English.
1. Please define the *natural classification system*.
2. Please define the *artificial classification system*.
3. What are the differences between the natural and artificial classification system?
4. What areas are used to classify the plants today?
5. How to classify the horticultural plants in common classifications?

B. Please translate the following paragraph into Chinese.

The information base for taxonomy is being continually increased by additional research. Plant taxonomists work to identify the different species of plants and to classify each plant to show its true relationship to all other plant life. Taxonomists strive to group plants on the basis of anatomic, morphologic, and physiologic, and genetic similarities and differences which are the expressions of the actual phylogenetic relationships. By analyzing these similarities and differences, a fairly orderly taxonomic system has been developed.

C. Please translate the following sentences into English.

1. 植物分类学是植物科学中的一门基础学科，植物学分类的目的在于确立"种"的概念和命名，建立自然分类系统。自然分类的理论基础是达尔文的生物进化论和自然选择学说，即按植物的亲缘关系和进化过程来分类。

2. 植物学分类的基本单位是"种"，是指生殖上相互隔离的繁殖群体，分类系统中唯一客观存在的最基本阶元；指物种间的生殖隔离和基因彼此不能交流，保证了物种的稳定性，使种与种可以区别。

Part B   How plants are named

Selected and rewritten from *Introductory Horticulture*, by H. Edward Reiley & Corroll L. Shry, Jr.

Most plants have more than one common name; some have several. For example, trout lily is also known as the tiger lily, adder's-tongue, dog's-tooth violet, and yellow snowdrop. The judas tree and redbud are the same tree, but are known by these different names in different parts of the United States. Common names can be confusing, since two totally different plants may have the same common name. The cowslip is one of these, in New York State, it is a marsh-loving, buttercup-like plant; in England, it is a primrose-like plant found on dry, grassy slopes. Both have yellow flowers; but, apart from their color, they have little else in common. Since common names can be so misleading, it is important that when plants from different areas are spoken of, the same name is used—to use common names when buying or selling could be disastrous.

The Binominal System of Naming Plants

The early scholars always wrote in Latin or Greek, so naturally, when they described plants or animals, they gave them scientific Latin or Latinized Greek names. However, this way of naming plants also caused problems; the names were often long and difficult. For example, *Nepeta floribus interrupte spicatis pedunculatis* was the name for catnip and *Dianthus floribus solitariis, squamis calycinis subovalis brevissimus, corollis crenatis* were the common name for carnation.

The famous Swedish botanist, Linnaeus, simplified the matter by developing the binomial (two-name) system for naming plants. This system is still used today. He gave all plants just two Latin names as their scientific name. For example, he renamed the catnip *Nepeta cataria*. The first name is known as the *generic name*, this is the plant's group name. All plants having the same generic name are said to belong to the same *genus*. All plants belonging to the same genus have similar characteristic and are more closely related to each other than they are to the members of any other genus. The second name is the *specific name* or special name. All plants with the same specific name belong to the same species. (The Latin word *species* means "kind".) It is difficult to define exactly what a species is, but we can say that plants of the same species have the same characteristics and will consistently produce plants of the same type. Today, species are often subdivided into varieties. One variety of a species resembles that of another variety, but there are always one or two differences that are consistent and inherited. For example, the peach tree is known as *Prunus persica*; the nectarine is *Prunus persica* var. *nectarina*.

The generic name is usually a noun and the species name is an adjective. Sometime, generic names are the names of early botanists; for example *Buddleja* was named in memory of Adam Buddle. Some common generic names include *Acer* (maple), *Chrysanthemum* (mum), *Dianthus* (pink), *Hibiscus* (mallow), *Mimulus* (monkey flower), *Sedum* (stonecrop), *Papaver* (poppy), *Pinus* (pine), and *Pelargonium* (geranium).

The species name, because it is an adjective, often gives important information about the plant. Sometime, it tells us the color of the plant. For example, *Betula lutea* is the yellow birch (*lutea* means "yellow"); Betula alba—the white birch (*alba* means "white"); *Quercus ruba*—the red oak; *Juglans nigra*—the black walnut. Sometimes, the species name tells us whether the plant is creeping or erect. For example, *Epigaea repens* is the scientific name for trailing arbutus.

Sometimes, the specific name gives geographical information about where a plant occurs naturally. For example, *Anemone Virginian* is the Virginia anemone; *Taxus canadensis* is the Canadian yew. *Macro* and *micro* are Greek words meaning "large" and "small". Therefore, a plant with the species name *macrocantha* could be expected to have large flowers, such as *Dianthus macrocanthus*—the large-flowered pink. Similarly, it would be expected that a plant with the species name *microphyllus* would have small leaves (*phyllis* means "leaf"); for example, *Philadelphus microphyllus* is the scientific name for the little-leaf mock orange.

When the meanings of the scientific names of plants are understood, the names are interesting and not difficult to learn. The easiest way to become familiar with them is to say them out loud; every time you transplant a seeding, dig a shrub or sow some seeds, say the Latin name. When scientific names are used the horticulturist is able to order plants from any part of the world, it is a universal language. The French, the Dutch, the Texan, and the New Englander all use the same Latin names. Where common names are often misleading, the scientific name never is. For example, people often confuse the red maple with the Japanese red maple. They are two completely different trees. The red maple (*Acer rubrum*) grows to be over 75 feet tall, it has green leaves in the summer and red foliage in the fall. The Japanese red maple (*Acer palmatum*), however, has red leaves throughout the year and does not grow above 25 feet tall.

Plant Families

Related genera (plural of *genus*) with similar flower structures are grouped together into major units known as *families*. For example, the rose family, known as Rosaceae, consists of several genera—*Prunus* (plum), *Fragaria* (strawberry), *Rubus* (bramble), and *Malus* (apple). All the members of each genus of the rose family have relatively simple flowers with separated petals. On the other hand, in the solanaceae, the potato family, the petals are fused or joined to form a corollatube. The Solanaceae includes the genera *Solanum* (potato), *Petunia*, and *Nicotiana* (tobacco). The Compositae (daisy family) is the largest of all the plant families. Members of the Compositae have two kinds of flowers packed together to form a single head or "flowers". The outer flowers (known as ray flowers) may have large or small petals. The inner flowers (disk flowers) always have small petals. The daisy family includes these genera. *Aster*, *Artemisia*, *Achillea* (yarrow), *Helianthus* (sunflower), *Chrysanthemum* (mum), *Senecio* (cineraria), *Calendula* (pot marigold), and many others. Other important families are the Cruciferae (cabbage family), Umbelliferae (carrot family or umbellifer family), Papaveraceae (poppy family), Liliaceae (lily family), and Graminae (grass family).

Expressing Scientific Names

Notice that when the Latin names of plants are printed, they are expressed in italics. This is because when names and phrases are written in a language other than our own, it is conventional to print them in italics or underline them if they are typewritten or hand written. Also, by convention, the generic name always begins with a capital letter; the species name with a small letter. Sometimes, when a number of species all belonging to the same genus is the subject, the generic name is abbreviated and the first letter is used. For example, to express several different types of oaks, the generic name for the oak (*Quercus*) is abbreviated to *Q*. The red oak may be expressed as *Q. rubra* and the pin oak as *Q. palustris*.

The Taxonomist

Scientists who identify and classify plants are known as *taxonomists*. An international set of rules has been drawn up to ensure that every different species has a different binomial name and that the scientific name assigned to that plant is the oldest binomial name ever used for that plant. This international set of rules is known as the *International Code of Botanical Nomenclature*.

Glossary

1. binominal system   二名制，两名制
2. carnation   *n.* 康乃馨
3. generic name   属名
4. genus   *n.* 种，类，属，种类
5. specific name   种名
6. *Buddleja*   *n.* 醉鱼草属，醉鱼草
7. *Acer*   *n.* 槭(树)属
8. *Dianthus*   *n.* 石竹，石竹属
9. *Hibiscus*   *n.* 木槿，木槿属，芙蓉花
10. *Mimulus*   *n.* 酸浆属，沟酸浆属植物
11. *Sedum*   *n.* 景天属植物，景天
12. *Papaver*   *n.* 罂粟，罂粟属
13. *Pinus*   *n.* 松属，松属植物
14. *Pelargonium*   *n.* 天竺葵属的植物，天竺葵，鼠掌老鹳草
15. *Philadelphus*   *n.* 山梅花属，山梅花
16. *Rosaceae*   *n.* 蔷薇科
17. *Prunus*   *n.* 李属
18. *Fragaria*   *n.* 草莓属
19. *Rubus*   *n.* 悬钩子属，悬钩子
20. *Malus*   *n.* 苹果属
21. *Solanaceae*   *n.* 茄科
22. *corollatube*   *n.* 冠筒，花冠筒；corollalobes   冠瓣
23. *Nicotiana*   *n.* 烟草，烟草属
24. *Compositae*   *n.* 菊科植物，菊科

25. *Aster*　　*n.*　紫菀属植物，紫菀；China aster　　翠菊
26. *Artemisia*　　*n.*　蒿属，艾属，蒿
27. *Achillea*　　*n.*　蓍属，蓍草属，蓍草类
28. *Helianthus*　　*n.*　向日葵，向日葵属
29. *Senecio*　　*n.*　千里光属，千里光，狗舌草，瓜叶菊，
30. *Calendula*　　*n.*　金盏菊属，金盏菊，金盏草
31. *Cruciferae*　　*n.*　十字花科，十字花科植物
32. *Umbelliferae*　　*n.*　伞形科，伞形花序植物
33. *Papaveraceae*　　*n.*　罂粟科，罂粟科植物
34. *Liliaceae*　　*n.*　百合科
35. *Graminae*　　*n.*　禾本科植物，禾本科
36. International Code of Botanical Nomenclature　　国际植物命名法规

Questions

1. What is the binomial system?
2. How to express scientific names of the plants?
3. How to name the plants according to the international rules?

Lesson 3

Part A Environments of the Tropics

Selected and rewritten from *Tropical Fruit*, by Henry Y. Nakasone and Robert E. Paull.

Climate is defined as the general temperature and atmospheric condition of an area, over an extended period of time. Atmospheric conditions include rainfall, humidity, sunshine, wind and other factors. Climates are subject to modification by various factors, such as latitude, elevation, cloudiness, whether the land mass is continental, coastal or oceanic, the direction of wind and ocean currents and the proximity to large bodies of water and mountain ranges.

The tropical region is a belt around the earth between the Tropic of Cancer at 23°30′ latitude north of the equator and the Tropic of Capricorn at 23°30′ latitude south of the equator. The Tropics of Cancer and Capricorn as boundaries are rather rigid and do not take into consideration the presence of areas that do not meet the various climatic characteristics generally established to describe the tropics. Some climatologists have extended the region to 30°N and S of the equator (Henderson-Sellers and Robinson, 1986); this increases the land mass in the tropics substantially, especially in Africa, China, South American and India, and would include approximately two-thirds of Australia.

Characteristics of the Tropics

The tropical zone is generally described as possessing the following characteristics:

1. It has an equable warm temperature throughout the year, and no cold season at lower elevations. The average annual temperature of the true tropics is generally greater than 25℃, with no month having an average less than 18℃. Others have described the tropics as areas with a mean temperature not lower than 21℃ and where the seasonal change in temperature equals or is less than the diurnal variation of temperature. The latter boundary is greatly influenced by continentality. Another boundary is the isotherm where the mean sea level temperature in the coldest months is not below 18℃; although it can include certain errors, these are relatively small on a world scale and reliable data which are available for its computation.

2. Rainfall is usually abundant, from seldom less than the semiarid 750mm to as high as 4300mm, indicating considerable variation. The heaviest rainfall occurs closest to the equator. Where rainfall is marginal for agriculture, its variability takes on great signifi-

cance.

3. Photoperiod varies little throughout the year at the equator, where day length is about 12h.

4. The position of the sun is more directly overhead, giving a year-round growing season.

5. Higher potential evapotranspiration is due to rainfall, temperature and solar radiation.

These characteristics describe the true tropics in and near the equator, with latitudinal changes towards the poles producing a variety of sub-climates. Even near the equator, mountain ranges and other geographical factors can produce various sub-climates. Since temperature, solar radiation and photoperiod are fairly constant in the tropics, the variety of sub-climates and vegetation is frequently dependent upon rainfall. A continuous succession of climates starts with long seasons of well-distributed precipitation and short dry seasons close to the wet tropics, and it gradually changes to short seasons of relatively low rainfall and long dry seasons as the latitude increases. Some seasonal variation in mean daily temperature becomes apparent, the temperatures are lowing with the increasing distance from equator.

Radiation Conditions

Day Length

The day length at the equator is about 12h. At low latitudes in the tropics, the increase in difference between the longest and shortest days is about 7 min per degree (Table 3-1), increasing to 28 min per degree at latitudes between 50° and 60°. The difference in photoperiod is associated with the earth being inclined on its axis by approximately 23°30′; hence the solar equator moves about 47° as the earth moves around the sun. The extremes are the Tropic of Cancer (23°30′N) and the Tropic of Capricorn (23°30′S); within this belt, the sun's rays are perpendicular at some time during the year. At the spring and autumn equinoxes, the lengths of the day and night are equal everywhere over the earth.

Day-length extremes in hours and minutes at various latitudes in the tropics and subtropics   Table 3-1

	Latitudes				
	0°	10°	20°	30°	40°
Longest day	12:07	12:35	13:13	13:56	14:51
Shortest day	12:07	12:25	10:47	10:04	9:09

Radiation

When compared with higher latitudes, the tropical latitudes have a smaller seasonal variation in solar radiation along with a higher intensity. The longer day length in summer at the higher latitudes means that these latitudes exceed the daily amounts of solar radiation received in the tropics. The highest annual energy input on the earth's surface of about 12MJ m^{-2} day^{-1} occurs in the more cloud-free subtropical dry belt at 20°~30° latitude. In the tropics, solar radiation received is reduced by clouds and water vapour in the air through reflection and absorption to a minimum of about 7 MJ m^{-2} day^{-1} at the equator. Over a large portion of the tropics, the average is 9 MJ m^{-2} day^{-1} ±20%.

Temperature

Near the earth's surface, temperature is controlled by incoming and outgoing radiation. Surface temperatures are modified spatially and temporally throughout the year by local factors more than radiation. The main modifying factors are continentality, the presence of large inland water bodies, elevation, topography and cloudiness. Highest diurnal temperatures occur in dry continental areas, at higher elevations and in cloud-free areas. The rate of decrease in temperature with elevation (lapse rate) varies with cloudiness (hence season) and the diurnal variation. The normal rate is about 5℃ per 1000m under cloudy conditions and can range from 3.1℃ to 9℃ per 1000m.

A human's perception of temperature is modified by the rate of evaporation. Evaporation from human skin is primarily influenced by humidity, wind speed and response to sunshine. A human can endure high temperatures if the humidity is low, but feels discomfortable in the tropics associated with high temperatures and humidity (>25℃ and >80% relative humidity (RH)). These conditions are also favourable for growth of microorganisms and insects. The problem of controlling plant diseases and insect pests in the tropics is compounded by the absence of a cold winter and aridity to limit their development. Field sanitation is crucial to disease and insect control.

Rainfall

Temperature determines agricultural activity in the temperate regions of the midlatitudes (30°~60°), while rainfall is the crucial factor in the tropics. The seasonal and diurnal distribution, intensity, duration and frequency of rainy days vary widely in the tropics both in the space and time. Maximum rainfall occurs near the equator, without dry season. Surrounding the equatorial zone in Africa and South America are areas with two rainy and two dry seasons alternating, rarely are the seasons of the same duration or intensity. Further from the equator is a region of minimum rainfall at 20°~30° latitude, associated with a subtropical high-pressure area, with one rainy season, frequently due to the monsoons. Topography can significantly modify the generalized rainfall pattern: examples include the western coast of India and Borneo and the coastal areas of Sierra Leone, where monsoonal winds are forced to rise because of mountain ranges. Trade winds can bring considerable rainfall and are subjected to the forced rise by topographical features. Other factors influencing rainfall include changing and slowing down of wind speed as it approaches the equator and continentality, such as in South-west and Central Asia. The above factors lead to complicated rainfall patterns with generalization possible when there are numerous variations.

Strong Winds, Frost and Hail

In the equatorial zone, strong winds are associated with localized thunderstorms (diameter <25 km) having greater intensity than those in the middle and upper latitudes and lasting from 1 to 2 h. Most occur outside the 0°~10° latitude zone and are convectional in origin, associated with intense solar heating; others are due to sea or land breezes and unstable warm and humid air associated with a land mass. Hail occurs rarely in the tropics, but it is known to damage tea in Kenya and tobacco in Zimbabwe.

Tropical cyclones (hurricanes, typhoons) are an almost circular storm system, ranging in diameter from 160 to 650 km, with winds from 120 to 250 km · h^{-1}, originating over water in the warm summer and early autumn season. Most develop within latitudes 20°N and S of the equatorial belt and may turn north-east in the northern hemisphere or south-west in the southern hemisphere to 30°~35° latitude. These systems bring violent winds and heavy rains. The Philippines is very prone to such systems. Crop damage, especially to trees, can be very severe, due to the high winds in vulnerable areas, making wind-breaks essential.

Monsoon depression is a less intense weather phenomenon. It brings 80% or more of the precipitation to the Indian subcontinent, with considerable year-to-year variation. It occurs when there is at least a 120° directional shift in prevailing wind direction between January and July. It is a characteristic of the seasonal wet and dry tropics and spreads from Asia to Africa. The intensity of rainfall can lead to considerable flooding.

In the subtropics, frost is a major limiting factor to tropical horticultural production. In isolated tropical high mountainous areas, frosts can occur frequently. Frost in the subtropics is associated with incursions of cold air masses (advection frost), while on tropical mountains it is mainly due to rapid cooling on clear nights (radiation frost).

Summary

Whereas temperature is the major limitation to plant growth in temperate areas, while in the tropics the rainfall plays that role. Year-round plant growth is generally only limited in the tropics by moisture availability. There is considerable variation in tropical climates, caused by altitude, continentality and the presence of large bodies of water. Disease and insect problems are more severely in high-rainfall warm tropics. Good soils are available in the tropics, and the high value of horticultural crops means that they can command the use of more favoured areas.

Glossary

1. atmospheric *adj.* 大气的，大气层(压)的，常压的
2. rainfall *n.* 降雨，降雨量
3. humidity *n.* 湿度
4. latitude *n.* 纬度
5. elevation *n.* 海拔，标高
6. cloudiness *n.* 云量，多云状态；(混)浊度
7. environment variable　环境变量
8. phenotype *n.* 表(现)型

9. isotherm　*n.* 等温线
10. photoperiod　*n.* 光（周）期
11. evapotranspiration　*n.* 蒸（散）发量，蒸发蒸腾（作用）
12. precipitation　*n.* 下雨，降水；降水量；降落，落下；沉淀（作用）
13. Tropic of Cancer　北回归线
14. Tropic of Capricorn　南回归线
15. perpendicular　*adj.* 垂直的，直立的；*n.* 垂线，垂直面
16. equinoxes　*n.* 二分点（春分点与秋分点）
17. solar radiation　太阳辐射，日射
18. cloud-free　*adj.* 无云的
19. reflection　*n.* 反射
20. topography　*n.* 地形（势），地形学，地形测量学；局部解剖学（图）
21. diurnal temperature　昼夜温度
22. perception　*n.* 知觉；［生理］感觉；看法
23. relative humidity　相对湿度
24. microorganism　*n.* 微生物
25. aridity　*n.* 干旱，干燥（旱）度；荒芜
26. sanitation　*n.* 环境卫生（卫生设备，下水道设备）
27. midlatitude　*n.* 中纬度
28. duration　*n.* 持续，持久
29. monsoon　*n.* 季风，季风期；monsoonal winds　季风
30. thunderstorm　*n.* 雷暴，雷暴雨（大雷雨）
31. hail　*n.* 雹，冰雹
32. Kenya　*n.* 肯尼亚
33. tobacco　*n.* 烟草；烟草属
34. Zimbabwe　*n.* 津巴布韦，津巴布韦人
35. cyclone　*n.* 旋风
36. hurricane　*n.* 飓风（12级以上大于 32.7m/s）
37. typhoon　*n.* 台风
38. Philippines　*n.* 菲律宾
39. windbreak　*n.* 防风林带，防风障
40. frost　*n.* 霜，雪面；*v.* 结霜，冰冻，冻坏，使（植物）受霜害

Exercises

A. Please answer the following questions in English.
1. Please list the characteristics of the tropics.
2. Please list some typical fruits and flowers which can be planted in tropics.
3. Please discuss the characteristics of the radiation and evaporation conditions in tropics.
4. How to lower the loss by strong wind, frost and hail in tropics and subtropics?

5. Please discuss the advantages and disadvantages of environments in tropics.

B. Please translate the following paragraph into Chinese.

Climate control cannot be seen as separate from the crop, for which one tries to create optimal conditions. The crop plays a double role: it changes its surroundings and it reacts to them. As a result of evaporation, photosynthesis and respiration, the crops influence the mass balances of CO_2 and water vapor pressure of the air, as well as the energy balance. In controlling the production process, a distinction can be made between slow and fast-reacting processes. Slow-reacting processes are, for example, leaf and flower development, morphogenesis, and dry matter accumulation and distribution. Fast-reacting processes include photosynthesis and transpiration. The production rate is determined primarily by crop photosynthesis. This is determined largely by the amount of photosynthetically active radiation (PAR), to a lesser extent by the CO_2 concentration.

C. Please translate the following sentences into English.

1. 海南岛属热带季风海洋性气候。基本特征为：四季不分明，夏无酷热，冬无严寒，气温年较差小，年平均气温高；干季、雨季明显，冬春干旱，夏秋多雨，多热带气旋；光、热、水资源丰富，风、旱、寒等气候灾害频繁。

2. 热带雨林气候终年高温多雨；热带沙漠气候终年高温少雨；热带季风气候雨季高温多雨，旱季高温少雨；热带草原气候湿季高温降雨丰富，草茂动物肥，干季高温少雨、草枯动物瘦。

Part B Cultural Requirements of Plants

Selected and rewritten from *Horticulture: A Basic Awareness*, by Robert F. Baudendistel.

Before they can grow plants well, the grower must have a complete understanding of its cultural requirements, which include:

1. The intensity and duration of light needed.
2. The method of watering and its frequency.
3. The most nearly ideal growing temperature.
4. The frequency and method of fertilization.
5. The preferred soil type and most desirable pH.

This rule applies to the homeowner, the nurseryman, the florist, and the truck farmer alike.

The cultural requirements for most plants are merely suggested guidelines to provide the grower with sufficient flexibility to insure proper plant growth. However, there are certain plants that have very specific growth or cultural requirements which must be adhered to before success is possible. Under natural conditions, the successful grower must accept the environmental conditions, but he must have the knowledge necessary to alter these conditions to guarantee ideal plant growth. For example, during periods of high light intensity, the grower should know when to shade and which plants must be shaded.

Light Requirement All green plants produce some of their food by the process of photosynthesis. This unique process involves a chemical reaction in which plant cells manufacture carbohydrates from carbon dioxide and water in the presence of light and the green plant pigment, known as chlorophyll. The leaves are noted for most of the carbohydrate production, but stems and buds are also capable of photosynthesis. This process is totally dependent upon the plant's receiving quantities of light. Many plants thrive in complete sunlight while others desire a partial or completely shaded environment. The grower must be aware of the best light environment for each plant grown and position the plants accordingly.

The plant symptoms associated with low light intensity are the following: leaf tips become discolored, leaves and buds drop, leaves and flowers become light in color, there is a lack of plant vigor, showing a decrease in growth, and the new growth appears stunted and weak.

The symptoms connected with too high light intensity are the plant wilts, and light-colored leaves may become gray in color.

Experimentation has shown that plants receiving continuous light of either high or low intensities become stunted and display a general lack of vigor when compared to plants given a normal light period followed by darkness.

Certain plants show a definite response to the length of their exposure to light. Knowledge of this response, known as *photoperiodism*, has enabled commercial growers to develop a program insuring production for a specific date or holiday. The poinsettia, popular Christmas potted plant, is known as a short day or long night plant, since it flowers naturally in December when the day length is short.

Watering Requirements Watering requirements varies with the type of plant, the texture of the soil, the time of year, and the growing temperature. During cloudy periods throughout the year, and during the winter months, light intensity, it is decreased, causing a decrease in growth. During these periods, plants require much less water. When transplanting any plant, whether it is a seedling or a mature tree, the addition of proper amounts of water helps to success.

The symptoms associated with underwatering are the following: crisp, brown leaf spots form, older leaves drop, leaf color becomes bleached, the plant wilts, flowers do not last and buds may drop, stems become weak and limp, suggesting a general lack of plant vigor, and the soil becomes dry and hard packed.

Overwatering may produce the following symptoms: leaves become curled and drop, leaf tips turn brown and die back, soft dark areas form on the leaf surface, new leaves grow soft and sometimes become discolored or even rotten, and the plant wilts because of root deterioration caused by a water-logged soil.

Temperature Requirements The growing temperature is another important consideration. Plants grown outdoors must be able to withstand wide fluctuations in temperature, while indoor plants are usually more specific in their temperature requirements. When the growing temperature is specified for a plant, it usually means the night temperature that will produce the best plant. These same plants are usually not affected by daytime temperatures 3~4.5℃ above specified night temperatures.

Humidity Requirements Most plants, with the exception of cacti and certain succulents, which are characterized by large, fleshy leaves capable of storing water, prefer a more humid atmosphere to the normal home provides. This condition can be corrected by positioning the plants near containers filled with water and away from drafts.

Symptoms associated with low humidity are injury to the leaf tip, wilting of the plant and new growth that appears weak and distorted.

Plants grown under high humidity conditions may exhibit the following symptoms: soft dark areas on the leaves, plus soft, mushy, rotted leaf and stem tissue.

Fertilization Requirements Since all growing plants require fertilization, it is important for the grower to know when to fertilize, how much to give each plant, and what is the best method of application.

Plants differ greatly in the quantities of fertilizer that they require, but all are similar in that they all must receive the same chemical elements. From the list of twelve elements known to be essential for proper plant growth, three are required in much larger amounts than the other nine and usually called the *macronutrients*. They are nitrogen (N), phosphorus (P), and potassium (K).

The remaining nine elements are needed by plants in every minute amounts and are, therefore, usually called *micronutrients*. They are calcium, sulfur, magnesium, iron, manganese, zinc, copper, boron, and molybdenum.

Fertilizer may be applied to the soil in a granular form or a liquid form; it becomes much more readily available to the plant than in the granular form, which must be first broken down into a soluble form. The advantage of the granular form is that it is much longer lasting than the liquid form. Fertilizer may also be sprayed directly on the leaves of certain plants. Some fertilizers are labelled as *organic*, being slowly released to the plants, and others as *inorganic* are characterized by being water soluble and giving a fast response; others on the market are a combination of both types.

Overfertilization causes crisp dark spots on the leaves, lack of flowers on flowering plants, wilting of the plant, and root injury.

The symptoms caused by underfertilization are dropping of the older leaves, lack of flowers on flowering plants, pale bleached leaves, lack of plant vigor with stunted growth, and leaf veins yellow in color.

Soil pH Receiving an ample supply of the essential chemical elements is not a guarantee that a plant's growth will be normal. The degree of acidity or alkalinity of soils greatly affects growing plants. Most plants thrive best in the pH range of 6, which is slightly acid or sour, to pH 7, which is neutral, being neither acid nor alkaline. The plants may be survival in an undesirable pH, but they usually grow abnormal.

Other Cultural Requirements Additional, cultural items that can not be overlooked by any grower are the spacing between of plants, disease and insect control, cultivation of the surrounding soil, the presence of agents responsible for pollution, and the pruning, shaping, or shearing demands of each plant.

Glossary

1. carbon dioxide 二氧化碳
2. chlorophyll *n.* 叶绿素
3. photoperiodism *n.* 光周期性，光周期现象
4. poinsettia *n.* 一品红，猩猩木
5. deterioration *n.* 恶化，降低，退化
6. water logged 浸透水的；半淹没的，沼泽化的
7. macronutrient *n.* 大量元素，常量营养元素
8. micronutrient *n.* 微量元素，微量营养元素
9. granular *adj.* 颗粒状的，由小粒而成的，粒状的
10. acidity *n.* 酸度，酸性
11. alkalinity *n.* 碱度，碱性

Questions

1. What are the cultural requirements for most temperate fruits?
2. What are the light and temperature requirements for most tropical fruits?
3. What are the water and fertilization requirements for most plants?

Lesson 4

Part A The Tropics Soils and Fields Management

Selected and rewritten from *Tropical Fruit*, by Henry Y. Nakasone and Robert E. Paull.

The Tropics Soils

Soils using the US classification system are separated into ten groups, based on parent material, soil age and the climatic and vegetative regime during formation. Tropical soils are diverse, having formed from different parent materials and climatic conditions. These soils have formed in areas where the soil temperature at 50 cm differs by less than 5°C between the warm and cool seasons. The parent rock materials are as different in the temperate zone as in the tropics, erosion and deposition are similar, and soil formation could have been from recent volcanic or alluvial flood plains to 1 million years old. The difference in temperate regions lies in soil-forming factors such as glaciations and movement of loess that have not occurred in the tropics.

The majority of tropical soils come under the US orders included Oxisols, Aridisols, Alfisols, Ultisols and Vertisols and these are spread widely throughout the tropics. The soil orders are separated on the presence or absence of diagnostic horizons or features that indicate the degree and kind of the dominant soil-forming process. It is very difficult to make generalizations about tropical soils other than that they have less silt than temperate soils and that surface erosion and deposition have been more significant. There are greater volcanic deposits in the tropics while the temperate region has a larger proportion of younger soils. Only a small proportion (2%~15%) of the tropics has so-called lateritic soils (Oxisols and Ultisols), defined as soils that have high sesquioxide content and harden on exposure. The red color of tropical soils does not mean that they have low organic matter.

The more intensively farmed, fertile soils of the tropics generally developed from alluvium and sediment and are high in calcium, magnesium and potassium. This gives them a high base status with no acidity problem. Phosphorus deficiency can be readily corrected. A large group of tropical soils (Oxisols, Ultisols and others) are low base status. Phosphorus deficiency can be significant as it is fixed by the iron and aluminum oxide in these soils, which also often have aluminum toxicity problems, with sulphur and micronutrients [zinc (Zn), boron (B), and molybdenum (Mo)] deficiencies. However, they have good physical properties. The high-base soils (Aridisols) in tropical deserts can be very productive with irrigation. Nitrogen deficiency and sometimes salinity can be problems.

Soil physical characteristics are of primary concerns for tropical-fruit production, with soil nutrients being secondary because they can normally be readily corrected. Soil texture and structure, soil-water storage and drainage are crucial. Deficiencies in these characteristics are major constraints to production because they are difficult and expensive to correct. Under natural conditions, most soils considered for fruit crops in the tropics have a good topsoil structure. This includes the highly weathered Oxisols and Ultisols. Loss of organic matter may lead to loss of structure and crusting of these soils after heavy rains. Some soils, however, do not favor root development, due to a dense subsoil layer, which needs to be broken during soil preparation to avoid shallow root systems. Heavy machinery may also cause the formation of a compact subsurface layer in medium-textured Oxisols with low iron and in fine-textured Oxisols. Low calcium and phosphorus and high aluminum contents in the subsoil can also restrict root growth.

Tropical fruit crops have shown a wide range of adaptability and have been observed to grow and produce well in a wide variety of soil types, provided other factors are favorable. In some cases, considerable management skill is required to maintain the crops in good growth and production. Soil pH can be corrected by liming during field preparation, with most trees preferring pH 5.5~6.5. Papaya is one of the few fruit crops that are adapted to a wide range of soil pH, growing and producing well in soil pH ranging from 5.0 to well into the alkaline range. Deficiencies in phosphorus associated with adsorption and excess aluminum need to be addressed in the Oxisols, Ultisols and some Inceptisols. Soil organic matter can be maintained by use of manure, ground-cover crops and mulches to preserve soil moisture and structure and improve the rhizosphere. Magnesium, zinc and boron deficiencies may also be encountered in some tropical soils, but these are relatively easy to correct in a management program. Saline and alkaline soils, along with deep peat soils, should be avoided for fruit production because of their difficult natures. Acid sulphate soils require specialized management strategies such as raised beds, to be productive.

A prime soil requirement for all crops is good drainage to prevent waterlogging, which leads to root diseases. Drainage is crucial for crops that are susceptible to *phytophthora* root rot, such as avocado, papaya, passion-fruit and pineapple. Mango and avocado have been observed to show branch dieback in parts of fields in western Mexico with a water-table around 50~60cm below the soil surface.

Nutrient Requirement and Fertilization

Plant tissue analysis is less influenced by site and situation than soil tests. Plant analysis data needs to be standardized to the plant part, its age at sampling, and the crop phenology and in some cases the cultivar. Soil analysis is more widely used for annual and short-term crops, while plant analysis is used to monitor the nutrition of a permanent crop having more extensive root systems and to compute nutrient uptake and fertilizer need. The analysis of a standardized tissue integrates the effects of soil, plant, climate and management. Use of "crop logging" to monitor nutrition over seasons helps to maintain the tissue level in the desired range. Deficiency symptoms and low levels in early growth are indicative of some nutrient deficiencies. However, by the time plant analysis indicates a problem, it is often too late to correct without yield loss. Tissue levels that are toxic, causing poor growth and reducing yield, are frequently not known.

Adequate levels of nutrients need to be maintained for growth and production and to replace the nutrients lost in production. Non-seasonal monoaxial-plant fruits (banana, papaya) remove more nutrients than seasonal polyaxial-tree fruits (durian, mango, rambutan, and litchi). Pruning, leaf fall, leaching and runoff also need to be taken into account. The fertilizer program should be designed to meet nutrient needs for vegetative growth and fruiting. Application times are adjusted to meet the different seasonal needs at the various phenological stages. These nutrient needs can be met from organic and inorganic fertilizer sources.

Field Management

Preparation

Field preparation is determined by the terrain and the equipment available. In hilly areas, terracing is preferred for erosion control. On gently sloping or level lands, conventional methods of clearing and plowing and planting rows on the contour are suitable. If the area to be cleared is wooded, wind-rows should be created by leaving lines of existing tree vegetation for wind-breaks. For grassland or shrub land, only planting rows are opened, and the wild vegetation between rows is left undisturbed to prevent erosion and conserve moisture. Planting holes are dug manually, trenched by use of a backhoe, or with a 46~61cm diameter auger attached to a tractor. In moist, heavy, clay soils, an almost impervious glazed surface is formed by the auger blade on the walls of the holes. This glazed surface must be broken to re-establish permeability.

In field where the soil has been compacted, subsoiling or ripping to 50~200cm is desirable to break up the hardpan in order to improve drainage and soil aeration. In the pineapple plantations of Hawaii, soils are ploughed below 60cm. Subsoiling provides better subterranean drainage if done parallel to contour lines. Discing, leveling and furrowing follow standard practice for all crops. Discing to break up clumps of soil and improve soil texture is an important phase of land preparation, especially if polyethylene sheets are to be used for mulching. Soil fumigation is also more efficient when soil clumps are broken down.

When root-rot-susceptible crops, such as papaya, passion-fruit, avocado and pineapple, are grown on level land with excessive seasonal rains, raised beds or berms are recommended. The deep furrows between the beds drain water from the field, if properly constructed. These furrows may be used for ground irrigation during dry seasons.

Weed Control

Weed control is a year-round problem in the tropics, except for regions with well-defined dry seasons. If irrigation is practiced during the dry period, some form of weed control is necessary. Weed control is troublesome during the first 2~3 years of orchard establishment when the trees have not yet developed substantial canopies to shade weed growth. For example, neglect of weeding can result in a 20%~40% decrease in pineapple yields. Weed growth can be reduced in the young orchards by heavy mulching with organic materials, such as straw, dried grass, wood shavings or whatever materials are easily available at low cost. Black polyethylene sheets cut to about 1m^2 and placed around the newly transplanted trees reduce weed growth and minimize weeding. Planting low-growing ground-cover crops is useful.

Methods of weeding vary from manual weeding to tractor-operated discing, mowing or application of herbicides, depending upon the orchard size and financial status of the grower. Growers of small orchards control weeds manually or with herbicides. Mechanical discing is rapid, with minimal cost, but is not considered to be a good practice in as much as it destroys feeder roots that are close to the soil surface.

Chemical weed control is efficient and rapid if done correctly at appropriate times. Pre-emergence application, either before or immediately after planting, is effective, least costly and a desirable management practice. Spray apparatus ranges from simple knapsack sprayers to the more sophisticated boom-type sprayers. Herbicides are generally not recommended in young orchards due to the possibility of damage from spray drift or direct contact with the stems, unless the crop is resistant to the rate used. Young avocado and papaya trees are especially sensitive to herbicides, so weeding around young transplants is usually done manually. For young seedlings and newly transplanted orchards, glyphosate, a systemic herbicide, may be applied by rope wick or weed wipers saturated with the herbicide solution and then wiped on the weed leaves. These applicators eliminate spray drift and can be applied close to the stem. Applicators of herbicides are through the irrigation system. There are restrictions on herbicide use imposed by manufacturers and government agencies, and all applicators must know the proper uses. Growers who intend to export fruit should become acquainted with regulations of the consuming countries governing the use of registered chemicals, residue levels and other precautions.

Intercropping in orchards with vegetables, leguminous crops and cucurbits is a common practice in some areas. In Mexico, fruit orchards have been observed with excellent intercrops of beans (*Phaseolus vulgaris*), watermelons (*Citrullus vulgaris*), cantaloupes (*Cucuning melo* var. *cantalupensis*) and chili (*Capsicum annuum*). Good weed control is obtained under this intercropping system.

Glossary

1. erosion   *n.* 侵蚀
2. deposition   *n.* 沉积
3. alluvial flood plains   冲积平原
4. glaciation   *n.* 冰河作用，冰蚀现象

5. oxisol n. 氧化土
6. aridisol n. 旱成土
7. alfisol n. 淋溶土，淀积土
8. ultisol n. 老成土（在美国土壤分类学中的，是高度风化和淋溶的一种黄色至红色的土壤）
9. vertisol n. （土壤学用语）变性土，转化土
10. sesquioxide n. 倍半氧化物，三氧化二物
11. topsoil structure 表层土壤结构
12. rhizosphere n. 根际，根围（指在土壤中围绕植物根系的一个区域）
13. *Phytophthora* n. 疫霉属，疫霉，疫霉菌
14. plant tissue analysis 植物组织分析，植物组织分析法
15. phenology n. 物候，物候学，生物气候学
16. soil analysis 土壤分析，土壤分析法
17. deficiency symptom 缺素症
18. monaxial adj. 单轴
19. polyaxial adj. 多轴
20. plough v. 翻地，犁耕，耕
21. permeability n. 透性，透水性，通透性
22. soil fumigation 土壤消毒，土壤熏蒸法
23. root-rot-susceptible 易感染根腐病的
24. glyphosate n. 草甘膦
25. herbicide n. 除草剂，除锈剂
26. intercropping n. 间作，套种，间混作，间套作
27. leguminous crop 豆类作物，豆科作物
28. Cucurbit n. 葫芦科植物，葫芦，瓜类
29. cantaloupe n. 哈密瓜，罗马甜瓜，香瓜

Exercises

A. Please answer the following questions in English.

1. How many kinds of tropical soils come under the US orders?
2. Please list the physical and chemical characteristics of tropical soils.
3. What are the nutrient requirements of tropical soils?
4. How to manage the field in tropics?
5. Please discuss the advantages and disadvantages of chemical weed control.

B. Please translate the following paragraph into Chinese.

Farmyard manure has been the traditional soil amendment in horticulture. This can be explained by its role as a source of plant nutrients, as well as its positive effects on soil structure. Increase in soil organic-matter content, improved aggregation and water infiltration, a decrease in bulk density and soil crusting following the addition of large amounts of manure to the soil have been reported.

C. Please translate the following sentences into English.

1. 土壤母质是由矿物岩石经风化而成。土壤母质的性质取决于矿物岩石的化学成分、分化特点和分解的产物。土壤矿物质一般占土壤固体物质的95%左右，是构成土壤的最基本物质。形成岩石的矿物称为造岩矿物。

2. 土壤的形成受自然因素和人为耕种等影响，经过不同的成土过程形成了不同的土壤发育层次和剖面形态特征，从而形成各种各样的土壤。

Part B Plant-growing Media and Soil Properties

Selected and rewritten from *Greenhouse Ecosystems 20*, edited by G. Stanhill and H. Zvi Enoch, and *Associate Horticulturist*, by Frank J. Peryea.

Plant-growing Media

For discussion in this unit, the word media will be used to mean the material that provides plants with nourishment and support through their roots systems.

Types of Media Media come in many forms. The oceans, rivers, land, and man-made mixtures of various materials are the principal types of media for plant growth. Seaweed, kelp, plankton, and many other plants depend upon water for their nutrients and support. It is only recently that we have come to understand the tremendous amount of plant life in the sea. The plant life in oceans and rivers is important for feeding the animal life of the sea and bodies of fresh water. Humankind has used fish as a staple food since the beginning of time.

It has long been known that water could be used to promote new root formation on the stems of certain green plants and completely support plant growth on a limited basis. Recently, however, it has been found that food crops can be grown efficiently in structure where plant roots are submerged in or sprayed with solutions of water and nutrients. These solutions feed the plants, while mechanical apparatus provide physical support. The practice of growing plants without soil is called hydroponics. Hydroponics has become an important commercial method of growing green plants.

Soil Soil is defined as the top layer of the Earth's surface, suitable for the growth of plant life. It has long been the predominant medium for cultivated plants. In early years, humans accepted the soil as it existed. They planted seeds using primitive tools and did not know how to modify or enhance the soil to improve its plant-supporting performance.

Ancient civilizations discovered that plant-growing conditions were improved on some land where deposits were left after river waters flowed over the land during flood season. Similarly, other land was ruined by flood waters. Therefore, early effort to improve plant-growing media was a matter of moving to better soil. Obviously, good soil was a valuable asset and, therefore was the cause of intense personal disputes and wars among nations.

Other Media In addition to water and soil, certain other materials will hold water and support plant growth. Ironically, some of the best non-soil and non-water media are partially decomposed plant materials. One common material available around most homes is leaf mold and compost. Leaf mold is partially decomposed plant leaves. Compost is a mixture of partially decayed organic matter such as leaves, manure, and household plant wastes. It is mixed with lime and fertilizer in correct proportions to support plant growth.

There is a group of pale or ashy mosses called sphagnum. These are used extensively in horticulture as a medium for encouraging root growth and growing plants under certain conditions. Peat moss consists of partially decomposed mosses which have accumulated in waterlogged areas called bogs. Both substances have excellent air-and water-holding qualities.

Many other sources of plant and animal residues may become plant-growing media. For instance, a fence post may rot on the top and hold moisture from rainfall. In time, a plant seed may be deposited in the rotted wood medium, germinate, root in the wood, and start to grow. Even horse manure mixed with straw is used extensively as a medium for growing mushrooms. In this instance, both animal residue (manure) and plant residue (straw) combine to make an effective medium.

Some mineral matters also become non-soil and non-water media. For instance, volcanic lava and ash remain black, gray, and barren only briefly. Soon the layer cools and cracks and seeds settle on it. Then moisture causes the seeds to germinate and roots to penetrate the volcanic residue. Soon the area is covered with the plant life.

Horticulturists use certain mineral materials in plant-growing areas, too. Perlite is a natural volcanic glass material having water-holding capabilities. Perlite is used extensively for starting new plants. Vermiculite is mineral matter from a group of mice-type materials that is also used for starting plant seeds and cuttings.

Soil Properties
  Soil chemical properties

The colloidal soil particles [i. e. the clay fraction ($<2\mu$m) and the humus (decayed organic matter)] determine the cation exchange capacity. This is the storage for nutrients and other ions, determining the nutrient supply or soil fertility. The greater the cation exchange capacity, the greater the buffer capacity of the soil and the greater the margin for error in fertilization.

Soil pH is another important chemical property, determining the availability of nutrients. The pH recommended for most greenhouse crops is 6.0~7.0; lower pH (more acid) causes aluminum and manganese toxicity, while higher pH (more alkaline) causes precipitation of phosphorus and problems with micronutrient uptake. Soil pH can be increased by liming, and can be decreased by proper composition of the nutrient solution.

Soil salinity affects plant growth by increasing the osmotic potential of the soil solution, causing plant water stress and decreasing water uptake. Specific ions may cause toxic effects. For salt-sensitive plants, even lower threshold values apply. Excess salts should be leached from the soil prior to greenhouse construction. Problems of salinity are associated in many cases with the quality of irrigation water.

Soil physical properties

The soil is a three-phase system, that consists of solid particles (the soil matrix) and voids (the soil pores), that may either be filled with water or with air. Hence, distinction is made between a solid, a liquid and a gaseous phase, respectively. The distribution between the three phases depends on the composition of the solid phase, particularly on the particle size distribution of the soil, which is denoted as the soil texture. There are three particle size classes distinguished: <0.002 mm, $0.002 \sim 0.05$ mm and $0.05 \sim 2$ mm, defined as clay, silt, and sand, respectively. The ratio between these fractions classifies the texture of the soil of interest according to the texture triangle.

Soils with high clay content are more difficult to handle, tend to hold excess water and drain slowly, and are therefore less suitable for greenhouse culture. On the other hand, sandy soils are less fertile, have a low water capacity and need better fertilization and frequent irrigation. The most important soil physical property is soil structure, this being the nature and stability of the bonds between soil particles, causing aggregation and large soil pores. Good and stable soil structure is enhanced by organic matter, which should be added to the soil if not present originally. Soil texture and structure determine the rate of water movement in the soil, the water holding capacity and the drainage. Soils which tend to drain slowly show aeration problems, since soil pores filled with water prevent oxygen diffusion and the uptake of oxygen by the plant roots, necessary for respiration and ion uptake. If a soil has severe drainage problems, artificial drainage is necessary. One should bear in mind, however, that artificial drainage would remove excess water from the soil only when the water table is close to the soil surface.

Glossary

1. kelp   *n.* 巨藻，大型海藻，海草灰
2. plankton   *n.* 浮游生物
3. sphagnum   *n.* 冰苔，水藓，泥炭藓
4. leaf mold   腐殖土，腐叶土壤
5. peat moss   泥炭沼，泥炭藓，泥煤苔，泥炭土
6. bog   *n.* 沼泽，沼泽地
7. horizon   *n.* 土层，层位；地平线
8. unconsolidated   *adj.* 松散的
9. volcanic lava   熔岩，火山岩
10. perlite   *n.* 珍珠岩
11. profile   *n.* 断面，剖面
12. residual soil   残积土
13. alluvial deposit   冲击物

14. vermiculite *n.* 蛭石
15. mice-type 云母型
16. colloidal *adj.* 胶状的，胶质的
17. clay fraction 粘粒
18. humus *n.* 腐殖质
19. cation exchange capacity 阳离子交换能力
20. equilibrium *n.* 平衡，均衡，保持平衡的能力
21. water stress 水分胁迫
22. precipitation *n.* 沉淀
23. buffer capacity 缓冲能力
24. osmotic potential 渗透势
25. threshold value 极限值，域值
26. salt-sensitive plant 盐度敏感植物
27. texture triangle 土壤结构三角图
28. fertile *adj.* 肥沃的，能繁殖的；*n.* 多产，肥沃
29. water table 地下水位

Questions

1. Please compare the soil with plant-growing media.
2. What does the soil salinity mean? How to deal with the salinity stress in the soil?
3. What do the soil physical properties include? Why is it said that the physical properties of the soil are quite important for success in culture?

Lesson 5

Part A Physical Control of Growth

Selected and rewritten from *Introductory Horticulture*, by H. Edward Reiley & Corroll L. Shry, Jr., and *Horticulture*, by R. Gordon Halface & John A.

Plant growth is modified for functional and aesthetic reasons. Control of growth by removing plant parts dates back to the Egyptians and is among the oldest of horticultural practices. More recently, dwarfing by rootstocks, scion cultivars, genetic mutations and chemicals has been used to control growth.

Pruning is the removal of plant parts, such as buds, developed shoots and roots, to maintain a desirable form by controlling the direction and amount of growth. If the natural form of the plant is undesirable, growth can be directed to a limited degree to the desired form through pruning techniques. Constant follow-up must be practiced to maintain the desired form. Although pruning is an invigorating process, it is also a dwarfing process because growing points are removed and the total weight of a pruned plant is usually less than that of an unpruned plant. Growth is frequently quite rapid following pruning, because the top-root ratio (balance) is temporarily altered; but this does not compensate for the portions of the plant removed. Removal of foliage and branches reduces stored carbohydrates and—more importantly—reduces the leaf area available for carbohydrate production. The new leaves which develop after pruning may be larger than the older leaves, but they will be fewer in number.

It is not only the practice of pruning itself which governs the results obtained, but the condition of the plant. Pruning can influence the number and quality of flowers and fruits. Pruning can repair injuries. Pruning is utilized to remove diseased parts, insect-damaged parts, or wood which was killed by winter injury. Pruning helps to develop a strong and durable framework, which is critical for fruit and nut-bearing trees and very desirable on ornamentals.

Pruning Techniques

Dormant pruning is done after autumnal leaf fall, while summer pruning is done during the growing season. Both dormant and summer pruning are dwarfing, which reduce the potential for shoot growth and delay flowering and fruit bearing of the pruned trees. Summer pruning of fruit trees can be practiced for training, for growth control, for better sunlight exposure, to stimulate flowering, and to improve fruit quality. This practice has a place in training young trees, and is useful in increasing fruit colors in some climates. However, care must be taken to avoid fruit size reduction. Thinning-out cuts at some distance from fruits have little effect on fruit sizes. Many studies indicate that summer pruning is no more effective than dormant pruning for limiting tree sizes and suppressing shoot growth.

Pruning procedures are determined by the life span, structure, and growth habits of the individual plants. Pruning may consist of as little as pinching buds to produce a more compact and bushy plant or as much as removing large branches. Herbaceous perennials generally are pruned either to remove dead or diseased parts or to thin the plants. Chrysanthemum buds are pinched to control the number of flowers and thereby increase the size of the flowers. Most frequently it is the woody, deciduous, and evergreen plants that are pruned. They can be grouped into two main categories: shrubs, which have several trunks and trees, which have only one or a few distinct trunks.

The two major types of pruning cuts, heading back and thinning, cause different responses in plants. Both thinning and heading-back cuts are normally used in almost every type of pruning.

In heading back, the terminal portion of the shoot is removed, but the basal portion is not. (Fig. 5-1) When heading back is used on flowering plants and foliage plants to increase branching, it is referred to as *pinching*. This method can be used effectively on all plants. Heading back can also be used to rejuvenate vegetative growth in older trees and shrubs.

In thinning, entire shoots are removed; thus thinning is an extension or complement of heading back. Growth and light penetration are more evenly distributed, since thinning produces an open type of growth. Thinning can be used to rejuvenate old fruit trees. Old and weak wood is removed, this results in better-quality fruit on the remaining branches. When removing an entire branch, make the cut clean and smooth and as close to the trunk as possible.

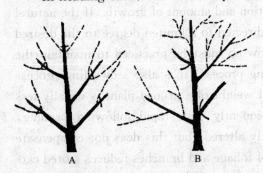

Fig. 5-1 A is the heading back results B is the thinning results

After pruning cuts have been made, rapid healing is essential. Cuts less than 2 cm in diameter heal rapidly and usually do not need protection from disease or insects. If the cut is over 2 cm in diameter, a wound dressing is desirable to prevent desiccation. A good wound dressing should be waterproof and durable and should include an antiseptic to kill fungi.

Training Methods

Central Leader Training In central leader training, a single central leader is selected and subordinate side branches are developed along this leader. Attention is given to selecting well-spaced lateral branches and maintaining the proper degrees of subordination among these laterals. The result is a tall, narrow tree ("Christmas-tree" shape). Some fruit types, such as apples, really lend themselves to this system; but others, such as plums, are difficult to train.

Modified Leader Training The modified leader system combines the best qualities of the central-leader and open-center systems. A leader develops on the young tree until it reaches the height of 2~3 m. It is dominant until the tree is formed and is then restricted.

Open Center Training In open center training, the main stem is terminated and growth is encouraged from the upper end of the trunk, where a number of branches originate. Three to five primary lateral branches are trained to equal dominance by pruning each year.

Espalier Training Espalier training is one of the most intense cultural practices that a horticulturist uses. Espalier plants are much used today, as a result of the limited space characteristic of urban living. Espalier plants are trained in a pattern on a flat surface, such as a fence or wall. With proper care, plants can be trained to almost any shape. However, unless constant maintenance is planned to continue such training indefinitely, it is better not to espalier plants.

Trellis Training Many vines and annual herbaceous plants are trained to a trellis. This is another rigid form of training. Grapevines may be trained on a trellis with canes—previous season's growth from the arm or trunk—tied to wires.

Bonsai Training Bonsai is a very highly specialized training system involving root pruning and top pruning to control growth. Bonsai is pinching, bending, and tying rather than cutting back the growth after it has occurred. The objective is to keep the plant attractively healthy in a miniature form. Bonsai pruning consists of reducing the size of branches, changing their direction, and thinning dense growth that hides the line of trunk and roots.

Pruning Equipment

Hand Pruners Hand pruners are of two types. In one type, sharpened blades overlap, producing a cut similar to that made by household scissors. The second type, the anvil-type pruner, has a straight-edged top blade which comes down on a soft-metal anvil. Either type is acceptable; however, a closer, cleaner cut can be made with the first type.

Power Pruners Electric hedge shears are commonly used today. Most of the large-scale pruning in orchards is done with power pruners, which take much of the hard work out of the job. Both power loppers and saws are available. These operate by the use of hoses and compressed air from a compressor powered by a power take off on a tractor.

Mechanical Pruners An innovation of recent years has been mechanized pruners. These vary widely in design, operation, and power source but are all made to prune a plant (usually a fruit tree) mechanically. They include large circular saws which rotate on arms, small overlapping circular saws, and cutter-bar type mechanisms.

Positioners In recent years fruit growers have found it increasingly difficult to hire willing, able, and skilled workers for winter pruning. One partial solution has been the purchase and use of positioners which put the pruner up in the tree, eliminating the need for climbing the tree or using ladders. Positioners are expensive, but they not only increase the efficiency of workers but make the job more attractive. Many of the positioners are attached to a tractor or are equipped with a power source so that pneumatic pruners can also be hired.

Glossary

1. rootstock *n.* 砧木
2. scion cultivar 嫁接品种，嫁接栽培品种
3. genetic mutation 基因突变，遗传变异
4. top-root ratio 根冠比
5. stored carbohydrate 贮藏的碳水化合物，碳水化合物
6. dormant pruning 冬季修剪，休眠期修剪；summer pruning 夏季修剪，夏剪
7. thinning-out cut 疏剪
8. herbaceous perennial 多年生草本植物
9. thinning *n.* 疏剪，间苗，疏苗
10. heading-back 短截
11. pinch *v.* 摘心，打顶
12. rejuvenate *v.* 复壮，使年轻，使恢复
13. vegetative growth 营养生长
14. light penetration 透光度
15. desiccation *n.* 干燥，除湿，脱水
16. waterproof *adj.* 不透水的，防水的；*v.* 使防水
17. antiseptic *adj.* 防腐的，杀毒的，无菌的；*n.* 防腐剂，杀毒剂
18. fungi *n.* 真菌，真菌科，真菌类
19. central-leader training 中心干树形，中轴式整枝
20. subordinate *n.* 隶属，下属；*adj.* 下级的
21. modified leader training 变则中心干整枝
22. open-center systems 开心形系统
23. espalier training 篱形整枝
24. trellis training 棚架式整枝
25. grapevines *n.* 葡萄藤，葡萄树
26. bonsai training 盆景整形，盆栽整枝
27. pruner *n.* 修枝(根)剪；lopper *n.* 修枝剪
28. positioner *n.* 定位器

Exercises

A. **Please answer the following questions in English.**

1. What is the difference between dormant pruning and summer pruning?
2. What are the different responses in plants when taking the pruning methods of thinning and heading-back?

3. Please tell the differences among the different training systems.

4. What are the factors one should take into consideration when pruning fruit trees?

5. Compare the advantages and disadvantages of hand pruning and mechanical pruning.

B. Please translate the following paragraph into Chinese.

Pruning is an important cultural practice used to maintain the size of fruit trees. It involves the removal of plant parts, which stimulates vegetative growth, and reduces fruitfulness. Removal of a branch not only eliminates stored carbohydrates, but also reduces potential leaf surface. As a result, root growth is reduced, too. However, pruning increases fruit size and N per growing point and stimulates growth near the cuts. Large cuts result in excessive stimulation of sprouts, while well-distributed small cuts spread the stimulus better over the entire tree.

C. Please translate the following sentences into English.

1. 植物的生长调控，有生物方法，如用矮化或乔化的砧木，用矮性品种；有化学方法，如应用植物生长调节剂；有通过改变环境的方法，如干旱、营养贫乏抑制生长；还有物理方法，主要是修剪和植株调整。

2. 果树修剪是用工具短截或疏除果树枝条的工作。其目的是形成良好的树形结构，调节生长与结果的矛盾，维持营养生长与生殖生长的平衡，为果树创造良好的光照环境条件，以实现早结果，并且维持丰产，获得优质果品。

Part B Chemical Control of Growth

Selected and rewritten from *Evergreen Orchards*, by William Henry Chandler, and *Horticulture*, by R. Gordon Halface & John A. Barden Mcgraw.

Today, the use of chemicals in the regulation of plant growth is becoming more widespread. Some chemicals have a very broad and general use, and others are very specific for individual species or cultivars.

Chemical Pinching

Hand pinching the apical portion of plant shoots is a time-consuming and expensive method of pruning. Chemicals can be used to increase the number of new shoots per plant, to control the shape of the plant, to increase the number of flowers, and to control the time of flowering. Pruning with chemicals is, therefore, a very necessary part of growing ornamental plants.

The chemicals, referred to as *chemical pruning agents*, are not translocated to other parts of the plant and kill only the meristematic cells. Lower alkyl esters of fatty acids destroy terminal buds, effectively pinching the plant; but the effectiveness varies with the concentration of the chemical and woodiness of the tissue.

Chemical pruning has become adapted to azaleas and chrysanthemums. Chemical pinching stimulates branching of azaleas and increases the number of flowers per plant. Growth of treated plants is suppressed initially, but within several weeks the growth may exceed that of an unsprayed plant. Chemicals such as methyl caproate, methyl caprylate, methyl laurate, and methyl stearate are effective chemical pinching agents.

Another area of chemical pruning is root pruning. Often dominant taproots develop if the root is not pruned to induce strong, fibrous growth. Since hand pruning requires time, chemicals are used to treat layers in the seedbed. When the roots reach these layers, they are pinched.

Flower and Fruit Thinning

The fruit industries, specifically the apple industry, use chemicals for flower and fruit thinning. The general purpose of fruit thinning with chemical sprays is to encourage annual bearing and to improve fruit size. Each orchard owner may experience different results because of variables such as timing of application, cultivar, weather conditions, vigor of trees, pollination, and frost damage. Many cultivars of apples tend to develop a biennial bearing habit in which very heavy flowering occurs every other year with a light crop the alternate year. The only effective way to get annual flowering is to thin in the "on year", but this must be done early in the year. Flower bud initiation occurs within 30 to 60 days after bloom; to affect next year's crop, therefore, this year's crop must be thinned well before hand thinning is practical, so that chemical thinning is the only genuine alternative.

Height Control of Plants

The floriculture industry is dependent upon chemical growth control. In floral crops these chemicals change plant growth so that the crop can be grown without extra labor. Growth regulators are extensively used in the production of flowering pot plants. These are frequently used to produce more salable compact plants. Chemicals used for this purpose have the desirable effect of reducing internode length without reducing the number of leaves.

In 1950, the growth retardant AMO 1618 was developed. The compound was very effective for dwarfing plants, but it was too expensive for commercial use. Later, a related material, Phosphon, appeared on the market; it is now used for retarding the height of chrysanthemums and lilies. This material is applied as a solution to the soil. Cycocel, a more recent introduction, can be used as a foliar spray or a soil drench for controlling the height if poinsettias and azaleas. Daminozide (succinic acid 2, 2-dimethylhydrazide) used as a foliar spray effectively controls the height of chrysanthemum, bedding plants, poinsettia, azalea, and hydrangea. One of the newest growth retardants is A-Rest [α-cyclopropyl -α- (4-methoxyphenyl)-5-pyrimidinemethanol]. This chemical controls plant height and is active in a low concentration.

Glossary

1. chemical pinching 化学摘心；hand pinching 手动摘心
2. chemical pruning agent 化学修剪剂

3. meristematic cell 分生细胞
4. alkyl ester 烷基酯
5. fatty acid 脂肪酸
6. azalea n. 杜鹃花
7. chrysanthemum n. [植]菊花
8. methyl caproate 己酸甲酯；methyl caprylate 辛酸甲酯；methyl laurate 月桂酸甲酯；methyl stearate 硬脂酸甲酯
9. root pruning 切根修剪，剪根
10. internode n. 节间
11. growth retardant 生长抑制剂
12. phosphon n. 氯化磷
13. cycocel n. 矮壮素
14. poinsettias n. 一品红
15. daminozide n. 丁酰肼
16. bedding plants 花坛植物
17. poinsettia n. 一品红
18. hydrangea n. 绣球花

Questions

1. Compare the advantages and disadvantages of physical pruning and chemical pruning.
2. How to pinch the plants by chemical control?
3. What chemicals are applied to control the height of the plants?

Lesson 6

Part A Mechanisms of Plant Sexual Propagation

Selected and rewritten from *Horticulture*, by R. Gordon Halface & John A., and *Horticulture: A Basic Awareness*, by Robert F. Baudendistel.

Biologically, all living things reproduce and thereby perpetuate the species. Plants are unique in their ability to reproduce asexually. In plants, the unique thing called *totipotency* for reproduction is achieved. Totipotency is the ability to generate or regenerate a whole organism from a part. Generally, all cells in all living organisms have the potential for totipotency, but only plants can use the generative process.

Plants reproduce in two ways, by sexual and asexual. *Sexual reproduction* is the reproduction of plants through a sexual process involving meiosis. The sexual cycle results in the production of seed or spores. A seed (embryo) results from the fertilization of the egg (female gamete) by pollen (male gamete). Recombination of genetic information, sexual reproduction takes advantage of natural genetic variation inherent in the two parent plants. *Asexual reproduction* is defined as the duplication of a whole plant from any cell, tissue, or organ. It takes advantage of the precise duplication of genetic information inherent in mitosis and is possible by totipotency. Through mitotic cell division and differentiation, a clonal population can be duplicated exactly for hundreds of years, leading to the production of thousands of genetically identical plants. Plants are unique among life forms in that they have the capacity to reproduce asexually.

It is generally agreed that sexual reproduction is more highly evolved than asexual reproduction. With sexual reproduction more opportunity exists for variability, adaptability, and change. Therefore, it is not surprising that several asexual organisms have developed a form of reproduction which may resemble, approach, or actually be sexual reproduction.

In nature most plants reproduce from seed and thereby maintain variation. But many plants reproduce asexually because they have a strong characteristic which competes effectively with the environment. The procedure or method for propagating plants commercially is dependent upon the time required, the cost, and the method required by each plant.

Sexual Propagation

The most common type of plant propagation is the sexual method, or production of plants from seed. The sexual method used involves the fertilization of the ovary of female part of the flower by the pollen from male anthers. (Fig. 6-1) Most plants reproduce themselves through seeds. Most agronomic, vegetable, and forest crops, in addition to many annual and perennial flower crops and some woody ornamentals, are seeds propagated. Propagation by seeds is usually cheaper and easier than other methods, which is used whenever possible. Certain limitations exist, however, plants (such as hydrangea and snowball viburnum) which do not produce viable seeds cannot be propagated from seeds. When propagating from seeds, one has fewer problems with possible diseases of the mother plant than with vegetative propagation. It is important that the seed is harvested when it is ripe and that the dormancy is broken, so that a high rate of germination can be realized. Many plants, such as apple, pear, plum, peach, and raspberry, display such genetic variability in seed that they are not propagated sexually. Seeds planted from these fruits usually result in the production of inferior plants and fruits.

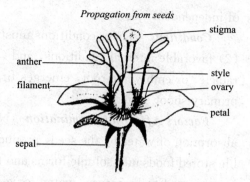

Fig. 6-1 Typical flower diagram

Sexual reproduction results in the creation of plants with new genotypes. In some ways, seed propagation can approach the genetic and phenotypic features of asexual propagation, provided that the plant material is genetically homozygous. Southern Corn Leaf Blight, which caused a near disaster in corn production in the early 1970s, resulted from mutations in fungi that were able to parasitize the male sterile T source of cytoplasm. Much commercially available hybrid corn seed had this T cytoplasm, because it was the cytoplasm of the female parent that prevented the formation of viable pollen, thus allowing seed companies to sell hybrid corn seed without incurring the cost of hand detasseling. This procedure is critical to the collection or loss of germ plasm, and it is increasingly done for world population of seed-reproduced plants that have very narrow genetic backgrounds and thus very limited genotypes. However, the process is similar to incest and could lead to serious problems in such crops. Through natural selection, seeds from sexual cycles result in variability and lessen the vulnerability of a plant species to disease or insects. Humans should honor the fact and work within available sources of germ plasm.

Seed Propagation

Initially, the success of seed propagation is dependent upon the production of flowers, normal meiotic behavior in the formation of the microspores and megaspores, fusion of there male and female gametes to from the zygote, and the subsequent development of the embryo and endosperm to from the seed. Finally, it is dependent upon the germination of the seed and the establishment of the seedling.

The Germination Process Germination is the initiation of active growth by the embryo, resulting in the rupture of seed coverings and the emergence of a new seedling plant capable of independent existence.

Conditions These conditions must be met for germination to occur: (1) viable seed, (2) favorable internal conditions, and (3) favorable environmental conditions. Usually the radicle, or embryonic root, emerges first, and the plumule pushes upward to develop the primary shoot system.

Factors Affecting Germination Necessary factors accompanying germination are the absorption of water by the seed, production of enzymes and hormones hydrolysis of insoluble stored foods into soluble forms and the translocation of there soluble foods to the growing points. Food reserves, water, oxygen, and temperature affect the germination process. In some cases light and physiological factors may also affect germination.

Seed Planting

Small areas, flats, greenhouse beds, and home gardens are usually planted by hand. Larger areas and fields are usually planted by machine. Seed drills which are used for planting may be operated by hand or may be part of the accessory equipment for a tractor. Grain drills may also be used to plant seed and are advantageous in that they place the fertilizer as a side dressing at the time of planting. A correctly adjusted drill places the seed at a uniform depth and at a uniform distance apart and firms the soil around the seed. Depth of planting depends upon the size of seed, soil structure, time of year, and moisture and oxygen content. Since small seed have less stored food, they must be planted nearer the surface to decrease the time and energy needed for the seedling to develop and start photosynthesizing.

If water is limiting factors, as it usually is during the germination period, the seed should be planted at a greater depth to prevent desiccation of the emerging seedlings. If the soil is nearly saturated, as it is during late fall, winter, and early spring, the seed should be planted rather shallow, since oxygen is necessary for respiration. Seedling to a depth where the oxygen supply is limited may result in failure.

Temperature requirements of the crop and temperatures of the location determine the best time for planting. Warm-season crops are usually sown after the last killing freeze of spring, cooling-season crops may be planted earlier.

Seed Tapes and Pelleting

When seeds are small or irregular, even the distribution is often difficult to obtain. To make the seed round and uniform in size, they are pelleted or coated with montmorillonite, finely divided clay. Pelleting permits more uniform planting, eliminates a great deal of thinning, and permits the incorporation of fungicides onto the coat. Seed tapes or ribbons are available for many flower and vegetable cultivars. The seed is attached and spaced at the proper intervals on a plastic tape. The tapes are buried in a shallow furrow. The tapes disintegrate from moisture as the seed germinates.

Glossary

1. totipotency   *n.* 全能性
2. organism   *n.* 生物,（尤指）微生物,有机组织
3. sexual reproduction   有性繁殖；asexual reproduction   无性繁殖
4. meiosis   *n.* 减数分裂；meiotic behavior   减数分裂特性,减数分裂行为
5. spores   *n.* 孢子,胚种；microspore   *n.* 小(型分生)孢子；megaspore   *n.* 大孢子
6. embryo   *n.* 胚,胚胎,胚芽(期),萌芽期；in embryo   初期的；萌芽时期的
7. fertilization   *n.* 受精
8. egg   *n.* 卵；fertilized egg   受精卵
9. gamete   *n.* 配子；female gamete   雌配子；male gamete   雄配子
10. variability   *n.* 变异性,变异,变异度；genetic variation   遗传变异
11. parent plants   亲本
12. genetic information   遗传信息,基因信息
13. mitosis   *n.* 有丝分裂；mitotic cell division   有丝细胞分裂
14. differentiation   *n.* 分化
15. clonal   *adj.* [生]无性(繁殖)系的
16. hydrangea   *n.* 八仙花,八仙花属,绣球,绣球属
17. viburnum   *n.* 荚蒾属植物
18. vegetative propagation   无性繁殖,营养繁殖
19. genotype   *n.* 基因型,遗传型；genetic   *adj.* 遗传的,基因的
20. phenotypic   *adj.* 表型的；phenotype   *n.* 表型,显型
21. homozygous   *adj.* [生]同型结合的,纯合子的
22. parasitize   *v.* 寄生,寄生于
23. male sterile   雄性不育
24. cytoplasm   *n.* 细胞质,细胞浆
25. hand detasseling   人工去雄
26. seed-reproduced plant   种子繁殖型植物,实生繁殖植物
27. genetic background   遗传背景,遗传基础
28. natural selection   自然选择
29. germ plasm   种质,种质资源
30. zygote   *n.* 合子,受精卵
31. endosperm   *n.* 胚乳
32. hydrolysis   *n.* 水解
33. insoluble   *adj.* 不溶性的
34. growing point   生长点
35. photosynthesize   *v.* 光合作用
36. desiccation   *n.* 干燥作用,干燥法,脱水,干化,干化适应
37. seed tapes and pelleting   种子包衣和丸粒化

38. montmorillonite   *n.* 蒙脱石，蒙脱土
39. fungicide   *n.* 杀菌剂

Exercises

A. Please answer the following questions in English.
1. Please define the ***totipotency***.
2. What are the advantages and disadvantages of sexual propagation?
3. Please list the main factors which affect seed germination.
4. What we should pay attention to in the seed germination process?
5. How to tape and pellet seeds for some plants?

B. Please translate the following paragraph into Chinese.

In the cultivation of pot plants, propagation using seed takes place primarily with species of flowering plants that have hybrid cultivars (*Cyclamen*) and species with true breeding cultivars (*Aechmea fasciata*). When propagating from seed, one has fewer problems with possible diseases of the mother plant than with vegetative propagation. It is important that the seed is harvested when it is ripe and that the dormancy is broken, so that a high rate of germination can be realized.

C. Please translate the following sentences into English.

1. 植物在营养生长后期进入生殖生长期，经双受精后，由合子发育成胚，由受精的极核发育成胚乳，由种被发育成种皮，即通过有性过程形成种子，凡由种子播种长成的苗称为实生苗。

2. 种子有生活力，但即使给予适宜的环境条件仍不能发芽，此种现象称为种子的休眠，种子休眠是长期自然选择的结果。造成休眠的原因主要有种皮或果皮结构障碍、种胚发育不全、化学物质抑制等。

Part B   Asexual Propagation

Selected and rewritten from *Horticulture*, by R. Gordon Halface & John A., Horticulture: *A Basic Awareness*, by Robert F. Baudendistel, and *Protected Cultivation of Ornamental Crops*, by J. Berghoef, K. L. Jeutscher and P. A. van de Pol.

Asexual propagation is the duplication of a whole plant from any living cell tissue or organ of plant. Asexual propagation is possible, because normal cell division (mitosis) and cell differentiation occur during growth and regeneration. Mitotic cell division is involved whether the form of propagation is initiation of roots and shoots or formation of callus tissue in the process of budding and grafting. A single cell can generate a new plant, because each cell contains all the genetic information necessary to reproduce the entire organism. When a group of plants originate from a single individual and are propagated by vegetative means, this group is referred to as *clone*. Clones may be maintained by humans for hundreds of years or may exist in nature by reproduction of plants by bulbs, rhizomes, runners, and tip layers. Since clonal plants are genetically identical to the parent, the desirable characteristics of the cultivar can be perpetuated.

In addition to the perpetuation of clones, plants may be asexually propagated for other reasons. Many crops, if propagated by seeds, will not reproduce true to type. The seedling progeny may not bear much resemblance to the parent and may be much less desirable. Generally, most horticultural species propagated by asexual means have heterozygous genotypes. They are phenotypically variable because of the environment, along with a heterozygous genotype when grown from seeds. Thus, valuable individuals are perpetuated through asexual means allowing for uniformity in phenotype.

Because of the season of flowering, genetic incompatibility or sterility, many valuable plants produce little or no seed. Another common problem occurs when a seed is difficult to germinate. This difficulty may be due to a hard, impervious seed coat, seed dormancy, or an immature embryo. American holly and viburnum are examples.

Dwarfing effects, resistance to certain insects and diseases, better adaptability to a given soil, and hardiness of certain parts of a plant can also be obtained by combining two clones. Disease resistant rootstocks make it possible to grow cultivars susceptible to soil-borne diseases.

Cuttings

Cuttings are detached vegetative plants parts which, when placed under conditions favorable for regeneration, will develop into a complete plant with characteristics identical to the parent. Any vegetative plant part that is capable of regenerating the missing part or parts when detached from the parent can be a cutting; hence, roots, stems, leaves, or modified stems such as tubers and rhizomes can all be used as cuttings. The type of cutting used to propagate a given plant is determined by many factors, such as ease of root or shoot formation, availability of leaves, facilities available for propagation, and season of the year.

Types of Cuttings Cuttings are classified as stem cuttings, leaf cuttings (Fig. 6-2), leaf-bud cuttings, and root cuttings. Stem cuttings are usually taken from mother plants, but with some plants (*Ficus benjamina*) these are also taken from plants which are destined for sale, and in a few cases (although this is not recommended) cuttings are taken from a cut flower production crop (e.g. *Rose*), and also sometimes taken from young plants in order to stimulate their branching (*Kalanchoe blossfeldiana*). Cuttings are usually treated with a hormone (auxin) in order to stimulate rooting.

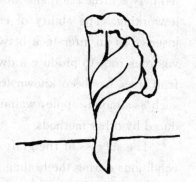

Fig. 6-2 Partial leaf cutting—Begonia rex

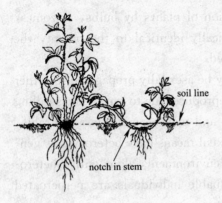

Fig. 6-3 Ground layering

In some cases, the rhizomes or stolons of mother plant is divided (Marantaceae) by removing or dividing.

Layering

Layering (Fig. 6-3), a vegetative method of propagation produces new individuals by producing adventitious roots before the new plant is severed from the parent. Conditions necessary for layering are quite similar to those necessary for rooting cuttings. The wood should be young, so that it will form adventitious roots easily. When the new plant has developed a self-sustaining root system, it can be severed from the parent. Species that are hard to root lend themselves to layering since the parent plant provides the food and water for as long as it takes the roots to develop. This method has two basic disadvantages. One is that only a few individuals can be started from a given stock plant at any one time, the other is that the expense of layering. This involves considerable hand labor for the small number of plants, is prohibitive for most large-scale usages. Brambles, grapes, blueberries, and other plants which naturally propagate by layering are sometime propagated this way by growers. Various modifications of layering are used: tip layering, simple layering, and trench layering.

Grafting

Grafting (Fig. 6-4) consists of joining two separate structures, such as a root and stem or two stems, so that tissue regeneration they form a union and grow as one plant. The upper part of the union is the scion, and the lower part is the stock (rootstock). Some graft combinations contain an interstock or intermediate stem piece, which is grafted between the scion and stock. This is called double-working. The ability of certain dwarfing clones, inserted as an interstock between a vigorous top and vigorous root to produce a dwarfed and early-bearing fruit tree, has been known for centuries. Grafting is used to reproduce clonal cultivars, such as almond, apple, walnut, and eucalyptus, which are not easily or successfully reproduced by other methods.

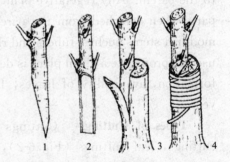

Fig. 6-4 Grafting of *Osmanthus*

The success of the graft depends on several predetermined factors and environmental conditions during the healing process. The first phenomenon of importance is compatibility. A second consideration is the kind of plant involved in the combination and the kind of graft to be used. Third, environmental conditions, especially temperature and moisture, exert a definite on the graft union.

Propagation using bulbs or tubers

Some important horticultural plants are bulb or tuber crops, which is actually a stem tuber. Stem tubers are solid structures with buds and internodes, comprised of a swollen stem base which may or may not be surrounded by dry leaves. The stem base has become swollen from the storage of reserve food in the parenchyma tissue. The apex produces the leaves and the flower shoot. The other buds usually do not grow out. Propagation takes place via lateral buds. In contrast, a bulb is a complete plant on a reduced stem. The buds of shoots, flowers, and sometimes even the roots for the next season, are already present in the bulb. Bulbs can be structured in various ways: bulbs with scales enclosing the entire bulb, e. g. tulip, daffodil, or bulbs with scales partially enclosing the bulb, e. g. lily.

The number of scales can vary from one to many. Bulbs may be enclosed by a bulb tunic (dehydrated scale). This protects the bulb against diseases, dehydration and damage. The propagation of bulbs and tubers usually takes place at specialized operations in the open field.

Micropropagation

Micropropagation (in vitro culture, tissue culture), which grew to be an important branch of horticulture with increasing commercial importance during the 1970s and 1980s, is used on a large scale with ornamental crops such as *Gerbera*, *Nephrolepis*, Orchid, *Ficus*, and *Anthurium*. In vitro culture is the cultivation of plants or parts thereof in sterile, conditioned surroundings. With this method, plants can be propagated from every part of the plant. The greatest application of micro-propagation is the rapid propagation of selected plant material. This method is relatively expensive due to the labor-intensive production process.

Glossary

1. callus tissue 愈伤组织
2. bulb *n.* 鳞茎，球茎，种球，球状物
3. rhizome *n.* [植]根茎，根状茎，地下茎
4. heterozygous genotype 杂合基因型
5. compatibility *n.* 亲和，亲和性；genetic incompatibility 遗传不亲和
6. sterility *n.* 不育
7. soil-borne disease 土传病害
8. stem cutting 枝插；leaf cutting 叶插；leaf-bud cutting 叶芽插；root cutting 根插
9. *Ficus benjamina* 垂叶榕
10. *Kalanchoe blossfeldiana* 落地生根，长寿花
11. hormone *n.* 荷尔蒙，激素；auxin *n.* （植物)生长素
12. marantaceae *n.* 竹芋科
13. stolon *n.* 匍匐枝，芽茎走根，匍匐菌丝，匍匐丝

14. tip layering 顶压条,先端压条; simple layering 普通压条,单枝压条;
    trench layering 沟槽式压条,开沟压条
15. scion *n.* 接穗; stock *n.* 砧木
16. eucalyptus *n.* 桉树
17. parenchyma tissue 薄壁组织
18. tulip *n.* 郁金香
19. daffodil *n.* 黄水仙,水仙花
20. tunic *n.* 鳞茎皮,膜皮,原套,膜
21. dehydrated scale 脱水鳞片
22. micropropagation *n.* 微繁,微体快繁,微繁殖
23. in vitro culture 离体培养,体外培养; tissue culture 组织培养,组培
24. labour-intensive production process 劳动密集型生产

Questions

1. What methods are used in ornamental asexual propagation?
2. What are the merits and faults of micropropagation?
3. Please define *vegetative propagation*.

Lesson 7

Part A   Plant Tissue Culture

Selected and rewritten from *Principles of Horticulture*, by Adams C. R., Bamford K. M., Early M. P., and *Genetics and Plant Breeding*, by Rhitu Rai.

Tissue culture is a method used for vegetative propagation by using a plant part or single cell or group cell in a container under very controlled and hygienic conditions.

Totipotency, the phenomenon that any part of a plant from a single cell to a whole apical meristem can grow into a whole plant, is the central to understanding tissue culture. A cell exhibits totipotency because it contains the entire genetic information in its nucleus. This information is expressed when it becomes necessary.

The concept of totipotency was suggested by German biologist Haberiandt in 1902 on the assumption that each cell of an organism being derived from the mitotic divisions of a zygote must be able to produce the entire organism. In the 1950s Steward and his co-workers succeeded in growing carrot plants from isolated phloem cells which turned the assumption into reality. Totipotency is known to be present in plant cells; however, this capacity is comparatively limited in animal cells. Totipotency has today formed the basis for tissue culture.

Besides the principal totipotency, another principal plasticity can make us deeply understand tissue culture. Plants, due to their sessile nature and long life span, have developed a greater ability to endure extreme conditions and predations than animals. Many of the processes involved in plant growth and development adapt to environmental conditions. This plasticity allows plants to alter their metabolism, growth and development to best suit their environment. Particularly important aspects of this adaptation, as far as plant tissue culture and regeneration are concerned, are the abilities to initiate cell division from almost any tissue of the plant and to regenerate lost organs or undergo different developmental pathways in response to particular stimuli. When plant cells and tissues are cultured in vitro they generally exhibit a very high degree of plasticity, which allows one type of tissue or organ to be initiated from another type. In this way, whole plants can be subsequently regenerated.

The pieces of a whole plant used for tissue culture are termed 'explants'. Explants may consist of pieces of organs, such as leaves or roots, or may be specific cell types, such as pollen or endosperm. Protoplasts (a cell without cell wall), meristems, nodes, anthers, ovules, embryos and seeds can be used as explants as well. Many features of the explants are known to affect the efficiency of culture initiation. Generally, younger, more rapidly growing tissue (or tissue at an early stage of development) is most effective.

In plant tissue culture, plants or explants are cultured in a specific plant medium. The plant medium, liquid type is prepared by mixing inorganic salts, organic nutrients (sucrose), vitamins, minerals and plant growth regulators (auxin and cytokinin). In addition to these ingredients, solid medium contains gelling agent (agar). Nutrient and plant hormones amounts vary, depending on the objective of plant tissue culture. For example, in order to induce more roots, auxin amount should be high.

Aseptic environment during tissue culture is required to avoid contamination from microorganisms. Since plant cell division is slower compared to the growth of bacteria, fungi and even minor contaminants can easily overgrow the plant tissue culture. Therefore, all the materials like glassware, instruments, media, explants etc. to be used in culture work must be fred of microbes by using several techniques. The techniques available used for sterilization consist of steam sterilization/autoclaving (for nutrient media, culture vessels, glassware and plastic ware), filter sterilization (for thermolabile substances like growth factors, amino acids, vitamins and enzymes), alcohol sterilization (for worker's hands, laminar flow cabinet), flame sterilization (for scalpel, forceps, needles etc. and mouth of culture vessel) and dry heat (for scalpel, forceps, needles, glassware, pipettes, tips and other plastic ware).

To start with plant tissue culture, one should wipe his/her hands, forceps and other equipments with alcohol or other sterilizer to prevent microbial contamination. Then the explants are surface sterilized by using chemical solutions such as bleach or alcohol. Though mercury chloride is an effective sterilizer, it is rarely used due to its potential toxicity. After sterilization, the explants are introduced into a plant medium, which can be either solid or liquid. The cells divide and differentiate into plant parts, thus give rise to a complete plant.

Plant tissue culture has wide applications. It is used directly for the propagation of plants especially for those hard to propagate in natural conditions. Horticultural plants such as orchids, roses, bananas, strawberries, potatoes, apples, etc. are successfully cultured in in-vitro conditions. Tissue culture is also used for the propagation of medicinal herbs on a large scale. With plant tissue culture, it is possible to generate virus-free plantlet of vegetatively propagated plants.

In experimental biology such as plant breeding, cell biology, biotechnology and genetics, plant tissue culture is applied to solve plant related problems. It allows screening of cells for the desirable characters such as early fruit bearing, disease resistance and drought resistance. Another important application is generation of a novel hybrid by crossing two distantly related species having advantageous traits. In-vitro fertilization and/or pollination of plants are possible, irrespective of the hindrances in natural conditions.

Furthermore, Plant tissue culture is used for the conservation of germplasm especially for those seedless plants species. Some plants with valuable secondary products are grown in the controlled conditions by using plant tissue culture technique.

Glossary

1. tissue culture　组织培养
2. hygienic　*adj.* 卫生学的，卫生的，保健的；有益卫生的；　hygienics *n.* 卫生学
3. vegetative propagation　营养繁殖，无性繁殖
4. plasticity　*n.* 可塑性，适应性，柔软性
5. totipotency　*n.* 全能性，细胞全能性
6. sessile　*adj.* 固有的，固着的，无柄的，无腹柄的
7. predation　*n.* 捕食，捕食现象，掠食
8. in response to　响应；适应
9. manifest　*n.* 表现，征候，显示，清单，声明
10. explant　*n.* 外植体；移植，外植
11. mercury chloride　氯化汞，二氯化汞，升汞
12. medium　*n.* 培养基
13. gelling agent　胶凝剂
14. agar　*n.* 琼脂
15. protoplast　*n.* 原生质体
16. propagation　*n.* 繁殖
17. auxin　*n.* 生长素
18. meristem　*n.* 分生组织
19. node　*n.* 节
20. anther　*n.* 花粉
21. ovule　*n.* 胚珠
22. embryo　*n.* 胚[胎]

Exercises

A. Please answer the following questions in English.
1. What is tissue culture?
2. What is the central concept to understand tissue culture?
3. Why aseptic environment is very important during tissue culture?
4. How to eliminate or avoid contamination during plant tissue culture?
5. What aspects should we pay attention to in plant tissue culture?

B. Please translate the following paragraph into Chinese.

Plant tissue culture technology is playing an increasingly important role in basic and applied studies, particularly in crop improvement. In modern agriculture, only about 150 plant species are extensively cultivated. Many of these are reaching the limits of their improvement by traditional methods. The application of tissue culture technology, as a central tool or as an adjunct to other methods, including recombinant DNA techniques, is at the vanguard in plant modification and improvement for agriculture, horticulture and forestry.

C. Please translate the following sentences into English.

1. 组织培养技术也存在着一些不利之处，如设备成本较高、程序复杂、需要耗费较多精力以及会产生变异等。

2. 植物组织培养是根据植物细胞具有全能性的理论，利用植物体离体的器官（根、茎、叶、茎尖、花、果实等）、组织（如形成层、表皮、皮层、髓部细胞、胚乳等）或细胞（如大孢子、小孢子、体细胞等）以及原生质体，在无菌和适宜的人工培养基及光照、温度等人工条件下，诱导出愈伤组织、不定芽、不定根，最后形成完整植株的技术。

Part B Tissue Culture in the Banana Industry

Selected and rewritten from *Tissue Culture in the Banana Industry*, by Agustin B. Molina Jr.

Tissue culture is one biotechnology that has been extensively and productively used in the banana industry. Compared with other reproductive methods tissue culture possesses obvious advantages in several aspects. The followings aim to introduce the uses and importance of tissue culture in bananas.

Rapid mass production of planting materials

Traditionally, bananas are propagated vegetatively using suckers or corms. Unlike seeded commercial cultivars of other crop species, production of planting materials through suckers takes a long time and very few quantity of planting materials are produced per mother plant. Realizing the potential of in-vitro propagation, shoot-tip cultures have gained popularity over the world for rapid mass multiplication of planting materials. Since the first report of banana in-vitro clone propagation in the 1960s, the tissue culture technology in banana has undergone significant improvement and now used widely in banana production worldwide.

The ability to produce big number of planting materials in relatively short period of time had allowed growing bananas in a bigger parcel of land in a given timeframe, which otherwise be limited by limited availability of suckers. With this technology, one can plan to plant the desired number of plants in a desired area of land.

Efficient distribution and transport of planting materials

One distinct advantage of tissue culture over suckers is the ease of transport of large quantities of planting materials with distance. Thousands and even millions of rooted tissue culture plant (meriplants) can be transported in long distances. For instance, in the early

1990s, millions of rooted tissue culture plantlets sourced from Israel by multinational companies were planted vast areas of land in Central America. Several thousands of hectares of banana plantation in southern Philippines also used tissue culture materials from Israel in the late 1990.

Production of disease-free planting materials

Several major diseases of bananas are known to be transmitted through vegetative planting materials, like suckers and corms. In addition, some pathogens like nematodes and those causing fusarium wilt and moko are also transmitted through the soil and root tissues.

Nematodes, fungal and bacterial pathogens are not transmitted through tissue culture. While virus diseases such as BBTV, BBrMV, BSV, and CMV may be transmitted through tissue culture, a procedure may be used to exclude infected mother plants. Antibodies of these viruses have been developed to detect their presence in a mother plant used in tissue culture mass production. This process of virus indexing ensures that the tissue culture materials are free from the pathogens.

Safe exchange of germplasm

Tissue culture technology coupled with virus indexing allows a safe movement and exchange of germplasm. The INIBAP Transit Centre ensures that germplasms requested by various national partners are virus indexed so that germplasm exchanges are free from virus pathogens. Tissue culture is the most common method used for germplasm exchange.

Germplasm conservation

Because of seedlessness of many *Musa* accessions, tissue culture is commonly used in in-vitro conservation. The INIBAP-ITC maintains more than a thousand *Musa* germplasms in tissue culture under low temperature. While tissue culture has a drawback in germplasm conservation due to its propensity to somaclonal variation as a result of in-vitro culture and repeated sub-culturing, it is still the most common method of in-vitro germplasm conservation, pending the full implementation of cryopreservation in *Musa* genebanking.

Annual cropping/Crop timing

Due to diseases, environmental and market considerations, annual cropping or crop timing were adopted in several countries. Traditionally, bananas are grown as perennial crop where banana farms are perpetuated from year to year through taking care of daughter plants (suckers) after harvesting the mother plant. This type of banana culture, while simple, is vulnerable to build up damages and suffer subsequent damages by pests and diseases.

To alleviate the adverse effects of typhoon and low temperature problems, bananas are grown in such a time that the adverse effects of these climatic factors are minimized or avoided. Hence, annual cropping is adopted. With this seasonal planting, or annual cropping, tissue culture technology provides large quantities of planting materials in such a narrow window of planting time of large areas of farms. In Taiwan Island, the TBRI (Taiwan Banana Research Institute) first developed the commercial planting of large quantity of tissue culture disease-free planting materials in 1982. Since then, this became a standard practice in Taiwan banana industry.

Crop timing is also used to time the volume of production to coincide with market demands. Market demands and prices follow a certain seasonal trend. Manipulating volume of fruit harvests for this seasonal demand fluctuation require good scheduling of planting of appropriate hectarage. The use of tissue culture planting materials in such a cropping system is essential.

Another cropping system that improves productivity employed by export banana companies is high density planting. This system is done with annual/crop timing production systems and it involves higher density of planting coupled with good pruning system. The yield per unit area of land is improved. Tissue culture planting materials are used in such a system.

Tissue culture in *Musa* Improvement

One of the drawbacks of tissue culture especially during the early phase of its commercial introduction in the 1980s is the occurrence of soma clonal variants. These "off-types" were mostly morphological in nature, such as shorter plants, narrow leaves, leaf deformation, etc. Refinements of tissue culture production methods have reduced these undesirable soma clonal variations. However, with the extensive planting of millions of tissue culture materials in Taiwan Island, and in the presence of field selection pressure against Fusarium wilt, TBRI, together with growers, were able to make use of their "undesired" soma clonal variation selecting variants which have desirable agronomic traits such as shorter plant height, bigger bunches, shorter maturing, and most importantly, resistant to Fusarium wilt, race 4. This somaclonal breeding approach was started by TBRI since 1983. This innovative approach has resulted to improved commercial varieties that have been released and used commercially in Taiwan Island. This program has contributed significantly to the rehabilitation of the Taiwan Island banana industry.

While the use of tissue culture has been shown to bring about numerous advantages, there are also some problems associated with it. There are strong evidences indicating that tissue culture materials are generally more susceptible to diseases than suckers (if the sucker is also disease-free). Cucumber mosaic virus (CMV) has been observed to be more prevalent and severe in tissue culture plants than those originated from suckers. There is also evidence that tissue culture materials are generally more susceptible to Fusarium wilt and other soil-born diseases.

Tissue culture plants were also observed to be more susceptible to herbicide damage especially at early growth stage. In general, tissue culture plants tend to develop "floating mats" and therefore prone to toppling over after shooting.

Glossary

1. sucker   *n.* 吸芽
2. corm   *n.* 球茎
3. mother plant   母株
4. in-vitro   体外的
5. pathogen   *n.* 病菌，病原体
6. nematode   *n.* 线虫
7. hectare   *n.* 公顷
8. germplasm   *n.* 种质
9. propensity   *n.* 嗜好，习性
10. somaclonal variation   体细胞克隆变异，体细胞无性系变异
11. subculturing   *n.* 传代培养，接种，移种
12. inocula   *n.* 接种物
13. disease incidence   发病率
14. rehabilitate   *vi.* 复原，恢复，康复；*vt.* 使修复，整顿，使复兴，更新
15. ravage   *n.* 破坏，蹂躏；*v.* 毁坏，破坏，掠夺
16. epidemic   *adj.* 传染性的，流行性的；*n.* 传染病，流行病
17. demand fluctuation   需求波动
18. banana bunchy top virus (BBTV)   香蕉束顶病病毒
19. INIBAP (International Network for the Improvement of Banana and Plantain) 国际香蕉和大蕉品种改进网络的简称
20. Fusarium wilt   镰刀霉枯萎病，凋萎病，干腐病
21. Cucumber mosaic virus (CMV)   黄瓜花叶病毒
22. hectarage   *n.* 公顷数，作物产量(通常以公顷衡量)

Questions

1. What are the advantages of tissue culture over conventional propagation techniques used in the banana industry?
2. Why tissue culture is used in *Musa* improvement?
3. Why banana tissue culture seedlings are used for crop timing?
4. What are the problems associated with the use of tissue culture in the banana industry?

Lesson 8

Part A Genetic Engineering and Tropical Horticultural Industry

Selected and rewritten from *Papaya (Carica papaya L.) Biology and Biotechnology*, by Jaime A. *et al.*; *Genetically manipulated pineapple: transgene stability, gene expression and herbicide tolerance under field conditions*, by S. Sripaoraya, *et al.*; *Ripening in papaya fruit is altered by ACC oxidase cosuppression*, by Rodolfo López-Gómez, *et al.*; and *Transgenic Virus Resistant Papaya: New Hope for Controlling Papaya Ringspot Virus in Hawaii*, by Dennis Gonsalves, *et al.*

Genetic engineering is a laboratory technique used by scientists to change the DNA of living organisms. DNA is the blueprint for the individuality of an organism. The organism relies upon the information stored in its DNA for the management of every biochemical process. The life, growth and unique features of the organism depend on its DNA. The segments of DNA which have been associated with specific features or functions of an organism are called genes.

Molecular biologists have discovered many enzymes which change the structure of DNA in living organisms. Some of these enzymes can cut (endonuclease) and join (ligase) strands of DNA. Using such enzymes, scientists learned to cut specific genes from DNA and to build customized DNA which offers the organism more advantageous features needed by people. They also learned about vectors, strands of DNA such as viruses, which can infect a cell and insert themselves into its DNA.

With this knowledge, scientists started to build vectors which incorporated genes of their choosing and used the new vectors to insert these genes into the DNA of living organisms. Genetic engineers believe they can improve the foods we eat by doing this.

Nowadays, genetic engineering has been widely used in the improvement of horticultural crops. By manipulating the synthesis of ethylene, an important phytohormone, playing a critical role in plant ripening and senescence, through genetic engineering, researchers have created the ripening delayed tomato cultivars and senescence delayed carnation cultivars. To change flower color is not only a commercial but also an exciting challenge for companies and researchers through genetic engineering approach. Creating the "blue rose" which means the impossible or the unattainable, now has been a reality. Japan's Suntory Ltd said in October 19, 2009, that it would start selling the world's first genetically-modified blue roses next month. The blue roses are created by implanting the gene that leads to the synthesis of the blue pigment Delphinidin in pansies. Besides these described above, genetic engineering has been used in researches such as modification of plant lipids, plant architecture construction, chilling tolerance and disease and pest resistance. The successful applications of genetic engineering encourage researchers to exploit it in more variety crops.

Tropical horticultural crops play an important role in world's agriculture industry and people's daily life. Many tropical fruits (e. g. banana, papaya, mango, litchi, longan and pineapple) and tropical flowers (Orchids, *Euphorbia*, *Heliconia*, Bromeliads, *Anthurium*, etc.) are familiar to us. The genetic engineering is also adopted in cultivar improvement of tropical horticultural species, resolved some severe problems as well. The following descriptions focus on a few of remarkable applications of genetic engineering on tropical horticultural crops which have and would impact the tropical horticulture industry.

Disease and Pest Resistance

Plant viruses result in considerable loss in tropical horticulture industry and genetic engineering has been successfully used in the improvement of anti-virus cultivars of tropical fruits. Papaya ringspot virus (PRSV) is devastation for the papaya industry. Papaya with resistance to PRSV has been the first genetically modified tree and fruit crop and also the first transgenic crop developed by a public institution that has been commercialized.

PRSV was discovered in the 1940s in Hawaii, by 1995, it caused the whole papaya industry of Hawaii in a crisis situation. Genetic engineering was successfully used to rescue Hawaii's papaya industry. By using the concept of pathogen-derived resistance, a coat protein gene of a mild mutant of a PRSV strain from Hawaii was used in ballistic transformation of embryogenic cultures of red-fleshed Sunset cultivar and yellow-fleshed cultivar Rainbow. The field trial results showed that the transgenic papaya plants were PRSV resistance and the yield of transgenic papaya was much higher than that nontransgenic as well.

The transgenic papaya was deregulated within two years after documents were submitted to the Animal Plant Health Inspection Service (APHIS), the Environmental Protection Agency (EPA), and the Food and Drug Administration (FDA). APHIS considered the impact on agricultural environments, EPA considered the pesticidal aspect of the viral coat protein produced by the transgenic papaya, and consultation was held with FDA which considered the food safety aspect of the transgenic papaya. Licenses that were needed to commercialize the transgenic papaya were obtained by April 1998. Seeds were distributed to growers on May 1, 1998. Efforts to deregulate the transgenic papaya were carried out by the investigators and funding for deregulation and licensing was provided by the Papaya Administrative Committee (PAC), a grower organization regulated under a USDA marketing order. The transgenic papaya could now be used in efforts to translate the hope of controlling PRSV into a reality.

Banana, the most important tropical and subtropical fruit, its production has been seriously endangered by insects and various diseases caused by fungi and viruses. The conventional banana cultivar improvement approaches for insect and disease resistance have obvious limitations, which include the lack of germplasms with resistance needed and the triploid chromosomes. Furthermore, genetic transformation is of great interest in banana because (1) the cultivated varieties are triploid and sterile, (2) some resistance sources are not available among genetic resources (i. e. virus resistance) and (3) the foreign gene within the genetically modified plant cannot be transferred to another plant because the triploid plants will not produce fertile pollen. Therefore, the risk of direct gene contamination is minimized both for other plants and for the environment.

Through genetic transformation technologies, transgenic plants have been produced for some banana cultivars Williams, Gros Michel, Bluggoe and Three Hand Planty, using gene constructs encoding for various antifungal peptides which have previously been proven highly active in-vitro against major pathogenic fungi of bananas.

Nematode and weevil account for severe production lost of bananas and plantains. Transferring of genes encoding Protease Inhibitors (PIs) into banana plants to enhance the pest resistance has been proven effective methods. In addition to PIs, genes available for genetic engineering for pest resistance include Bacillus thuringiensis (Bt) toxins, plant lectins, vegetative insecticidal proteins and alpha-amylase inhibitors. Some of these genes have been engineer in bananas and in greenhouse research or in commercial release.

Molecular Farming

Over the last few years there has been a growing interest in "molecular farming" for the production of added value compounds of pharmaceutical, cosmetic and industrial importance. Out of these, edible vaccines are of prime importance for human health care. The production of antigens in genetically engineered plants is anticipated to provide an inexpensive source of edible vaccines and antibodies in the fight against infectious diseases such as hepatitis B. In this regard, banana and papaya are recognized as the ideal systems for the production and delivery of edible vaccines. Ganapathi *et al*. (2002) sub-cloned hepatitis B surface antigen (HBsAg) and transformed embryogenic banana cells using *Agrobacterium*-mediated transformation in order to produce transgenic banana plants for edible vaccines against hepatitis B. In this research, the embryogenic cells of banana cv. Rasthali (AAB) were transformed with the "S" gene of HBsAg using *Agrobacterium*-mediated transformation. The transgenic nature of the plants and expression of the antigen were confirmed by PCR, Southern hybridization and reverse transcription (RT)-PCR. HBsAg obtained from transgenic banana plants was similar to human serum derived one in analogous density properties. Transgenic papayas that carry the epitopes KETc1, KETc12, and GK-1, three promising candidates for designing a vaccine against *Taenia solium* cysticercosis, were developed by Hernández *et al*. (2007). Cysticercosis the most common parasitic infection of the central nervous system world-wide is caused by the pork tapeworm, *Taenia solium*. Infection occurs when tapeworm larvae enter the body and form cysticerci (cysts). In this research, nineteen different transgenic papaya clones expressing synthetic peptides were found to confer resistance against cysticercosis. Complete protection against cysticercosis was induced with the soluble extract of the clones that expressed higher levels of transcripts of up to 90% of immunized mice. The results indicate that transgenic papayas may be a new antigen-delivery system for subunit vaccines. An initial study to develop a vaccine against tuberculosis in papaya was done by Zhang *et al.* (2003) by introducing the esat-6 gene from Mycobacterium tuberculosis under the control of the CaMV 35S promoter and using the hpg gene as selection marker for *Agrobacterium*-mediated transformation. Selected transgenic papaya plantlets were shown to have incorporated the gene. However, it still needs to be shown if the protein produced by the transgenic plant is immunogenic when injected into test animals.

The results of banana and papaya as a molecular vaccine farm are significant as there is an urgent need for affordable and reliable vaccines in developing countries. Costs associated with the production, maintenance and delivery of traditional vaccines are often very high resulting in limited distribution of vaccines in these countries. Theoretically, the expression of recombinant proteins in transgenic plants offers inexpensive vaccines that could be produced directly "on site".

Ripening and Senescence

Compared with temperate fruit crops, tropical and subtropical fruit often present greater problems in storage and transportation because of their greater perishability and fruit overripening. The phytohormone ethylene is confirmed playing a major role in regulating fruit ripening and senescence especially the climacteric fruit. Manipulating the synthesis of ethylene by genetic engineering has been successfully used in many horticultural crops which enlighten the researchers to adopt this approach to improve tropical horticultural crops' keeping quality. It has been clear that, in higher plants, ethylene is synthesized from methionine via S-adenosyl methionine and 1-aminocyclopropane-1- carboxylic acid. The role of the two key enzymes of the pathway, ACC synthase and ACC oxidase, during fruit ripening has been the focus of research of many groups over several years. By antisense inhibition of ACC oxidase, or RNAi or ACC synthase antisense it has been possible to delay fruit ripening. Other studies have further demonstrated that introduction of truncated gene constructs in the sense orientation; can result in suppression of homologous host genes, a phenomenon called co-suppression. Rodolfo *et al.* reported a study on ACC oxidase cosuppression and its effects on papaya fruit ripening. The transgenic papaya fruits showed a delay in ripening rate and reduction in mRNA level for ACC oxidase in transgenic fruit was clearly detectable although more studies are necessary before this technology can be used to extend the shelf life of papaya fruit, it is undoubtedly that genetic engineering is an efficiency approach in retarding the ripening of papaya fruit. The same work is progressed in banana and other tropical fruits crops.

Genetic engineering is also used in some tropical ornamental crops such as Orchids and *Anthurium* but no striking progresses being reported. In spite of the controversy about the potential biosafety risks of transgenic varieties, genetic engineering will influence the industry of tropical horticultural crops extensively and widely.

Glossary

1. genetic engineering   基因工程
2. Papaya ringspot virus (PRSV)   番木瓜环斑花叶病
3. embryogenic culture   胚发生培养
4. Animal Plant Health Inspection Service (APHIS) （动植物卫生检验局），是美国农业部(USDA)的一个下属机构
5. Environmental Protection Agency (EPA) （美国）环境保护局
6. Food and Drug Administration (FDA) （美国）食品和药物管理局
7. USDA   美国农业部
8. nematode   *n.* 线虫
9. weevil   *n.* （香蕉）假茎象甲
10. pharmaceutical   *adj.* 药的，配药的，配药学的，制药的
11. cosmetic   *n.* 化妆品，装饰品；*adj.* 化妆用的，化妆品的
12. vaccine   *n.* 疫苗
13. hepatitis B surface gene (HBsAg)   乙型肝炎表面抗原，乙肝表面抗原
14. *Taenia solium*   猪肉绦虫（学名）
15. pork tapeworm   猪肉绦虫
16. cysticerci   *n.* 囊状虫；幼虫
17. (RT)-PCR (reverse transcription PCR)   反转录 RCR
18. overripening   *n.* 过熟
19. S-adenosyl methionine   腺苷蛋氨酸
20. 1-aminocyclopropane-1- carboxylic acid   1-氨基环丙烷-1-羧酸
21. RNAi (RNA interference)   RNA 干扰，是指外源 dsRNA 引发生物体内基因的同源序列降解，从而表现出的基因转录后沉默现象
22. shelf life   货架期

Exercises

A. Please answer the following questions in English.

1. What is genetic engineering?
2. Is genetic engineering approach widely used in horticultural industry?
3. How did genetic engineering confer papaya the resistance to PRSV?
4. How to confer nematode or weevil resistance to banana by genetic engineering approach?
5. Is the Molecular Farming a reality now?

B. Please translate the following paragraph into Chinese.

Relative success in genetic engineering of bananas and plantains has been achieved recently to enable the transfer of foreign genes into plant cells. Protocols for electroporation of protoplasts derived from embryogenic cell suspensions, particle bombardment of embryogenic cells, and co-cultivation of wounded meristems with *Agrobacterium* are available for bananas and plantains. *Agrobacterium*-mediated transformation offers several advantages over direct gene transfer methodologies like particle bombardment and electroporation.

C. Please translate the following sentence into English.

基因工程技术既可以用于提高作物对不利生物因素的抗性还可用于克服那些由非生物环境因素如土壤贫瘠造成的低产问题。

Part B Mango Cultivar Improvement and Genetic Engineering

Selected from *The Mango: Botany, Production and Uses*, by Richard E. Litz.

Mango (*Mangifera indica* Linn.) is a typical tropical fruit tree and plays an important part in the diet and cuisine of many diverse cultures. Mango are regarded as one of the most popular and esteemed tropical fruits. There are over 1000 named mango varieties (cultivars) throughout the world, which is a testament to their value to humankind.

Although exists a tremendous of cultivars, the mango cultivars with overall excellent traits, such as taste, appearance and resistance, are rare. To keep the mango industry progressed sustainably and normally, the improvement of mango cultivars is absolutely necessary.

Mango cultivar improvement program currently exist in several countries, and they address significant production problems that have a genetic basis. Classical breeding of mango has obvious limitations, which include, the long juvenile period of mango trees (7 or more years), the low frequency of fruit set following controlled pollination, the period required for seedling trees to be evaluated for fruit production, tree architecture, and the cost of maintaining large populations of seedling trees in order to observe segregation of important horticultural traits. There is no single ideotype for mango; however, the most important attributes for scion cultivars must include: compact size, resistance to anthracnose and other limiting diseases, fruit production (which would include annual bearing and factors that affect fruit quality, i.e. shape, color, flavor and size).

Biotechnology confers an efficiency approach for mango cultivar improvement. Biotechnology refers to the application of molecular biology and somatic cell genetics to the improvement of plants. Biotechnology can resolve some of the most serious production problems of important mango cultivars and improve breeding methodologies. Genomic studies will ultimately associate genes with specific functions, and this will impact genetic engineering and molecular breeding of mango. Marker assisted selection (MAS) would facilitate the screening of seedling populations for important horticultural traits. Genetic engineering, maybe the most attractive biotechnique nowadays, would permit the targeting and alteration of specific horticultural traits in existing cultivars, without altering the integrity of clones. Mango improvement by modern genetics will be freed from the constraints of the lengthy juvenile period of the species and the additional years required for tree evaluation. Moreover, the efficient management of mango plant genetic resources should be greatly facilitated within the next decade by advances that have been made in molecular biology, cell culture and cryopreservation.

Genetic transformation is currently the only practical solution for improving existing elite selections of perennial species for specific horticultural traits and for investigating gene function by interference RNA. Transformation of mango has been reviewed most recently by Gomez-Lim (2002,2005) and Litz (2007).

Mathews et al. (1992, 1993) first reported the genetic transformation of mango using embryogenic cultures of polyembryonic "Hindi" and of a monoembryonic "Keitt" zygotic embryo-derived embryogenic line, respectively. These two studies utilized two different disarmed, engineered strains of Agrobacterium tumefaciens: (1) strain C58C1 containing the plasmid pGV 3850::1103 with the selectable marker gene for neophosphate transferase (NPTII) which confers resistance to the antibiotic kanamycin, both of which were driven by the CaMV constitutive 35S promoter (Mathews et al., 1993); and (2) strain A208 containing the plasmid pTiT37-SE::pMON9749, a co-integrate vector, with genes for NPTII and the scorable marker β-glucuronidase (GUS or uidA) with the 35S promoter (Mathews et al., 1992). A report by Cruz Hernandez et al. (1997) utilized A. tumefaciens strain LBA4404 containing NPTII, β-glucuronidase (GUS) and genes that mediate a horticulturally useful trait in binary plasmid pBI121 with the CaMV 35S promoter. Mathews and Litz (1990) earlier had demonstrated that 12.5 μg/ml kanamycin sulfate is toxic to embryogenic suspension cultures; whereas, much higher levels (200μg/ml kanamycin) are toxic to embryogenic cultures that are grown on semi-solid medium.

These genetic transformation reports have followed a similar two-step (Mathews et al., 1992; Cruz Hernandez et al., 1997). Embryogenic suspension cultures in their logarithmic phase of growth are separated by passing them through sterile filtration fabric (1000 μm pore size), and the large fraction (>1000μm) is abraded with a sterile brush on sterile filter paper. The abraded PEMs are then incubated with acetosyringone-activated A. tumefaciens for 3 days in liquid maintenance medium, with subculture into fresh medium at 24 h intervals. The PEMs are then transferred onto semi-solid maintenance medium supplemented with 200 mg/L kanamycin sulfate and 500 mg/L cefotaxime. After 10 months on this selection medium, the PEMs are transferred to semi-solid maintenance medium containing 400 mg/L kanamycin sulfate. Proliferating cultures are subcultured in liquid maintenance medium containing 100 mg/L kanamycin sulfate, and somatic embryo development is initiated by subculture onto semi-solid maturation medium. Mathews et al. (1993)

regenerated transgenic mango plants derived from a "Keitt" zygotic embryo embryogenic culture and which had been transformed with pGV 3850∷1103 containing the selectable marker gene NPT II. Genetic transformation was confirmed by: (1) growth in selection medium containing inhibitory levels of kanamycin sulfate, (2) positive histochemical reaction for GUS with X-GLUC (Jefferson, 1987), and (3) Southern hybridization.

Transient gene expression in embryogenic polyembryonic "Kensington" and polyembryonic "Carabao" cultures has been described using a biolistic approach using two vectors: (1) pBI426 with GUS-NPTII under the control of a double CaMV 35S promoter, and (2) pBinGFP-SER, which contains NPTII and the green fluorescent protein gene (GFP) (Cruz Hernandez *et al.*, 2000).

Loss of mango fruit due to spoilage in storage and en route to markets accounts for a significant proportion of total production in many developing countries that have poorly developed infrastructure (i.e. cold storage facilities, poor roads, unreliable transportation, etc.). Mango has become an important export commodity for several developing countries. Extended shelf life and absence of physiological disorders that cause internal breakdown of fruit (e.g. "soft nose" and "jelly seed") of the most important export cultivars (e.g. monoembryonic "Tommy Atkins") are potentially very important, therefore, for the valuable export trade and for domestic markets.

The mango is a climacteric fruit, and ethylene therefore is a critical regulator of the biochemical processes that occur during ripening. Certain rate-limiting genes that mediate ethylene production in mango have been cloned. Cruz Hernandez *et al.* (1997) described the genetic transformation of embryogenic polyembryonic 'Hindi' mango cultures with mango ACC oxidase, ACC synthase and ACC alternative oxidase cloned in the antisense orientation and under the control of the CaMV 35S constitutive promoter in the pBI121 binary vector in *A. tumefaciens* strain LBA4404. Embryogenic cultures were transformed by the two-step procedure described above. Although the phenotype of the transformed lines was not reported, the genetic transformations were confirmed in each case by the XGLUC reaction for GUS, growth in the presence of inhibitory levels of kanamycin sulfate, Southern blot hybridization and NPTII amplification by PCR. Successful regeneration of plants and inhibition of ethylene production by mature mango fruit could possibly resolve the production problem of premature ripening (jelly seed) and post-harvest loss due to spoilage.

Glossary

1. improvement   *n.* 改进，改良，改善，改正
2. cultivar   *n.* 品种
3. juvenile period   童期
4. fruit set   坐果
5. controlled pollination   人工授粉

6. tree architecture 树形
7. ideotype *n.* 理想株型，模式株型；（分类）表意标本
8. scion *n.* 接穗，嫩枝，幼芽
9. anthracnose *n.* 炭疽病
10. rootstock *n.* 砧木
11. abiotic stress 非生物胁迫
12. polyembryony *n.* 多胚性，多胚现象
13. monembryony *n.* 单胚
14. somatic cell 体细胞
15. methodology *n.* 方法学，方法论
16. genetic engineering 遗传工程
17. marker assisted selection (MAS) 标记辅助育种
18. elite *n.* 良种，原种
19. perennial *adj.* 常年性，多年生的 *n.* 多年生植物
20. interference RNA RNA 干扰
21. kanamycin *n.* 卡那霉素
22. β-glucuronidase *n.* 葡萄糖醛酸苷酶
23. binary plasmid 二元质粒
24. suspension culture 悬浮培养
25. logarithmic phase 对数期，对数生长期
26. acetosyringone *n.* 乙酰丁香酮
27. cefotaxime *n.* 氨噻肟头孢菌素
28. proliferate *v.* 增生，增殖
29. subculture *n.* 继代培养；次培养基；次培养菌；*v.* 次培养
30. histochemical *adj.* 组织化学的
31. Southern hybridization Southern 杂交，基于 DNA 与 DNA 杂交的分子技术
32. spoilage *n.* 变质，酸败，腐败
33. climacteric fruit 呼吸跃变型果实

Questions

1. What are the disadvantages of traditional improvement of mango cultivar?
2. Is biotechnology an efficiency approach for mango cultivar improvement?
3. What is marker assisted selection?
4. What is transient gene expression?

Lesson 9

Part A Seed Production for Horticulture Crops

Selected and rewritten from *Horticulture: A Basic Awareness*, by Robert F. Baudendistel.

Most flower and vegetable seeds are produced in the inner valleys of California, which provide favorable growing and harvesting conditions, consisting of a mild climate with limited amounts of rainfall. Because of the lack of rainfall, most seed-producing fields are watered by irrigation.

Seed production

Seed production is widespread, and its scale ranges from the home gardener to large commercial enterprises. Seed collecting from plants in their natural habitat is often done both by amateurs and commercialist. Commercially, seeds from ornamental shrubs and forest trees are collected in large-scale operations.

Plant breeders are constantly cross-pollinating a wide variety of flowers in test fields in an attempt to provide the home gardener with seeds having improved characteristics, which can range from larger-size flowers or fruits to total resistance to a specific disease organism. The entire process of developing new varieties is both complex and time-consuming and requires critical examination by the plant breeder during the new seeds' first year of growth.

Seeds that have finally reached the stage of public acceptance are planted continuously from November to May. Each seed grown, however, has its own specific schedule of planting, growing conditions, pollination, and harvest. The growth requirements or culture of one species of seed may be entirely different from another species.

The grower must also know whether the seed species entrusted to him are to be self-pollinated by either wind or insects or cross-pollinated by hand, which requires the emasculation or removal of the male components of the flower and the transfer of the desired pollen from other plants grown in another location to the ripened pistil. Seeds obtained in this manner are given the designation of hybrid seeds (F_1 hybrids) and must be harvested by hand. Seeds with high market desirability may be grown in enclosed structures, either glass or plastic, where both growing conditions and pollination can be more adequately controlled.

Environmental conditions necessary for production of high-quality seed determine the location of commercial operations. Different environmental factors affect the expression of the hereditary characteristics. The temperature, irradiance level, photoperiod, and relative humidity are considered. However, many industries producing vegetable and flower seeds are located in environmental areas different from those in which the crops will later be grown, since low humidity and minimum summer rainfall are desirable conditions for drying seed for harvesting. Also, seeds for many plants are produced in areas that are more likely to exhibit symptoms of the presence of a latent virus. This is especially important in asexually propagated crops, such as potatoes, strawberries and many cut flowers. A problem encountered in areas of low humidity is premature shattering of the seed pod during harvesting. Therefore, many flower seeds are produces in the Lompoc Valley in California, in Puerto Rico, and in Florida, where the moist winds from the ocean and frequent night and morning fogs aid in preventing the pods from dehiscing before or during harvest. Isolation is important in wind and insect pollinated crops.

Both flower and vegetable seeds are harvested from June to December. At the proper time, each seed-producing crop is cut and gathered into rows. For economical reasons, machinery is used for both operations whenever possible.

Cleaning

Hand labor is necessary to harvest flower and vegetable seeds. This is especially true when the seed head or pod shatters easily or when seeds mature over a long period of time, so that flower buds, flowers and mature seeds may be on the same plant at the same time. The chief advantage of hand picking is that the cleaning process is greatly reduced. With some crops, such as carnation, hollyhock and sweet pea, the entire plant must be cut, placed on canvas and dried so that the seeds can be threshed out. Many crops, especially the fleshy fruits, require that the seeds should be milled from the fruit and then cleaned. The seed of tomato is removed after maceration of the fruit and fermentation of the pulp removed may reduce germination.

Differences in size, density and shape of seed in comparison with plant debris and other undesirable objects generally determine the cleaning practices to be followed. Screens with different sieve sizes are used to separate the larger particles from the seeds. Smaller, light-weight particles can be removed by blowing an air current through the seeds as they pass from one screen to another or as they pass across a porous bench or against an inclined plane. The heavier seed remain at the base while the lighter materials are blown into another plane. By using an "indent machine", desirable seeds are separated from other seeds or particles of the same density but of different shape. A wheel covered with indentations—the size and shape of which are determined by the particular crop being cleaned—is passed through a batch of seed, and each "indent" picks up a seed. Some seeds can be separated on the basis of color (beans and peas). A single seed is picked up by suction through perforations on a hollow wheel and then passed through a photoelectric cell; upon detection of an object of the wrong color, the vacuum is released and the seed is ejected. Seeds separation and cleaning is a delicate operation. The machinery must be adjusted carefully so that the seed is not damaged or chipped. Damaged seeds may fail to germinate, or may show reduced viability, or may produce weak seedlings.

Storage

It is usually necessary to stored seeds after harvest. The viability of seeds after the storage period depends on: (1) the initial viability of seed at harvest, which is a result of the production factors and handling methods; and (2) the rate of physiological deterioration inherent in the particular species and influenced by the environmental conditions under which the seeds are stored. The approximate longevity of well-stored seed of some common vegetables and flowers is presented. (Table 9-1)

Approximate longevity of well-stored seeds of some common vegetables and flowers   Table 9-1

1 year	Sweet corn, onion, parsnip, okra, parsley
	Delphinium, candytuft (*Iberis umbellata*)
2 years	Beet, pepper, leek, chives
	Aster, strawflower, sweet pea
3 years	*Asparagus*, bean, carrot, celery, lettuce, pea, spinach, tomato
	Aster, *Phlox*, *Verbena grandiflora*
4 years	Cabbage, cauliflower, Brussels sprouts, Swiss chard, kale, squash, pumpkin, radish, rutabaga, turnip
5 years	Cucumber, endive, muskmelon, watermelon
or more	Shasta daisy, cosmos, *Petunia*, *Scabiosa*, marigold, pansy, sweet alyssum pink, hollyhock, stock, *Nasturtium*, *Zinnia*

Source: Christopher. E. P. Introductory. New York: McGraw Hill, 1958.

The seed is thoroughly cleaned and tested for germination by highly skilled registered seed technologists, who are regulated by germination standards set by the federal government for each species of seed.

Seeds, like all living organisms, carry on respiration even when dormant. The respiration rate of seeds is largely dependent on water content and temperature. Most seeds have the ability to retain a certain moisture level by absorbing moisture from the air. The respiration increases with increasing temperature. The storage life of many seeds can be extended by lowering the relative humidity of the storage atmosphere and by lowering the storage temperature.

Pregermination moisture relationships can also influence germination percentages in many species. Before storage, the seed is often dried to approximately $5\% \sim 7\%$ of its dry weight. Only $10\% \sim 12\%$ is needed to prevent decay. Storage temperature of $-18 \sim 0°C$ appears to be optimal for most species. A common rule for most seeds is that for each $1°C$, storage life is doubled. But the seed of some species (wild rice, silver maple, citrus, oak, and hickory) lose viability if their moisture content is decreased. The seeds of a few species, such as apples and pears, must be kept moist in prier to maintain food viability.

Seeds dried to low moisture content are often stored in airtight cans or other containers. Again, the seeds must be dried to 5%~7% of the dry weight. Any fluctuation in the moisture content of seeds during storage will usually reduce longevity.

In some cases, it is possible to modify the storage atmosphere with beneficial results. A vacuum can be created, carbon dioxide content raised, or oxygen replaced by nitrogen or other gases not affecting respiration.

Home gardeners who have been pleased with the performance of a particular plant often save the seeds of the plant for the next growing season. However, they may be disappointed with the performance of cross-pollinated and produced seeds of different and undesirable genetic characteristics. A home gardener may have been planting hybrids produced from a particular cross, such as hybrid corn from inherent lines. Such seed will segregate in the F2 generation, and the results will be undesirable.

Packaging

After receiving its necessary period in storage and its specific pregermination treatments, the seed is ready for packaging. A specified number of seeds are counted out, either by hand or by machine, into a dry, moisture-proof packet providing the eventual purchaser with sufficient seed to sow one row. Because of their delicate nature, great care must be exercised during the entire packaging procedure to prevent damage to the seeds.

Once the seeds have been packaged, they are kept cool and dry until they are distributed to the consumer. The seed companies may sell their seeds either through their colorful catalogues, which they disseminate to interested gardeners, or on display racks found in both retail and wholesale outlets. Most seeds packets have planting instructions and other important information clearly printed on the outside cover.

Longevity

The seeds of maple, elm, willow, and some other trees lose their viability very rapidly. Desiccation—the drying out or loss of moisture from the seed—plays a role in reducing the longevity of seed. Seed of medium life are those which normally retain their viability for 2 to 3 years and can remain viable as long as 15 years, depending on storage conditions. Certain weed seeds have even germinated after hundreds of years, and seed of the Egyptian lotus that were found in pyramids have also germinated.

Glossary

1. breeder   *n.* 育种工作者
2. cross-pollinating   *adj.* [植]异花授粉的
3. self-pollinate   *v.* [植]自花传粉
4. emasculation   *n.* 去雄
5. pollen   *n.* 花粉
6. pistil   *n.* [植]雌蕊

7. hybrid seed   杂种种子
8. germination   *n.* 发芽，萌芽
9. pregermination   *n.* 发芽处理，催芽
10. ornamental shrub   观赏灌木
11. forest tree   林木
12. hereditary character   遗传特性，遗传性状
13. irradiance level   辐照度
14. photoperiod   *n.* 光周期
15. asexually propagated crop   无性繁殖作物
16. strawberry   *n.* 草莓
17. carnation   *n.* 康乃馨（一种花）
18. hollyhock   *n.* 蜀葵
19. sweet pea   [植]香豌豆，麝香豌豆花
20. respiration rate   呼吸速率

Exercises

A. Please answer the following questions in English.

1. Why the process of developing new varieties requires critical examination during the new seed's first year of growth?
2. As a breeder, what kind of knowledge should be got before producing seeds?
3. How do the environmental conditions affect the quality of seeds?
4. How to deal with the seeds after harvesting?
5. How to prolong the longevity of seeds during the storage?

B. Please translate the following paragraph into Chinese.

Production of genetically pure and otherwise good quality pedigree seed is an exacting task requiring high technical skills and comparatively heavy financial investment. During seed production strict attention must be given to the maintenance of genetic purity and other qualities of seeds in order to exploit the full dividends sought to be obtained by introduction of new superior crop plant varieties. In other words, seed production must be carried out under standardized and well-organized condition.

C. Please translate the following sentences into English.

1. 种子是裸子植物和被子植物特有的繁殖体，由胚珠经过传粉受精后逐步发育形成，一般由种皮、胚和胚乳三部分或种皮和胚两部分组成。可通过杂交育种、基因工程等技术手段改良遗传特性来获得高品质的植物种子。

2. 目前对种子实施有机处理主要有四种方法：一是用热水或干热空气消毒，防止种子携带病菌；二是用微生物包衣种子，以控制各种土传性病害及苗期病害；三是用共生微生物处理，以增强作物的自然防御能力；四是用自然生长促进剂处理种子，促进幼苗的生长并增加其抗性。

Part B Seed Treatment for Disease Control

Selected and rewritten from *Seed Treatment for Disease Control*, by Marcia P. McMullen.

Most seed treatment products are fungicides or insecticides applied to seeds before planting. Fungicides are used to control diseases of seeds and seedlings, insecticides are used to control insect pests. Some seed treatment products are sold as combinations of fungicide and insecticide.

Fungicidal seed treatments are used for three reasons: (1) to control soil-borne fungal disease organisms (pathogens) that cause seed rots, damping-off, seedling blights and root rot; (2) to control fungal pathogens that are surface-borne on the seed, such as those that cause covered smuts of barley and oats, bunt of wheat, black point of cereal grains, and seed-borne safflower rust; and (3) to control internally seed-borne fungal pathogens such as the loose smut fungi of cereals. (Fig. 9-1)

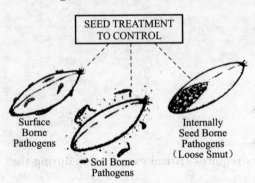

Fig. 9-1 Reasons for seed treatment

Most fungicidal seed treatments do not control bacterial pathogens and most will not control all types of fungal diseases, so it is important to carefully choose the treatment that provides the best control of the disease organisms present on the seed or potentially present in the soil. The degree of control will vary with product, rate, environmental conditions and disease organisms present. Some systemic fungicidal seed treatments may also provide protection against early-season infection by leaf diseases.

Fungicide-insecticide combination products or an addition of insecticide for wireworm control should be considered if planting newly opened land or land that has had a history of wireworms. Consult current recommendations for insecticides registered for wireworm control. A fungicide-insecticide combination may also be useful for dry beans. The insecticide used on dry beans should be one that provides control of the seed corn maggot.

Seed Treatment Application

Fungicide seed treatment products come in a variety of formulations and in a variety of packaging sizes and types. Some are registered for use only by commercial applicators using closed application systems; others are readily available for on-farm use as dusts, slurries, water soluble bags, or liquid ready-to-use-formulations. Whatever the formulation used or application method chosen, some precautions should be taken to assure applicator safety and appropriate seed coverage.

Cautions Follow label directions when handling seed treatment chemicals. These products are potentially poisonous if mishandled or misused. Extreme caution must be used when handling seed treatment chemicals; some are toxic, others may be irritating. An approved chemical respirator and goggles are recommended even if not specifically required by the fungicide label.

The rate of application prescribed by the label must be used; overtreatment may injure the seed and undertreatment may not provide good disease control. To apply the correct rate, it is essential to calibrate application equipment carefully and to check calibration frequently. Metering cups of commercial applicators should be cleaned daily to prevent a buildup of chemical that might result in reduced application rates.

Treated seed should not be used for food or feed, and treated grain should not contaminate grain delivered to elevators or be placed in bins or in trucks delivering to elevators.

Containers should be triple rinsed with the rinse water added to the treatment mixture. The rinsed containers should be punctured and crushed for disposal in an approved landfill.

Lentils

Lentils should be treated with captan, fludioxonil (Maxim), mefenoxam (Apron XL) or metalaxyl (Allegiance). Captan and fludioxonil provide broad spectrum protection against *Rhizoctonia* and *Fusarium* seedling blights. Mefenoxam (Apron XL) and metalaxyl (Allegiance) provide excellent control against *Pythium* seedling blight, but do not provide protection against *Rhizoctonia* or *Fusarium*.

Peas

Common seedling blights of peas can be controlled with captan, fludioxonil, PCNB or thiram. The water mold fungi *Pythium* and *Phytophthora* are common problems on peas and can be controlled with mefenoxam, metalaxyl or oxydixyl treatments. No seed treatment is registered for *Ascochyta* blight on peas, but data from Manitoba indicates that thiram provides good suppression of seed-borne *Ascochyta*.

Sugarbeets

Pythium, *Aphanomyces*, and *Rhizoctonia* are fungi that may cause stand establishment and seedling disease problems in sugarbeets. The *Pythium* fungus occurs in most sugarbeet soils. It causes seeds rot, pre-emergence damping off, and post-emergence damping off. Post-emergence damping off caused by *Pythium* may occur when the seedlings are so tiny that they dry up and blow away within a day or two. Consequently, *Pythium*-induced seedling death is seldom noticed by the grower. The only thing noticeable may be an unusually poor emergence and stand.

Most sugarbeet seeds are sold treated, but different treatments vary in their effectiveness against these three fungi. Certain fungicides have specific activity: mefenoxam (Apron XL), metalaxyl (Allegiance) and oxadixyl (Anchor) are highly effective against *Pythium*; thiram is moderately effective against *Pythium*; PCNB, chloroneb and fludioxonil (Maxim) are effective against *Rhizoctonia*. Growers planting in fields with known *Rhizoctonia* problems may wish to request a special or supplemental seed treatment from their seed supplier or else use a planter box overtreatment. Hymexazol (Tachigaren) is effective against *Aphanomyces* and *Pythium*. It is available in specially pelleted seed, the 75 g rate provides protection for four weeks.

Glossary

1. fungicide *n.* 杀菌剂
2. insecticide *n.* 杀虫剂
3. soil-borne *adj.* 土壤带有的，土壤传播的
4. fungal *adj.* 真菌的
5. pathogen *n.* 病原体
6. damping-off *n.* 猝倒病
7. blight *n.* 枯萎病
8. rust *n.* 锈病
9. wireworm *n.* 线虫
10. maggot *n.* 五谷虫
11. poisonous *adj.* 有毒的
12. toxic *adj.* 有毒的
13. lentil *n.* 扁豆
14. captan *n.* 克菌丹（一种用硫醇制的杀真菌剂和杀虫剂）
15. fludioxonil *n.* 咯菌腈，勿落菌恶（由瑞士诺华公司开发）
16. mefenoxam *n.* （精）甲霜灵
17. metalaxyl *n.* 甲霜林
18. *Rhizoctonia* *n.* ［微］丝核菌
19. *Fusarium* *n.* 镰刀菌
20. *Pythium* *n.* ［真菌］腐霉属
21. *Phytopbthora* *n.* 辣椒疫霉菌
22. thiram *n.* ［药］二硫四甲秋兰姆，福美双，双硫胺甲酰（杀菌药）
23. sugarbeet *n.* 糖用甜菜
24. chloroneb *n.* 地茂散（杀真菌剂）
25. hymexazol *n.* 恶霉灵
26. tachigaren *n.* 土菌消

Questions

1. Why the seeds should be treated before planting?
2. How to control the diseases of seeds?
3. Please list some fungicide-insecticide combination products for seed treatment.

Lesson 10

Part A Plant Pathogens in Horticulture Crops

Selected and rewritten from *Greenhouse Management*, by J. J. Hanan • W. D. Holley & K. L. Goldsberry.

Plants are subject to infection by thousands of species from every diverse group of organisms. Most are microscopic, but a few are macroscopic. The infectious agents are called pathogens and can be grouped as follows: bacteria, fungi, viruses and viroids, nematodes, and parasitic seed plants, of which the first three will be discussed in this article.

In general, bacterial and fungal diseases are encouraged by high temperatures and high humidity. There are exceptions such as *Phialophora* wilt of carnations, which develops faster at low temperatures. Most bacteria and fungi are spread by splashing water and require free water for spore germination. However, free water is lethal to the conidia of powdery mildew on roses.

Bacteria

Although bacteria are capable of causing rots, leaf spots, blights, and wilts, they are often classified separately as there are relatively few important genera. Predisposing conditions are high humidity, poor air movement and high temperatures—conditions commonly prevalent in propagation beds. Infected plant material is a major means of introduction, but disease can be spread by dirty tools, insects, inoculated soil, splashing water and often gains entry to the host through wounds as may occur in propagation or cutting. Infection can occur through roots, stems, and leaves.

For bacterial leaf spots, the classical symptoms are circular or angular, water-soaked areas on the leaves. These spots may be first dark to light green, gradually turning yellow, then brown or black. In some instances, a halo may be seen around the center when held to the light. Under moist, humid conditions, bacterial ooze may be observed, yellow, reddish, clear, or white in color. The spots may coalesce and there can be premature leaf drop. Spots may be sunken, can have reddish brown borders or purplish concentric rings as on carnations.

Rots and blights caused by bacteria are nearly always characterized as soft rots, leading to complete tissue disintegration and a slimy, often ill-smelling, black mess. The bacteria may gain entry and develop internally as in wilts or stunts. Development may be fast or slow, depending upon environmental conditions and growth stage of the host. In slow wilt of carnation, plants usually show an unthrifty appearance, lighter color, and loss of bloom. Bacterial wilt of carnations, however, may cause sudden wilting without any previous indication. Bacterial blight of chrysanthemums commonly shows terminal wilting with a dull, grayish, water-soaked appearance of the stem at a point one-half to two-thirds of the way up the stem. The vascular tissue of infected plants may be affected on only one side, or all, of the stem, usually black, streaky, slimy, and sticky to the touch. Stickiness and a foul odor of ooze from lesions is a good indication that the causal agent is bacterial.

Fungi

In many instances, definite diagnosis of disease requires the services of a trained specialist to isolated and identify the pathogen. This is often required for intelligent control and eradication, and is particularly important for fungal diseases. The number of fungal genera that can attack plants is practically without end. We have classified fungal diseases into broad groupings of blights, rots, leaf spots, wilt, rusts, mildews, and cankers. The easiest way to identify are mildews and rusts. Powdery mildew grows a white powdery to cottony mycelium on leaf surfaces, sometimes confined to a single side of the leaf causing leaf deformation and stunting. High humidity is a predisposing condition. Control is directly related to humidity manipulation and outside climatic conditions. Downy mildew of snapdragons is favored by lower temperatures. Rusts are identified by pustules filled with reddish-orange or brown spore masses erupting through the leaf epidermis. The spores require water to germinate, and rust is usually found on plants under drips, or if water is allowed to stand on leaf surfaces for a considerable period.

Wilts, blights, and rots are often difficult to distinguish as; depending upon method of entry and plant part, the same organism may cause symptoms of rotting, blighting, or wilting. Wilts are usually systemic and spread by infected plant material. The organism may invade the root system and grow up one side of the stem so that branches on that side are affected. Or, if young plants are invaded, they may suddenly topple over, wither and die. There is usually a general browning of the vascular tissue, with some black necrosis of the basal stem tissue in the case of *Aster* and *Chrysanthemum*. The plant may appear unthrifty, off-color, stunted, and produce smaller blooms. The base of the stem can be water soaked. With the exception of *Phialophora* wilt, high temperatures generally hasten growth of the pathogen. No symptoms can be seen until flowering in the case of *Fusarium* wilt of cyclamen. In advanced stages of azalea leaf blight, there may be a sparse to luxuriant brownish mycelium on lesions with powdery white masses of conidia of the fungus *Phytophthora*.

Viruses

Plant viruses are generally composed of complex nucleoproteins that are visible under the electron microscope. However, recent research has shown that some diseases formerly though to be caused by viruses are actually mycoplasma organisms without cell walls that can exist in two or more forms in one life cycle. More than one virus may infect a plant and sometimes two are required to produce visible symptoms. Symptoms may vary with the season and host development, with some detectable only by grafting, and transmitting the virus to a variety that will produce visible symptoms. Often, the only visible symptom will be a reduction in vigor which cannot be ascertained without comparison with a virus-free plant. At other times with some viruses, damage will be readily apparent leading to ultimate death of the host.

Transmission can be sucking insects, such as thrips, aphids, and leafhoppers, or by juice carried on hands and tools. Control is commonly exclusion of the insect as the case of aster yellows, transmitted by leafhoppers, or careful washing and disinfecting of tools and hands as in the case of tobacco mosaic. Tobacco should never be allowed in tomato greenhouses as the tobacco mosaic readily infects tomatoes.

Viruses are often classified into broad categories as mosaics, yellows, mottles, and streaks. The names roughly characterize the disease symptoms. Mosaic viruses generally produce chlorotic symptoms in a manner described by the term "mosaic"; whereas, "mottling" can be a more or less random yellowing, chlorotic pattern. "Vein clearing", or the loss of green color along the veins, is a common symptom with yellow and mosaic. Tulip "breaking" is probably the oldest known virus disease of plants. Flowers become variegated with leaves striped with light green or even with the white. Variegation in flowers consists of bars, stripes, flames, streaks, or feathering of a darker color overlaying a lighter shade of the same color, or on a pure white or yellow. There is reduced size and vigor of the plant with fewer offsets or bulbils. On *Peperomia*, the leaves are distorted and disfigured with concentric zonal markings with each ring beginning as a small translucent spot that grows larger by addition outwardly of narrow bands or lines. The serious stunt virus on chrysanthemums generally causes reduction in size which cannot be diagnosed without a healthy plant for comparison, or by grafting on varieties that produce definite symptoms. Streak virus on carnations generally produces white to purplish-brown flecks in order leaves. With cineraria, the symptoms are roughening and curling of the leaves of young plants. Fleck in Easter lily is a combination of two viruses, neither one of which alone will cause symptoms. Geranium leaf cupping is probably the most distinctive and destructive virus disease. The virus changes the shape of the plant to one no longer characteristic of the species with leaves changed to incurved, hairless cups and sinuous veins. Aster yellows may cause a peculiar spindling growth with stems a light, greenish-yellow and abnormal production of side shoots. Chrysanthemum flowers may be greenish with weak lateral shoots, pale, and upright.

Glossary

1. microscopic *adj.* 微小的，细微的，显微镜的，用显微镜可看见的
2. macroscopic *adj.* 肉眼可见的，宏观的

3. pathogen   *n.* 病原，病原体
4. viroid   *n.* 类病毒
5. parasitic   *adj.* 寄生的，寄生虫的，由寄生引起的
6. infectious   *adj.* 侵染性的，易传播的
7. carnation   *n.* 麝香石竹，康乃馨
8. spore   *n.* （细菌、苔藓、蕨类植物）孢子
9. powdery mildew   白粉病，白粉菌
10. coalesce   *vi.* 联合，合并
11. purplish   *adj.* 略带紫色的
12. chrysanthemum   *n.* 菊花
13. streaky   *adj.* 有斑点的，有条纹的，容易变的
14. slimy   *adj.* 似黏液的，黏滑的
15. lesion   *n.* 损害，损伤，身体器官组织的损伤
16. pathogen   *n.* 病菌，病原体
17. deformation   *n.* 损形，变形，畸形
18. snapdragon   *n.* 金鱼草
19. pustule   *n.* 脓疱
20. necrosis   *n.* 枯斑，坏死，坏疽
21. cyclamen   *n.* 樱草属植物，仙客来，仙客来属
22. azalea   *n.* 杜鹃花
23. mycelium   *n.* 菌丝（体）
24. nucleoprotein   *n.* 核蛋白质
25. thrips   *n.* 牧草虫
26. leafhopper   *n.* 叶蝉
27. aster yellow   紫菀黄化病
28. chlorotic   *adj.* 萎黄病的，变色病的
29. bulbil   *n.* 鳞芽，球芽
30. zonal   *adj.* 带状的
31. translucent   *adj.* 半透明的

Exercises

A. Please answer the following questions in English.

1. How many categories can infectious agents be grouped?
2. What symptoms are there when fungal diseases infect a plant?
3. What are main reasons for bacteria diseases?

B. Please translate the following paragraph into Chinese.

Flowers are very often affected in storage if the spores are present when blooms are stored or transported. First symptoms may be small, water-soaked lesions, enlarging rapidly, and becoming brown to black with age. Petal blight of azalea, caused by the genus

Ovulinia, results in eventual rotting and disintegration of tissue, which turns dark brown to black with petals becoming slimy and falling apart if rubbed gently. Tiny purple spots, soon developing a broad, yellow-green border, are typical for alternaria blight of carnations.

C. Please translate the following sentences into English.

1. 由微生物侵染而引起的病害称为侵染性病害。由于侵染源的不同，又可分为真菌性病害、细菌性病害、病毒性病害、线虫性病害、寄生性种子植物病害等多种类型。

2. 植物侵染性病害的发生发展包括以下三个基本环节：病原物与寄主接触后，对寄主进行侵染活动，病原物数量得到扩大，并在适当的条件下传播开来，不断进行再侵染，使病害不断扩展；由于寄主组织死亡或进入休眠，病原物随之进入越冬阶段，病害处于休眠状态；到次年开春时，病原物从其越冬场所经新一轮传播再对寄主植物进行新的侵染。这是侵染性病害的一个侵染循环。

Part B A Greenhouse Without Pesticides: Fact or Fantasy?

Selected and rewritten from *Crop Protection*, by J. C. van Lenteren.

Biological control and integrated pest management (IPM) are reliable crop protection methods and are economically profitable endeavours for growers of greenhouse crops. The fast evaluation and introduction of a number of natural enemies in situations where chemical control was either insufficient, impossible or undesired, has taught growers and crop protection specialists that biological control, within IPM programs, is a powerful option in pest control.

The total world area covered by greenhouses is about 300,000 ha, 50,000 ha of which are covered with glass, and 250,000 ha with plastic. Vegetables are produced on 195,000 ha and ornamentals on 105,000 ha. Developments in biological control in this cropping system have been unexpectedly fast and illustrate the great potential of alternatives to chemical methods. Greenhouses offer an excellent opportunity to grow high-quality products in large quantities on a small surface area. For example, in the Netherlands only 0.5% of the area in use for agriculture is covered with glasshouses. On this small area of 10,000 ha, about 20% of the total value of agricultural production is realised.

Few specialists in biological control anticipated being able to employ natural enemies in greenhouses, because growing vegetables and ornamentals in this protected situation is very expensive and pest damage is not tolerated. This means that the usually well-trained, intelligent greenhouse growers will not run the risk of any damage from insects, just because of ideological reasons such as reduced environmental side effects compared to chemical control. If chemical control works better, they will certainly use it. In tomatoes, for example, pest control represents less than 2% of the total overall cost of production, so costs is not a limiting factor for chemical control. The same situation occurs in ornamentals where the cost of pest control using chemicals (including material and application) is usually less than 1% of the overall cost of producing the crop. Yet despite the serious constraint that chemical control is comparatively simple and inexpensive, adoption of biological control has been remarkably quick in greenhouses first in north-western Europe, and later in other greenhouse areas. The growers now clearly see the specific advantages of biological control in greenhouses. The main reason for use of biological control methods in the 1960s was the occurrence of resistance to pesticides in several key pests in greenhouses. Nowadays, other important stimuli include demands by policy makers for a reduction in usage of pesticides, and consumers requiring production of residue-free food and flowers.

Integrated pest and disease management in greenhouses

IPM is used on a large scale in all main vegetable crops. In the Netherlands for example, more than 90% of all tomatoes, cucumbers and sweet peppers are produced under IPM. Worldwide, 5% of the greenhouse area is under IPM, and there is potential for increase to about 20% of the area in the coming 10 years. A good example of an IPM program is the one for tomato used in Europe. It involves 10 natural enemies and several other control methods like host-plant resistance, climate control and cultural control. When tomatoes are grown in soil, soil sterilization by steaming is used shortly before planting the main crop to eliminate soil borne diseases such as tomato mosaic virus(TMV), *Fusarium*, *Verticillium* and pests such as *Lacanobia oleracea* (tomato moth) and three *Liriomyza* spp. (leaf miners). Previously, cultivars lacking TMV resistance were inoculated as young plants with a mild strain of the TMV virus to make them less susceptible. Now, TMV-resistant cultivars are available. Furthermore, many tomato cultivars in Europe are resistant to *Cladosporium* and *Fusarium*. Some cultivars are also tolerant to *Verticillium* and rootknot nematodes. Problems with soil diseases can also be strongly reduced by growing the crop in inert media, which has become common practice in Western Europe. In tomatoes, therefore, only foliage pests and *Botrytis cinerea* require direct control measures. The few pest organisms that "overwinter" in greenhouses and survive soil sterilization are the greenhouse red spider mite (*T. urticae*) and the tomato looper (*Chrysodeixis chalcites*). Transferring young plants free of the other pest organisms into the greenhouse is important to prevent early pest development. For 20 years, the bulk of greenhouse tomatoes have been grown on rockwool systems, which makes soil sterilization redundant. With the cessation of soil sterilization more organisms, such as *Liriomyza* spp. and their natural enemies, and *L. oleracea* "overwinter" in greenhouses. A recent development which gave a strong stimulus to the application of biological control is the use of bumblebees for pollination.

Development of IPM for ornamentals is more complicated than for vegetables. The first problem is that many different species and cultivars of ornamentals are grown. In Western Europe for example, more than 100 species of cut flowers and 300 species of potted plants are cultivated, and for several ornamentals more than 100 cultivars are produced. Other problems for implementation of IPM in ornamentals are that (1) more pesticides are available than for vegetables, (2) the whole plant is marketed, instead of only the fruits, so no leaf damage is allowed, and (3) a zero tolerance is applied to export material. But, since the 1990s use of biological control is steadily growing in cut flowers (gerberas, orchids, roses and chrysanthemums) and pot plants (poinsettia). In gerberas the developments have been particularly fast and natural enemies were used on 78% of the Dutch gerbera area in 1998. Biological control was applied on more than 10% (600ha) of the total greenhouse are a planted with flowers and ornamentals in 1998 in the Netherlands.

Specific advantages of biological pest control in greenhouses

Why do greenhouse growers use biological control? There are, of course, the general advantages of biological control such as reduced exposure of producer and applier to toxic pesticides, the lack of residues on the marketed product and the extremely low risk of environmental pollution. These, however, are not of particular concern for the grower. More important are the specific reasons that make growers working in greenhouses prefer biological control:

(1) with biological control there are no phytotoxic effects on young plants, and premature abortion of flowers and fruit does not occur;

(2) release of natural enemies takes less time and is more pleasant than applying chemicals in humid and warm greenhouses;

(3) release of natural enemies usually occurs shortly after the planting period when the grower has sufficient time to check for successful development of natural enemies, thereafter the system is reliable for months with only occasional checks; chemical control requires continuous attention;

(4) chemical control of some of the key pests is difficult or impossible because of pesticide resistance;

(5) with biological control there is no safety period between application and harvesting fruit, with chemical control one has to wait several days before harvesting is allowed again;

(6) biological control is permanent: once a good natural enemy— always a good natural enemy;

(7) biological control is appreciated by the general public.

Costs of biological control are similar to those of chemical control, and this, in combination with points (1), (2) and (5), makes it an attractive pest management approach. Consumers demand for pesticide-free food also stimulate the use of biological control.

Glossary

1. integrated pest management   害虫综合防治
2. glasshouse   n. 玻璃暖房，温室
3. side effect   副作用
4. host plant   寄主植物
5. sterilization   n. 消毒

6. tomato mosaic virus 番茄花叶病毒
7. *Fusarium* *n.* 镰刀霉，镰刀菌属
8. *Verticillium* *n.* 轮枝孢属，轮生菌属
9. *Lacanobia oleracea* 西红柿夜蛾
10. leaf miners (*Liriomyza* spp.) 斑潜蝇
11. susceptible *adj.* 易受影响的，过敏的，易感染的
12. *Cladosporium* *n.* 分子孢子菌属
13. root-knot nematodes 根结线虫
14. *Botrytis cinerea* 灰葡萄孢菌
15. looper *n.* 尺蠖
16. red spider mite 红蜘蛛，螨
17. redundant *adj.* 不需要的，多余的
18. cessation *n.* 停止，中止
19. bumblebee *n.* 大黄蜂，雄蜂
20. gerbera *n.* 非洲菊，大丁草
21. poinsettia *n.* 一品红，猩猩木
22. phytotoxic *adj.* 植物性毒素的，对植物有毒的
23. abortion *n.* 败育

Questions

1. Please give the exact definition of IPM in your own word.
2. What is biological control in plant disease and pest prevention, and why have it been turned to good use?

Lesson 11

Part A Handling and Storage before Marketing

Selected and rewritten from *Horticulture*, by R. Gordon Halface & John A. Barden Mcgraw.

Preparation for Marketing

Fruits and Vegetables

After harvest, many steps are necessary for the preparation of fresh fruits and vegetables for market. The number and type of treatments vary with the particular product, but with most, the following steps are involved: cleaning, sorting, sizing, and packaging. With some crops, additional treatments are typical: these may include removing held heat, trimming, treating with disinfectant or fungicide, waxing and curing.

During the harvest operation, fruits and vegetables are put into a diversity of containers for hauling to the packing house. A few vegetables such as head lettuce are trimmed and packed in the field as are many table grapes and most hand-harvested berries. Certain vegetables are packaged by a crew of workers on a moving packing house which travels through the field with the pickers. Examples of crops packed with this system are sweet corn and cantaloupes. The great majority of fresh fruits and vegetables are hauled to a cannery or to a central packing house where they are prepared for market. Containers used for the trip from the field to the packing house or processing plant include field crates holding from 10 to 40 kg and pallet boxes or bulk bins which hold from 15 to 22 bushels. Some of the fruits and vegetables are loaded directly onto trailers and trucks. The type of container used varies with many factors including the type of harvest (hand or mechanical), the perishability of the item, its resistance to damage, and the equipment available. The major advantages of bulk handing are lower cost, lower risk for bruising, and much lower labor requirements.

Removal of Field Heat Crops which are particularly perishable can have their market life extended significantly by prompt removal of field heat. The two most widely used techniques are vacuum cooling and hydrocooling.

Unloading Containers The transfer of produce from the field container to the packing line has changed markedly with the transition from the use of field crates to large containers. Produce in field crates was hand-poured onto the grading line, but bulk containers are mechanically emptied. When initially introduced, bulk bins were mechanically tipped to pour the product out, but this method resulted in considerable bruising. Many modern plants are now using hydrohandling systems in which the bin is mechanically submerged in a tank of water, and the fruits are floated out. A stream of water floats the apples or any other product out of the bin and onto a conveyor. The conveyor takes the fruit to the washer. This method results in a minimum of bruising.

Cleaning Before fresh fruits and vegetables are marketed, various amounts of cleaning are necessary. Cleaning typically involves the removal of soil, dust, adhering debris, insects, and spray residues.

Sorting After cleaning, the next operation required is sorting. This entails the removal of items which are unsuitable for packing. In most packing operations sorting is done by hand as the product moves along a roller or conveyor in front of the workers. Items damaged by insect, disease, or mechanical injury, which are obviously unfit for sale, are separated from the better produce. It is also a common practice for sorters to segregate fruit into grades on the basis of color or other visible characteristics on which a grade is based.

Waxing Some fresh fruits and vegetables are waxed as a part of the packing operation. With cucumbers, waxing is done to suppress moisture loss, thereby keeping the cucumber fresh and turgid. With apples, the waxing is usually for improved appearance only.

Sizing In normal marketing channels, fruits and vegetables are bought on the basis of both grade and size. With most items, the larger size command higher prices, but regardless of this consideration, uniformity of size is necessary. Uniform-sized fruits and vegetables are demanded by retail outlets for several reasons. Most consumers prefer uniform-sized items for a particular use.

Presizing and Presorting Once cleaned, sorted, and sized, fruits and vegetables may be handled in several ways. Some may be packed for immediate marketing, but in the peak season some may be returned to bulk bins for storage. Formerly, putting apples and other fruits into storage immediately after harvest without any sorting or sizing was standard practice. However, with the rising cost of cold storage, growers now commonly presize and presort before storage. This has two major advantages: avoiding the expense of storing low-grade fruit and facilitating packing of fruit out of storage to meet orders as received. With other products, where storage costs are low, such as potatoes stored in common or air-cooled storages, presorting may not be advantageous. Another approach is to size, sort, and package before storage. The major disadvantage of this technique is the possibility that the product will have to be repacked if a storage disorder occurs or if the pack does not match what is desired by the buyer.

Packaging The degree to which a particular product is prepared for marketing depends to a large degree on the marketing channel to be used. Current packaging for fresh market ranges from putting watermelons in a bulk bin which travels all the way to the retail store, to the use of a broad spectrum of consumer packages such as polyethylene bags, shrink films, plastic boxes with overwraps, plastic net bags, and paper bags.

Whether packaging is done at harvest or after storage, the process is the same. After cleaning, sorting, and sizing, the fruits or vegetables are packed in market containers. The package varies widely with the item.

A fresh produce grower may have a packing house in which the fruit is cleaned, sorted, sized, and packaged or may belong to a cooperative packing house which handles crops for many growers. In some areas packing is offered by custom packing houses which charge a fee.

Cut Flowers

The preparation of cut flowers for marketing is less involved than most fruits and vegetables. The grower must cut, grade, and package the cut flowers. A major goal should be cutting flowers at the proper stage of development to ensure optimum quality upon receipt and resale by the retail florist. The flowers must be graded, usually on the basis of flower size, stem length and freedom from defects. After grading, the flowers are packed "dry" in rigid cardboard cartons. Very expensive and perishable flowers, such as orchids, may be put into vials containing water as a preservative. For maximum retention of quality, cut flowers should be refrigerated. A grower may refrigerate flowers before shipment especially if a load is shipped only every 2 or 3 days. For this holding period the stems would be put in water. Upon receipt by the wholesaler, flowers are refrigerated. Long-distance shipping is usually by air freight, short hauls are typically by truck.

Pot Plants, Nursery Stock, Foliage Plants

These items usually require minimal preparation for marketing with the exception of field-grown nursery stock which must be dug, balled, and burlapped. Since the nursery business is tending more and more toward the use of container stock, these tasks are gradually being eliminated. Most of these items are now loaded on trucks for shipment. Since these plant materials are not nearly as perishable as cut flowers, considerably more flexibility in handling is possible.

Storage

Types Several types of storages are used for holding horticultural plants and products: common, cold, and controlled-atmosphere (CA) storages. A common storage is unrefrigerated storage but utilizes cooler outside air in fall and winter to hold temperatures at acceptable levels. The underground "root cellars" of earlier days would be an example. Cold storage is mechanically refrigerated to provide both rapid products cooling during loading and accurate temperature control during the holding period. Normally a room is filled gradually to prevent over-loading the cooling equipment and to lower the temperature of the product as soon as possible. Particularly perishable crops are precooled by hydrocooling, vacuum cooling, or the use of ice before being placed in storage. Most fruits and vegetables suitable for long-term holding are cooled in the storage room. Stacking containers to provide good air circulation is an absolute necessity if adequate cooling and temperature control is to be maintained.

Controlled-atmosphere storages utilize not only cold temperature but altered levels of CO_2 and O_2 to maximize storage life. By lowering the oxygen from the normal atmospheric level of 21 percent to 2 to 3 percent and elevating CO_2 from the normal concentration of 0.03 percent to 2 to 5 percent, the storage life of certain product can be extended, largely by lowering the rate of respiration. The atmosphere may be modified by sealing the fruit in a completely airtight room and allowing respiration by the fruit to utilize O_2 and generate CO_2. To provide the desired atmosphere more quickly and to reduce the necessity for completely airtight rooms, many storages now use gas generators to produce the desired atmosphere. One such system burns propane gas, and the burner is vented into the storage. In any case, frequent gas analysis is mandatory to prevent injury from excessively low O_2 or high CO_2. Controlled-atmosphere storage is widely used with apples and pears and seems to hold promise with other horticultural products.

The most recent development in storage technology is the principle of hypobaric storage. (Other terms are subatmospheric and low-pressure storage.) The product is held at a stable, subatmospheric pressure in a refrigerated vacuum chamber which is ventilated with fresh humid air. The principle behind hypobaric storage is that at low pressure the concentration of oxygen is reduced so that respiration is suppressed, and internal ethylene concentrations are dramatically reduced. Ethylene is known to be an extremely active ripening hormone, and by hold the product at low pressure, the ethylene concentration is lowered in the fruit and its diffusion rate is increased. Early results with this technique are indeed exciting, not only for fruits and vegetables, but for flowers, cuttings and potted plants as well.

Storage Nursery Stock For short-term holding, as in a garden center, little extra care is necessary other than providing adequate moisture. With balled and burlapped stock, the root ball is often wrapped in polyethylene, or a group of plants are held upright and the root balls covered with sawdust. Long-term storage becomes necessary for several reasons. Because they are handled bare-root, such products as fruit trees, strawberry plants, and asparagus roots must be shipped in late winter and early spring to enable planting as soon as the soil can be worked. To meet their shipping schedule, most northern nurseries dig their stock in late fall and early winter and thus must store it for a few months. Similar conditions exist in the handling of deciduous ornamentals which are also dug and shipped bare-root. Evergreens must be handled quite differently as they remain in full leaf. If field-grown, they are balled and burlapped; but increasing proportions are being produced and sold in containers. If field-grown, some may be dug in the fall and held in storage, like deciduous stock; but container stock is usually overwintered outdoors or in minimal-expenditure structures. In Northern parts of the country, much of the nursery stock is held in common storage. In warmer regions, such storages may be under ground with dirt floors. High-value crops which require minimal space are usually held in refrigerated storages to maintain optimum quality.

Glossary

1. packing house   包装房，包装车间
2. trim   *n.* 整齐，装饰，修剪；*adj.* 整齐的；*v.* 整理，修剪
3. pack   *n.* 包装，一群，一副；*v.* 包装，捆扎，塞满
4. sweet corn   甜玉米
5. cantaloupe   *n.* 罗马甜瓜，香瓜，哈密瓜
6. crate   *n.* 板条箱，篓子
7. trailer   *n.* 挂车，拖车
8. field heat   田间热，场热
9. vacuum cooling   真空冷却，真空预冷
10. hydrocooling   *n.* 用水冷却，水冷
11. grading line   分级生产线
12. sorting   *n.* 分等（根据外观），分选
13. waxing   *n.* 涂蜡，打蜡
14. sizing   *n.* 分级（根据大小）
15. presizing   *n.* 预先筛分，填孔处理
16. presorting   *n.* 预先分类，发货前清点
17. packaging   *n.* 封装，包装
18. polyethylene bag   聚乙烯袋
19. shrink film   收缩薄膜
20. cut flower   切花，鲜切花，插瓶花
21. wholesaler   *n.* 批发商
22. short haul   短途运输
23. pot plant   盆栽植物，盆栽花卉
24. nursery stock   定植苗，出圃苗，苗木
25. foliage plants   观叶植物
26. controlled-atmosphere (CA) storage   气调贮藏
27. cold storage   冷藏
28. hypobaric storage   减压储藏
29. sawdust   *n.* 木屑
30. asparagus   *n.* 芦笋
31. burlap   *n.* 粗麻布，粗麻袋，打包麻布

Exercises

A. Please answer the following questions in English.

1. Please list the handling steps of most fruits and vegetables products before marketing.
2. What materials can be used to package the fruits and vegetables?

3. How to handle the cut flowers before marketing?
4. Please define the **CA storage**.
5. What are the characteristics of cold storage?

B. Please translate the following paragraph into Chinese.

The two most widely used techniques to remove the field heat are vacuum cooling and hydrocooling. Most head lettuce is vacuum-cooled today. After packing, water is sprinkled over the lettuce and the cartons are closed. The lettuce is placed in large vacuum chambers. The pressure is lowered. As the water vaporizes, it absorbs tremendous quantities of heat. For leafy vegetables, vacuum treatment allows rapid cooling, eliminate the need for ice, and thus allow the use of fiber cartons. Hydrocooling has become standard commercial practice with many fruit and vegetables. The market today demands hydrocooled peaches because hydrocooling improves quality and shelf life.

C. Please translate the following sentences into English.

1. 国外蔬菜水果的商品化处理设备有大、中、小三种类型，自动化程度较高的机器可以自动洗果、吹干、分等分级、打蜡、称量、装箱，甚至可以操作电脑鉴别产品的颜色、成熟度，剔除伤果和病虫果。

2. 在果品贮藏中适当降低温度，减少氧气含量，提高二氧化碳浓度，可以大幅度降低园艺产品的呼吸强度，抑制乙烯的生成，延缓产品的衰老。

Part B Marketing of Fruits and Vegetables

Selected and rewritten from *Horticulture*, by R. Gordon Halface & John A. Barden Mcgraw.

Marketing of Fruits and Vegetables

Types Large chains of food stores handle the biggest part of the fresh fruit and vegetable business today. Even the independent grocers are often served by a large cooperative distribution center, serving 50 to 200 stores in a particular region. Tremendous buying power is in the hands of the produce buyer, who can buy in railcar and tractor-trailer loads rather than small quantities. Such centers assemble products from producers all over the country and the world and then distribute them to the local stores. Perhaps the major drawback of this system is that most of the decisions concerning the produce to be sold are in the hands of the distribution center's buyer; the local store manager, therefore, may have little choice. This disadvantage is often overcome by the buying power of a large distribution center.

Farmers markets are regaining some of their lost popularity as means of marketing fresh produce. These markets are designed so that individual producers can market their produce directly to consumers, often directly off the back of a truck. Some cities are encouraging the reactivation of farmers' markets by providing modern facilities and renting areas to individuals who wish to sell their produce. Such markets are often attractive to small and part-time farmers because they draw large numbers of potential customers with whom these producers might otherwise not be able to make contact.

Another alternative in the marketing scheme is roadside marketing. By selling their produce directly to the consumer, growers realize many advantages. These include minimal costs for packaging and the elimination of shipping and brokerage fees. By dealing directly with the customer, it is also possible to market a wider group of cultivars and thereby reduce the problems associated with the 3 to 4 major cultivars which are most in demand in wholesale marketing channels. By growing 8 to 10 cultivars, the harvest operation can be spread out over a longer period of time, thereby putting much less strain on labor, equipment, and cooling facilities during storage.

Diversification into several tree fruits, small fruits, and vegetables can reduce the gamble with a particular crop. For example, if a spring freeze destroys the apple crop, another crop may salvage the season's profits; but a wholesale apple grower would be much more severely affected.

Greatly increased adoption of "pick you own" is taking place in much of the country. In this system, since the customer picks the produce, the grower has eliminated much of the peak-harvest labor problem. Often such an operation can market crops from early summer through late fall. For example, a sequence might include strawberries, raspberries, blueberries, cherries, peaches, nectarines, apples and pears intermixed with vegetables such as green beans, squashes, tomatoes, peppers, corn and potatoes. Pick-you-own marketing seems to appeal to today's consumers in several ways. A major feature is the recreation offered to a family by getting out in the country and visiting a farm. Many operators encourage families by providing picnic facilities and recreation areas. The educational aspect is also important. Many urban children are totally unfamiliar with how crops grow, and visits to a farm can certainly be informative in this regard.

The pick-you-own system offers one of the few remaining ways in which a young person can break into the fruit or vegetable business without great financial resources. It is quite possible to start small and expand as the business grows.

Marketing Costs for Fruits and Vegetables

With the previously mentioned diversity of product preparation and marketing systems employed, it is certainly not surprising that the consumer's dollar is distributed in different ways. Taking lettuce, canned tomatoes and frozen orange juice as examples, we can see considerable variation. The lettuce and tomato producer gets only 12 to 14 percent of the consumer's dollar, whereas, an orange grower gets 28 percent. Assembly costs vary little but processing ranges from 16 percent on lettuce to 48 percent on canned tomatoes. Wholesaling and transportation take 29 percent of the lettuce dollar, but only about half as much on the other two products. Retailing takes a very large proportion of the lettuce dollar because of perishability, required refrigeration, and wrapping.

In the marketing costs for orange juice and canned tomatoes, about 25 percent is for labor, 20 to 30 percent is for packaging, and about 10 percent is for transportation. The remainder of the cost is split among many functions such as advertising, taxes, and interest.

Glossary

1. grocer *n.* 杂货商，食品商
2. distribution center 配送中心
3. railcar *n.* 轨道车，动车，滑轨车
4. tractor-trailer 拖拉机挂车
5. farmers market 农贸市场，农夫市集
6. part-time farmer 兼营农场主
7. roadside marketing 路边市场
8. pick-you-own marketing 自选市场
9. picnic facility 野餐设施

Questions

1. How many marketing types of fruits and vegetables are there in this text?
2. What are the advantages of the farmers markets?
3. Please take one fruit as an example to analyze its marketing cost.

Lesson 12

Part A Horticulture and the Home

Selected and rewritten from *Fundamental of Horticulture*, by J. B. Edmond, A. M. Musser, F. S. Anderews.

Every home presents some kinds of pictures to all who approach or pass by, as well as to those living in the home. This picture may be pleasing, attractive, and inviting, or it may be bleak, barren, and ugly. A beautiful home with well-landscaped grounds not only increases the value of the property but also increases the usefulness of the property. It is a source of pride to the family, visitor, and passer-by. Landscaping the home grounds involves more than planting "bushes" around the base of the building. Landscaping is the improvement of the home grounds to combine appearance with usefulness for the family living on the property. It includes the maintenance of the property as well as the planning and planting of the property.

Beautifying the home is not necessarily an expensive proposition. Many attractive and useful native plants can be secured for little or no cost. A few dollars' worth of well-selected shrubs and trees in their proper place will make a world of difference in the looks of a home. Quite often, the home grounds can be more completely landscaped through the proper use of trees and lawn grasses than through an abundant use of shrubs.

To beautify the home effectively certain objectives should be attained. These are: (1) to secure attractive grounds; (2) to provide natural, easy approaches; (3) to obtain privacy for the family; (4) to provide for the recreational needs of the family; and (5) to harmonize the home, buildings, yard, garden, and orchard into one complete unit.

The Landscape Plan

A plan for beautification is necessary not only to obtain these objectives and to effectively use plant materials, but also to relate the landscape developments to the needs of the family. It must be "custom-built" for the family. In other words, the plants that look well around one home may not suit a neighbor's home, or a flower garden may be a source of pride and recreation to an office worker but a burden to a farmer. Since the entire planting may not be completed in one season, with the aid of a plan each year's work can be coordinated without loss of effort. It is easier to change the location of a tree or shrub on the plan than it is to remove the tree or shrub on the grounds. In general, the plan is made to scale and shows the location of each area, building, drive, fence, tree, and shrub.

The home grounds consist of three areas: front or public, private, and service. The front or public area includes the front lawn, entrance, front walk, drive, and base planting. It is developed primarily to serve as an attractive foreground and frame for the house and property. By no means should the front area be used to exhibit some exotic plant that the owner may like, unless the plant fulfills a definite landscape need. The following guides are suggested for use in the development of the public area: (1) make the lawn open and spacious in proper proportion; (2) confine shrubs to the borders, corners, and base of the buildings; (3) balance the plantings, both trees and shrubs, about an imaginary line through the entrance of the house or property; and (4) use only those trees and shrubs which will compliment the house to best advantage.

As stated previously, the lawn should be open and spacious. Important factors in obtaining a satisfactory lawn are: (1) thoroughly prepared, well-drained, fertile soil; (2) use of well-adapted seed or lawn plants; (3) application of an adequate supply of nutrients and water; and (4) suitable maintenance practices. Lawns have many functions. They markedly reduce erosion, they reduce glare and cool the immediate surroundings, and they serve as an outdoor carpet. Lawn plants may be placed in two groups: warm-season and cool-season. Some of the most common lawn plants are presented. (Table 12-1)

Warm-season and Cool-season Lawn Plants   Table 12-1

Kinds of plants	Leaf		Plant height, inches	Sod[3]	Ability to maintain itself	How propagated
	Width[1]	Color[2]				
Warm-season Plants						
Bermuda···	n.	d. g.	2~3	d.	Low	Sod, springs, seed
Fine-leaved Bermuda	n.	d. g.	2~3	d.	Low	Sod, springs
St. Augustine···	m. b.	l. g.	3~4	m. d.	High	Sod, springs
Centipede···	b.	l. g.	3~4	d.	High	Sod, springs
Carpet···	b.	l. g.	2~3	d.	High	Seed
Zoysia···	n.	d. g.	3~4	d.	High	Sod
Cool-season Plants						
Kentucky Blue···	n.	l. g.	3~4	m. d.	High	Seed
Italian Rye···	n.	g.	6~8	m. d.	High	Seed

Note: 1 inch=2.54cm.
[1] n., narrow; m. b., moderately broad; b., broad.
[2] l. g., light green; g., green; d. g., dark green.
[3] d., dense; m. d., moderately dense.

The entrance is located near the corner of the lawn in the direction of the most travel and at right angles to the main highway. The approach to the farmstead should be direct, though not necessarily straight to any of the buildings. However, it should be adapted to the ground form and at the same time be the most convenient and direct approach to the house and service area.

The base planting is the planting around the base of the house. Its function is to unite and harmonize the dwelling with the remainder of the grounds. The extensiveness of the planting depends on: the size of the house and grounds, the height of the house, and the prominence of various features of the house. In general, with a large house and spacious grounds, large groups of plants are used. On the other hand, with a small house and small grounds, small groups of plants or even single specimens are used. Similarly, tall shrubs are used at the corners or angles and short plants at the steps or doorway. As a rule, shrubs are placed at least 91.44 cm from the building. Although some shrubs thrive best in shade and others thrive best in the sun, most shrubs grow satisfactorily in sun or partial shade.

The private area consists mainly of recreational areas for the family and includes such features as the barbecue pit, family area, children's play ground, flower garden, specimen shrubs or flowers, bird bath, lily pond, or rock garden. It is sometimes called the outdoor living room. The following guides are suggested for use in the development of the private area: (1) enclose the area to insure privacy and to form a background for landscape features; (2) arrange flower beds, rock garden, barbecue pit, or other features around the perimeter; (3) allow the center to remain open; and (4) make the area easily accessible to the house and to other parts of the property.

The service area includes the outbuildings, laundry yard, vegetable garden, home orchard, or similar features. This area is sometimes screened from the front and from the dwelling. It should always be convenient to the kitchen and entrance drive.

Arrangement of Trees In general, trees are planted in groups rather than in rows. With spacious grounds, the groups may consist of eight, ten, or twelve trees, and with non-spacious grounds they may consist of one, two, or three trees. Trees in the rear and on the sides of the lawn provide an effective frame and background and balance the landscape planting. For example, a group of trees at the southwest corner of the property with a corresponding group on the southeast corner frames and balances the planting. The planting of rapidly growing, short-lived trees such as cottonwood, box elder, and soft maple with slowly growing, long-lived trees such as oak and elm to provide temporary shade in a relatively short time is advisable.

Arrangement of Shrubs There are three general types of arrangement: the angle or corner, the entrance, and the group.

The angle or corner arrangement is adapted to the inside or outside of corners and extends in two ways. The tall plants are planted in the back, the medium-sized next, and the short to the extreme outside. To give stability, angle and corner plantings should be triangular in outline. This arrangement is particularly useful in designating the limits of the yard or lawn, breaking the angles where the back and side lawn meet, and hiding objectional views.

The entrance arrangement may be single plants or groups of plants, formal or informal in character, depending on the type and arrangement of the entrance unit. This planting should be the most outstanding planting in the front area, since it is used to attract attention or to set off and scale the entrance unit. The formality of the planting is determined by whether the entrance unit appears formal or informal.

The group arrangement usually is used for mass effect. The tall plants are planted in the middle and the medium and short plants to the sides. This arrangement is particularly useful in separating the private and public lawn and planting along borders.

Hedges and Vines Hedges and vines are used as screens, fences, or barriers and to provide seclusion in the private area. Vines are very valuable to screen unsightly buildings and to secure privacy.

In general, a satisfactory landscape planting has the following characteristics: (1) it fills a definite landscape need, (2) the plants are adapted to the soil and climate of the locality, (3) the size of the house and purpose for which used, and (4) the plants require a minimum of care. In particular, shrubs provide more unity when large groups of one or two kinds are used, and a more finished appearance when relatively wide spaces are used. Overplanting, a rather frequent occurrence, should be avoided. It results in shading of the leaves and in severe competition for water and nutrients. This results in a low rate of photosynthesis, poor growth, winter injury, and death. Thus, the use of large, healthy plants will avoid this undesirable condition.

Glossary

1. bush   *n.* 灌木，灌木丛
2. lawn grass   草坪草
3. orchard   *n.* 果园
4. drive   *n.* 快车道
5. imaginary line   假想线，假设线，虚线
6. lawn   *n.* 草地，草坪
7. well-adapted seed   适应性强的种子
8. lawn plant   草坪植物
9. erosion   *n.* 流沙
10. farmstead   *n.* 农庄
11. specimen   *n.* 样本，标本
12. barbecue pit   烧烤炉
13. lily pond   睡莲池塘
14. rock garden   岩石庭院，假山花园
15. perimeter   *n.* 周界
16. cottonwood   *n.* 杨木
17. box elder   [植]梣叶槭
18. soft maple   糖槭，银槭
19. specimen tree   园景树

20. mass effect   质量效应
21. hedge   *n.* 树篱
22. vine   *n.* 攀爬植物，藤，蔓
23. overplanting   *n.* 移植
24. photosynthesis   *n.* 光合作用
25. winter injury   冻害

Exercises

A. Please answer the following questions in English.

1. Why do people like beautifying home with some plants?
2. Normally, what kinds of objectives should be attained to beautify the home effectively?
3. How to make a landscape plan for beautifying home?
4. Please list some plants used in your home.
5. What are the three areas of the home grounds?

B. Please translate the following paragraph into Chinese.

Homes built in wooded areas or where mature trees have been carefully left by the developer offer the home gardener a wonderful opportunity for naturalistic landscaping. If the home already exists on a wooded plot, spend some time considering how you want to make use of the property. Lawns require constant maintenance and are not always in harmony with a naturalistic setting. It is practical to plant grass only where required for play areas or where a uniform carpet of turf will give the landscape effect you desire. Plus, establishing turf in shade is not always easy.

C. Please translate the following sentences into English.

1. 家庭园艺是园林艺术在居家设计上的具体应用，是人们对精神生活的一种高层次追求。它不但可以美化家居环境、自给部分果蔬，还可以陶冶身心、让人感受原生态的自然家居生活，令人轻松、舒适，越来越受到人们的喜爱。

2. 作为室内绿化装饰的植物材料，除部分采用观花、盆景植物外，大量采用的则是室内观叶植物。从观赏的角度讲，居室绿化不外乎赏花、赏叶、赏果和赏气味四种，有的兼而有之。具体考虑时还要注意色彩与室内主调是否相配，植物间气味是否相投，植物形态是否为人喜欢，大小是否适宜等。

Part B   House Plants

Selected and rewritten from *Horticulture: A Basic Awareness*, by Robert F. Baudendistel.

At some time during his life, almost everyone has either purchased or received some type of house plants. Sometimes a house plant is selected because of a special day or holiday and at other times simply to fulfill a desire to grow and care for a living plant.

Like all living things, house plants have scientific or generic names. Some are sold by their genus or scientific names, while others are sold by a variety of common names. Because of this, three people can refer to the same house plant by three different names.

To grow a specific house plant, its owner should become familiar with the cultural requirements of that plant, such as its temperature, light watering, and fertilization requirements. Certain plants are extremely specific in their growth requirements, while others will survive the most adverse conditions.

House plants are generally divided into the following five groups:

1. *Flowering plants*. These usually need day light to produce the desirable flowers.
2. *Foliage plants*. These plants are able to exist without much available sunlight.
3. *Fruit-bearing plants*. They need abundant light, warm temperatures, and sufficient water to produce their fruits.
4. *Succulents*. These plants are capable of living at very high temperatures, they need very little water.
5. *Vines*. Some vines are grown for their flowers, others for their foliage, and still others are selected because they can be trained to grow on foreign objects.

New house plants can be obtained from seeds, cuttings, bulbs, tubers, leaves, and roots. Certain plants have plant patents, which restrict completely any propagation without payment to their originators.

The balance of this chapter will be an alphabetical presentation of the more commonly grown house plants. Important information will be given with each house plant to enable the reader to achieve a much greater degree of success in growing a specific plant.

Bougainvillea can withstand a variety of growing conditions but prefers a soil on the dry side. This plant will bloom all winter, if pruned to maintain a bushy, pot-size plant.

Bromeliads are native American plants whose flowers and foliage make them desirable as house plants. They adapt readily to all indoor conditions. The pineapple is a member of this family.

Burn plant or *Aloe vera* is a small succulent with heavy leaves originating from a central base. The leaves may be plain green or variegated. Its common name is associated with the fact that the gelatinous pulp oozing from a removed leaf has analgesic properties for the treatment of simple burns.

Chinese cactus or *Zygocactus* is commonly referred to as crab's claw. It flowers freely in December and January when kept dry from mid-September until November except for a light sprinkling every ten days and when kept in the dark during the evenings, because it responds to short-day conditions.

Chrysanthemums flower naturally during periods of short days. They now can be programmed to flower on a specific date. Chrysanthemums come in a variety of sizes, shapes, and colors, and can be grown as either cut flowers or as potted plants.

Dieffenbachia is also called dumb cane, because a piece of the leaf placed on a person's tongue is supposed to render him temporarily speechless for about 24 hours. All species of this genus tolerate poor growing conditions.

English ivy or *Hedera helix* is a favorite vine grown in the home. Its leaves may be green or variegated and varied in shape, depending upon the variety selected.

Flamingo flower or *Anthurium* prefers high humidity, but resents transplanting. Varieties of this plant offer long-lasting flowers in a variety of colors.

Fuchsias are the favorite of many for their hanging baskets. They are not true house plants and will become dormant during the fall months after flowering has occurred.

Geranium is a very common house plant that does much better outdoors than it does inside the house. During the winter months, most plants become elongated, lose many of their leaves and produce few flowers, but even then, most homeowners do not discard them. There is wide range of differing varieties of *Geranium*, which is increasing each year with the new hybrid varieties.

Hoya is a flowering vine that is commonly called *wax plant*. The plants grow slowly and will not flower until they reach a certain size or age. It is sometimes planted in hanging baskets.

Impatiens is grown from seed, producing a variety of colors. These plants come as close to continuously flowering as any house plant grown. Their most important growth requirement is sufficient water, and new plants are easily obtained from the parent plant by taking stem cuttings.

Jasmine is a fragrant flowering plant that is easily grown indoors if it receives sufficient sunlight, a temperature about 65°F (19°C), and regular watering. The name jasmine is a general name that encompasses a wide variety of house plants.

Monstera is sometimes called Philodendron pertusum, Swiss cheese plant, or split leaf philodendron. The fruit, if it ever forms, would taste like a cross between a banana and a pineapple.

Orchids, once thought to be impossible to grow by the amateur grower, are becoming more popular. These are many types and varieties that can be successfully grown by the homeowner. The growing conditions vary somewhat from one variety to another, but they all desire a more humid atmosphere than the average home can provide. This problem is normally solved by placing pans of water near the plants.

Palms are durable, slow-growing, tolerant of high temperatures and insufficient light, and require little care, except for a regular schedule of watering.

Pilea is an easily grown house plant having glossy, dark green, flat leaves with interesting veins. They have small clusters of flowers that appear to originate from the leaves. Another variety of *pilea*, aluminum Plant, has already been mentioned.

Sansevieria or *snake plant* is a member of the lily family that may eventually produce green flowers. It is one of the toughest house plants, surviving both poor growing conditions and amazing abuse. New plants are easily propagated by placing a one-inch leaf section in sand.

Sensitive plant is a unique house plant whose leaflets collapse when touched. New plants are started from seed. Its genus is *Mimosa*, a member of the legume family.

Spider plant or Anthericum has narrow green leaves, striped with white, that grow in small tuffs. Additional plants can be quickly obtained by removing the tufts that hang over the side of pot and potting them. This plant does yield small white flowers, which are normally hidden by the mass of foliage.

Glossary

1. generic name　属名
2. scientific name　学名
3. adverse condition　不利条件，逆境条件
4. foliage plant　观叶植物
5. fruit-bearing plants　结实植物，观果植物
6. succulents　*n.* 肉质植物
7. bulb　*n.* 球茎
8. tuber　*n.* 块茎
9. plant patent　植物专利
10. bougainvillea　*n.* 叶子花
11. bromeliad　*n.* 凤梨科植物
12. pineapple　*n.* 菠萝
13. *Aloe vera*　[植]芦荟（芦荟属植物）
14. zygocactus　*n.* [植]蟹爪兰
15. chrysanthemums　*n.* 菊，菊花
16. *Dieffenbachia*　*n.* 花叶万年青属植物
17. *Hedera helix*　常春藤
18. flamingo flower　彩斑芋
19. fuchsias　*n.* 倒挂金钟属（*Fuchsia*）植物
20. geranium　*n.* 天竺葵，[植]老鹳草属植物
21. hoya　*n.* [植]球兰
22. *Impatiens*　*n.* [植]凤仙花属植物
23. jasmine　*n.* 茉莉花
24. lemon　*n.* 柠檬
25. monstera　*n.* [植]蓬莱蕉
26. orchids　*n.* [植]兰科植物，兰花
27. palms　*n.* 棕榈植物
28. *Pilea*　*n.* 冷水花属
29. sansevieria　*n.* [植]虎尾兰

30. sensitive plant　　[植]含羞草
31. spider plant　　[植]吊兰

Questions

1. How many groups can be divided into among house plants?
2. How to get new house plants according to the introduction of the text?
3. Please list some commonly grown house plants in your city.

Lesson 13

Part A Organic Farming——Agriculture with a Future

Selected and rewritten from *Organic Farming*, by Nicolas Lampkin.

Organic farming took on a new lease of life during the 1980s, not just in Britain but around the world. These problems of overproduction in the industrialized countries, underproduction in developing countries and the environmental impact of agriculture have concentrated minds and brought about a dramatic reassessment of the achievements of the post 1945 era. The effect can be seen not only in the range of policies which give greater weight to environmental considerations, but also in the growth of the organic movement and the market for organically produced food.

Organic farming is increasingly being recognized as a potential solution to many of the policy problems facing agriculture in both developed and developing countries. Denmark, Sweden, Germany and Switzerland have introduced schemes to support farmers financially during the critical conversion period; more European Community countries are set to do so under the new extensification legislation. Other countries like Israel and New Zealand have given considerable support to the development of export-oriented marketing strategies and research. The Government of Burkina-Faso in West Africa hosted the 1989 conference of the International Federation of Organic Agriculture Movements(IFOAM) and is committed to following an ecological approach to the development of its own agricultural resources. Ecologically oriented projects are being developed in many other countries in the so-called Third World.

What is Organic Farming

There are several problems which arise when presenting an explanation or definition of organic farming. Firstly, there are a number of misconceptions surrounding the topic which tend to a prejudicial view and divert attention from the main issues. Secondly, the nomenclature varies in different parts of the world, causing understandable confusion to the uninitiated observer. Thirdly, many existing practitioners believe that successful organic farming involves conceptual understanding as well as the employment of specific practical techniques.

These problems prevent the framing of a short, sharp, clear definition of organic farming. It has, therefore, become commonplace to define what it is by stating what it is not. Definitions and descriptions are frequently framed around negatives. What organic farmers do not do or use is summarized in the phrase that 'organic farming' is farming without chemicals'. While such a definition has the advantage of being concise and clear, it is unfortunately untrue and misses out on several characteristics which are of fundamental importance.

The principles and practices that lie behind different names, such as biological farming, regenerative farming, sustainable farming and organic farming, are essentially similar. They have been concisely expressed in the standards document of the International Federation of Organic Agriculture Movements (IFOAM) as:

① to produce food of high nutritional quality in sufficient quantity;

② to work with natural systems rather than seeking to dominate them;

③ to encourage and enhance biological cycles within the farming system, involving microorganisms, soil flora and fauna, plants and animals;

④ to maintain and increase the long-term fertility of soils;

⑤ to use as far as possible renewable resources in locally organised agricultural systems;

⑥ to work as much as possible within a closed system with regard to organic matter and nutrient elements;

⑦ to give all livestock conditions of life that allow them to perform all aspects of their innate behaviour;

⑧ to avoid all forms of pollution that may result from agricultural techniques;

⑨ to maintain the genetic diversity of the agricultural system and its surroundings, including the protection of plant and wildlife habitats;

⑩ to allow agricultural producers an adequate return and satisfaction from their work including a safe working environment;

⑪ to consider the wider social and ecological impact of the farming system.

For organic farmers in the World, these principles provide a basis for day-to-day farming practice. They directly give rise to the techniques of organic agriculture, such as composting; the use of wide rotations which utilize leys and green manures; the avoidance of soluble fertilisers; the prohibition of intensive livestock operations; the avoidance of antibiotic and hormone stimulants; the use of mechanical and thermal methods of weed control; the emphasis towards on-farm processing and direct sales to the consumer; and the use of extra labor when not strictly necessary, as a positive contribution to the farm and rural community.

The United States Department of Agriculture has framed a handy definition of organic farming which, although it misses out some important aspects, provides a description of the key practices:

Organic farming is a production system which avoids or largely excludes the use of synthetically compounded fertilizers, pesticides, growth regulators and livestock feed additives. To the maximum extent feasible, organic farming systems rely on crop rotations, crop residues, animal manures, legumes, green manures, off-farm organic wastes, and aspects of biological pest control to maintain soil productivity and tilth, to supply plant nutrients and to control insects, weeds and other pests.

This definition can be divided into three parts:

1. What organic farmers do not do;
2. What positive things they do instead;
3. An indication of the underlying view of the soil as a living system that the farmer, in harmony with nature, should seek to develop.

This idea of the soil as a living system is part of a concept which maintains that there is an essential link between soil, plant, animal and man. Many people involved with organic agriculture believe that an understanding of this is the prerequisite for sustaining a successful organic farming system. This concept has been described as "holistic", but it can be discussed in a less pretentious way.

Simplified, and put into a practical context, it is the recognition that—within agriculture, as within nature—everything affects everything else. One component cannot be changed or taken out of the farming or the natural system without positively or adversely affecting other things. For example, on an organic farm there is not one method of weed control or of supplying nitrogen. The ley, green manures and appropriate cultivations do both of these things, as well as their more obvious other functions.

Here indeed is the key to understanding what organic agriculture is about. It concentrates primarily on adjustments within the farm and farming system, in particular rotations and appropriate manure management and cultivations, to achieve an acceptable level of output. External inputs are generally adjuncts or supplements to this management of internal features.

Why Organic Farming

Several factors have come together in recent years which highlight the necessity for a fundamental review and revision of agricultural policy in Britain and other European countries. The traditional goal of maximizing output is being countered by widespread concern over the countryside and environment, and by the growing realization that finite natural resources need to be more carefully managed. At the same time, subsidized overproduction in Europe has brought about unendurable financial strain and political embarrassment.

While increased productivity has resulted in European food self-sufficiency and the arrival of surplus, the real cost of support for the Common Agricultural Policy has increased by 28% since the mid 1970s as farm incomes in Britain have fallen by 50%. The current cost of the storage and export of the EC cereal surplus is of the order of £12.5 billion, equivalent to approximately £137 per year for every taxpayer in the United Kingdom.

Dramatic changes in farming practices have resulted in a loss of natural habitat and species: for example, a loss of one fifth of hedgerows and more than three quarters of wetland habitats. Environmental pollution of ground and surface water from agricultural sources is an increasing problem, with supplies in some parts of Britain at EC maximum permissible levels. The Soil Survey of England and Wales estimates that nearly 44% of the UK arable land is at risk from erosion.

It is not really surprising, therefore, that increasingly people within and outside agriculture are questioning the desirability of its continuing in its present form. A recent NOP poll, for example, showed that almost 60% of those questioned felt that farmers should avoid using "modern methods of farming", and more than 25% of respondents thought that farmers should be paid for changing from these methods.

Glossary

1. Burkina-Faso 布基纳法索(非洲国家)
2. nomenclature n. 系统命名法，(某一学科的)术语，专门名称
3. microorganism n. 微生物
4. compost n. 混合肥料，堆肥
5. antibiotic n. [微]抗生素，抗菌素；adj. 抗菌的
6. stimulant n. 刺激物；激励物
7. feed additive 饲料添加剂
8. tilth n. 耕种，耕作(深度)，翻耕，整地，耕作地，已耕地
9. cereal n. 谷类植物，谷物
10. hedgerow n. 灌木树篱；栅栏；隔板

Exercises

A. Please answer the following questions in English.

1. What is the difference between conventional farming practices and organic ones?
2. Why the definition of organic agriculture is generally expressed around negatives?
3. Have such a possibility do you think that organic agriculture is a substitute for conventional agriculture? Please tell us your reason.

B. Please translate the following paragraph into Chinese.

IFOAM is the worldwide umbrella organization for the organic movement, uniting more than 750 member organizations in 108 countries. Organic trade is a rapidly growing reality all over the world. The growth rates of the organic sector demonstrate that organic products are moving from the "niche" and entering mainstream markets. The total land under certified organic production worldwide has reached over 26 million hectares. IFOAM is at the center of this development.

C. Please translate the following sentences into English.

1. 有机农场会运用不同的方法，其中包括作物轮作、绿肥、堆肥、选择合时作物和设置农田覆盖物等，以控制水土流失，促进生物多样性，并加强土壤健康。

2. 从1990年代早期，发达国家的有机农业市场每年成长20%，主因是消费者需求的上扬。小型独立生产者和消费者促成了有机农业的兴起，有机产品的量与种类也同步增加。

使得相关生产大幅成长。

Part B Organic Gardening

Selected and rewritten from *Horticulture: A Basic Awareness*, by Robert F. Baudendistel.

  Organic gardening is a specific method of growing vegetables without the use of commercial pesticides or inorganic fertilizers. It emphasizes the recycling of a variety of waste materials either by composting or by direct addition of these materials to the soil. Organic matter is invaluable as an addition to any soil, no matter whether it is applied as manure, as a cover crop, or as a soil-improving crop.

  The fertility of the soil is maintained by a complex interaction between the available organic matter and the soil microorganisms, plus the periodic applications of lime, to raise the soil pH, and organic fertilizers. In early spring, organic fertilizes are not very effective, because the soil temperatures necessary for their breakdown by the soil microorganisms are too low.

  It must be understood by everyone that even though organic gardening can be extremely successful for most home gardeners, it would be completely impossible to employ its principles on a wide commercial scale to feed the population of this country.

Soil-improving Crops

  Soil-improving crops, also known as green-manure crops, should be turned under before they become mature, because then their rate of decay is much faster than when they become thoroughly dry. These crops are grown during the same growing season as vegetables for the purpose of preparing the soil for the growth of future crops grown in succeeding years.

  Cover crops are usually grown during the dormant season when vegetable crops are not grown for the combined purpose of soil improvement and soil protection.

  Both the soil-improvement and soil-cover crops should be turned under before they become mature and at a time when the soil is both warm and well supplied with moisture.

  To help the inexperienced gardener achieve some degree of success with an organically grown vegetable garden, the following suggestions or remedies are offered.

1. Select disease-resistant varieties.
2. Use the following "organic" materials for insect and disease control.
1) Dormant oil spray for aphid, scale and mite.
2) Nicotine sulfate for aphid and pear psylla.
3) Rotenone for aphid.
4) Ryania for aphid, codling moth, and Japanese beetle.
5) Wettable sulfur for diseases, such as scab and brown rot.
3. Use beneficial insects, such as ladybugs and praying mantises, to devour other insects.

4. Use certain "companion plant" to rid certain plants of specific pests. (Table 13-1)

Companion plants — Table 13-1

Companion plant	Desired plant	Removes
Garlic	Roses	Blackspot, mildew, aphids
Parsley	Roses	Rose beetles
Beans	Potatoes	Mexican bean beetle, Potato beetle
Soybeans	Corn	Chinch bugs, Japanese beetles
Chives	Peach	Peach borer
Radishes	All cucurbits	Striped or spotted, Cucumber beetle
Chives and garlic	Lettuce, peas	Aphids
Herbs	Cabbage	Cabbage butterflies

5. Use certain "plant traps" so that insects attack the trap, and leave the more valuable plant material alone. (Table 13-2)

Plant traps — Table 13-2

Plant trap	Valuable plant	To lure
Marigolds	Tomato, bean, eggplant	Nematodes
Marigolds	Cucurbit	Cucumber beetle
Sunflower	Corn	Most corn insects
Sage	Broccoli	Jap. beetle
Geraniums	Rose, grape	Jap. beetle
Marigolds	Corn	Cabbage moth
Mint or rosemary	Cabbage	Colorado potato beetle
Nasturtium	Bean	Mexican bean beetle
	Broccoli	Aphids
	Cucurbit	Cucumber beetle

Glossary

1. green-manuré crop   绿肥作物
2. aphid   *n.* 蚜虫
3. mite   *n.* 螨
4. psylla   *n.* 木虱
5. rotenone   *n.* 鱼藤酮[杀虫药]
6. ladybug   *n.* 瓢虫
7. praying mantis   螳螂
8. parsley   *n.* 欧芹,洋芫荽,洋香菜
9. chive   *n.* 细香葱
10. marigold   *n.* 金盏草,万寿菊
11. broccoli   *n.* 花椰菜,花茎甘蓝,西兰花

Questions

1. How to maintain soil fertility in organic gardening?
2. What are cover crops, and what functions do they have?

Lesson 14

Part A Subtropical and Tropical Fruits

  Selected and rewritten from *Tropical Fruits of Thailand & SE Asia*, edited by Kim Inglis, and *Horticulture*, by R. Gordon Halface & John A. Barden Mcgraw.

  Although fruits can be classified in many ways, perhaps the first distinction should be on the basis of climatic requirements, the three major divisions being *temperate, subtropical, and tropical*. Temperate fruits are those which require a cool period and are deciduous. Subtropical fruits are intermediate between the temperate and tropical types; some are deciduous, and others are evergreen, like the tropicals. The subtropicals can ordinarily withstand temperatures slightly below freezing but are seriously injured by temperatures of -4 to $-5°C$. The tropical species are evergreen, can withstand no temperatures below freezing, and some—such as bananas—suffer chilling injury at temperatures above freezing.

  Although subtropical and tropical fruits can be grown commercially only in very limited parts of Asia, they account for a large part of the total Asian fruit crop markets. Major production areas are confined to Thailand, China, Philippines, Indonesia and Vietnam.

Banana (*Musa* spp.)

  Those accustomed to the commercially popular bananas exported to the West—large pale yellow bananas with white, somewhat bland flesh and virtually no fragrance—are astounded by the range of sizes, shapes, skin colors and flavors of bananas found in tropical Asia.

  The banana plant is native to the region and may be seen growing wild on hillside and in secondary forests. The fruit of these is generally full of hard seeds and inedible. Bananas are high in food value, containing vitamins B and C, as well as minerals. Not only the fruit is utilized, banana leaves serve as an all-purpose wrapping for steamed or baked food and as a disposable plate. The center of the stem is treated as a vegetable and is the basis of what might be regarded as the Burmese national dish, a soup called *mihinga*. And after cooking, the center of the banana bud tastes surprisingly like an artichoke.

  The banana is a fast-growing herbaceous plant which develops suckers (pseudostems) from underground rhizomes and reaches a height of 1.5 to 1.8 m (Fig. 14-1). The leaves are large—up to 3.5 m long—and dark-green. The false stem is composed of compressed leaf sheaths. After growing for several months, the flower stalk emerges from the top and usually bends downward. Female flowers with abortive stamens produce the hands of bananas, thus, the fruit develops parthenocarpically. Later developing flowers abort, and the flowers at the end of stem are male and abortive. Since a sucker fruits only once, it is cut back to the ground after the fruit is harvested. Bananas are harvested when mature but green; they develop excellent quality when ripened. Ripening is done at the distribution center by exposing the fruit to approximately 0.1 percent ethylene for 24 hours. The ethylene treatment not only accelerates ripening but makes a shipment of bananas ripen more uniformly.

Fig. 14-1 Banana

Pineapple (*Ananas comosus*)

The pineapple (Fig. 14-2), native to South America, is cultivated throughout tropical Asia. The name comes from the Spanish word for pine cone, which the fruit vaguely resembles with its scaly skin. Ripe pineapples have a juicy sweet flesh with just a hint of acidity to make them even more refreshing. Pineapple is not only good raw or cooked in savoury dishes, it also makes food pickles, chutney and jam, as well as delicious juice.

Fig. 14-2 Pineapple

Several types of pineapple are found in the region. Some are grown only for ornamental use, their decorative leaves making them a popular pot plant. Small varieties that tend to be somewhat acid, or unripe fruits, are used as a vegetable or in sour fruit salads—and also made into pineapple curry. Freshly peeled and sliced ripe pineapple is found everywhere in the region. If buying a whole fruit, check that it is ripe by smelling to see if it is fragrant and try to tear one of the leaves sprouting from the top. If it comes away easily, the fruit is ready to eat.

The pineapple is a member of the Bromeliaceae family. It has many features which make it resistant to desiccation such as sunken stomates, narrow leaves, and funnel-shaped leaf bases which hold water.

Since the pineapple is seedless, it is propagated vegetatively by slips which arise beneath the fruit (shoots originating lower down the stem), suckers or most commonly the crown (the shoot arising from the top of the fruit). During the harvest of pineapples for processing plants, workers wearing heavy chaps and gloves walk between the rows, placed on a long conveyor which carries it to a truck or trailer, and the crown is tossed on top of the plants to day. One or two weeks later the crowns are collected from the field and are planted, often in fumigated the soil using black plastic mulch. From newly set crowns, it normally takes 18 to 24 months for the plants to flower, a process sometimes accelerated and commonly synchronized by the use of selected growth regulators such as ethephon. The first crop consists of a single, large fruit on each plant; the second crop (called *the first ratoon crop*) consists of two smaller fruits per plants and is mature about 12 months after the first crop. The third crop, consisting of four smaller fruits (called *the second ratoon crop*), is harvested about 12 months after the second crops. After this crop is harvested, the field is prepared for replanting and after the three-crop cycle repeated.

Dragon's Eye Fruit (*Dimocarpus longan*)

The dragon's eye fruit (Fig. 14-3) is the true longan, one of many Southeast Asian natives which now grows in China and Thailand. A smaller fruit with very thin flesh, also called cat's eye(*D. longan* spp. *malesianus*) grows only in Southeast Asia, and is a vastly inferior fruit.

Dragon's eye fruits are small and round and have a single shiny brown round seed inside. They grow in clusters and should be bought when still firm to the touch. The flesh is white, with a delicate flavor and a good balance of sweetness and acidity. There is a faint, indescribable fragrance to this fruit—almost woody but pleasant. To open, simply squeeze gently with the fingers.

Fig. 14-3 Dragon's eye fruit

Dragon's eye fruits are reported to maintain their flavor after cooking, though most people eat them raw. Dried, they have an intriguing smokey flavor and are sometimes used to make a fruit "tea". Tinned fruits are available, but their flavor—like that of tinned lychees—is a poor substitute for the real thing.

Mango (*Mangifera* spp.) (Fig. 14-4)

There are dozens of varieties of mango family, varying in fragrance and flavor from sublime to unpleasant. Each country has developed its own varieties and a mango lover is hard-pressed to choose, say, between the very long, almost white-fleshed flower mango of Thailand, the small orange-fleshed Philippines mango dripping with sweet juice and the stronger-smelling and slightly sharp arumanis mango of Indonesia.

All these fruits are hybrids, as most of the varieties native to the region have somewhat stringy flesh with a sour, almost turpentine, flavor. There mangoes are generally made into a pickle or preserve.

Fig. 14-4 Mango

Mangoes can be divided into two broad categories: those that are eaten green (unripe) and dessert mangoes enjoyed for their sweetness. Unripe mangoes are the perfect answer to the Asian love of sharp sour flavors. These fruit are peeled and eaten in salads or with savoury or chilli-hot dips; unripe mangoes are also cooked to make various pickles and chutney. Dessert mangoes vary in size, skin color and shape, some being fat, green-skinned and almost round, others being pale golden and slender, still others having a reddish tinge. All fruits have a large elongated seed inside and a non-edible skin.

Mango slices served with sweet sticky rice mixed with coconut cream are regarded as the ultimate dessert in Thailand and the Philippines. Their color, texture and flavor combine well with milk products: mangoes make good ice-creams, yoghurts and souffles, but as they are so good fresh from the tree this is like girding the lily.

Durian (*Durio zibethinus*)

The durian (Fig. 14-5), Southeast Asia's most highly prized fruit, is also it's most controversial because of the overpowering odor. It is the only fruit banned from airline cabins, hotels and some public transport.

Native to Southeast Asia, the fruit of the very tall durian tree is roughly the size and shape of a spiky football. Inside the tough skin are five white segments enclosing two or three portions of soft cream-colored flesh, each wrapped around a single large beige seed. Both the flesh and the seed (after boiling) are edible.

Fig. 14-5 Durian

The durian is surrounded by folklore. It is reputed to be an aphrodisiac. It is also claimed to be dangerous to drink alcohol when consuming durians. The Chinese believe the durian is very "heaty" to the body. Durians should be eaten within hours of their falling or being harvested, and fruits which have split open should be avoided as the flesh deteriorates quickly when exposed to the air.

Papaya (*Carica papaya*)

The papaya (known in some countries as the papaw), is renowned for is high vitamins A and C content and for its medicinal properties, while papain—an enzyme found in both the fruit and leaf—is used as a meat tenderizer.

A native of Mexico, there are many different varieties, ranging in size from long pendulous fruits of 35~40 cm to dainty little egg-shaped fruits. The skin is green, usually turning to yellow or orange as the fruit ripens. Inside the papaya is a cavity which contains a mass of shiny black seeds, which are discarded (although they are edible). The ripe flesh, ranging from golden to salmon pink, is always eaten raw, usually accompanied by a squeeze of lime juice; however, unripe papayas are used in salads or cooked as vegetables throughout Southeast Asia.

Many of the modern commercially grown hybrids, which are usually smaller in size than the old-fashioned fruit and known as Hawaiian or Solo papayas, have a richer flavour than older varieties.

Papaya is a tropical herbaceous plant which grows to a height of 8 m or more (Fig. 14-6). The normally single-stemmed plant grows rapidly, and fruit are borne in the axils of

Fig. 14-6　Papaya

the leaves, which are progressively shed from the base upward. Although the papaya plant continues to produce fruit, the planting is usually cut down and replanted when the fruit can no longer be harvested from the ground.

　　Papaya plants are staminate (produce staminate flowers only), pistillate (produce pistillate flowers only), or hermaphroditic (produce staminate and hermaphroditic flowers). The "solo" cultivar produces hermaphroditic and pistillate plants in a 2∶1 ratio. To establish a new planting, from three to five seeds are set in each location as the sex of the plants cannot be ascertained until flowering is initiated. At that time, the pistillate plants are removed, leaving the preferred hermaphroditic plants to fruit.

Glossary

1. temperate fruit　温带水果
2. chilling injury　冷害
3. secondary forest　次生林
4. artichoke　*n.* 朝鲜蓟
5. sucker　*n.* （植物的）吸芽，根蘖，根出条
6. pseudostem　*n.* 假茎（由叶鞘组成的茎）
7. bud union　芽接口，愈合处
8. rhizome　*n.* 根茎，根状茎，地下茎
9. leaf sheath　叶鞘
10. female flower　雌花
11. parthenocarpically　*adv.* 单性结实地
12. scaly skin　鳞状表皮
13. Bromeliaceae　*n.* 凤梨科
14. seedless　*n.* 无核，无子；*adj.* 无核的
15. slip　*n.* 根出条，萌蘖枝，接枝，插枝；*v.* 分蘖
16. crown　*n.* 树冠，根颈
17. fumigate　*v.* 熏蒸，烟熏
18. synchronize　*v.* 同步，同时发生
19. growth regulators　生长调节剂
20. ethephon　*n.* 乙烯利，乙烯
21. ratoon　*n.* 块茎芽，根蘖，宿根
22. dragon's eye fruit　龙眼
23. tinned fruit　水果罐头
24. turpentine　*n.* 松节油，松脂
25. dessert　*n.* 甜食

26. durian   n. 榴莲
27. meat tenderizer   嫩肉粉
28. pendulous   adj. 悬垂的，下垂的
29. staminate   adj. 雄蕊的，有雄蕊的，只有雄蕊的
30. pistillate   adj. 雌蕊的，有雌蕊的
31. hermaphroditic   adj. 两性的，雌雄同体的

Exercises

A. Please answer the following questions in English.

1. Please list the main tropical fruits and subtropical fruits in China.
2. How do you understand the term **parthenocarpy**?
3. How many types of the pineapple are found in the Asia region?
4. What are the differences between the green mangoes and dessert mangoes?
5. Why Chinese believe the durian is very "heaty" to the body?

B. Please translate the following paragraph into Chinese.

The date palm (*Phoenix dactylifera*) is a crop which thrives best in arid climates and is thought to be native to northern Africa. Both high temperatures and low humidity are requirements for normal fruit ripening. The date palm is an evergreen monocot and is dioecious. Hand pollination is often carried out to ensure adequate fruit set. Most dates are dried.

C. Please translate the following sentences into English.

1. 荔枝：常绿乔木，高 8～20m。茎上多分枝，灰色；小枝圆柱形。双数羽状复叶互生；小叶对生，具柄，叶片披针形或矩圆状披针形。春季开花，圆锥花序，花杂性。核果球形或卵形，果皮暗红色，有小瘤状突起。种子外被白色、肉质、多汁、甘甜的假种皮，易与核分离。种子矩圆形，褐色至黑红色，有光泽。

2. 椰子：常绿乔木。高 15～30m，单项树冠，整齐。叶羽状全裂，裂片多数，革质，线状披针形，叶柄粗壮。佛焰花序腋生，多分枝，雄花聚生于分枝上部，雌花散生于下部。坚果倒卵形或近球形，顶端微具三棱，内果皮骨质，近基部有 3 个萌发孔，种子 1 粒；胚乳内有一富含液汁的空腔。

Part B   Constraints of Lychee Development in China

Selected from *Lychee Production in China*, by Huang Xuming.

Lychee (*Litchi chinensis* Sonn.) originated in the northern tropical and southern subtropical regions of South China. Wild lychee trees can be found as one of the dominant tree species of tropical rainforests in southern provinces such as Hainan, Guangdong, Guangxi and Yunnan.

As the original home of lychee, China was the first country to cultivate the fruit. The recorded history of lychee cultivation in the country is more the 2,100 years. Lychee is the most competive fruit in China for the international market. As long as there is a great domestic potential and international market, there is great room for further development. In addition, China possesses the best climate for lychee, plenty of sloping land that can be constructed into lychee orchards, and an incomparable rich germplasm and labor resource. However, lychee production development in China is still strongly limited by several constraints.

The constraints limiting development in China are:

Short shelf-life, Poor storability and Short Production Season

The lychee production season is short, about one and half months from late May to early July. The large quantity of lychee produced within such a short time must be marketed immediately since the fruit turn brown and rot rapidly (within 3 days) after harvest under ambient temperature. Short shelf-life strongly limits the extension of the lychee market in terms of time and space and causes heavy loss when the produced fruit cannot be marketed immediately. Cold storage houses are thus constructed in some large lychee orchards in order to provide a temporary buffer between production and marketing. Although low temperature storage ($3 \sim 5°C$) plus fungicide treatment (0.0005 TBZ or $0.00025 \sim 0.0005$ Sportak) has been able to keep fruit in fresh condition for $30 \sim 40$ days, the capacity of the presently available cold storage houses is far from enough for the large quantity of lychee fruit produced in such a short season. Moreover, the poor storability of lychee fruit casts a high risk for cold storage companies to store the fruit. Lychee fruit become even more vulnerable to browning and rotting when taken from low temperature to ambient temperature. Therefore, cold chain is important to market cold-stored fruit. Unfortunately, there is a serious shortage of cold chain for the huge domestic market in China. Part of the reason is the high cost of cold chain. A much cheaper alternative involving transportation of lychee fruit packed in heatproof foam boxes plus ice has recently been widely used. However, the fruit in this type of package experience gradual temperature rise and cannot endure for more than 2 days.

Absence of an Efficient and Nationwide Marketing System

Because of the short shelf-life and short production season of lychee, an efficient marketing system is urgently needed to enable lychee fruit produced in large quantity within a short period to be marketed before they turn brown. Presently, large number of small fruit dealers are playing the major role in fruit marketing system, which usually involves local dealers who purchase lychee fruit from the growers, transporters, wholesaler at the destination, and retail sellers. Most of the dealers do not have the financial strength to invest transportation means of large volume, cold storage and cold chain. Their business is therefore limited to a small volume and to a small region. They are functioning in an unorganized manner with a low handling capacity, far below the demand of the ever-increasing lychee production in the country. In some lychee production regions such as Gaozhou, the local government has set up an efficient information system to attract wholesalers from all parts of the country and a sound marketing system is running involving only growers, wholesalers, retail sellers and consumers. However, such a system awaits further development so as to cover all the lychee production regions as well as the nationwide market in China.

Unorganized Production by Individual Farmers

Most of the lychee orchards in China are managed by unorganized individual farmers or smallholders. This production system functioned well before the local market was saturated. With the rapid expansion of lychee production and the saturation of local markets, its disadvantages become apparent. Most of the farmer households are weak in financial strength and their limited investment is put into the management of their orchards, which are usually small in size. They lack enough technical support, market information and channels for marketing their fruit beyond local market. As a result, farmers and smallholders compete bitterly on the local market. In years with bumper harvest they produce more than the local market can digest, and most of them suffer big losses. The orchard management standard and cultivation techniques are different among orchards, and thus the yield and quality of fruit produced by different farmers differ. Such a production system can no longer produce high economic benefit.

Climatic Constraints

Although lychee cultivation techniques have improved a lot in the past 10 years, lychee production is still largely dependent upon climate. In general, the climate in the lychee production regions in China is favorable for lychee growth and development, but there are still unfavorable climatic conditions in South China that cause crop loss and/or irregular bearing. They are:

Frost Lychee is susceptible to frost. Though it is rare in lychee production regions, its damage is severe once it occurs. In late December of 1999, a frost resulted in massive damage to lychee orchards, especially the new ones and those in low places. Lychee production loss caused by this frost damage in Guangdong alone was estimated to be 400,000 tons.

Humid Autumn and Warm Winter In South China, autumn is usually dry and winter is dry and chilly. The long autumn and winter drought plus chilly winter (temperature below 15℃ in the day and 10℃ in the night) is essential for lychee flower induction. Humid autumn and warm winters are unfavorable for winter shoot growth. Such kind of weather occurred in 1998 and most mid-to late-season cultivars failed to flower resulting in an off-year for these cultivars.

Cold and Rainy Spring Most lychee cultivars flower in spring, when cold and rainy weather frequently occurs. Cold or rainy weather inhibits bee activity and causes disease to the trees. This kind weather happening during the lychee bloom period is very harmful to pollination and subsequent fruit set and may cause severe crop loss.

Typhoons The typhoon season usually starts from June in China, when lychee fruit of mid- and late-season cultivars are maturing. The strong wind of typhoons causes heavy damage to trees and severe fruit drop. The heavy rainfall brought by typhoons usually causes serious fruit cracking to some susceptible cultivars like "Nuomici" and "Guiwei".

The development of lychee fruit happens to be in the rainy and humid spring and summer in South China. Rainy and humid weather not only increases the incidence of fruit drop and cracking, but also brings diseases and pests as well as difficulties in their management. Rainy weather during the harvesting period reduces the storability of lychee fruit remarkably and brings difficulty in post-harvest handling and heavy post-harvest loss.

Although lychee production has a long history in China, it did not become an important industry until the 1980s. The current output of lychee has saturated the local markets in South China. There is a very large potential domestic and international market for the future development of lychee production.

Glossary

1. germplasm *n.* 种质资源
2. shelf-life *n.* 货架期，货架寿命
3. ambient temperature 环境温度
4. fungicide *n.* 杀菌剂
5. TBZ {N/2}-特-丁基-{N/4}-乙基-6-甲硫基-1,3,5-三嗪-2,4-二胺
6. Sportak *n.* 是一种新型咪唑类广谱杀菌剂
7. heatproof foam 隔热泡沫
8. wholesaler *n.* 批发商
9. retail seller 零售商
10. smallholder *n.* 小农，小农地主
11. frost *n.* 霜冻，结霜，冻
12. mid-to late-season cultivar 中晚熟品种
13. off-year *n.* 小年
14. typhoon *n.* 台风
15. rainfall *n.* 降雨，降雨量
16. fruit cracking 裂果
17. post-harvest loss 采后损失，采后耗损

Questions

1. Why the lychee has short shelf-life, poor storability and short production season?
2. What are the climatic constraints for the lychee production in China?
3. Please discuss the advantages and constraints of the lychee production in China.

Lesson 15

Part A Flowers and Fruit Setting of Evergreen Fruits

Selected and rewritten from *Evergreen Orchards*, by William Henry Chandler.

Flowers

In many of the orchard species in which clonal selection has been in progress for hundreds of years, failure of trees in clones that are apt to be grown commercially, to produce flowers enough for a good crop is not one of the greatest sources of loss, but in some species such as the mango it may be. In most species, failure of the flowers to set fruit is a greater source of loss. Even in species that usually set flowers enough when the trees are old enough, however, there are apt to be times when, if a grower could produce flowering on his trees at will, he might improve his profits greatly. And in home planting, where there may not be room enough for normal growth of the tree in unshaded positions, there is apt to be special reason to want knowledge for obtaining adequate flowering in spite of shade and of excessive pruning to keep them small enough for the space available.

In this evergreen orchard species, as in deciduous species, flowers develop from apical meristem, terminally or in the axils of leaves of current shoots or shoots formed in a preceding growth flush.

A meristem that produces an inflorescence might, under different influence, produce a shoot instead, or it might remain dormant, growing only enough each year to keep its apex in the bark. How long flower induction may precede first evidence of differentiation will depend upon the species and the environment. We do not know just how flowering is induced. We know certain influences that tend to promote flower induction.

Nitrogen and Other Nutrients Nitrogen deficiency, great enough to cause leaves to be considerably smaller than normal and much paler green and the shoots to be short with few leaves, will prevent flower bud formation in some orchard species. The same seems to be true in the rare situations when phosphorus is this deficient. Copper deficiency seems to have a still greater tendency to prevent flowering. Zinc or potassium deficiency may reduce flowering but usually only when the deficiency is great enough to cause serious leaf distortion or scorching.

An excess of nitrogen has been considered likely to reduce flowering, to cause growth to be too succulent for flowering, but this effect is exceedingly rare unless other influences such as shading or severe pruning accompany the high nitrogen supply.

The Carbohydrate Supply We have seen that cell wall materials, such as cellulose, hemi-cellulose, and pectic substances, do not seem to be important food reserves for most orchard species and sugars rarely accumulate to high concentrations except in maturing fruit and germinating seeds. Starch is the great carbohydrate storage material. We may wonder how an insoluble material like starch can be active toward inducing flowering. Yet we must remember that all starch in the leucoplasts is from sugar that passed through the cytoplasm to the plastids, as sugar. A number of influences that reduce or increase the starch reserve also reduce or increase flower induction.

1. Effect of a Heavy Crop A heavy crop on a tree reduces the accumulation of starch and usually reduces the number of flowers to form, especially if the fruit remains on the tree until time for flower induction. Trees in some clones of some species have a very strong tendency toward alternate bearing: a heavy crop in one year, followed by a light crop, or no crop, in the succeeding year.

2. Starch-Nitrogen Ratio We have seen that an excessive nitrogen supply is supposed to be antagonistic to flower induction. Some stress the view that the excessive nitrogen causes such strong, succulent growth that the carbohydrates are used for this growth and do not accumulate to the extent necessary for flower induction. No carbohydrate-nitrogen ratio in the tree tissues has been found to be the one that is most favorable for flower induction, a wide range in nitrogen content in the tissue and in carbohydrate-nitrogen ratio may be equally favorable for flower induction.

3. Shade Dense shade causes prolonged succulence in growth, longer but more slender shoots, with a lower percentage of dry matter. Such growth tends not to accumulate much starch and may not form many flower buds.

4. Chilling Temperature and Drought A number of influences tend to cause starch accumulation and increase the degree of flower induction. In some of the species, either a cool winter period or a dry period will stop growth and increase starch accumulation and may cause flowering to be heavy during the period or soon afterward.

5. Ringing, Scoring, Bending On trees that are not bearing a heavy crop, cutting out a ring of bark at certain times of the year, may increase the number of flowers to be formed. It will also cause starch to accumulate in tissue of the part of the tree above the ring. On trees of some species, scoring, making a knife edge cut through the bark around the trunk or branch, may increase concentration of material above the ring enough to cause flower induction. Bending a branch downward sometimes checks growth and causes accumulation of organic material in the branch and greater flowering.

Sap Concentration Another change tends to be taking place in the cells of a plant when its growth declines and starch begins to accumulate faster than it dose during rapid growth: the concentration of molecules and ions dissolved in the cell tends to be increasing. Not nearly all these are of sugar and mineral compounds. Some of them are organic acids or salts of these acids. Treatments such as ringing and bending that increase starch formation also tend to increase sap concentration. In other words, the protoplasm is in contact with a stronger medium and perhaps with a greater concentration of some specific substances. I see no reason for thinking that starch formation is more apt to be associated with flower induction than this other change in the environment of the protoplasm.

Is There a Flower-Inducing Hormone?

There seems to be more correlation of heaviness of flowering with leaf surface on the tree, in proportion to fruits and meristem activity, than with starch formation. If there were a hormone formed in the leaves, or from a precursor formed in the leaves, that induces flowering, leaf surface rather than accumulation of carbohydrates might be the dominant influence toward flowering. From ringing and fruit thinning experiments in which flowering is increased , we can be certain that if flowering in orchard species is induced by a hormone, that hormone must be a substance that moves in the phloem toward the roots and it must be used and the supply depleted by fruit growth, or these facts must be true of a precursor from which the hormone is formed; or the hormone may be formed only when food is accumulating in the plant or when living cell sap concentration in the leaves is increasing.

Fruit Setting

Normally for fruit setting, the ovules in the flower must be fertilized, or at least some of them must, and seed must develop. Then some tissue associated with the flower, under the stimulus of these developing embryos becomes fleshy fruit.

Because the flesh of so many fruits develops from carpel tissue, the term parthenocarpic is applied to fruits that develop without fertilized ovules, regardless of the tissue from which the edible part develops. Parthenocarpic fruits are, of course, seedless, but seedless fruits are not all parthenocarpic. In some clones a fertilized ovule is necessary to prevent abscission of the flower but the embryo later disintegrates without causing abscission or arresting development of the fruit.

In a variety such as the navel orange that sets fruit parthenocarpically, environmental influences on the tree determine whether a fruit will develop from a flower or the flower or young fruit will be abscised. In a variety that requires ovule fertilization; two sets of influences determine whether or not a fruit will mature from a flower: those that determine whether or not an ovule will be fertilized, pollination influences, and the environmental influences that determine whether or not a flower or young fruit will be abscised.

1. Pollination   Some seedling trees are self sterile; pollen from flowers on such a tree cannot fertilize ovules on that same tree. A variety (clone) from scions from that tree will be self sterile; pollen from any tree in the variety cannot fertilize ovules on that tree or any other in the variety. A seedling tree or a clonal variety may be self-sterile,(1) because it is a dioecious species as the date palm is; pollen and ovules are borne on different trees, (2) because it is dichogamous; pollen is shed either before the pistils are receptive or after they

have become senile, (3) because it produces no viable pollen, or (4) because it is self-incompatible: although its pollen is viable it cannot fertilize ovules on that seeding tree or in that clone. Self incompatibility may be complete or partial: a clone may be unable to produce any seed by fertilization with its own pollen, while another may be able to fertilize some of its ovules with its own pollen but will have more ovules fertilize and will set more fruits if it has pollen from another, compatible clone. If the degree of self-incompatibility is not great enough to reduce the number of fruits that can become large enough for the markets, partial self-incompatibility may be beneficial, may reduce the cost of thinning or increase the market value of the fruit.

2. Abscission of Flowers and Fruits   When flowers or young fruits fall, the process is not a passive one, but is due to the formation of layers of corky cells across the pedicel at an abscission zone. At this zone the nonliving elements such as tracheids and fibers seem usually to have less strength than in other parts of the pedicel and are broken by the pressure of these new thickening corky cells. Abscission of a flower or young fruit may be at more than one zone, at the base or the apex of the pedicel for example. If a shoot grows from the apex of this inflorescence axis, the layer of an abscission cells does not form.

Ovules in all or nearly all flowers that fall have not been fertilized. And fruits that fall before they are about 1/4 inch in diameter may not contain fertilized ovules: apparently even in varieties that do not set fruit parthenocarpically, some temporary stimulus from the ovary delays abscission. Many fruits with fertilized ovules are abscised, however, in some environments much too many.

Auxin seems necessary to prevent abscission. Auxin sprays on the blossoms of some self-unfruitful clones have caused the setting of parthenocarpic fruits. And such sprays have been found very effective in delaying the dropping of mature fruits in some species and giving more time for harvest.

Very many flowers or young fruits are abscised, in such heavy blooming species as the olive, the avocado, and the mango, probably nearly always as much as 99 percent. Many young fruits with fertilized ovules fall, usually the greater the number of fruits to begin growth the greater will be the number and percentage abscised. This may be a highly desirable thinning process and highly effective too.

Nutrient deficiencies may cause abscission. A nitrogen deficiency at blossoming time is one of the most common causes of too much abscission. Usually the deficiency must be great enough to restrict growth rather greatly. Phosphorus deficiency also may cause abscission of flowers or young fruits much as nitrogen deficiency does. Zinc deficiency is apt to cause very many flowers to fall before they are fully open.

Perhaps the most common cause of excessive abscission is water deficits. Both flowers and young fruits have considerably lower osmotic pressure than the leaves. Sometimes the water deficits in sunny dry days and in shallow, poorly-aerated soil may be great enough to stimulate abscission. Trees of varieties that set their fruit parthenocarpically seem more apt to drop it badly under such soil and weather conditions than trees of seedy varieties. As the fruit grows older, until it is nearly ripe, stronger influences, such as greater leaf water deficits are required to cause it to be abscised.

Glossary

1. meristem   *n.* 分生组织，分裂组织；apical meristem 顶端分生组织，茎尖分生组织
2. inflorescence   *n.* 花序
3. bark   *n.* 树皮，茎皮
4. cellulose   *n.* 纤维素，纤维素酶
5. pectic substances   果胶质，果胶物质
6. starch   *n.* 淀粉；*adj.* 淀粉的
7. leucoplast   *n.* 白色体
8. cytoplasm   *n.* 细胞质，胞浆，胞质
9. plastid   *n.* 质体，成形粒
10. alternate bearing   大小年结果
11. flower induction   成花诱导
12. sap concentration   汁液浓缩，汁液浓度
13. protoplasm   *n.* 原生质，原浆
14. ringing   *n.* 环割
15. fruit thinning   疏果
16. hormone   *n.* 激素，荷尔蒙
17. phloem   *n.* 韧皮部，韧皮
18. precursor   *n.* 先质，前体
19. ovule   *n.* 胚珠
20. embryo   *n.* 胚胎，胚，胚胎体
21. carpel tissue   心皮组织，果瓣组织，聚瓣组织
22. parthenocarpy   *n.* ［植］单性结实
23. abscission   *n.* 脱落，脱离
24. disintegrate   *v.* 分裂，解体，分解
25. dioecious   *adj.* 雌雄异体的，雌雄异株的
26. dichogamous   *adj.* ［植］雌雄（蕊）异熟的
27. pistil   *n.* 雌蕊
28. senile   *adj.* 衰老的，高龄的
29. self-incompatible   *adj.* 自交不亲和的，自交不孕的
30. thinning   *n.* 疏除
31. tracheid   *n.* 管胞（木材学词汇），木材的管胞
32. pedicel   *n.* ［植］花梗，［解］茎，蒂
33. corky cell   木栓细胞
34. auxin   *n.* 生长素

35. osmotic pressure   渗透压
36. poorly-aerated soil   通气性不良的土壤

Exercises

A. Please answer the following questions in English.
1. Summarize the influences that reduce or increase flower induction.
2. Is there a flower-inducing hormone?
3. State the process of the fruit setting.
4. What are the influences of pollination?
5. What are the environmental factors that influence the young fruit abscise?

B. Please translate the following paragraph into Chinese.

   Florigen, the hypothetical flowering hormone, presumably is responsible for changing a vegetative bud into a floral initial. Much of the evidence for a flowering hormone comes from photoperiod-sensitive herbaceous plants, but some work has been done with woody perennials. Florigen is said to be synthesized in relatively mature leaves and translocated in the phloem to the nearby bud where initiation occurs. The movement of the flowering stimulus from leaves to buds is quite local and is not detected some distance from the leaves. Studies with apple showed that buds on defoliated spurs did not initiate flowers even though there were leaves on nearby spurs.

C. Please translate the following sentences into English.

   1. 花芽分化是指叶芽的生理和组织状态向花芽的生理和组织状态转化的过程，是植物由营养生长转向生殖生长的转折点。花芽分化一般从芽内生长点向花芽方向发展开始，直至雌、雄蕊完全形成为止。它主要包括两个阶段：生理分化阶段和形态分化阶段。

   2. 影响花芽分化的因素主要有：园艺植物自身遗传特性的制约，植株的营养生长状况，温度、光照、水分、土壤营养等环境因素。

Part B   Fruits of Evergreen Tree

Selected and rewritten from *Evergreen Orchards*, by William Henry Chandler.

   An approximate definition of a fruit based on common or literary usage and on horticultural usage might be: the edible product from the growth of some part of the flower or tissue associated with the flower of trees, bushes, or vines. In technical usage of the botanist, a fruit is the ripened ovary with its seed and any other tissue that may adhere and mature with the ovary. Since this definition includes fruits of all seed plants, relatively very few of the fruits that come under it are succulent or edible.

   The influence of the seed on development of the fruit is different in different species. In the avocado, for example, seedless fruits are much smaller and more oblong than normal ones, while in *Citrus*, seedless fruits are not measurably different in form or size from seedy fruits of the same variety. While the presence of seed within a fruit may, in some species, have a striking effect on the nature of that fruit, the genetic nature of that seed usually dose not determine the influence. A yellow apple may have in it seeds that will grow trees that bear red apples; those seeds in the yellow apple do not modify its color. An influence of the genetic nature of the seed on the size and form and time of maturing of fruit of date varieties has been shown.

In many kinds of fruits that have been studied, cell division ceases while the young fruit has less than 10 percent of the size it will have at maturity. After this stage, growth is by cell enlargement. In evergreen orchard species there are some exceptions to this behavior, possibly many. Cell division in the rind of mature citrus fruits has been reported. Cells in mature avocados are reported little, if any, larger than those in small young fruits. Increase in size of such a fruit throughout its life must be by cell division. Whether growth of the fruit during part of the time is by cell enlargement only or by cell division and enlargement throughout its life on the tree, the increase in dry matter of the crop on the tree is large.

Size of Fruit and Thinning A nutrient or water deficiency may lower the size of the fruit. In a well-managed orchard in good soil, and in a climate suitable for the species concerned, however, size of fruit is largely determined by leaf-surface in proportion to number of fruits on a tree or a main branch, if the crop is heavy. Thinning of some kinds of fruits as soon as heavy dropping has ceased is a necessary but expensive annual practice. The earlier the thinning is done the greater the effect will be on size of fruit left, or the more fruit can be left and still develop to required size.

Fruit Color Two general classes of pigments give color to ripe fruits, plastid pigments and pigments dissolved in cell sap. Plastid pigments are carotinoids, mostly bright yellow or orange but some red. They are precursors of vitamin A so that fruit rich in carotinoids especially carotene $C_{40}H_{56}$ is a good source of vitamin A. Water soluble pigments are flavones, yellow pigments, and anthocyanins that give blue, red, and purple colors. The waxy covering of fruits brightens their color.

Flavor In some of these evergreen orchard fruits, as in most of the deciduous fruits, pleasant flavors are given by happy blending of sugars with organic acids and very small quantities of esters, known sometimes as odorous constituents. Much of the pleasure of eating a fruit is due to its texture, to the thickness and composition of its cell walls. If these are thick and composed too largely of cellulose rather than pectic substance, or if too many fibers are among the living cells, chewing the fruit may not be a pleasant experience and may not rupture enough cells to free enough of the pleasant juices.

Food Value Most fruits except those of legumes have little protein or fat and considerably less of mineral substances than leafy vegetables have. They tend to be fairly high in carbohydrates. Perhaps only a few of them, such as the date and the banana, could be grown in competition with grain crops or sugar cane for the carbohydrates they contain. Some of them are good to excellent sources of certain vitamins, especially A and C. And, for people with whom they agree, most of them promote health in the digestive tract.

Ripening and Breaking Down Ripening changes tend to make the fruit edible. In those that contain starch, this is gradually changed to sugar. The process seems to be hastened by ethylene and certain growth substances and delayed by some tannin compounds. In the banana, at least, hemicellulose content declines to ten or fifteen percent of the amount in green fruit. This decline in hemicellulose is not all accounted for by increase in sugar or by sugar used in respiration. Some of its products seem to be oxidized to dibasic acids.

If the fruit contains either the enzyme invertase or a considerable amount of acid, sucrose present is slowly changed to glucose and fructose in equal quantities. If the concentration of sucrose in the fruit sap is less than ten percent, the change to equal quantities of the less-sweet glucose and the sweeter fructose will reduce the sensation of sweetness it will give, but if the concentration is 12 to 15 percent or higher, the change to glucose and fructose may increase the sensation or sweetness it will give.

Total acid content tends to decline considerably during the ripening process. Active acidity usually declines at about the same rate, but not precisely so, owing to varying degree of buffering; One orange, for example, may have higher total acid content than another, but about the same pH reading.

Easters are not present in large enough quantities for dependable estimation of changing concentration. Their influence on flavor, however, seems to increase until the fruit has reached its maximum palatability and then to decline sharply.

In oily fruits such as the olive and the avocado, oil content may be increasing even after the fruit is too ripe for best uses.

Soluble tannin compounds that give astringency may become insoluble slowly during the ripening process, but in some fruits are carried down in insoluble masses with hardening colloidal material that includes them. This last process is hastened in some fruits by ethylene or related gases.

In the cell walls, insoluble rather rigid pectic compounds, protopectin, change to pectin, a less rigid substance when mixed with water. The fruit thus becomes mellow. The change of protopectin to pectin also is hastened by ethylene.

Harvest Time The time of harvest for most commercial, evergreen orchard fruits is not as sharply fixed by ripening processes as for deciduous fruits. Abscission processes in the pedicel and ripening processes while still on the tree tend, with a few conspicuous exceptions, to be slower. In some varieties of citrus fruits and avocados there is a period of three or four months or longer during which a fruit may be harvested and reach the consumer in good condition.

Glossary

1. cell division 细胞分裂
2. pigment *n.* 色素

3. carotinoid   *n.* 类胡萝卜素
4. anthocyanin   *n.* 花青素，花色苷
5. mineral substance   矿物质
6. tannin compound   单宁类化合物
7. dibasic acid   二元酸，二碱价酸
8. sucrose   *n.* 蔗糖
9. glucose   *n.* 葡萄糖
10. fructose   *n.* 果糖
11. palatability   *n.* 适口性，风味，口感
12. astringency   *n.* 涩味
13. colloidal   *adj.* 胶状的，胶质的
14. protopectin   *n.* 原果胶
15. mellow   *adj.* 熟透的，黄熟的，松软的；*v.* (使)成熟

Questions

1. State the process of the fruit ripening.
2. How to improve fruit color by culture practices?
3. How to determine the harvest time of the fruits?

Lesson 16

Part A Physiology in Evergreen Fruit Tree——Building Materials, Photosynthesis and Respiration

Selected and rewritten from *Evergreen Orchards*, by William Henry Chandler.

Tree Building Materials

Water is considerably the largest constituent of the living tree: 50 percent or mature wood, 65 percent or more of the fresh fruit excepting a few such as dates. Excepting water, much the largest constituents are cell walls. Varying quantities of starch and sugars are present and acids from partial oxidation of sugars. The protein molecule is built up largely from carbohydrates, only about 15 to 17 percent of it's built up largely nitrogen, a much smaller percentage of sulfur and a small percentage of phosphorus in some molecules. Nitrogen, sulfur, and phosphorus, are from the soil and are in all cells, nitrogen and perhaps sulfur in all protoplasm, phosphorus at least in some protoplasm. Magnesium is a constituent of chlorophyll and iron, though not a constituent of chlorophyll, must be present in the chloroplast for chlorophyll development and maintenance. Calcium is combined with pectin in the cell walls and is necessary for healthy root growth. Potassium in rather large quantities, larger than of any of these other elements except nitrogen, is necessary for healthy tree growth. Besides these substances taken into the plant in measurable quantities, much smaller quantities of manganese, zinc, copper, boron and molybdenum are necessary. A pound each of manganese, zinc, copper, and boron, may be used per year by 8 to 20 acres of mature tree lacre=4046.86m^2, still less of molybdenum. All of them together constitute less than 5 percent of the dry weight of most trees and fruit, but deficiencies of any of them may cause striking injury.

Photosynthesis

  Photosynthesis The carbon compounds, more than 90 percent of the dry weight of the tree, its leaves, and its fruit, are derived from the sugar synthesized in chloroplasts of the leaves. The reaction is sometimes written $6CO_2 + 6H_2O +$ about 673 kg Cal. Light energy $= C_2H_{12}O_6 + 6O_2$. The products are sugar and oxygen, but no such reaction has been brought about in the laboratory. The reaction in the plant is much more complicated than this equation indicates(Fig. 16-1). It is accomplished in large part through the agency of light and two compounds in the chloroplasts: chlorophyll a, and chlorophyll b. These compounds reflect and transmit more wave length in the green part of the spectrum than in others and therefore appear green.

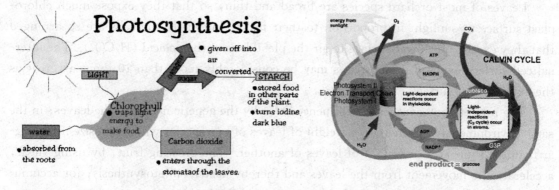

Fig. 16-1 Model of photosynthesis(downloads from http://images.google.cn/imglanding?imgurl)

    Chlorophyll and sunlight cannot be the only agents in producing sugar from carbon dioxide and water, for the reaction does not take place except in the plastids. Indirect evidence is strong that two reactions or series of reactions are involved: one, photochemical is influenced little if at all by temperature within the noninjurious range for plants of the species concerned, usually 10 to 25℃; the other, known sometimes as the dark reaction because it is not dependent upon light, or the dark reaction for the discoverer shows within the range 10 to 25℃. approximately the normal response of chemical processes to temperature, the rate being approximately doubled by a rise in temperature of 10℃. If the carbon dioxide supply and light intensity are both optimum, the rate of photosynthesis will be determined by the dark reaction and may be approximately doubled by a temperature rise of 10℃(within the range of 10 to 25℃). If the supply of carbon dioxide is adequate but light intensity is considerably below the optimum, the rate of photosynthesis will be determined by the light reaction and will not increase much with rise in temperature.

    Leaves exposed to full sunlight receive more radiant energy than they require for maximum photosynthesis even when the carbon dioxide supply is as large as it is apt to be. On a tree, however, a large percentage of the leaves receive very much less than full sunlight; Light is apt to be the limiting factor for these shaded leaves and carbon dioxide for those most exposed.

    When the temperature and soil conditions are favorable for rapid growth respiration to use the products of photosynthesis, the small carbon dioxide supply in the atmosphere, rarely more than about 0.03 percent by volume, is probably a limiting factor for photosynthesis at least in leaves that are exposed to optimum light. The supply of carbon dioxide in the atmosphere tends to be nearly constant. That which is removed is partly replaced by respiration of plants and animals, much of this by organisms in the soil that decompose plant products there. Sometimes the amount rising from the soil is enough to keep the content of air nearest the soil higher than that in air surrounding the highest leaves in the tree. In other words, leaves carbon dioxide may be in atmosphere containing a little less carbon dioxide than that around lower leaves that, because of shade, cannot use as much.

Leaves of most orchard species are broad and thin, so that they expose much chloroplast surface to sunlight in proportion to their mass. Internally the cells are so arranged that they expose much wet surface to air the plastids as carbonic acid (H_2CO_3). The internal cell surface exposed to air spaces may be considerably more than 10 times as great as the external leaf surface.

The rate of photosynthesis is influenced also by the genetic nature of the leaves; in the same environment, a given area or weight of leaves of one species will synthesize more sugar than the same area or weight of leaves of another. The growing fruit, by using sugar, accelerates its movement from the leaves and thereby hastens photosynthesis; for accumulation in the leaf of the products of photosynthesis retards that process.

Tree Food and Other Carbon Compounds Throughout this text the term food will be used for tree as it is for animals, meaning carbohydrates, fats, and proteins, the substances that are obtained by the tree through photosynthesis.

Two hexose sugars, d-glucose and d-fructose, are important in the tree. Glucose may be the only sugar formed directly by photosynthesis, but if so, some of it is quickly changed to fructose, and the two combine with loss of a molecule of water to form sucrose, $C_{12}H_{22}O_{11}$. The fact that sucrose suggests that it may be the first sugar formed. However, when a leaf is shaded until it has lost all sugar formed. However, when a leaf is first sugars to appear seem to be hexoses. But these are quickly changed to sucrose and starch. Of course, starch, being insoluble, must be changed to sugar before it can be moves out of the plastid. When carbohydrates are not all used in growth and respiration, they are stored mainly as starch, in the leucoplasts. Sugars rarely accumulate to high concentration except in germinating seeds, in fruits, and in winter wood of temperate zone tree. Much the largest part of the sugar from photosynthesis is used in forming the cell wall material, especially cellulose, which has the same formula as starch except than in the cellulose formula, and stands for a much larger number of glucose molecules.

Other compounds in the walls of most cells in woody tissue are lignins that tend to increase the resistance of cells to compression. Cutin, and suberin, condensation products of different fatty acids with perhaps other fatty substance, tend to render cell walls less permeable to water. Cutin, especially on the outer surfaces of epidermal cells, greatly reduces loss of water. Suberin has a similar effect in cork cells and seems to be in the walls of many other cells, if not most.

Among organic nitrogen compounds, some amino acids are important for their own role in the cells and because they are building materials for proteins. Nitrates(NO_3^-) entering the plant from the soil are reduced to nitrites and further to NH_2 and NH_3 compounds and in some way combined with carbohydrates, or products of carbohydrates, to form amino acids.

Proteins are constituents of protoplasm and some of them are reserve foods. Some are soluble and some insoluble. They are formed by condensation of very many molecules of amino acids, the protein molecules being from about 100 to more than 1000 times as large as that of sucrose.

Fatty substances, or lipids, including phosphatides, which contain nitrogen and phosphorus in the molecule, are present in the protoplasm but mostly as food. Some fatty substance are regular forms of reserve food in trees of some species, they can be formed from carbohydrates and readily changed back to carbohydrates in trees of such species.

Transport of Food and Nutrients Food moving from its source in the leaf or from any situation where it has been stored in large quantities, to other parts of tree must pass in solution through cells. Starch and insoluble fatty substances must first be changed to sugar. Soluble organic acids and other soluble organic compounds must move as the sugar does, when they leave the cells in which they are located. Some soluble pigments seem to remain in the cells in which they are formed. Sugar does not readily enter the protoplasm from the protoplasm in one cell is immersed, but apparently passes readily from the protoplasm in one cell to that in another.

Rather large amounts of food must be used for respiration and new cell material in the apical meristems. This must pass from the leaves below the tip of a shoot up through differentiating and dividing cells to any cell in which it is needed. Movement along shoots, branches and trunks toward the roots is mainly in the phloem. In most dicotyledonous species this is in the bark, though in some there is also phloem in tissue beneath the bark.

There is still some disagreement concerning the tissues in which mineral nutrients move from the young roots to the leaves. The best evidence, however, seems to me to indicate that these, when in inorganic compounds pass through the living root cells into the nonliving elements of the xylem and are carried up with the water.

Respiration

The tree does not use as building material or reserves all the sugar formed in its chloroplasts. Some must be broken down in respiration to supply energy. The gram-molecule of glucose (180 grams) required for its formation 673 kg calories of energy from the sun and can release that much energy when completely oxidized to carbon dioxide and water. Many processes in the cells require energy, and respiration releases it from carbon compounds. Energy is required even for the entrance of nutrients into the root cells; if the carbohydrate supply to the roots for respiration is low, intake of respiration in every living cell, the rate depending in part on the processes in the cells concerned and also on the food supply. It seems to be more rapid in active meristematic tissue than in others and may be higher than necessary for the energy needed if the supply of soluble carbohydrates is large. Rapid changes of sugar to the insoluble starch may be protection against excessive respiration.

The proportion of a tree's product of photosynthesis that is used in respiration will depend on the rate of photosynthesis, which is greatly influenced by light intensity, and on the rate of respiration, which is greatly influenced by temperature. A plant in the shade of a dense forest in a hot climate may use nearly all its products of photosynthesis in respiration and have little for growth, while in full sunlight a plant may respire even more rapidly at the same temperature but photosynthesis may be rapid enough to supply food for its and for growth, a heavy crop, and a considerable amount of stored starch.

Respiration and growth tend to be reduced more than photosynthesis by cool weather; and accumulation of starch begins sooner after the depletion during a growth flush in a cool district than in a warm one, unless the plant in one that is injured by cool weather.

Respiration does not proceed by the simple equation $C_6H_{12}O_6 + 6O_2 \longrightarrow 6CO_2 + 6H_2O +$ 673 kg calories of energy; a number of steps are involved, catalyzed by a system of enzymes, but glucose and possibly fructose are used in respiration.

Glossary

1. starch *n.* 淀粉
2. protein molecule 蛋白质分子
3. carbohydrate *n.* 碳水化合物
4. nitrogen *n.* 氮
5. sulfur *n.* 硫
6. phosphorus *n.* 磷
7. protoplasm *n.* 原生质
8. magnesium *n.* 镁
9. chlorophyll *n.* 叶绿素
10. chloroplast *n.* 叶绿体
11. calcium *n.* 钙
12. pectin *n.* 胶质
13. potassium *n.* 钾
14. manganese *n.* 锰
15. zinc *n.* 锌
16. copper *n.* 铜
17. boron *n.* 硼
18. molybdenum *n.* 钼
19. plastid *n.* 质体
20. photochemical *adj.* 光化作用的，光化学的
21. noninjurious *adj.* 无害的
22. dark reaction 暗反应
23. light reaction 光反应
24. hexose sugar 己糖

25. d-glucose   d-葡萄糖
26. d-fructose   d-果糖
27. sucrose   *n.* 蔗糖
28. leucoplast   *n.* 白色体
29. cellulose   *n.* 纤维素
30. lignins   *n.* 木质素
31. cutin   *n.* 表皮素，蜡状质
32. suberin   *n.* ［生化］软木脂
33. fatty acid   脂肪酸
34. amino acid   氨基酸
35. nitrate   *n.* 硝酸盐
36. lipid   *n.* 脂质，油脂
37. phosphatide   *n.* 磷脂
38. pigment   *n.* 色素
39. meristem   *n.* 分生组织

Exercises

A. Please answer the following questions in English.

1. What do the mainly tree building materials include and where are they from?
2. What does photosynthesis mean to trees? How do the temperature and sunlight affect photosynthesis?
3. What does respiration mean to plants? Can we suppress it completely?
4. Please describe the synthesis process of carbon compounds in the plant briefly.
5. How do the tree foods transport from its source to the other part of plant?

B. Please translate the following paragraph into Chinese.

Green plants are the only plants that produce oxygen and make food, which is called photosynthesis. Photosynthesis means "putting together with light". This takes place in chloroplasts, which have chlorophyll in them. Chlorophyll absorbs the sunlight. From sunlight, green plants combine carbon dioxide and water to make sugar and oxygen. Green plants use sugar to make starch, fats, and proteins. There are tiny pores called stomata. Carbon dioxide and oxygen enter and leave through the stomata respectively.

C. Please translate the following sentences into English.

1. 光控制植物生长、发育和分化的过程，称为光形态建成。红光和远红光可以决定光形态建成的改变，其光受体是光敏色素。光敏色素是一种易溶于水的色素蛋白质，生理作用很广泛，可控制种子萌发、器官分化、生长和运动、光周期和花诱导等。

2. 绿色植物光合作用是地球上最为普遍、规模最大的反应过程，在有机物合成、蓄积太阳能量和净化空气等方面起很大作用，是农业生产的基础。叶片是进行光合作用的主要器官，叶绿体是光合作用的重要细胞器。呼吸作用是高等植物代谢的重要组成部分，与植物的生命活动关系密切，可为植物体内的各种生命活动提供所需能量和合成重要有机物的原料。

Part B Freezing Injury in Evergreen Orchard

Selected and rewritten from *Evergreen Orchards*, by William Henry Chandler.

For trees in some of the evergreen orchard species, growth at temperature of 20℃, will be very much more than twice that at 10℃. In fact, some of them will not grow at temperatures between 10℃ and 15℃, and will eventually shed the leaves they had when planted and die slowly. Trees of some species show pronounced chilling injury symptoms. In coastal districts of southern California, the leaves on average summer may turn yellow and the shoots may die back in an especially cool summer. On the other hand, strains of avocados apparently native to a latitude of about 20℃ make rather strong growth in the climate of around the San Francisco Bay where the mean summer temperature is about 18℃ or lower. Trees of some species such as citrus grow very slowly in such a cool climate but survive such as citrus grow very slowly in such a cool climate but survive and fruit.

At such temperature, even if the trees grow and blossom well, they may not set much fruit. This is true of avocado varieties that have been tried. If fruit is set it may tend to be below normal size and to have poor flavor. This tends to be true of citrus fruits. Even in the tropics at elevations of about 3,000 feet or greater(one foot=30.48cm), the flavor of some kinds, such as grapefruit, may be poor, owing to the coolness.

In some districts a daily wind from the ocean may be cool enough to impair flavor of the fruit. A thick hedge of tall trees on the ocean side may deflect such a wind over a rather wide strip of trees if the orchard is nearly level, a narrow strip if the orchard slopes rather steeply toward the ocean.

Freezing Injury

Although trees of many evergreen, fruit-bearing species are limited to frost-free districts by their susceptibility to injury by chilling temperatures above the freezing point, a considerable percentage of the total investment in evergreen orchard species is in districts where killing frost damage trees and fruit. Trees of many varieties of species such as oranges, grapefruits, enough to survive, without much injury, temperatures as low as 16℃ to 20℃, while trees of other may be badly damaged at temperatures of 26℃ to 27℃, or higher, by very small amounts of ice in their tissues. This killing by ice formation in the tissue is much more rapid than chilling injury; for example, thin plant parts placed in a freezing room for only twenty minutes may, if ice forms in them, show the symptoms of death upon thawing. Tissue of some species does not show browning, shows death slowly by turning nearly white. Of course a large, thick piece of tissue, such as a mature fruit or a large piece of tree branch or trunk, would not be killed in such a short time, even in air well below its killing temperature that soon, because it would not lose its heat fast enough to reach a killing temperature that soon, but only a few minutes with the critical amount of ice in its tissue is enough to kill it.

How Freezing Kills We know that ice formation in the tissue is necessary to cause freezing to death; for tissue can be undercooled. If kept very still around a thermometer bulb in cold air, it can sometimes be lowered to well below its killing temperature and held at that temperature for many minutes and warmed back up to room temperature without having had any ice formed in it. And it will not be killed. If it had been touched with a piece of ice when below its killing temperature, ice would have formed in it quickly and it would have been killed.

In very tender tissue ice forms in the cells. If the temperature fall is very rapid it forms within the cells of resistant tissue also and kills it at a considerably higher temperature than if the fall had been slower. When the temperature fall from the freezing point is not a very tender one, ice does not form within the cells but begins to form first in the intercellular spaces. As the temperature falls, water moves out of cells and adds to the size of the ice masses.

In some way ice formation kills cells by a physical effect on the protoplasm. When ice forms within the protoplasm, it may rupture the plasma membrane. This may be the way all very tender tissue is killed. Protoplasm does not shrink away from the walls evenly, but adheres at some points, possibly held by plasmodesma, and shrinks away at others. In tissue that is not killed at temperature above 15°C to 18°C or a little higher, shrinking of the protoplasm with temperature fall must be slow, for most of the water has moved out of the cells and frozen at higher, non-injurious temperatures. We know protoplasm that has shrunk away fro the walls of cells in a strong plasmolyzing solution can be so killed by being transferred directly to distilled water, although if it is transferred through weaker and weaker solutions and finally to distilled water, it will not be killed.

This view may seem out of harmony with the fact that, excepting a very few tissues such as ripe apple and ripe pear flesh, the rate thawing in air has no measurable influence on the amount of injury at a given temperature. However, when the temperature of frozen tissue begins to rise, the water does not seem to leave the ice particles until it has collected in droplets large enough to cause rather rapid expansion of the protoplasm at its point of entrance, regardless of how slow the rise in temperature may be.

Cause of Frost Resistance Some plants have little or no ability to acquire resistance to freezing; in any condition of growth they are tender. Others are very tender when in a succulent, growing condition, more resistant between growth flushes, and can be made considerably more resistant by exposure for several days or several weeks to temperatures near the freezing point. The process of acquiring increased resistance during exposure to cold is known as hardening, becoming hardy. What differences in the plant are associated with this greater resistance? There may be a greater concentration of substances dissolved in the cell sap, and possibly a greater amount of colloidal material that holds a little water. These will tend to lower the temperature at which ice is formed in the plant and lower the rate of water loss from the cells with lowering temperature. However, before the hardened tissue can be killed, considerably more of its water must be ice than in tender tissue. In other words, the protoplasm has acquired the ability to withstand without injury a greater loss of water to ice formation than it had in an unhardened condition. Studies of this hardened protoplasm have shown that it has increased the danger of ice formation within it, that it will remain a somewhat fluid sol after loss of a percentage of its water that would cause unhardened protoplasm to be a rather stiff or brittle gel, and that it will withstand a higher degree of plasmolysis and be uninjured when placed directly in distilled water than will unhardened protoplasm.

While this hardening process makes much greater differences in resistance of deciduous orchard species than in these evergreen species, such resistance as these can develop is dependent upon their being prevented from starting any of the activities that precede visible growth. Water deficits may help toward this, but the most important influence seems to be chilling weather, for species that can withstand chilling. Even young, succulent avocado shoots, subjected to a considerable period of chilling before a frost, seem to develop a considerable degree of resistance.

Flooding Water has a high specific heat, and a high heat of fusion that is given to the air if the water freezes. Heavy irrigation of the orchard before a killing frost will increase the amount of heat the soil can give to the same weight of dry soil, and upon freezing gives up 80 times as much as that given by cooling a degree centigrade at temperatures above freezing.

Surface Influences Degrees of resistance of the cells may not be the only influence on amount of injury by given low temperature. Leaves or flowers that are dry on the surface may not show as much injury as leaves or flowers with equally resistant cells but with wet surface. And a waxy coating increases resistance.

Atmospheric Conditions and Frost Damage The air temperature is not an exact measure of the temperature of plant parts exposed to the sky on a still clear night. Objects lose heat at night by radiation, and if nothing but air is between them and the cold sky, no heat is radiated back to them, and if there is no wind to bring the warmer air into contact with them, they receive little heat from the air. The number of degrees below the air temperature that of a plant part may fall will depend in part on the completeness of its exposure to the sky, the clearness and stillness and dryness of the air, and the nature of the surface of the plant part.

Cold air may come into the district with a wind, but before morning the air may become still and the tree parts may fall to a temperature well below that of the air.

Clear, still nights are apt to be followed by bright, sunny mornings. Fruits or flowers most exposed to the sky at night may be most exposed to the sun in the morning. People may conclude that rapid thawing caused the greater damage when the real cause was the lower night temperature of flowers or fruit owing to their greater heat loss by radiation.

In an area without trees or shrubs I leaf, the coldest air on a still, clear night is next to the soil. It is cooled by contact with the soil. In an orchard in leaf, however, as healthy evergreen orchard always will be, these leaves are colder than the soil and the air 5 or 6 feet above the soil is apt to be colder than that below. In some nights frost damage in an orchard is considerably worse if the soil is very dry or its surface is freshly worked and loose. In an orchard with a thick cover crop, frost damage is sometimes considerably greater than in one with bare, compact soil.

When the air is not cold enough to cause damage but radiation by flowers or young fruits or tree parts is apt to lower their temperature dangerously, any material between them and the sky may radiate back to them about as much heat as they lose and so keep them at the air temperature. A few layers of some material such as corn stalks close around young trees may save them. A thick layer spread out at the bottom to direct heat from the soil up around the tree wound be necessary.

Horticulturists thought at one time that smoke and moisture, from burning around the orchard material that was a little wet, would serve to prevent or greatly reduce the loss of heat from an orchard. They realized that such fires around the edge of an orchard could not raise its temperature, but if the fires were started long enough before the air temperature began to be dangerous, they were excepted to prevent or impede further temperature fall and save the flowers or fruit.

Orchard Heating The effectiveness of orchard heating depends almost entirely on the heat from the fires and very little if at all on the blanket of smoke. Much the large part of the expenditure in the world for orchard heating is in evergreen orchards such as citrus and the avocado. Besides saving a crop, heating in these species may prevent serious damage to the trees.

Cost of equipment for heating with oil in citrus orchards in California may be $300 an acre for lemons; a supply of oil must be in the orchard before the cold night comes and this involves, in addition to the heaters, oil, and lighters, tanks for storage and tank trucks for hauling.

If the orchard were under a cover so that heated air could not escape, very much less fuel would be required to heat it. The hotter the individual fires, the higher the heated air rises, and the more heat is wasted. The smoke stacks add to efficiency by radiating heat outward so that a much larger volume of air is heated but not so hot, and it does escape above the orchard as fast as a small mass of air over an open flame would.

Glossary

1. chilling injury   冷害
2. avocado   *n.* 鳄梨，油梨
3. citrus   *n.* 柑橘属果树
4. grapefruit   *n.* 葡萄柚

5. frost damage   霜冻害
6. browning   *n.* 褐变
7. undercooled   *adj.* 过冷却的
8. killing temperature   致死温度
9. freezing point   冰点
10. plasma membrane   质膜
11. plasmolyzing   *adj.* 胞质皱缩的，质壁分离的
12. frost resistance   耐霜性
13. cell sap   细胞液
14. colloidal material   胶体物质
15. deciduous   *adj.* 落叶的
16. water deficit   水分亏缺，水分不足

Questions

1. What will happen if plants meet with chilling injury?
2. Why the freezing injury in the tissue is much more rapid than chilling injury?
3. How to alleviate the chilling injury for plants?

Lesson 17

Part A Postharvest Physiology of Tropical Fruit

Selected and rewritten from *Postharvest Physiology and Storage of Tropical and Subtropical Fruits*, by S. K. Mitra.

Postharvest problems cause tremendous loss in tropical-fruit production. The estimates of tropical-fruit postharvest loss vary widely (10%～80%) in both developed and developing countries. The losses given in published reports highlight the total postharvest losses of products, but do not consider the loss of quality or downgrading that may reduce the price received. Losses may be due to mechanical injury, physiological damage or pathogens. The reduction of the losses in a systematic way requires a knowledge of postharvest physiology, its applied technical aspect, handling, and the appreciation of its biological limitation represented as storage potential.

Tropical-fruit physiology does not differ from the basic knowledge gained from studies of temperate and subtropical fruits. There are differences in the major substrates involved in ripening, the rate of ripening and senescence and, in some cases, variation in the order in which various components of ripening occur. The aspects of tropical-fruit physiology that make these fruits unique are the chilling sensitivity of most tropical fruits, the generally more rapid ripening of climacteric tropical fruits when compared with temperate fruit and the frequent need in postharvest handling of tropical fruit to expose them to high temperatures or other stresses during insect disinfestation prior to sale in markets.

Like temperate fruits, tropical fruits can be divided into climacteric and non-climacteric (Table 17-1). This division is based on the respiratory pattern after harvest. In climacteric fruit, there is generally a dramatic and rapid change in respiration during ripening. In commercial handling, ethylene can lead to earlier ripening of climacteric fruit but not of non-climacteric fruit.

Classification of selected tropical fleshy fruits according to their respiratory pattern

Table 17-1

Climacteric	Non-climacteric
Avocado (*Persea americana* Mill.)	Carambola (*Averrhoa carambola* L.)
Banana/Plantain (*Musa* spp.)	Litchi (*Litchi chinensis* Sonn.)
Breadfruit (*Artocarpus altilis* Parkins Fosb.)	Mountain apple [*Syzygium malaccense* (L.) Merr. & Perry]

Climacteric	Non-climacteric
Cherimoya (*Annona cherimola* Mill.)	Pineapple [*Ananas comosus* (L.) Merr.]
Durian (*Durio zibethinus* J. Murr.)	Rambutan (*Nephelium lappaceum* L.)
Guava (*Psidium guajava* L.)	Rose apple [*Syzygium jambos* L (Alston)]
Mango (*Mangifera indica* L.)	Star apple (*Chrysophyllum cainito* L.)
Papaya (*Carica papaya* L.)	Surinam cherry (*Eugenia uniflora* L.)
Passion-fruit (*Passiflora edulis* Sims)	Mangosteen (*Garcinia mangostana* L.)
White sapote (*Casimiroa edulis* La Llave)	
Soursop (*Annona muricata* L.)	
Chiku (*Manilkara zapota* L.)	

Tropical fruits vary widely in their respiration rate and ethylene production, varying with stage of ripening and senescence as well as variety, preharvest environment and culture. However, knowing the rates of respiration is essential for determining heat loads in refrigerated cold rooms and containers. The ethylene-production rate is also essential information, because it relates to mixed loads and the effect of one commodity on another; for example, ethylene is used to ripen banana fruit.

Respiration rate and storage life are related. Fruit with high respiration rates have shorter postharvest lives——hence the need to reduce respiration and thereby increase postharvest life. Temperature management is the major method of controlling respiration rate to extend the postharvest life of tropical fruit, but it is limited in most tropical fruit by their chilling sensitivity. The symptoms of chilling injury are similar for most commodities and include pitting, skin darkening, failure to ripen completely and increased susceptibility to decay.

In any discussion of chilling, two aspects must be considered: the temperature and the time spent at that temperature. Although there is not an exact, fruit-specific, reciprocal relationship between temperature and time, it takes a longer time at a higher temperature to develop injury than at a lower temperature. As the storage temperature is lowered from 30℃, duration of storage life increases, the limitation being fruit ripening and senescence. Storage life reaches a maximum at 15℃ for Brazilian banana, 10~12℃ for papaya, 8℃ for rambutan and 5℃ for carambola. Lowering the temperature further leads to a shorter storage life, but the limitation changes from ripening to the development of chilling injury, that ripening being completely inhibited. Recommendations for optimum storage of most tropical fruits are just inside the chilling range (8~12℃), as this allows ripening to be controlled and, if removed before the chilling-stress threshold is exceeded, the fruit still has a number of days of useful marketing life as it ripens. Unfortunately, similar data are not available or are fragmentary for many tropical fruits. The actual relationship between storage temperature and duration can vary with cultivar, preharvest conditions, stage of ripeness and postharvest treatments. Carambola and the subtropical fruits longan and litchi are crops that are somewhat resistant to chilling injury, requiring a considerable time (>14 days) at 1℃ before injury occurs, but some standard tropical fruits, for example, durian, mangosteen, mango, jackfruit *et al.* apt to injured at 1℃ for s a short time.

Water loss is a severe problem affecting the storage life of tropical fruits. Frequently, injury induced by water loss is confused with chilling injury. Loss of mass in tropical fruits postharvest, mainly a loss of water, is dependent upon the commodity, cultivar, preharvest conditions, water-vapour pressure deficit (WVPD), wounds, postharvest heat treatments and the presence of containings or wraps. Tropical fruit can be grouped from low moisture-loss rate (coconut) to medium (avocado, banana, pummelo) to high (guava, litchi, mango, papaya, pineapple). On a per-unit-area basis, the stem scar is frequently the site of highest water loss, although most water is lost through lenticels, stomata and skin cuticle. Tropical fruit have water-loss rates between about 0.1% and 0.3% day^{-1} mbar WVPD^{-1}. Fruit that lost 6%~8% of their fully turgid initial weight begin to show signs of mass loss. Usually the initial sign is skin wrinkling, although skin discoloration is the first symptom in some fruits. Loss of mass, besides affecting overall appearance, is also an economic loss if fruit is sold by weight.

Glossary

1. postharvest   *n.* 采后
2. tropical and subtropical fruits   热带亚热带果树
3. physiology   *n.* 生理学
4. respiration   *n.* 呼吸作用
5. climacteric and non-climacteric   呼吸跃变和非呼吸跃变
6. avocado   *n.* 鳄梨，油梨
7. plantain   *n.* 大蕉
8. breadfruit   *n.* 面包果
9. cherimoya   *n.* 番荔枝
10. durian   *n.* 榴莲
11. guava   *n.* 番石榴
12. mango   *n.* 芒果
13. passion-fruit   *n.* 鸡蛋果，又名百香果、计时果
14. white sapote   山榄果，白柿，又名白人心果、香肉果
15. soursop   *n.* 刺果番荔枝
16. chiku   *n.* 人心果，即 sapodilla，泰国称作 Lamoot，印度尼西亚称作 Chiku，中国台湾称为吴凤柿
17. pineapple   *n.* 菠萝，凤梨
18. optimum storage condition   最佳贮藏条件
19. papaya   *n.* 番木瓜
20. rambutan   *n.* 红毛丹

21. carambola *n.* 杨桃
22. rose apple 蒲桃
23. star apple 金星果
24. surinam cherry 番樱桃，苏里南樱桃，毕当茄（pitanga），红果仔
25. mangosteen *n.* 山竹子，又名莽吉桔、凤果、倒稔子
26. water-vapour pressure deficit（WVPD） 水汽压差
27. lenticel *n.* 皮孔
28. stomata *n.* 气孔
29. cuticle *n.* 角质层，表皮（层）
30. discoloration *n.* 变色，褪色
31. disinfestation *n.* 灭虫，灭昆虫法
32. tephritid fruit fly 白色条纹果蝇
33. quarantine *n.* 检疫，隔离（期），检疫所；*vt.* 对⋯进行检疫，对⋯进行隔离
34. fumigation *n.* 熏蒸

Exercises

A. Please answer the following questions in English.

1. What are the reasons that result in the tropical-fruit postharvest loss?

2. What are the differences of fruit physiology between tropical fruits and temperate fruits?

3. What phytohormone is tightly associated with fruit ripening?

4. How does the temperature affect the storage life of tropical fruit?

B. Please translate the following paragraph into Chinese.

Mechanical hazards can be defined as those caused by impact, vibration, and compression and puncturing. Impact damage is likely if packages are carelessly dropped or thrown. The fruits inside move around, and contact between fruit and fruit and packaging leads to bruising. To reduce the effect on the produce the package should immobilize and spread the load on individual pieces and provide cushioning.

C. Please translate the following paragraph into English.

根据呼吸代谢的特性，热带果树的果实可分为呼吸跃变型果实和非呼吸跃变型果实。香蕉、芒果、番木瓜、油梨及人心果等果树的果实属于呼吸跃变型果实，而菠萝、杨桃、荔枝、红毛丹和山竹子等果树的果实属于非呼吸跃变型果实。

Part B Harvesting and Postharvest Handling of Tropical and Subtropical Fruits

Selected and rewritten from *Postharvest Physiology and Storage of Tropical and Subtropical Fruits*, by S. K. Mitra

Compared with temperate fruit crops, tropical and subtropical fruits often present greater problems in storage and transportation because of their greater perishability and overripening. Many factors can result in postharvest fruit deterioration which consists of respiration, ethylene production, water loss, mechanical damage, pests and diseases and physiological disorders. In addition, postharvested fruits may be influenced by a range of environmental conditions, including temperature, humidity and atmospheric composition. All may be manipulated by careful management of the postharvest handling system to obtain the best possible results (quality and storage life) for the produce. All fruits (and even different cultivars of the same fruit) have highly specific requirements and tolerances to storage. As a consequence, the mixing of loads for storage and transportation is done with care, paying attention to requirements for temperature and humidity, as well as ethylene production and sensitivity. In attempting to improve the quality of the produce reaching the final market the harvesting and postharvest handling described below must be pay more attention to.

Harvesting of Tropical and Subtropical Fruits

Harvest the fruit at the correct time physiologically can influence its performance postharvest. In the case of climacteric fruit that is allowed to ripen after transportation, the more physiologically immature the fruit is at harvest the longer its storage life; if it is too immature, however, it may never ripen to a good eating quality. With non-climacteric crops the changes are not so dramatic and the natural storage life longer. Harvest maturity is the point at which the fruit has reached a minimum level of development such that it has sufficient life to withstand transportation and ripening, yet will still ripen normally to produce a fruit of good quality. The harvest maturity of a fruit depends on its required postharvest life. In commercial terms this often equates to whether it will be air-freighted or sea-freighted. Fruit to be air-freighted will have a shorter journey time and may therefore be harvested slightly more mature than that going by sea.

Once fruit suitable for harvest have been identified they are carefully removed from the plant, either by hand or by using knives or clippers. Ladders and supports or picking poles may be needed to reach fruit high off the ground. Fruit should not be allowed to fall to the ground because of the potential for damage and contamination. Once picked, the fruit should be placed either in a small picking container, worn or carried by the picker, or directly into a field container, thereby avoiding placing the fruit on the ground. The use of the picking container reduces the number of times the picker has to go back and forth between the trees and the field containers. All containers being used must be clean and not damage the produce.

It is possible to make an initial selection for quality in the field to reduce the amount of rejects taken into the packhouse. Proper training of the pickers for judging harvest maturity and for fruit handling helps to reduce wastage from harvesting unsuitable fruit and also from damaged fruit. Hygiene in the field is important and rejected and fallen fruit should not be left in the field to act as sources of inoculum for future infection, they should be removed at regular intervals.

Having harvested the crop into field containers these should be assembled in the shade, to reduce heating of the crop, until they can be transferred carefully to the packhouse. The temperature of the harvested crop can also be kept as low as possible by harvesting early in the morning or even at night. There is a danger that considerable mechanical damage can be caused while transporting crops between the fields and the packhouse especially if poorly packed produce is transported in trucks driven at inappropriate speeds on poorly surfaced roads. Such damage can be avoided by educating the workforce in the problems of fresh produce. The produce requires packing correctly into suitable containers so that the containers take any applied forces rather than the produce inside. The loaded vehicles should then be driven with care to prevent the load from moving and produce being damaged.

Postharvest Handling of Tropical and Subtropical Fruits

The objective of the postharvesting handling is to keep the freshly harvested fruit into the form acceptable to (and often specified by) the consumer. This is usually a case of cleaning, grading, packaging and temperature and atmosphere regulating.

Field boxes or bins may be unloaded and emptied dry or may be dumped into water depending on the requirements for cleaning (for example, the removal of latex from bananas and mangoes) and the nature of the produce. Cleaning may also be by brushing rather than by washing.

Even where pickers are well trained and experienced, not all the fruit reaching the packhouse will be of good quality. It is therefore essential to sort out the poor-quality fruit (by appearance, maturity, degree of blemish, damage, bruising, disease and size) and either discard it or divert it for alternative uses (local markets, institutions, catering or processing), depending on the type of defect. The fruit defects may be regarded as stable or unstable depending on their effect on keeping quality. Stable defects are usually caused preharvest and are mainly cosmetic, being easily removed by grading. The unstable defects influence keeping quality since they develop further during storage. They are difficult to detect at grading and include both mechanical damage arising during handling and physiological disorders. Much quality sorting is done by visual assessment on tables or, in the larger mechanized packhouses, on conveyors. Automated sorting (for example, by colour) is also possible in situations where there are large throughputs of suitable fruit. Automated sorting methods utilizing other properties of the fruit (including light reflection or transmission, fluorescence, delayed light emission, image processing, acoustical or electrical properties and mechanical methods for determining firmness) are being examined for their potential. Consumers require fruit to be sized and this may be done by eyes, often as the fruit are being packed, although mechanical sizers (for both weight and dimensions) are available for many commodities should the commercial and economic situation warrant their use. Some fruit may be packed directly into transport containers in the field; this reduces the amount of postharvest handling but depends heavily on good field hygiene and on trained staff capable of good selection at harvest. It also requires that the crop needs no further treatment after being packed that can not be conducted on boxed fruit.

Treatments should be given to fruit in packhouse to control postharvest diseases which include the simplest way of diping or drenching fruits into fungicides and an integrated approach starting with good field hygiene and following through the packhouse, storage and transportation. Currently temperature treatments including heat treatments and cold treatments are being used for elimination of both fungal pathogens and insect pests. In addition, wax is applied to some fruits and this, as well as reducing water loss and to some extent modifying the internal atmosphere, can also act as carrier for fungicides.

Each tropical fruits need an optimum storage temperature (Table 17-2). Proper temperature management can be a very effective tool in ensuring that produce remains in good condition throughout storage and transportation. Reducing the temperature slows down metabolism (including respiration, and also ethylene production and action), delaying changes in the produce and reducing the heat produced from respiration. It also slows water loss and the development of pathogens. But the benefit that can be derived from temperature control is limited by the susceptibility of the fruit to damage at low but nonfreezing temperatures (chilling injury). When in storage or transportation the appropriate temperature should be provide for the selected fruit.

Recommended storage conditions for a range of tropical and subtropical fruits   Table 17-2

Product	Temperature/℃	Relative humidity /%	Storage life (weeks)	Controlled atmosphere	
				O_2/%	CO_2/%
Avocado	7~13	90~95	2~4	2~5	3~10
Banana	13~14	90~95	1~4	2~5	2~5
Grapefruit	10~15	85~90	6~8	3~10	5~10
Lemon	10~13	85~90	4~24	5~10	0~10
Mango	10~14	85~90	1~4	2~5	5~10
Orange	1~9	85~90	3~12	5~10	0~10
Papaya	7~13	85~90	1~3	2~5	5~8
Pineapple	7~13	85~90	2~4	2~5	5~10

For temperature management to be effective it is necessary to consider the whole postharvest system from the field to the consumer. Temperature managements should start with harvesting during cool times of the day (or night), shading the harvested crop and keeping delays between harvest and cooling as short as possible. A more technical approach may involve the use of expensive equipment with sufficient cooling capacity to remove heat from the produce. For crops which have very short postharvest lives it is essential to remove the field heat rapidly, bringing them to their optimum storage temperature as quickly as possible to obtain the maximum period of storage. Once the produce has been cooled to the final holding temperature it should maintained at this temperature throughout the subsequent marketing chain to the final destination. The produce may be cooled by placing it in a cool room, or it may be allowed to cool during transportation. This does not cool highly perishable produce quickly enough, however, although the rate of cooling can be increased by improving air circulation and using open stacking. The two effective principal methods of cooling for fruits are forced-air cooling and hydrocooling.

The use of controlled and modified atmospheres is becoming more popular. This is particularly true for tropical and subtropical fruit where the benefit of refrigeration is limited because of chilling injury. Atmospheric modification through reducing the concentration of oxygen and increasing the concentration of carbon dioxide helps to retard senescence and ripening by reducing respiration and ethylene production and sensitivity. It has beneficial effects in reducing some physiological disorders and in both directly and indirectly the growth of pathogens and the survival of some insects. Some physiological disorders are caused by the treatment, however, and in addition there may be irregular ripening and the development of off-flavors and odors.

Under controlled-atmosphere conditions the levels of oxygen and carbon dioxide are maintained at predetermined levels. For modified atmospheres, however, the development of the beneficial atmosphere is dependent principally on two factors: the respiration rate of the produce and the permeability of the packaging materials. The respiration is determined by the type of produce, the cultivar, its maturity and condition as well as the temperature. The permeability of the packaging materials is dependent on the type, thickness and surface area of the film used. Other factors influencing the development of the modified atmosphere include the initial free volume of the package and the atmospheric composition both within the package and in the environment. Good temperature management is therefore critical with modified atmosphere packaging to ensure that respiration remains within predetermined levels. If the temperature rises too high the increased respiration can result in damage to the produce through either anaerobic respiration or production of too much carbon dioxide.

An additional atmospheric component of importance to the handling is ethylene. When storing different commodities in the same area it is important to determine the ethylene production and sensitivity of the products. Fruit responds to ethylene at levels between 1×10^{-7} and 1×10^{-6} in the atmosphere, causing premature ripening in unripe climacteric fruit and stimulating the growth of some fungi. Good postharvest practice separates ethylene producers from commodities which are sensitive to ethylene. Storage areas for ethylene-sensitive commodities may also be kept ethylene-free through good ventilation or the use of ethylene-scrubbing equipment. Alternatively, ethylene-absorbing films can be used as overwraps, or sachets of ethylene absorbent in the packages. In many cases climacteric fruit are both ethylene-sensitive and ethylene producers, depending on their ripeness. For example, ripe bananas are high ethylene producers, whereas unripe, preclimacteric are sensitive to low levels of ethylene which can initiate ripening.

Glossary

1. postharvest handling　采后处理
2. deterioration　*n.* 腐烂
3. perishability　*n.* 易腐性
4. climacteric fruit　呼吸跃变型果实
5. non-climacteric fruit　非呼吸跃变型果实
6. harvest maturity　采收成熟度，可采成熟度
7. hygiene　*n.* 卫生学，保健法
8. grading　*n.* 分级
9. catering　*n.* 饮食界，提供餐饮服务
10. sorting　*n.* 分选
11. packhouse　*n.* 货仓
12. conveyor　*n.* 传送带
13. fluorescence　*n.* 荧光
14. delayed light emission　延迟发光
15. acoustical　*adj.* 听觉的
16. firmness　*n.* 硬度
17. pathogen　*n.* 病菌，病原体
18. chilling injury　冷害
19. flavor　*n.* 风味，气味，滋味
20. odor　*n.* 气味，臭气
21. oxygen　*n.* 氧气
22. carbon dioxide　二氧化碳
23. permeability　*n.* 透性
24. commodity　*n.* 商品
25. premature　*n.* 早熟
26. ventilation　*n.* 通风

Questions

1. Why do tropical fruits often present greater problems in storage and transportation?
2. What factors influence the storage of tropical fruits?
3. Why must the fruit be harvested at proper maturity?
4. How do you harvest the tropical fruits for a long distance transport?
5. What temperature range is appropriate for the storage of banana?

Lesson 18

Part A   Getting the Orchard Established for Macadamia

Selected and rewritten from *Macadamia Grower's handbook*, by Paul O'Hare, Russ Stephenson, Kevin Quinlan and Noel Vock.

Setting up an orchard that will be profitable in the long term requires careful planning. Mistakes made with orchard layout, land preparation, variety selection and tree spacing are difficult or impossible, and costly, to rectify later on. There are 14 important steps:
1. Assess the orchard site
2. Plan the orchard layout
3. Choose varieties and tree spacing
4. Order trees
5. Start to prepare the land
6. Plant windbreak trees (where necessary)
7. Mark out the rows
8. Deep rip along the rows
9. Control water flow within the orchard
10. Do a soil analysis and apply required fertilizers
11. Prepare the tree rows
12. Mark out the tree planting sites
13. Install the irrigation system (where required)
14. Plant the trees

Assess the Orchard Site

No all of an orchard site may be suitable for profitable macadamia production. Important elements to consider are soil depth/drainage, surface stoniness and slope.

Soil Depth/Drainage   As macadamias are susceptible to decline and trunk canker disease in poorly drained soils, check the depth of well-drained soil across the orchard site. A minimum depth of 0.5 m of free-draining soil without impermeable clay or rock layers is required, with 1 m preferred.

Surface Stoniness   While checking soil depth/drainage, also check the soil for small stones of a similar size to macadamia nuts. It is best to avoid such areas as the stones may cause excessive wear on harvesting machinery, and in some cases even preclude its use.

Slope As slope determines the risk of soil erosion and the safety of machinery operation, check the angle of slopes across the orchard site. Slope can be measured in degrees using a clinometer, or as a percentage using a simple spirit level. Note that other factors need to be considered in initially selecting the site. These include severity of frosts, exposure to strong winds, and proximity to neighbors in relation to noise and spraying conflicts.

Plan the Orchard Layout

The aim of this step is to achieve maximum productivity with minimal environmental impact. Important points to consider include machinery access and use, water retention and runoff, and the impact of orchard operation on neighbors.

The process of planning the orchard layout involves marking on a map of the intended orchard site the existing features such as roadway, standing timber, gullies and slope direction, and then developing an overlay plan showing proposed access roads, buildings, windbreaks, tree rows, surface drains to control runoff, and dam sites.

Choose Varieties and Tree Spacing

Varieties Because macadamias are a long-term crop, great care must be taken in choosing varieties. Unfortunately, there are no easy short cuts to identifying the best varieties, as the choice depends on a number of factors that different people will weight differently. However, here is a general process to follow:

1. Identify the varieties that yield best in your district in terms of sound kernel.
2. Analyze these varieties for any tree or nut characteristics that may affect performance.
3. Seek additional opinions from local growers, consultants and nursery tree suppliers.
4. From your list, identify those varieties that suit your proposed tree spacing and management system.
5. From these, select as many varieties as is appropriate to adequately spread the risk and harvesting workload.

Row and Tree Spacing This is a balance between maximising yield during the early life of the orchard and minimising cost and management requirements. Closer spacings provide earlier cash flow, but cost more to establish and require side trimming from early in the life of the orchard. On the other hand, wide spacings are suitable for all varieties and require little or no side trimming, but take much longer to provide a positive cash flow.

Variety Arrangement in the Orchard There are a number of reasons for carefully considering the way the varieties are arranged in the orchard.

Cross-pollination Cross-pollination between varieties is believed to increase the number of nuts, the percentage of first grade kernel, kernel recovery and nut size. To obtain any benefits of cross-pollination, we recommend that at least two varieties are interplanted within each major block of trees.

Harvesting and orchard management It is important to try to match the nut drop periods of the two (or more) varieties selected above for each sub-block. This will help to make subsequent harvesting more efficient. There will be spin-offs for orchard management as well.

Processing Where possible, avoid mixing hybrid varieties (for example some of the HVA varieties) with *Macadamia integrifolia* varieties (for example HAES varieties and Daddow) in the one block. Processors may require these to be consigned separately in the future. Seek advice on this from processors.

Order Trees

Once you have your varieties and worked out your row and tree spacing, calculate the number of trees you need. Order your trees at least 12 months before intended planting from a specialist macadamia nursery. Give preference to nurseries using non-soil potting mixes, using a minimum pot size of 6 L, and where trees are in the pot for no more than two years.

Start to Prepare the Land

In previously cultivated sites where clearing is unnecessary, start rehabilitating the soil at least 12 months before planting. This involves deep ripping and improving the nutrient and organic matter levels of the soil, as outlined in the following steps.

Plant Windbreak Trees (Where Necessary)

In general, permanent planted windbreaks are only recommended in sites highly exposed to strong winds, and then only where they are needed to supplement inadequate natural forest surrounds.

Mark out the Rows

Rows across the slope are marked parallel to a surveyed key line. Wire or rope is tightly stretched between two people at right to the key line and points marked approximately every 20 m along the row.

Rows up and down the slop are usually marked parallel to a fence line or windbreak or at right angles to the contour.

Deep Rip along the Rows

Where the land has been previously cultivated or grazed, deep rips to a depth of at least 60 cm along each row. Ripping will also help with the drainage of wet areas. If ripping downhill, lift the toolbar for a metre so every 30 m to avoid water scouring down the rip lines.

Control Water Flow within the Orchard

On sloping land, construct a major contour diversion drain above the orchard to divert water, where possible, into a stable waterway or dam. The drain should have a gradient of 2% to 5% and be large enough to handle water from the catchment above. Keep the steeper sections of the drain furtherest from the waterway or dam, unless you have very stable clay soils. Establish a creeping grass such as carpet grass, couch or kikuyu in the drain channel to prevent scouring. There are two options to control water flow within the orchard: establish a permanent ground cover such as sweet smother grass, which is tolerant of low light conditions, and will help to later protect the soil surface under the shady canopy of the trees; or, build shallow, wide, flat-bottomed V-drains grassed with sweet smother grass, carpet grass, couch or kikuyu in the centre of the inner-row area.

Do a Soil Analysis and Apply Required Fertilizers

Do a soil analysis at least 6 months before planting. This allows plenty of time for required fertilizers to be applied and the soil conditioned ready for planting.

Prepare the Tree Rows

Where the soil is loose and friable, move directly to the next step. Where it is compacted, cultivate a 1 to 2 m wide strip along the tree rows. As well as incorporating the fertilizer, cultivation along the tree rows aids tree establishment and reduces initial weed competition.

Mark out the Tree Planting Sites

Mark out each tree planting site. If there is grass or weed cover, spray a metre square at each planting site or a band 1 to 2 m wide along the row with glyphosate herbicide at least one month before planting.

Install the Irrigation System (Where Required)

As irrigation equipment is expensive and its design and operation will have long-term impact on production, we recommend that you use the services of a professional irrigation design consultant. The two most commonly used irrigation system are: under-tree minisprinklers (Fig. 18-1) with a micro-spray or micro-jet feature, drippers or trickle tape.

Fig. 18-1 Under-tree minisprinkler

Plant the Trees

Nursery Trees When you take delivery of your trees, check that the trees have:
1. dark green, well-formed foliage;
2. no stem damage or trunk canker;
3. a sound graft union (for trees that have been grafted);

4. at least two growth flushes above the graft or bud;
5. no pests such as felted coccid and latania scale;
6. no infestations or serious weeds such as tropical chickweed;
7. a well developed root system with a taproot that is not distorted;
8. not become root-bound by being in the pots for too long.

Also make sure the trees have been hardened to full sunlight.

When to Plant Unless there is risk of frost damage, trees are best planted in the autumn. This takes advantage of the normally good soil moisture from the summer wet season. Where a site may be frost-susceptible, plant in spring. However, take care to monitor soil moisture closely through the normally hot and dry spring and early summer.

Planting Procedure One to two days before planting, water thoroughly too wet tree sites to a depth of 30 cm. Follow these planting steps:

1. Dig a hole slightly deeper and wider than the pot bag (Fig. 18-2). Backfill with some of the topsoil and firm them down so that the surface of the potting mixture will be at the same level as the soil surface.
2. Before planting, water the tree well.
3. Cut the pot bag from the tree and inspect the roots.
4. Place the tree in the hole, ensuring that the roots at the bottom are spread.
5. Mulch trees with a coarse mulch such as grass, cereal or legume stubble to a depth of 10 to 15 cm.
6. Prune the tree to a central leader (if this as not already been done in the nursery).
7. Ensure any grafting tape is removed as soon as any constriction at the graft is noticed. This could be required several months after planting.
8. Do not allow the root ball to dry out after planting. Irrigation or hand water 2 to 3 times per week for the first few weeks, particularly where conditions are dry.
9. Paint exposed trunks immediately with white water-based paint to reduce the risk of sunburn and heat stress.

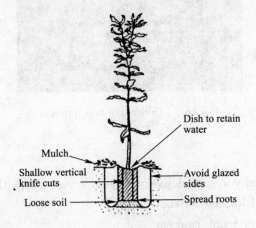

Fig. 18-2 A correctly planted tree

Glossary

1. macadamia　　*n.* 澳洲坚果，澳洲坚果属
2. canker　　*n.* 溃疡病，癌肿病
3. clinometer　　*n.* 测斜仪，倾斜仪，量坡仪，倾斜计
4. cross-pollination　　*n.* 异花授粉，杂交授粉
5. interplant　　*n.* 套种，间作，间种物
6. contour　　*n.* 等高线，外形，轮廓线，轮廓
7. carpet grass　　地毯草
8. kikuyu　　*n.* 隐花狼尾草，西非狼尾草（*Pennisetum clandestinum* Hochst.）
9. smother grass　　窒息草
10. glyphosate　　*n.* 草甘膦
11. minisprinkler　　*n.* 微喷灌装置
12. drippers or trickle tape　　滴灌带
13. felted coccid　　毡蚧
14. latania scale　　拉塔尼亚芭蕉蚧
15. sunburn　　*n.* 日灼，晒伤
16. heat stress　　热胁迫

Exercises

A. Please answer the following questions in English.

1. How to plan the orchard layout for macadamia?
2. How to choose varieties for macadamia?
3. How to prepare the land and how to plant windbreak trees before planting macadamia?
4. How to apply required fertilizers in orchard before planting fruit trees?
5. Please state the planting procedure of macadamia.

B. Please translate the following paragraph into Chinese.

New product innovations will bring precision agriculture to a new level. There will be a point where a grower can control each emitter or each emitter would act independently, depending on the condition of the soil it is in. The emitter will measure the moisture level and then irrigate automatically to maintain the most beneficial watering schedule. The future systems will monitor each plant automatically and deliver to the plant the exact requirements including fertilizers, chemicals and biologicals.

C. Please translate the following sentences into English.

1. 园艺植物的种植园，即通常意义上的果园、菜园、花圃、苗圃、风景绿化区或绿地等。这些种植园的设计、建立及不断变化的种植制度，都要有事先的构思、策划和论证。盲目的播种和栽植会给以后的生产管理带来麻烦和巨大损失。

2. 种植园规划设计的主要内容有：水土保持工程，种植园小区的规划设计，作物种类、

品种的配置,防护林体系,排灌系统,道路设计,建筑用房和其他等。

Part B Managing Young Trees of Macadamia

Selected and rewritten from *Macadamia Grower's handbook*, by Paul O'Hare, Russ Stephenson, Kevin Quinlan and Noel Vock.

During the first four years, the aim is to grow a strong, well structured tree that will produce well in future years. There are six important operations.

1. Protecting trees from frost and other damage
2. Fertilizing
3. Watering
4. Training and pruning
5. Weed control and mulching
6. Pest and disease management

Protecting trees from frost and other damage

Where a site is susceptible to frost, loosely wrap the trunks of the young trees before winter to a point above the graft or bud union with builder's insulation foil, corrugated cardboard, newspaper or plastic sleeves. This will also protect the trunk from herbicide damage and animals such as hares. Make the wrapping a little tighter at the top to prevent cold air from entering. Strip off the leaves below the graft or bud union before wrapping. Remove the wrapping after the danger of frost has passed. Depending on the climate and location, wrapping may be required for up to three winters.

Fertilizing

If the soil preparation recommendations from earlier in this chapter have been followed, no fertilizer will normally be needed for the first few months until trees start to put on new growth and this growth has hardened. Then, using soil analysis as a guide, apply small amounts at regular intervals (every eight weeks) during the growing season from spring to autumn. This is better than applying single large doses, which can easily kill young trees. It is also a better strategy on sandy soils, where leaching is more likely.

Where irrigation is available, fertigation is the best method of applying small amounts of fertilizer at regular intervals.

Watering

Do not allow the root ball to dry out after planting. Irrigation (or hand water where irrigation is not installed), for the first few weeks. Watering may be required up to two to three per week in very hot weather.

Once trees are well established, use a soil moisture monitoring system to help calculate how often and how much to water. The main choices include tensiometers or capacitance probes.

Training and pruning

Training Training trees to a central leader (a single dominant main trunk with smaller side branches). Keep the tip of the central leader at least 30 cm higher than the upper branches. A central leader system minimises breakage of limbs from strong winds and improves later machinery access, particularly for close planting. Limb breakage is likely to be a problem in varieties with a spreading tree shape and dense foliage.

Pruning Inspect the trees regularly during the first two years, particularly in summer and autumn when trees are actively flushing, and prune trees as follows:

1. Where a tree has produced a central leader without any branches below a height of 80 cm, prune off the top of the tree at 80 cm.

2. Where a tree has produced branches below about knee height, prune off these branches.

3. Examine the junction between branches and the main trunk or central leader, and remove any branches with a narrow crotch angle (more upright) where the bark is folded into the crotch.

4. Where there are multiple lateral branches at any one node, remove all but the two or three strongest lateral branches, remembering to maintain the central leader as well.

5. Remove any suckers at ground level and any shoots on the trunk below the graft or bud union.

6. To encourage the trunks of young trees to grow and thicken quickly, it is important to retain as much foliage as possible and avoid heavy, early pruning.

Weed control and mulching

Newly planted trees compete poorly with weeds for water and nutrients. Weed control within 50 cm of the trunk is vital.

Control weeds by maintaining a grassed inter-row area and mulching along the tree rows. Mulch not only minimises weeds, it also reduces soil moisture loss, maintains a more even soil temperature and improves the soil surface structure. Weeds that then grow through the mulch can be spot sprayed with herbicide.

The mulch can come from the grassed inter-row area by using a side delivery slasher or side delivery hay rake to divert the slashed grass along the tree rows. Fertilizing the inter-row grass and letting it grow to about 15 to 20 cm high, ensures that a reasonable volume of mulch can be produced. On small orchards, mulch such as coarse straw and composted nut husk may be brought in and placed along the tree rows. The mulched area should extend to just beyond the edge of the leaf canopy.

Pest and disease management

Pest The major pests likely to cause problems in young trees are:
1. macadamia felted coccid
2. scale insects

3. macadamia twig-girdler
4. macadamia leafminer
5. red shouldered leaf beetle
6. hares and kangaroos/wallabies.

From planting, inspect trees regularly for these pests. Low levels of scale insects, twig-girdler and leaf miner can be tolerated without spraying and will often be effectively controlled by beneficial insects. It is only if infestations become severe, that spraying is necessary. However, felted coccid and red shouldered leaf beetle are much more dangerous and if detected, spraying is generally required immediately.

Diseases The only major disease of young trees is trunk canker. Where cankers are small, pare back affected bark and wood with a sharp knife, and thoroughly soak trunks with a registered copper fungicide mixed with white, water-based paint. This helps to maintain contact with the fungicide and seals the wound. Where cankers are more extensive, and paring back affected bark and wood is impracticable, spray affected trees with phosphorous acid. Repeat the treatment two or three months later.

Glossary

1. leach   v. 过滤，萃取，水浸 n. 过滤，过滤器，滤灰槽
2. fertigation   n. 加肥灌溉，肥水灌溉法
3. tensiometer   n. 张力计，(流体)压强计
4. capacitance probe   电容探测器，电容探头
5. crotch   n. 分叉处，叉柱
6. sucker   n. (植物的)萌蘗，根蘗，根出条；suckering n. 萌条，分根蘗
7. bud union   芽接口，愈合处
8. slasher   n. 切碎器，茎秆剁碎机
9. scale insect   n. [昆]介壳虫
10. twig-girdler   环蛀蝙蛾(旋皮虫)
11. redshouldered leaf beetle   花生红肩叶甲
12. hare   n. 野兔
13. kangaroo/wallaby   n. 袋鼠/小袋鼠
14. leaf miner   潜叶蝇，甜菜麦蛾
15. infestation   n. 侵扰，侵袭，侵染，蔓延
16. phosphorous acid   磷酸，亚磷酸

Questions

1. How to protect macadamia trees from frost and other damages?
2. How to train and prune the young tree of macadamia?
3. What is the aim of weed mulching in macadamia orchards?

Lesson 19

Part A Olericulture

Selected and rewritten from *Horticulture*, by R. Gordon Halface & John A. Barden.

The vegetable industry is a very large and complex part of horticulture today. Despite the current trend toward increasing numbers of home vegetable gardens, the vast majority of the vegetables consumed are produced commercially. The commercial vegetable industry is a fast-moving, intensive, competitive business and in many respects differs significantly from the fruit business. With tree fruits, and to a somewhat lesser degree with small fruits, a long-term investment and commitment are made when the operation is started. Since most of the major vegetables are grown as annuals, some vegetable growers can adjust the relative proportion of different crops to meet changing market situations and—within the limits of equipment, soil type, and climate—can sometimes switch crops completely.

As with fruits, the early American colonists grew their own vegetables and stored as many as possible for winter use. Root cellars were common in many areas for the storage of crops such as potatoes, carrots, beets, cabbage, and turnips. A root cellar was an underground storage area which provided a moderate and steady temperature. Home canning, drying, or pickling was widely used for preservation of more perishable vegetables. The advent of home freezers has greatly facilitated the preservation of home-grown vegetables and has also improved quality and flavor.

As cities grew and fewer people were able to produce their own vegetables, commercial vegetable growing was started. Early vegetable growers grew a wide variety of vegetables and often "peddled" them in an adjacent city or town. They were called market gardeners, and their production was quite diversified. As transportation methods improved, the development of truck farming began. In the late 1800s larger vegetable farms developed in areas particularly well suited to specific crops along the newly developing transport lines, such as railroads, rivers, and canals. Thus truck farming involved larger plantings of fewer crops for shipment to distant markets.

The advent of refrigerated transportation for vegetables has had still further influence on where produce is grown. The railroads introduced the use of ice in refrigerated cars, and now mechanical refrigeration of railroad cars and also trucks is standard. Lettuce and other perishable produce can be harvested in the Salinas Valley of California and displayed on a supermarket shelf in Boston a few days later. This capability has led to very heavy concentration of production in areas most ideally suited for a particular crop. However, the leading vegetable-growing states in U. S. are determined more by climate than by proximity to market.

Vegetable production for processing is an increasingly important part of the total vegetable industry. The production of vegetables for the fresh market has been fairly stable since 1960, but processing vegetables have shown a gradual upward trend. Per capita consumption of vegetables is on a slight upward trend, with most of the rise attributed to processed vegetables. In addition to knowing about trends in consumption of fresh and processed vegetables, a vegetable producer must keep abreast of changes of particular crops. For example, per capita consumption of fresh corn, cabbage, and tomatoes is down, but onion and lettuce are up lettuce particularly. Even more striking are patterns in processed vegetables. Among frozen vegetables, sweet corn has increased remarkable while lima beans have declined in popularity.

In many areas of the country, an increasingly important aspect of the vegetable business is the pick-your-own and roadside-stand marketing systems. Although very small when considered on the scale of conventional vegetable farms, direct-marketing outlets have real advantages for both the grower and the consumer. In relatively high-population areas, the trend is definitely upward.

Although very difficult to monitor, the production of vegetables in millions of home gardens is a major factor in the vegetable situation. This has been reflected in the tremendous interest in the small package market for vegetable seeds. The production of vegetable seed is big business in certain areas of the country.

Roots to be stored for extended periods should be free from disease, excessive mechanical injury, and the injury associated with cold or wet soils. The normal procedure after harvest is to cure sweet potatoes at about 30℃ and 85 percent relative humidity for 4 to 8 days. These conditions encourage wounds to heal over and thereby greatly reduce losses due to rot and moisture loss during storage. Once the curing process is complete, the temperature should be lowered to 14~16℃ with a relative humidity of about 85 percent. Temperatures should not go below 10℃ or 12℃ because of chilling injury which results in increased decay, internal breakdown, and lowered quality.

Most sweet potatoes go to market in wax-impregnated cardboard containers of various sizes, bags have not been used widely because of increased damage to the roots. Retail sales are most commonly from bulk displays, although there is some trend toward prepackaging with overwraps. Polyethylene bags are not used, because the high relative humidity and 22℃ supermarket temperatures are ideal for the development of *Rhizopus*, or soft rot, the leading cause of postharvest sweet potato losses.

The major demand for fresh sweet potatoes is for medium-sized (5~8cm), well-shaped roots. Prices for jumbo sizes and small sizes are low, and thus many of these go to processing outlets. The major processed sweet potato product has been canned, either in a heavy syrup or vacuum-packed. Various other products, such as dehydrated sweet potato flakes, have been developed but are not widely marketed. It appears that new sweet potato products must be developed if the decline in per capita consumption is to be reversed.

Glossary

1. olericulture   *n.* 蔬菜栽培，蔬菜园艺，蔬菜学
2. annual   *n.* 一年生植物
3. root cellar   储藏根用蔬菜的地窖
4. turnip   *n.* [植]芜菁，萝卜
5. pick-your-own   *adj.* 由顾客自摘自采的（水果、蔬菜等）
6. preservation   *n.* 保存，保藏，储藏，保持
7. perishable   *adj.* 容易腐烂的
8. per capita consumption   按人口平均计算的消费量
9. wax-impregnated cardboard   石蜡浸过的硬纸板
10. prepackage   *n.* 事先做好的包装；*v.* 出售前预先包装
11. polyethylene   *n.* 聚乙烯
12. *Rhizopus*   根霉属菌
13. jumbo size   大尺寸
14. syrup   *n.* 糖浆，糖汁
15. vacuum pack   真空包装(品)
16. dehydrate   *v.* 脱水，失水，干燥

Exercises

A. Please answer the following questions in English.
   1. Why most vegetables are produced commercially?
   2. What role does vegetable preservation play in the market?
   3. What requirements for root vegetables before stored?

B. Please translate the following paragraph into Chinese.

Eggplant fruits are harvested when they reach one-half to two-thirds of full size because both the total yield and the quality tend to decline if the fruits are left until they reach full size. The most noticeable changes associated with leaving the fruit on the plant too long are a toughening of the flesh and a woodiness of the seeds. The fruits are harvested with a shape knife or clippers to cut the somewhat woody stem, leaving the calyx attached to the fruit.

C. Please translate the following sentences into English.
   1. 随着人们对蔬菜多样化稳定供应需求的提高，保护地栽培面积在大城市的郊区不断增长。在20世纪90年代，本地供应的黄瓜、番茄等在冬季的蔬菜市场上价格一路上扬，

既满足了消费者的需求，又为当地农民创造了可观的经济效益。

2. 蔬菜包装的根本目的，是为了延长产品的贮存期，同时也为了美化商品并给顾客提供方便。通过合理的选用包装材料以及容器结构设计，大大地减少了水果、蔬菜在运输、搬运和展销过程中的损伤和败坏。近年来，许多研究工作都致力于采取气体控制方法来延缓蔬菜在长途运输中的败坏期限。

Part B Tomato

Selected and rewritten from *Vegetable Science*, by H. D. Brown, and from *Vegetable Crops*, by Thompson and Kelly.

Tomatoes and possibly peppers originated in tropical America, and eggplants presumably originated in India. The tomato is the third most important vegetable in the United States, its value being exceeded only by potatoes and sweet potatoes. The fruits contain nearly twenty times as much vitamin A, the same amount of vitamin B_1, slightly more vitamin B_2, and over two-thirds as much vitamin C as oranges in spite of the fact that the fruits themselves contain on the average of 94.1 percent water. Tomatoes are indeed popular among home, community, industry, and farm gardeners. More tomatoes are canned than any other vegetable, and large quantities are grown in the southern states and Cuba, and Mexico for shipment to northern markets during the colder months. Tomatoes are the most important crop grown under the 2400 acres of glass (1acre=4046.85642 square meters) used for forcing vegetables in the United States.

Plant Characteristics Tomatoes grown from seed and not transplanted have a strong taproot which grows rapidly and may reach a length of 2 feet (1foot=30.48cm) or perhaps more. However, since most tomato plants are transplanted one or more times and the taproot is broken, the root system appears fibrous with many lateral roots developing in the upper 8 or 10 inches (1inch=2.54cm) of the soil. Adventitious roots also develop from any portion of the stem when sufficient moisture is present. The main stem reaches a height of 1 or 2 feet depending upon the variety. Laterals arise from each leaf axil and secondary laterals develop from these axils. Glandular hairs are found on the stems and the leaves and when ruptured release the soil fluid associated with tomato odor and strain. The leaves are alternate and pinnately compound. The flowers are borne on a two forked branched cymose inflorescence arise from the third node, while with small fruited varieties it arise from the sixth node. The peduncle is adnate, being united with the stem and for this reason it appears that the peduncle arises from the internode. The individual flower consists of a five-to ten-parted calyx, which persists to maturity of the fruit; the corolla tube, which is yellow and expands at the top into five or more lobes; and five or more stamens which are attached at the base of the corolla and from a cone around the pistil. There is an abscission zone formed in the pedicel, and various environmental factors may cause the flower bud, the flower, or the partially developed fruit to drop. The tomato fruit is a fleshy berry with from 2 to 10 locules. It is free of stomata. The length of the style is influenced by environment as well as by heredity. It elongates during hot weather and during short days. Short styles are preferred for greenhouse tomatoes so that the stigma is completely enclosed by the staminal cone, thus facilitating self-fertilization. The stigma is receptive before the anthers dehisce making it possible for plant breeders to emasculate and pollinate at the same time. Most of the large-fruited varieties contain from 5 to 10 locules. The tomato has a parietal type of placentation and a gelatinous pulp completely surrounds the seed and fills the seed cavity. In yellow and pink fruits the epidermis is colorless and the carotene ($C_{40}H_{56}$) and lycopersicin ($C_{40}H_{56}$) pigments are in the tissue below the epidermis. In orange- and red-fruited varieties the carotin and lycopersicin pigments are present both in the epidermis and in the underlying tissue.

Culture The tomato is a warm-season crop and cannot be grown in the field until after the frost-free dates. The greenhouse crop is practically always grown from seed planted in sterilized soil. About 10 days after the seed is sown the plant are transplanted to flats or pots and grown until they are large enough to set in a permanent growing bed. At no time should the plants be allowed to become crowded.

Plants grown for early crop, either in market-gardening or truck-gardening regions, are grown much the same as for the greenhouse crop. Four ounces of seed will produce enough plants for an acre. Care should be taken that the roots and tops are not injured during all handling processes. Injury may introduce several virus diseases into the plant and may cause several check due to mechanical disturbances. Seed sown directly in pots eliminates the necessity for some mechanical injury. Moreover, if the ball of earth is removed carefully from the pots, the plants can be set in a permanent growing position with little injury to the tender tops or roots. Very small seedlings can be transferred with little injury if the transfer is made before the roots begin to branch and if the plants are grasped by the cotyledon leaves instead of by the stem where plant hairs are bound to be broken thus providing injured cells through which disease organisms gain entrance more easily.

Harvesting If grown for canning, the fruits should remain on the vines until fully ripened. At the same time, it is essential to harvest the tomatoes as soon as they ripen. The yield is often reduced from one-fourth to one-half by careless pickers. Color blindness is one cause for ineffective pickers. During rainy periods, once every 7 days is sufficient.

Tomatoes grown by market gardeners are usually picked when there is still a little green showing on each fruit, as they are usually handled by one or two middlemen before reaching the ultimate consumer.

Tomatoes which are shipped long distances, as for example, those shipped from Florida, from California, from Mexico, or from Cuba to markets in New York City or other eastern cities are usually picked while still green and before red starts to show.

Glossary

1. forcing vegetables　蔬菜促成栽培
2. taproot　*n.*（植物的）主根，直根
3. fibrous　*adj.* 含纤维状，纤维状的
4. adventitious　*adj.* 偶然的，偶发的
5. pinnate　*adj.* 羽状的
6. glandular hair　腺毛，汗毛
7. forked　*adj.* 叉状的，有叉的
8. cymose inflorescence　聚伞状花序
9. peduncle　*n.* 花梗，（肿瘤或息肉的）肉茎
10. adnate　*adj.* 贴生的，联生的，并生的
11. internode　*n.* 节间，节间部
12. calyx　*n.* 花萼
13. corolla　*n.* 花冠
14. stamen　*n.* 雄蕊
15. pistil　*n.* 雌蕊
16. abscission zone　离区
17. self-fertilization　*n.* 自体受精
18. emasculate　*vt.* 阉割，使柔弱，使无力；*adj.* 阉割了的，柔弱的
19. gelatinous　*adj.* 胶状的
20. epidermis　*n.* 表皮
21. carotene　*n.* 胡萝卜素
22. lycopersicin　*n.* 番茄素
23. pulverize　*vt.* 粉碎，研磨

Questions

1. What are main stem characteristics in a tomato plant? How lateral stems developed?
2. What can we do if we would keep injury away from the tomato seedlings?

Lesson 20

Part A Cucurbits or Vine Crops

Selected and rewritten from *Vegetable Crops*, by Thompson and Kelly, and *Vegetable Science*, by H. D. Brown.

The vine crops include cucumber, muskmelon, watermelon, pumpkin, and squash——all of which are in the family Cucurbitaceae. Each is a tender annual crop and is grown for its fruit, all have similar cultural requirements.

Cucumber

The cucumber, *Cucumis sativus*, is a very popular vegetable in the United States as well as worldwide. It has been cultivated since very early times, presumably well over 3000 years. Its origin was probably in India, it was known by the Romans, and it was brought to the New World by Columbus.

Cucumbers, like squash, thrive under somewhat cooler temperatures than muskmelons or watermelons, but germination will not occur unless temperatures are as warm as 13℃, and germination is much more rapid at 30℃. Since the cucumber reaches harvest maturity in a relatively short growing season and will grow at relatively cool temperatures, it can be grown almost anywhere in the United States, although for success in the far North it may need to be transplanted. Since it can withstand no freezing temperatures, winter production even in Florida, is a risky venture. Greenhouse production of cucumbers was a sizable business in Ohio, but high fuel costs have raised serious questions about its feasibility in the late 1970s. In Europe, greenhouse cucumber production has been a large industry, especially in the Northern areas. The English and Dutch developed cultivars which are large (of 0.6m long) and usually seedless for this type of production. Production of these European types is gaining in the southern United States.

Cucumbers are used fresh primarily as a salad ingredient, for vegetable trays, or with any number of dressings, sauces, or marinades. Pickles are widely used in many ways.

The Plant The cucumber plant is an annual trailing vine with a spiny or hairy stem. Cucumbers have traditionally been monoecious (bearing both female and male flowers). Recently introduced hybrids are gynoecious and produce female flowers only. For commercial plantings, a small percentage of a monoecious type is included to provide pollen for pollination. Gynoecious cultivars are used because of their earliness, concentrated ripening, and increased yields. For mechanical harvesting these recently introduced cultivars are particularly beneficial.

Commercial cucumber production is totally dependent on pollination by insects, and honeybees are the primary pollinating agents. Research has shown that cucumber flowers must be visited several times by bees for normal fruit set, and that fruit weight increases with increasing numbers of visit up to 40 or 50. The number of honeybee colonies needed for adequate pollination varies with the type of cucumber being grown. With monoecious cultivars, one colony per hectare might be adequate, with high plant populations of gynoecious types for mechanical harvest; two or three times as many bees may be beneficial.

The great majority of cucumbers fall into one of two categories. Slicing cultivars are those grown for the fresh market. These are grown to a fairly large size and retain their dark-green color. The other major type is the pickling cultivars, which are smaller, somewhat lighter in color and more productive.

Propagation Cucumbers are usually direct-seeded in the field after the danger of damage from freezing weather is past, but market gardeners may transplant small acreages. Seeding rates vary with the cultivar and in particular, with the method of harvest. For once-over or "destructive" harvest, very high plant populations are used. With multiple harvests—the normal procedure for the fresh market—lower populations are used.

Harvest and Storage For the fresh market, cucumbers should be in the range of 12 to 20 cm in length with a diameter of 4 to 5 cm and dark-green in color. To supply top-quality cucumbers, the fields are picked every 2 to 4 days. Cucumbers which are too large or too ripe are removed and discarded because their presence will decrease subsequent yields of young cucumbers. Hand-harvested cucumbers are placed in containers or onto conveyors. Modern machines transport the pickers in a prone or sitting position, and the picked cucumbers are placed on a conveyor in front of the pickers.

For the pickling industry more and more cucumbers are being harvested by the once-over, or destructive, harvester. For this method to be economically practical, cultivars had to be developed which produced high tonnage of cucumbers of similar maturity at one time. Planting distances and cultural practices had to be modified to encourage maximum production.

Marketing Fresh-market cucumbers are brushed to remove the soil and spines, and are graded. Almost all are now waxed to improve appearance and suppress water loss to maintain the firmness and crispness so necessary in a cucumber. They should be cooled rapidly and held at 7°C to 10°C and 90 to 95 percent relative humidity during shipment. Under such conditions, cucumbers will hold for 7 to 10 days. Chilling injury will occur if temperatures remain below about 5°C for any extended period of time.

Watermelon

The watermelon, *Citrullus vulgaris*, is usually considered to have an African origin but was also being grown by Indians in the Mississippi Valley when early explorers arrived. Today, watermelons are grown worldwide.

In the United States, watermelons are grown in more than 15 states, but production is concentrated in Florida(33 percent), Texas(19 percent), Georgia(10 percent), and South Carolina(6 percent). A long, warm growing season is required for watermelons, but since leaf disease are less troublesome than on muskmelon, high humidity is less detrimental. The per capita consumption has declined from about 8 kg in 1947~1949 to about 6 kg in 1975~1976. Watermelons are used mostly as a cold, juicy dessert. They can be sliced or scooped out to make melon balls, or the flesh can be scooped out and cubed or balled and the shell filled with a mixed fruit salad of watermelon, muskmelon, and honeydew cubes or balls mixed with other fresh fruits such as strawberries, and raspberries.

The watermelon plant is a tender vine with deeply cut leaves, is most often monoecious, and is pollinated by bees. The fruits are round to oblong, ranging in weight from 4kg to more than 25kg. The small-fruited cultivars have been developed for the short growing season in the North, most of the commercial melons for the South are the larger cultivars. The commercial cultivars have red flesh, although yellow-fleshed types are available.

For optimum quality, watermelons should be mature but not overripe at harvest. For the inexperienced, it is most difficult to determine maturity as there is little if any change in the skin color. One of the best indices is the change in color from white to creamy yellow of the portion of the melon which is in contact with the ground. Another index is thumping the melon with a finger: a metallic ring indicates immaturity while a dull thud or hollow sound is a fairly good indication of maturity. The degree of desiccation of the tendril immediately proximal or distal to the point of fruit attachment to the vine is also used as an index.

Watermelons are harvested by hand and loaded onto trucks or trailers. Rail shipment was once common, but trucks are more commonly used today. Formerly the melons were stacked three to five high on straw, but the modern method uses bulk bins which may travel form the field to the supermarket.

Glossary

1. Cucurbitaceae   *n.* 葫芦科
2. thrive   *vi.* 兴盛，兴隆
3. ingredient   *n.* （混合物的）组成部分；配料
4. marinade   *n.* 腌泡汁；腌泡汁里泡的肉[鱼]等
5. dressings   *n.* 敷料剂
6. pickle   *vt.* 腌渍（泡菜等）；*n.* 腌菜
7. spiny   *adj.* 长满刺的；多刺的，带刺的
8. monoecious   *adj.* 雄雌同株的，雄雌同体的；*n.* 雌雄同体
9. gynoecious   *n.* 纯雌植物，雌株
10. slice   *vt.* 把……切成薄片；切开[下]；*n.* 片，薄片，切片
11. conveyor   *n.* 搬运者，输送机，输送设备
12. wax   *n.* 蜡；*vt.* 给……打蜡

13. detrimental *adj.* 有害的，不利的
14. per capita consumption 按人口平均计算的消费量
15. honeydew *n.* 甘汁，蜜露
16. raspberry *n.* 悬钩子(树)，木莓(树)，山莓(树)
17. indices index 的复数
18. metallic *adj.* 金属的，像金属的，金属般的
19. desiccation *n.* 干燥
20. tendril *n.* 卷须，蔓，卷须状之物
21. distal *adj.* 末梢的

Exercises

A. Please answer the following questions in English.

1. What are the differences between slicing cucumber cultivars and pickling cultivars?
2. What are the advantages of pollinating cucumber flowers by honeybees?
3. How to evaluate whether a watermelon is ripe or not?

B. Please translate the following paragraph into Chinese.

Most of the commercial lettuce crop in the United States consists of the crisphead type. Cultivars of crisphead lettuce are characterized by their firm heads and the brittle texture of the leaves. The heads are usually at least 15 cm in diameter and are solid enough to withstand the rigors of harvest, long-distance shipment, and final marketing. In this country lettuce is used almost exclusively as a fresh vegetable, although in some parts of the world it is cooked like spinach. Lettuce is particularly attractive as the main constituent of salad because of its mild flavor, crisp texture, low caloric content and attractive color.

C. Please translate the following sentences into English.

1. 瓜类苗期花芽分化以后，就开始生殖生长，以后生殖生长和营养生长同时进行，营养生长是生殖生长的基础，两者互相影响、互相制约，栽培上应处理好两者的关系。

2. 20 世纪 90 年代以来，我国西瓜生产有很大发展，主要分布在华北，约占总栽培面积的 45％，长江中下游地区约占总栽培面积的 32％。有些地区西瓜生产已成为当地一项产业。

Part B Muskmelon

Selected and rewritten from *Vegetable Crops*, by Thompson and Kelly, and *Vegetable Science*, by H. D. Brown.

The muskmelon, *Cucumis melo* var. *reticulatus*, is referred to as the cantaloupe in the United States. Muskmelons are thought to have originated in Asia, eventually spreading throughout Europe and the New World. Although the exact type varies, muskmelons are widely grown around the world. The muskmelon is distinct from some other melons because its netted skin, and also because of its much better keeping quality.

United States Industry   The muskmelon is available to the United States consumer primarily in the summer, with smaller quantities in the market during the spring and still less in the fall. California provided 62 percent of the muskmelon in the 1974~1976 period, Arizona and Texas grew 11 and 10 percent respectively.

Muskmelons are grown and marketed as a vegetable but utilized as a fruit. They are often served as a fresh breakfast fruit, but they are equally delectable in a fruit salad or with a scoop of vanilla ice cream or strawberries in the center as a refreshing dessert. The muskmelon fruit is from 11 to 14 cm in diameter, it has thick orange flesh and multiple seeds in the internal cavity.

The Plant   The muskmelon is a tender, trailing vine which needs warm temperatures and plenty of sunshine. Low humidity and low rainfall make the control of fungus diseases much easier; fungus diseases are particularly severe on muskmelons in humid climates. Improved disease resistance is being incorporated into new cultivars. Most of our crop of muskmelons comes from irrigated regions in the Southwest, and furrow irrigation is commonly used to avoid wetting the foliage. The plants produce both staminate flowers and perfect or hermaphroditic flowers. Pollination is by insects, especially by honeybees, which are often brought into the fields for this purpose. Excess moisture just before maturity results in poor quality, due to low sugars.

Propagation   For large plantings, muskmelons are direct-seeded; but for small areas or where the growing season is too short, seed may be started in greenhouse and transplanted. In many areas muskmelons are grown on black plastic mulch because they are particularly responsive.

Harvest and Storage   Maturity is very critical if top-quality muskmelons are to be offered to the consumer. Because a muskmelon does not increase in sugar level after harvest, immature fruits are not only hard but insipid as well. The most widely used index of maturity is the ease with which the fruit can be separated from the vine. A "full slip" melon breaks from the vane cleanly, leaving no stem attached. This is considered to provide a melon of adequate quality if handled properly, shipped under refrigeration, and marketed promptly. "Half slip" melons have some stem remaining with the fruit and are normally considered to be of inferior quality even after adequate softening.

Although many machines have been tested to harvest muskmelons mechanically, the majority are still picked by workers who carry a large bag on their back. Muskmelons should be hydrocooled or iced down as soon as possible and held at 4°C to 7°C during shipment. They should not be stored for more than a few days.

Marketing   Muskmelons are sold from bulk displays with no prepackaging. If the melons are ripe, which not on display should be refrigerated; most melons are not refrigerated while on display because of the normally rapid turnover.

Glossary

1. cantaloupe   *n.* 罗马甜瓜，香瓜，哈密瓜
2. cavity   *n.* 腔，洞
3. furrow irrigation   沟灌，畦灌
4. hermaphroditic flower   两性花
5. hydrocool   *vt.* 液体冷却

Questions

1. What is the reason for muskmelons being hydrocooled or iced down as soon as possible?
2. What are the main points in muskmelon propagation?

Lesson 21

Part A The Type of Tropical Flowers

Selected and rewritten from *Type of Tropical Flowers*, by Net Paper Editor.

The tropics are the geographic region of the Earth centered on the equator and limited in latitude by the two tropics: the Tropic of Cancer in the north and the Tropic of Capricorn in the southern hemisphere. The principal regions with a tropical climate are the Amazon Basin in Brazil, the Congo Basin in West Africa and Indonesia. The tropical flowers come from this core tropical region.

Tropical Flowers are those species of flowers that are native to the tropics and thrive naturally in tropical climatic conditions. Because tropical flowers have adapted to live in warm environments, they are generally last very well when kept in air conditioned or heated environments even in cold area or season, but the low temperature is dangerous to their life. Except the ecological characteristics, tropical flowers are different to the more traditional flower types in appearance in that their flowers usually have a "rubbery" appearance and texture. Hence, most tropical flowers are excellent cut flowers; they consume very little water, and should generally last at least two weeks when detached from plants. Tropical flowers hold a special place in the hearts of flower lovers due to their breathtaking fragrance and exquisite beauty.

The main types of tropical flowers consist of Orchids, Euphorbias, Bromeliads, Heliconias, Anthuriums, etc.

Orchids belong to the family Orchidaceae which is an extremely diverse family of flowering plants. The richest assortment species of this family is found in tropical and subtropical parts of the world, but one can find orchids in colder climates as well. All members of the family Orchidaceae is protected under CITES as potentially threatened or endangered, but hybrids are not included. Advanced orchids typically display five common characteristics. The flowers display bilateral symmetry and have a column (gynostemium). The pollen is glued into pollinia, a congregation of waxy pollens on filaments. The seeds are usually extremely small and have no food reserve, but there are exceptions to this general rule, including the well-known members of the genus *Vanilla*. The seeds form a symbiotic relationship with certain fungi, and without the presence of suitable fungi they can not germinate under natural circumstances.

The Euphorbias belong to family Euphorbiaceae which is also known as the Spurge family. All spurge species are flowering plants, some are herbs while others are shrubs or trees. Shrubs and trees are most common in the tropics. This type of tropical flower can resemble a cactus, but it is not a true cactus. The stipules are sometimes altered into spines, hairs or glands. In succulent species, they can be completely absent. In most cases, there will be male and female flowers present on the same specimen. This type of tropical flower is especially common in the Indo-Malayan region and tropical America.

The Bromeliads make up a broad family of flowering plants that includes both terrestrial plants and epiphytes. Christopher Columbus is generally recognized as the first European to encounter this type of tropical flower and he brought back *Ananas comosus*, the pineapple, to Spain. It is common for this type of tropical flower to have the ability to store water in a form of tank created by tightly overlapping leaf bases. The biggest known member of this family is the *Puya raimondii* which can reach a height of 4 m and form a 10 m tall flower spike.

The *Heliconia* is a genus of tropical flowers that can be found in the tropical parts of America and on some of the Pacific Ocean islands. A common name for the *Heliconia* is lobster-claw or sometimes false bird-of-paradise, this because a group of flowers most often resembles claws or bird wings. Heliconias produce rhizomes and erect shoots. The rhizomes branch off and produce new shoots. New branches and shoots develop from buds or eyes on the rhizomes. The shoots are composed of overlapping leaf sheaths which make up the above ground pseudostem and support the large leaf blades and inflorescences. Some heliconias have erect leaves with long petioles like bananas, others have horizontal leaves with short petioles resembling gingers, and some are intermediate with short to medium petioles supporting leaves at about a forty degree angle. The inflorescences are either erect or pendent with showy bracts containing varying numbers of small flowers.

The *Anthurium* was discovered by the Austrian botanist Heinrich Wilhelm Schott and can mostly be found in the wet tropical mountain forests of South-Central America. The leaves of this tropical flower can come in lots of different shapes and can be found growing out of the top of the rather short stem. The extremely small flowers are densely packed on a sort of spike and come on a long variety of colors. Just below the flower there usually is a leathery leaf called a spathe. This spathe is the most impressive part as it usually is brightly colored and changes color over time. This tropical flower has a wonderful exotic scent and can be a fine addition indoors.

Besides these mentioned above, tropical flowers comprise the Red Ginger, some Annonaceae plants and part of Cycadophyta plants as well.

Glossary

1. latitude *n.* 纬度
2. Tropic of Cancer 北回归线

3. Tropic of Capricorn　南回归线
4. Orchids　*n*. 兰花
5. Orchidaceae　*n*. 兰科
6. CITES　濒危野生动植物种国际贸易公约（Convention on International Trade in Endangered Species of Wild Fauna and Flora）的简称
7. *Euphorbia*　*n*. 大戟属，大戟属植物
8. Bromeliad　*n*. 凤梨科植物
9. *Heliconia*　*n*. 蝎尾蕉属，又名海里康属，蝎尾蕉属植物
10. *Anthurium*　*n*. 花烛属
11. gynostemium　*n*. 合蕊冠，合蕊柱
12. bilateral symmetry　两侧对称，左右对称
13. symbiotic　*adj*. 共生的
14. cactus　*n*. 仙人掌
15. stipule　*n*. 托叶
16. spine　*n*. 刺
17. gland　*n*. 腺[体]
18. spike　*n*. 穗状花序
19. rhizome　*n*. 根状茎，地下茎
20. leaf sheath　叶鞘
21. pseudostem　*n*. 假茎
22. petiole　*n*. 叶柄
23. bract　*n*. 苞片
24. Euphorbiaceae　*n*. 大戟科
25. Spurge　*n*. 大戟科
26. specimen　*n*. 标本
27. terrestrial　*adj*. 陆地的，陆栖的，陆生的
28. epiphyte　*n*. 附生植物，附生菌
29. pineapple　*n*. 菠萝，凤梨
30. inflorescence　*n*. 开花，花，花序
31. leathery　*adj*. 革质的
32. spathe　*n*. 佛焰苞

Exercises

A. **Please answer the following questions in English.**
1. How to define the term ***tropical flowers***?
2. Which types of tropical flowers is used mainly as cut flowers?
3. What characteristics do the tropical flower spurge species possess?
4. How many types of tropical flowers do you know?

B. **Please translate the following paragraph into Chinese.**

Tropical flowers, as their category name suggests, are native to the Torrid Zone (a. k. a. the tropics)—the section of the Earth between the tropics of Cancer and Capricorn and flowers, that are native to those regions immediately on the other sides of the tropics known as the subtropics, are known as subtropical flowers.

C. **Please translate the following sentences into English.**

1. 热带花卉种类繁多，兰科、大戟科、凤梨科、鹤鸟蕉科的很多植物都是热带花卉。

2. 热带花卉中，蝎尾蕉属植物起源于中南美洲及太平洋海岛，菠萝属植物起源于巴西和巴拉圭的南部，兰科植物既有起源于热带地区的也有起源于亚热带地区甚至更冷的地区。

Part B Tropical Orchids and its Adaption to Tropical Climate

Selected and rewritten from *Orchids in Your Home*, by Robert Atkinson E.

Orchids are very beautiful and unique plants, with amazing flowers. These flowers come in astonishing color combinations, and add an exotic touch to any location. In nature, orchids are usually aerial plants, so their roots grow in the air or attached to tree trunks.

There are over 25,000 known species of orchids growing worldwide. This number is always growing due to new discoveries in remote locations, as well as the creation of new hybrid varieties. Many of these varieties are found in rainforests and tropical areas where they thrive in the humid climate. There are three main types of orchids, although this by no means encompasses all of the known or commercially available orchid species.

Dendrobiums are among the most popular types of orchid plants. Some bloom with white flowers, while others are purple or yellow. These are usually found in Asia and other tropical areas, including the Philippines, Borneo, New Zealand, Australia, and New Guinea. Due to demand, there are many newly created hybrid species based on *Dendrobium* orchids. These are specially created to have large, exotic flowers, unlike those found on most other plants, and many bloom for longer seasons than most other orchids.

Cattleyas are another type of beautiful orchids. These are found in some South American countries, as well as parts of Asia. These are among the most extravagant species of orchids, and each plant produces from one to eight flowers per season. The amazing colors of these flowers range from white and yellow to dark purple. *Cattleya* orchids do not grow tall, but instead spread out along a tree trunk or other surface.

Another unique orchid species, the *Vanda*, is a very strange looking type of orchid. Their leaves grow on a single tall stalk, with flower stalks sprouting from the leaves' bases. These stalks can grow up to twenty individual booms of exotic flowers. *Vanda* orchids are found in India, China, the Philippines, Indonesia, the Himalayas, Australia, and New Guinea.

These three types of orchid species are just a few of the different species. There are many rarer or more exotic orchid species, as well as newly discovered species that have actually existed for hundreds of years in remote areas of the rainforest. For example, with special care for *Phalaenopsis*, in places very different from rainforests or tropical climates, such as the average home is very possible. Many hybrids, in fact, are grown particularly for adaptation to indoor climates.

In order to survive climate changes, orchids have evolved strange associations with other living organism. Co-existing within this alliance forms a symbiotic relationship, whereby both the orchid and the fungus become completely dependent upon each other for their survival. The mycelium releases nutrients that are absorbed by the orchid, which in turn becomes the host for the fungus. Most orchids have their own specific micro-fungi, so there must exist as many different fungi as there are orchids. For a seed to germinate, it needs contact with the fungus from the beginning. For this reason, orchids are often found in large colonies, rather than growing as individual plants, because this dose proximity to other orchids ensures that the necessary fungus is present. Tropical epiphytes will also only grow on particular species of trees. In dense rain forest that has remained undisturbed for centuries, it is only certain trees that play host.

The larger, more bulky orchids are confined to the main trunk or the first fork of a very large tree, while the smaller species will cling to the finer twigs and branches higher up on the outskirts of the canopy. As the leaf cover increases and becomes denser in evergreen forests, the orchids at the center of such cover produce healthier and darker-foliage specimens, but may not be as free-flowering as those growing on the edge. Here the plants will benefit from cooling prevailing winds and extra sunlight, flowering better as a result, although often with shriveling pseudobulbs and yellowing foliage.

To achieve pollination, orchid flowers have also developed special relationships with insects, hummingbirds and even small bats. In the case of insects, the relationship is formed with a group of insects or just one specific species. The insect is attracted to the bloom in its search for nectar, which is sometimes, but not always, given in return for facilitating pollination. The color, shape and size of the flower are all significant forms of attraction.

While some species grow in sandy soils in arid places, others flourish in marshy swamps, where their tubers remain submerged in water for much of the year. During the winter, only the underground parts of the plant survive to reactivate new growth in the spring. Other terrestrials, such as *Phaius* and the evergreen *Calanthe*, produce a creeping rhizome with pseudobulbs. Not all terrestrial orchids with underground rhizomes live in cold areas. Many of the tropical species adopt this way of life, becoming completely deciduous and remaining dormant below ground level during the dry season. Their green parts emerge when conditions are suitable.

Once the females emerge, the male bee will lose interest in the flowers. The timing of this flowering is therefore critical for pollination. There are some orchids, particularly among the *Bulbophyllum* species, that emit a strong odour of putrefaction. These have sepals or a lip in a dark reddish color that resembles decaying meat, just the place where carrion flies and wasps would normally lay their eggs. In contrast, other orchids such as *Brassavola nodosa* carry a delicious nighttime scent, relying on night-flying moths and other nocturnal insects for pollination.

The Australian terrestrials are worthy of study in their own right, but these plants are not generally found in cultivation, and knowledge of them outside Australia is gleaned mostly from other specialist publications. Although the terrestrial orchids are not cultivated, they still have enthusiasts who would seek them out, returning each year to a favourable location to search for them in bogs, on hillsides and wherever else they may appear. For many orchid enthusiasts, the opportunity of searching and observing tropical orchids in the wild is an unattainable goal, but where there is the easier option of finding terrestrial orchids, the satisfaction generated is just as great. One aspect that makes this so compelling year after year is the fluctuation in the number of flowering plants that may arise. In an area supporting hundreds of flowering plants in one season, you may be hard pressed to find a dozen the next. Terrestrial orchids are notorious for appearing sporadically over the seasons, and some species of orchids can remain in a dormant state underground for many its before suddenly reappearing.

Glossary

1. *Brassavola nodosa*　拉索兰属
2. *Calanthe*　*n.*　虾脊兰属
3. *Cattleya*　*n.*　洋兰，卡特兰属
4. deciduous　*adj.*　落叶的
5. *Dendrobium*　*n.*　石斛，石斛属植物
6. epiphyte　*n.*　附生菌，附生植物
7. exotic　*adj.*　外来的，非本地的，引进种
8. fungus　*n.*　真菌，霉菌，菌类
9. hummingbird　*n.*　蜂鸟
10. mycelium　*n.*　菌丝体
11. *Phaius*　*n.*　鹤顶兰属
12. *Phalaenopsis*　*n.*　蝴蝶兰属
13. symbiotic relationship　共生关系
14. *Bulbophyllum*　*n.*　石豆兰属
15. putrefaction　*n.*　腐烂，腐败
16. carrion flies　尸食性蝇类
17. night-flying moths　夜蛾类
18. nocturnal　*adj.*　夜间的，夜行的

19. *Vanda* n. 万代兰属

Questions

1. Are all *Dendrobium* orchids originated from tropical area?
2. What features do *Vanda* orchids possess?
3. What is the symbiotic relationship?
4. Why timing of flowering is critical for orchids' pollination?
5. How do orchids adapt to the tropical climate?

Lesson 22

Part A Foliage Plants and Bedding Plants

Selected and rewritten from *Horticulture*, by R. Gordon Halface & John A. Barden, and *Bedding Plants*, by David Beaulieu.

Foliage plants

Foliage plants are used indoors to create an interior landscape for a home or business. Public buildings often have areas set aside especially for indoor plantings which may include 12m palm trees and other small and large plants. Foliage plants may provide a point of interest, serve as a screen, or soften harsh lines in contemporary design.

Foliage plants generally come from the tropics or other mild climates not like the climate of some areas of the South and California. Greenhouses are necessary for Northern production. Many foliage plants are propagated and begun outdoors or in a protective structure in the South and shipped to Northern greenhouses for further growth. In the southern parts of Florida and in California, *Sansevieria*, *Caladium*, and palms are grown outdoors; but *Philodendron*, *Ficus*, *Dracaena*, *Croton*, *Dieffenbachia* and *Epipremnum* must be grown in plastic screen houses. In central Florida, foliage plants are grown in slat sheds, plastic screen houses and greenhouses. The stock plants of *Dieffenbachia*, *Maranta*, *Brassaia*, *Peperomia*, *Philodendron*, and *Epipremnum* are grown in heated slat sheds or plastic houses and transferred to greenhouses for propagation and finishing.

About 10,000 lux are necessary for most foliage plants; however, there are exceptions, as *Sansevieria* and *Peperomia* require 21,000 and *Aglaonema modestum* needs only 7500. Daylength does not affect foliage plants. The chief problem is providing light in interior design plantings or in dish gardens. Most foliage plants need a minimum of at least 325 lux for 12 h per day. Artificial light may be necessary to meet this requirement.

Temperatures of 21°C to 24°C and 75 to 80 percent humidity are necessary for ideal growth. Plants used in homes and buildings usually require less water because of the low irradiance level and resultant slow growth.

Foliage plants thrive in highly organic soil mixes with at least one-half peat moss or leaf mold. They require a balanced fertilizer. Liquid nitrogen should be applied only after the root system is well established. Generally, foliage plants grow well in slightly acid soils with pH of 5.5 to 6.5.

Bedding Plants

Bedding plants are plants (usually annuals) massed with others to produce the maximum in visual appeal. Bedding plants are used for flower gardens, window boxes, hanging baskets, and miniature gardens. Although some biennials and perennials are grown as bedding plants, annuals generally predominate and are replanted each spring when the danger of frost has passed. Generally, growers propagate bedding plants by seed because this is the most economical method.

Most bedding plants require full sun. Photoperiod cannot be considered because it generally cannot be controlled outdoors. Plants grown in low light or tightly spaced will have weak stems and flower more slowly. Artificial light may be used for seed germination and growing young seedlings. Fluorescent light of 10,000 lux obtained by spacing lights at 1m intervals 15 cm above the plants is effective. At least 16 h of light per day should be used until the plants are moved into full sunlight in the greenhouse. Although a warm temperature (21°C or higher) is required for germination, most bedding plans grow better under cool temperatures. Night temperatures of 13°C to 16°C and day temperatures of 18°C to 21°C are needed for slow growth and flowering with short, compact stems of desired diameter.

Seed is sown usually in vermiculite or peat-lite mix. Seedlings are then transplanted to artificial soil mixtures of peat moss and perlite, vermiculite, or fine sand in a variety of containers. Liquid fertilizer can be applied after germination.

Careful attention must be given to watering, since bedding plants are grown in small containers under light and temperature conditions which quickly dry the soil. However, overwatering should be avoided since it often leads to root rot problems.

The most common disease problem is damping-off, produced by the pathogens *Rhizoctonia*, *Pythium*, and *Phytophthora*. Seed decay, stem rot, root rot, and—in extreme cases—rot of the upper parts of the plant may result. It may be controlled by making the environment unfavorable for the pathogens or by the use of chemical treatments. Steam can be used to sterilize the soil, containers, benches, and equipment. Soil can also be sterilized with methyl bromide or vapam. Since damping-off pathogens thrive in constantly moist conditions, less-frequent irrigation, better-drained soil, sterile containers, and good air circulation can be used to counteract pathogen growth. A number of soil fungicide drenches give control, but prevention is best.

Bedding plants are also affected by botrytis blight, caused by *Botrytis cinerea*. This often develops in the upper portions of the plants, progressing downward. The elimination of old stems, leaves, and flowers will help eliminate sources of *Botrytis*. Irrigation early in the day, proper ventilation and air circulation are important in controlling *Botrytis*. Moisture on the leaves, especially at night when lower temperatures prevail, aids spore development. When the foliage stays moist for long periods, humid cloudy weather is the time of greatest danger. Aphids, slugs, thrips, and the white flies are all pests of bedding plants and should be controlled.

Glossary

1. *Caladium*　　*n.* [植]贝母
2. *Philodendron*　　*n.* 喜林芋
3. *Ficus*　　*n.* 榕树
4. *Dracaena*　　*n.* [植]龙血树属植物
5. *Epipremnum*　　*n.* 拎树藤属
6. *Maranta*　　*n.* [植]竹芋
7. *Brassaia*　　*n.* 澳洲鸭脚木
8. *Peperomia*　　*n.* 豆瓣绿属植物
9. *Sansevieria*　　*n.* [植]虎尾兰
10. peat moss　　泥煤苔(泥煤的主成分)
11. leaf mold　　腐叶土
12. bedding plant　　花坛植物
13. vermiculite　　*n.* 蛭石
14. perlite　　*n.* 珍珠岩
15. *Phytophthora*　　*n.* 疫霉属
16. sterilize　　*v.* 杀菌
17. methyl bromide　　溴甲烷
18. vapam　　*n.* 威百亩
19. botrytis blight　　灰霉病
20. *Botrytis cinerea*　　灰色葡萄孢
21. ventilation　　*n.* 通风
22. aphid　　*n.* 蚜虫
23. slug　　*n.* 蛞蝓，鼻涕虫
24. thrip　　*n.* 蓟马

Exercises

A. Please answer the following questions in English.
1. What is the application of the foliage plants?
2. How does the ecology environment affect the foliage plants?
3. Greenhouses are necessary for foliage plants production in the North, why?
4. How to use bedding plants properly?
5. Why do the bedding plants need more careful attention?

B. Please translate the following paragraph into Chinese.

Colorful flowers look wonderful in a yard, but foliage plants (plants grown primarily for their foliage) boast a reliability that is not to be scoffed at. Bedding plants are plants (usually annuals) massed with others to produce the maximum in visual appeal. With an eye to the five basic elements of landscape design (color, scale, line, form and texture), a landscape designer skillfully arranges each bedding plant in relation to the accompanying annuals, perennials, shrubs and trees.

C. Please translate the following sentences into English.

1. 观叶植物一般叶形叶色美丽可观，多原生于高温多湿的热带雨林中，需光量较少。可分为草本植物和木本植物，草本植物多属多年生宿根草本植物；木本植物大多属灌木或灌木状植物。

2. 花坛是应用各种不同色彩的草本花卉相配置，以花卉的群体效果来体现精美的图案纹样或盛花时艳丽色彩的一种花卉规则式应用形式。花坛根据表现主体不同可分为盛花花坛和模纹花坛两大类。盛花花坛主要由观花草本花卉组成，表现盛花时群体的色彩美。模纹花坛主要由低矮的观叶植物或花及叶兼美的植物组成，表现群体组成的精美图案或装饰纹样。

Part B Cut Flowers

Selected and rewritten from *Horticulture*, by R. Gordon Halface & John A. Barden.

Cut flowers are crops grown for the purpose of selling flowers and their stems rather the intact plant. Commercial cut flowers are grown both in greenhouses and outdoors. California produces 30 percent of all cut flowers; Florida produces 10 percent. Flower production is influenced by market demand, the general economy of the country, customs, and fashions. The popularity of mums has greatly increased because they can be produced year round. The decreased use of corsages has lessened the demand for such crops as camellias, gardenias, and orchids. Economically, carnations, chrysanthemums, and roses constitute the largest portion of cut flower crops.

Carnations, chrysanthemums, orchids, roses, and snapdragons are usually forced in temperature-controlled greenhouses. Irradiance level may be regulated by shade materials, and photoperiod can be decreased by the use of black cloth and increased with electric lights.

Cut flowers are grown in raised benches, ground beds, or pots. The optimum width of a bench is 1.2 m, and the width should not exceed 1.5 m. The length of the bench is dependent on the length of greenhouses and the arrangement of benches. Good drainage is critical in both benches and ground beds and is achieved by placing a layer of tile or gravel under the ground bed or placing a layer of gravel under the bench. Aluminum alloy, asbestos rock concrete, concrete slabs, steel, tile and wood (cypress or redwood) can all be used for bench construction.

Some cut flowers are field-grown. Outdoor production takes place throughout the United States, allowing a succession of crops to be produced. Chrysanthemums and asters are often grown in polypropylene or saran houses to keep out leaf hoppers which transmit disease. These houses decrease irradiance level, lower leaf temperature, and reduce scorching.

The life or keeping quality of cut flowers is determined by water absorption, transpiration, and plant cultivar. Since cut flowers can absorb water only through the stem, the absorption area is small in comparison with the transpiration area. Turgidity of the tissues, temperature, relative humidity, movement of the air, and absorptive area of the cut surface determine the amount of water absorption and transpiration. Lower temperature, and high relative humidity, will decrease transpirational losses.

Cut flowers with high sugar content usually last longer, and respiration can be decreased by lowering the temperature. Chemicals may be applied in the water to control the activity of bacteria and fungi that rot the stems, reducing the life of cut flowers. Examples are Floralife, a solution of hydrazine sulfate, manganese sulfate, and sugar; and Bloomlife, a solution of potassium aluminum sulfate, sodium hypochlorite, ferric oxide, and sugar. The sugar provides substrate for metabolic processes, and the chemicals control the growth of bacteria and fungi, which is stimulated by concentration of sugars in the water.

Chrysanthemums

As a cut flower, the chrysanthemum (*Chrysanthemum morifolium*) or "mum" ranks first in importance. It is native to Japan and in fact is the Japanese national flower. It was introduced to England and brought to America about 1795. The middle of the nineteenth century saw the introduction of the chrysanthemum as a greenhouse crop, before that time it was grown as a bedding plant.

A myriad of chrysanthemum cultivars allow for variation in size, flower type, and contribute to its popularity. Chrysanthemums are noted for their keeping quality. From the grower's standpoint, the ability to produce the desired grades and types at any time during the year adds to their popularity.

Stem-tip cuttings are used to propagate chrysanthemums. The plants are then grown under long-day conditions until the stem reduces the desired length. Thereafter, short days are provided for flower initiation, which occurs when the night is 9.5 h or longer. Depending on the cultivar, 9 to 15 weeks are needed for flower development. Temperatures at night should be 16℃ to 18℃ during vegetative growth and 13℃ to 16℃ after flower initiation.

Chrysanthemums have a variety of flower types, including incurved, spider, pompon, decorative, single, and anemone reflexed. The reflexed type has ray florets with long petals, but the outer florets reflex downward, forming a less formal flower.

Roses

Roses are produced year around, but demand is greatest around holidays. Today, all commercial roses (*Rosa* sp.) are hybrids. The Chinese were the first to cultivate the rose. The prevalent form today is the hybrid tea rose, but floribunda roses are also grown commercially. One large terminal flower per stem is usually formed by the hybrid tea, the lateral buds being removed.

Roses pruning usually involves one of two systems. In the systematic system, the plants are cut to a height of 0.6m or more. Successive pruning are performed 15cm above the previous year's cut to ensure the cutting of soft wood. Gradual pruning is generally done with a knife. Nit all stems are removed simultaneously, and each stem is cut so that at least one five-leaflet leaf per stem remains. Roses should be cut in the early morning, the late afternoon, or both.

It is crucial that roses be grown with their precise light, temperature, and moisture requirements. Roses should be isolated in one area to maintain these exacting requirements and to control disease and insects. Night temperatures should be maintained at 15.6℃ for most cultivars. Humidity should be raised during the day by wetting the walks and watering mulched beds. From late May through August it is desirable to lightly shade the plants to avoid burning of the flowers. Control of aphids, spider mites, mildew, and black spot must be programmed.

Orchids

Orchids are produced worldwide. They are long-lasting and are therefore of the used in corsages and contemporary floral designs. The orchid family has 20,000 recorded species, but most are tropical or jungle exotics, few genera are grown commercially.

Orchids are herbaceous perennials with a sympodial or monopodial growth habit. Sympodial orchids produce a prostrate rhizome with growth terminating periodically. Orchids require 4 to 8 years to produce flowers from seed. Propagation, therefore, is frequently done by "meristeming" or shoottip culture. Some cultivars respond to photoperiod and this can be used to alter production for better marketing. Cattleya flowering can be delayed by long days and promoted by short days, but *Cymbidium* do not respond to photoperiod.

Snapdragons

Snapdragons (*Antirrhinum majus*) are native to the Mediterranean area. They are one of the few commercially produced flowers with a raceme inflorescence. Snapdragons are popular in flower arrangements because they lend themselves to line development in the design composition. They are somewhat difficult to ship because the flowers shatter easily, and bended tips result from geotropism.

Irradiance level and temperature influence growth and flowering. Summer-grown plants will flower within 7 weeks after planting. Different cultivars require various light conditions; some require intense light and will flower only in summer, while others tolerate low light and can be grown in winter. Flowers are cut when expansion of the lower florets is complete and the tip florets are still tight. After cutting, a 4℃ air temperature is desirable. When the flowers are cut, the plants are removed.

Carnations

Although it is a native of southern Europe, the carnation has been a major floral crop in the United States since the late nineteenth century. Commercial production is sometimes programmed for only a single year, so that plants are benched in the spring, flowers cut in the fall, and plants removed the following spring after the second cutting. High light and low temperatures allow a more rapid development of the plants. During the calyx development stage, nights of 16℃ reduce the incidence of spilt calyx. Carnations require support, which is given by several layers of wire or wire and string grids. The first grid is placed about 15 cm above the soil, and the succeeding grids are spaced at increasing intervals, the top ones about 31cm apart.

Narcissus

Narcissus, or daffodils, include an abundance of cultivars, but only the cultivars grown in the Pacific Northwest or the Netherlands are used for forcing. Bulbs shipped to growers for forcing are distributed as early as September. Generally bulbs are planted in flats. Cold and forcing temperatures influence stem length. Forcing procedures must be carried out carefully for the production of quality flowers.

China Asters

Asters (*Callistephus chinensis*) are grown chiefly in cloth houses during the summer. Lighting is necessary during short days for stem elongation. As soon as they can be handled, the seedlings are benched. No pinching is required, since they are self-branching. Eight to ten flowers can be produced per plant. A market is beginning to develop for potted asters. They are long-lasting and offer colors not available in mums. Dwarf cultivars of lavenders and purples are increasing in demand.

Gladiolus

The gladiolus (*Gladiolus grandiflorus*), a native of South Africa, is usually field-grown. Greatest production is centered in Florida; North Carolina is second. Technically, the gladiolus produces a corm, but this thickened underground stem is often incorrectly referred to as bulb. It is day-neutral and has a rest period that can be broken by 4℃ storage for 8 weeks before replanting. High irradiance levels are necessary during forcing.

Other cut flowers

Stocks are largely grown outdoors in California and Arizona. Some retail growers still produce sweet peas on a small scale during the Christmas season and around. Valentine's Day Freesia is produced in southern California fields. These three crops, along with crops such as peonies, dahlias, and gypsophila, are commercial crops grown on a small scale for a limited market.

Glossary

1. cut flower　切花
2. corsage　*n.* 装饰的花束
3. camellia　*n.* 山茶

4. gardenia   *n.* 栀子
5. snapdragon   *n.* 金鱼草
6. aster   *n.* 紫菀属植物
7. polypropylene   *n.* 聚丙烯
8. turgidity   *n.* 膨胀
9. transpiration   *n.* 蒸腾
10. hydrazine sulfate   硫酸肼
11. manganese sulfate   硫酸锰
12. potassium aluminum sulfate   硫酸铝钾
13. sodium hypochlorite   次氯酸钠
14. ferric oxide   氧化铁，三氧化二铁
15. vegetative growth   营养生长
16. pompon   *n.* 彩球，绒球
17. floribunda roses   丰花月季
18. hybrid tea   [园艺学、植物]杂种香水月季
19. herbaceous perennial   [植物]多年生草本植物
20. sympodial   *adj.* [植]合轴的
21. monopodial   *adj.* [植]单轴的
22. cattleya   *n.* 洋兰
23. *Cymbidium*   *n.* [植]兰，兰花
24. narcissus   水仙
25. gladiolus   *n.* 剑兰

Questions

1. What is the definition of *cut flowers*?
2. How to prolong the life or keep quality for cut flowers?
3. Please list several kinds of cut flowers in your hometown.

185

Lesson 23

Part A Floral Arrangement

Selected and rewritten from *Horticulture: A Basic Awareness*, by Robert F. Baudendistel, and *Flower Arranging: Basic Flower Arrangements*, by Ron Morgan.

Flower arrangement is the combination of several elements to produce a visually pleasing display of fresh, silk or dried flowers. Flowers are arranged in several basic designs, including vertical, horizontal, triangular, crescent, and oval arrangements. Other options include a minimal arrangement, such as the lazy "S" or "Hogarth's Curve", and free-standing arrangements. Hogarth's curve is named for English painter William Hogarth who introduced designs shaped like the curves of the letter "S" into floral design.

When called upon, florists must blend their artistic talents with the knowledge of basic floral design. They are expected to know and make proper use of the available flowers and transform them into a lasting display of beauty.

Color Harmony

Color harmony in any floral arrangement may be obtained through the correct use of flowers, supporting greens, and the proper container. A complete understanding of the color wheel and how to use it will give any designer a good deal of flexibility in the creation of the final arrangement. The wheel contains a total of twelve colors of which three are known as primary colors (red, yellow, and blue), three are known as secondary colors (orange, green, and violet), and six as intermediate colors. Red and yellow are known as warm colors, while blue is considered a cool color.

Complementary colors are pairs of color exactly opposite each other on the wheel, and these can be used to good advantage in any arrangement whenever the background is neutral. Analogous colors are those colors next to or close to each other on the wheel; when used in equal intensity, they can make a pleasant arrangement. It is important to emphasize to the beginner that dark colors must be kept low in any arrangement.

Containers

Besides the flowers, the correct container is the most important ingredient of any arrangement. The container selected must be deep enough to guarantee a continuous supply of water to the flowers and large enough to adequately hold and display the flower stems.

The container should also be simple in color and design, so that it does not detract from the arrangement.

The beginning floral arranger should start with four basic containers, two of them having a height of 3.75~5 cm and the other two being 4~6 in. (10~15 cm) tall. One of the containers of each height should be circular, and the other should be rectangular in the shape.

Holding Materials

The holding material is necessary to keep the flowers in position within the arrangement. Shallow containers require a needlepoint holder held in place with florist's clay. When such a holder is employed, the flower stems must be cut straight across.

For deeper containers, crumpled chicken wire, shredded Styrofoam, or oasis can be used. The oasis is a sponge like material that can be easily cut to fit the shape of the container and then can be soaked with water. It is advisable to keep all three of these materials in place with floral tape. Usually, two pieces are necessary; they should be positioned to make an X across the holder, but not in the exact center of the container, because it may interfere with the positioning of the central flower in the arrangement.

Principles of Floral Design

The principles of design that guide a florist's creation are the following:

1. The natural habitat of the flowers selected must be known and used to good advantage. Flowers that grow in an upright manner naturally should be placed similarly in the arrangement.

2. The eventual design must be formulated in the florist's mind before he begins. To do this properly, the florist must consult with the purchaser first with respect to both price and purpose intended for the arrangement.

3. Selection of the proper container is very important. It should be large enough to hold the flowers, but not so large that it distracts from arrangement.

4. The addition of greens is the next step. The purpose of the green is to hide the material that is used as the holder for the flowers and to add both body and contrast to the arrangement.

5. The colors used, coupled with the size, shape, and texture of the materials chosen, must be selected with care to achieve the proper balance, so that all parts of the arrangement will be in harmony with each other.

6. The flowers must not cross in the arrangement but should follow one of three lines: vertical, horizontal, spiral, or a combination of all three.

Process for Floral Arrangement

The elements of flower arrangement include line materials, which are the first pieces placed in a design to establish the overall width and height. Next, the dominant materials are inserted. These are form flowers, such as lilies, irises or peonies.

Next, place smaller mass flowers, or secondary materials, in between the dominant selections. Filler flowers are an optional next step. Special materials, such as moss or vines, add texture to an arrangement. The accent of a flower arrangement might be a focal point including a statue or figurine or might be the impact of a single color. Open flowers also add accent to a flower arrangement.

Many tools make flower arrangement easier. Dried foam holds silk or artificial flowers in place. A "frog" is a metal device often used when dried foam will not work, for example in a clear glass vase. It holds flowers in place between its steel pins. Glass marbles and river rock hold stems in clear receptacles as well.

Spray a completed floral arrangement with floral spray paints to add special effects, a clear sealer adds shine. Hot glue guns and craft glue are both useful for silk and dried flower arrangements. A pick tool crimps a metal pick onto the stem of a flower, which simplifies arranging.

Tape, clay, and floral wire are immensely helpful for flower arrangement. Floral tape covers wire and flower stems. Clay anchors foam, frogs or prongs to the container. Wire supports flower heads and also lengthens stems for easier handling.

Several Basic Flower Arranging Designs

Horizontal Arrangements

1. Using a relatively shallow container, anchor foam with a lot of glue or use anchor pins, and position sprays of line flowers to establish the shape of the design.

2. Insert focal flowers in the middle so they gently droop over the lip of the container on both sides, reach towards the line material and extend on either side of the middle. Leave room for filler flowers.

3. Fill in and around focal area with filler flowers and foliage. (Fig. 23-1)

Fig. 23-1 Horizontal Arrangements

Vertical Arrangements

1. Wedge or secure foam in a vase with hot glue. Cut the stems of the tallest flowers or leaves to reach three or four times the height of the vase.

2. Place the focal flowers vertically within the diameter of the vase.

3. Fill in the areas as needed with filler flowers. (Fig. 23-2)

Triangular Arrangements

1. Secure floral foam. Determine the vertical height and horizontal width with the smallest line flowers and/or leaves. Make the height higher than the width.

2. Position the largest focal flowers in the heart of the arrangement and slightly lower to give weight and balance.

Fig. 23-2 Vertical Arrangements

3. Fill in with the filler flowers and foliage keeping within the triangular shape. (Fig. 23-3)

Fig. 23-3 Triangular Arrangements

Glossary

1. flower arrangement   插花
2. neutral *adj.* 中立的，中性的
3. analogous colors   类似色
4. ingredient *n.* 成分，因素
5. shallow containers   浅容器
6. chicken wire   铁丝织网
7. styrofoam *n.* 泡沫，聚苯乙烯
8. florist *n.* 花匠，花商，花卉研究者
9. vertical *adj.* 垂直的；*n.* 垂直线
10. spiral *n.* 旋涡，螺旋形之物；*adj.* 螺旋形的，盘旋的
11. lily *n.* 百合花
12. iris *n.* 鸢尾属植物
13. moss *n.* 苔藓，泥沼
14. glass marble   玻璃球
15. hot glue gun   热熔胶枪
16. anchor pin   锚定销
17. glue *n.* 胶，各种胶合物

Exercises

A. Please answer the following questions in English.
1. What do the basic designs for floral arrangement include?
2. What are the necessary factors for flower arranging?
3. What principles should be taken into account when design floral arrangement?
4. What are the normal processes of floral arrangement?
5. Please list several kinds of flower arranging designs you have saw in the past.

B. Please translate the following paragraph into Chinese.

The elements of flower arrangement include line materials, which are the first pieces placed in a design to establish the overall width and height. Next, the dominant materials are inserted. These are form flowers, such as lilies, irises or peonies. Next, place smaller mass flowers, or secondary materials, in between the dominant selections. Filler flowers are an optional next step. Special materials, such as moss or vines, add texture to an arrangement. The accent of a flower arrangement might be a focal point including a statue or figurine or might be the impact of a single color. Open flowers also add accent to a flower arrangement.

C. Please translate the following sentences into English.

1. 插花艺术，即指将剪切后的植物枝、叶、花、果作为素材，经过一定的技术（修剪、整枝、弯曲等）和艺术（构思、造型、设色等）加工，重新配置成一件精制完美、富有诗情画意、能再现自然美和生活美的花卉艺术品。

2. 插花的类型根据花材性状可分为鲜花插花、干花插花、人造花插花和混合式插花。鲜花插花主要用鲜花进行插制，具有自然花材之美，但不易维持；干花插花主要用干燥的植物材料进行插制，既不失原有植物的自然形态美，又可随意染色、组合，插制后可长久摆放；人造花插花所用花材是人工仿制的各种植物材料，易于造型，可较长时间摆放。

Part B Bonsai

Selected and rewritten from *Bonsai*: *Wikipedia*, *the free encyclopedia*, by Jimmy Wales.

Bonsai is the art of aesthetic miniaturization of trees, or of developing woody or semi-woody plants shaped as trees, by growing them in containers. Cultivation includes techniques for shaping, watering, and repotting in various styles of containers.

"Bonsai" is a Japanese pronunciation of the earlier Chinese term penzai（盆栽）. A "bon" is a tray-like pot typically used in bonsai culture. The word bonsai is used in the West as an umbrella term for all miniature trees in containers or pots.

Cultivation

Bonsai can be created from nearly any perennial woody-stemmed tree or shrub species, which produces true branches and remains small through pot confinement with crown and root pruning. Some species are popular as bonsai material because they have characteristics, such as small leaves or needles that make them appropriate for the compact visual scope of bonsai. The purposes of bonsai are primarily contemplation (for the viewer) and the pleasant exercise of effort and ingenuity (for the grower). By contrast with other plant-related practices, bonsai is not intended for production of food, for medicine, or for creating yard-sized or park-sized landscapes. As a result, the scope of bonsai practice is narrow and focused on long-term cultivation and shaping of one or more small trees in a single container.

Sources of Bonsai Material

All bonsai start with a specimen of source material, a plant that the grower wishes to train into bonsai form. Bonsai practice is an unusual form of plant cultivation in that growth from seeds is rarely used to obtain source material. To display the characteristic aged appearance of a bonsai within a reasonable time, the source plant is often partially-grown or mature stock.

Propagation

While any form of plant propagation could generate bonsai material, a few techniques are favored because they can quickly produce a relatively mature trunk with well-placed branches.

Cuttings In taking a cutting, part of a growing plant is cut off and placed in a growing medium to develop roots. If the part that is cut off is fairly thick, like a mature branch, it can be grown into an aged-looking bonsai more quickly than can a seed. Unfortunately, thinner and younger cuttings tend to strike roots more easily than thicker or more mature ones. In bonsai propagation, cuttings usually provide source material to be grown for some time before training.

Layering Layering is a technique in which rooting is encouraged from part of a plant, usually a branch, while it is still attached to the parent plant. After rooting, the branch is removed from the parent and grown as an independent entity. For bonsai, both ground layering and air layering can create a potential bonsai, by transforming a mature branch into the trunk of a new tree. The point at which rooting is encouraged can be close to the location of side branches, so the resulting rooted tree can have a thick trunk and low branches, characteristics that complement bonsai aesthetics immediately.

Nursery Stock A plant nursery is an agricultural operation where (non-bonsai) plants are propagated and grown to usable size. Nursery stock may be available directly from the nursery, or may be sold in a garden centre or similar resale establishment. Nursery stock is usually young but fully viable, and is often potted with sufficient soil to allow plants to survive a season or two before being transplanted into a more permanent location.

Collecting Collecting bonsai is the process of finding suitable bonsai material in its original wild situation, successfully moving it, and replanting it in a container for development as bonsai. Collecting may involve wild materials collected from naturally treed areas, or cultivated specimens found growing in yards and gardens. Mature landscape plants which are being discarded from a building site can provide excellent material for bonsai. Some regions have plant material that is known for its suitability in form. In North America, for example, the California Juniper and Sierra Juniper found in the Sierra Mountains, the Ponderosa pine found in the Rocky Mountains, and the Bald Cypress found in the swamps of the Everglades.

Techniques

The practice of bonsai development incorporates a number of techniques either unique to bonsai or, if used in other forms of cultivation, applied in unusual ways that are particularly suitable to the bonsai domain.

Leaf Trimming This technique involves the selective removal of leaves (for most varieties of deciduous tree) or needles (for coniferous trees and some others) from a bonsai's trunk and branches. A common aesthetic technique in bonsai design is to expose the tree's branches below groups of leaves or needles (sometimes called "pads"). In many species, particularly coniferous ones, this means that leaves or needles projecting below their branches must be trimmed off.

Pruning The small size of the tree and some dwarfing of foliage those result from pruning the trunk, branches, and roots. Pruning is often the first step in transforming a collected plant specimen into a candidate for bonsai. The top part of the trunk may be removed to make the tree more compact. Major and minor branches that conflict with the designer's plan will be removed completely, and others may be shortened to fit within the planned design.

Wiring Wrapping copper or aluminum wire around branches and trunks allows the bonsai designer to create the desired general form and make detailed branch and leaf placements. When wire is used on new branches or shoots, it holds the branches in place until they lignify (convert into wood), usually 6～9 months or one growing season. Wires are also used to connect a branch to another object (e. g. another branch, the pot itself) so that tightening the wire applies force to the branch.

Clamping For larger specimens, or species with stiffer wood, bonsai artists also use mechanical devices for shaping trunks and branches. The most common are screw-based clamps, which can straighten or bend a part of the bonsai using much greater force than wiring can supply. To prevent damage to the tree, the clamps are tightened a little at a time and make their changes over a period of months or years.

Grafting In this technique, new growing material (typically a bud, branch, or root) is introduced to a prepared area on the trunk or under the bark of the tree. There are two major purposes for grafting in bonsai. First, a number of favorite species do not thrive as bonsai on their natural root stock and their trunks are often grafted onto hardier root stock. Examples include Japanese red maple and Japanese black pine. Second, grafting allows the bonsai artist to add branches (and sometimes roots) where they are needed to improve or complete a bonsai design.

Defoliation Short-term dwarfing of foliage can be accomplished in certain deciduous bonsai by partial or total defoliation of the plant partway through the growing season. Not all species can survive this technique. In defoliating a healthy tree of a suitable species, most or all of the leaves are removed by clipping partway along each leaf's petiole (the thin stem that connects a leaf to its branch). Petioles later dry up and drop off or are manually removed once dry.

Deadwood Bonsai growers use deadwood bonsai techniques called jin and shari to simulate age and maturity in a bonsai. Jin is the term used when the bark from an entire branch is removed to create the impression of a snag of deadwood. Shari denotes stripping bark from areas of the trunk to simulate natural scarring from a broken limb or lightning strike. In addition to stripping bark, this technique may also involve the use of tools to scar the deadwood or to raise its grain, and the application of chemicals (usually lime sulfur) to bleach and preserve the exposed deadwood.

Glossary

1. bonsai   *n.* 盆栽，盆景
2. woody plant   木本植物
3. semi-woody plant   半木本植物
4. ingenuity   *n.* 智巧，创造力，精巧的设计
5. layering   *n.* 压条法
6. plant nursery   植物苗圃
7. juniper   *n.* 杜松
8. ponderosa   *n.* 美国黄松
9. dwarfing   *adj.* 矮化的
10. aluminum wire   铝丝，铝线

Questions

1. What is the definition of ***bonsai***?
2. How to propagate bonsai plants?
3. What are the normal techniques used in training bonsai?

Lesson 24

Part A Elements of Landscape Design

Selected and rewritten from *Horticulture*, by R. Gordon Halface & John A. Barden Mcgraw, and *Horticulture: A Basic Awareness*, by Robert F. Baudendistel.

Landscape design functions in preserving and protecting our natural environment. The development of the environment determines our reactions to the landscape. The environment can subdue us, dominate us, overpower us, or inspire us. Through design we can manipulate and control the environment to improve our relationship with it. Within the creative process of nature and art, growth may in be directed and developed to attain a better quality of life.

The renewed interest in the preservation and protection of the natural environment indicates sincere and determined efforts to heal the wounded earth around us. Thoughtless destruction and careless rebuilding have never been acceptable practices. Through the creative processes of art and science and with the judicious observance of the principles of nature, the foundation for a better environment can be built.

Landscape design is an art for people. To create landscape designs, an understanding of the basic principles (unity, focalization, balance, scale, proportion, and rhythm) common to all spatial arts is necessary. But the way these principles are ultimately applied depends on the imagination, spirit, and sensitivity of the designer. Because these principles serve as guides for design, they can help the inexperienced. Experienced designers must adhere to the principles to some extent, but they must also be flexible in situations that require variation. To fulfill a purpose, the landscape designer—like any other artist—must establish limits. The painter's canvas and the potter's clay impose limitations and, thus, form a point of reference. These limits do not indicate that the project may not be expanded, they are simply intended to give the artist a finite area with which to work. (Infinity is impossible to deal with.) The boundaries may be previously designated, such as streets or property lines, or they may be imposed by the designer. This may be done obviously (with the use of a wall, for example) or subtly (as with partial plantings). The treatment of these boundaries determines whether the project is completed within itself or will later be expanded.

Like a painter or sculptor, a landscape designer develops a composition by employing or purposefully eliminating the elements of design: line, pattern, color, light, texture, form, and space. Using these elements of design, the designer can compose a design with an overall concept.

Elements of Landscape Composition

Line may be perceived as the junction of two materials, such as a border of water and land or glass and a walkway. It is used to create and control patterns of movement and attention. Straight lines denote formality and pomp, implying strong, solid structural qualities. On the other hand, curved lines are less formal because they encourage slower movement. Vines can soften lines, while clipped hedges can strengthen them.

Pattern provides surface interest and enrichment. It is usually the repetition of a design motif. Pattern can be directional (like a path) or static (like a pattern of leaves against the sky).

Color brings the world to life. It invokes a variety of human responses. As with line, the abstract qualities of color can create moods and emotions through the landscape. Nature can be extravagant with color, especially in the spring and fall, but one must be cautious in its use. Almost any color can be made to harmonize where sunshine and foliage blend; however, too much color can be visually displeasing. Many flowers, such as oriental poppies, can be used freely, since they bloom for only a short time. Most shrubs are compatible, but some (such as azaleas) need to be carefully arranged in order to have a pleasing effect. In selecting colors, one should allow for some color during every season.

Colors harmonize by contrast or analogy. Contrasting colors are opposite on the color chart, e.g., blue and orange. Adjacent colors are analogous, such as green and blue.

Colors also project coolness and warmth; for example, bright red is a warm color which may not be pleasing around a patio, while blue would give a restful feeling.

Light is used in respect to colors and shadows. As light passes through the atmosphere, dust particles reflect the blue light waves giving a blue hue to the sky or to mountains viewed from a distance. This can be exploited by using blues with the proper transition in texture and size to create a feeling of depth or distance.

Light causes shadows. As the sun passes through the sky, forms created by shade continually change and move. The continual change and movement create interesting illusions, but shadows can interfere and confuse ground patterns. Artificial lighting at night for trees and shrubs casts intriguing patterns on ground or walls.

Texture is the variation of the surface of a material. Plants are classified as fine-textured, medium-textured, coarse-textured. Weeping willow, cottoneaster, and spirea have fine-textured foliage; azalea, sasanqua, and cleyera have medium-textured foliage; loquat and aucuba have coarse-textured foliage. As a general rule, fine-textured plants enrich architecture having smooth surfaces and fine lines; coarse-textured plants harmonize with large spaces and coarse building material. Differences in texture can be used for the development of depth or distance; fine texture gives the illusion of being farther away, while coarse texture gives the illusion of closeness. A sudden change in texture can also be used as an accent.

The form, or "architecture" of plants defines and qualifies space, giving it order. Plant masses are selected to achieve a desired visual effect. Vertical branching leads the eye upward, upright evergreens such as spruce or hemlock accent the high gables of a large house and the verticality of hilly terrain. On the other hand, horizontal branching pulls the vision to ground forms; for example, rounded shrubs echo the profile of a ranch house and the undulations of rolling terrain. Tall, upright, stiff plant forms, such as podocarpus, are useful as emphasis points, as in the repetition and regularity of formal gardens. Informal design usually calls for plants with loose form, such as *Rhododendron* and *Loropetalum*.

Density in growth habit also reinforces form. Boxwood and yew are heavy and compact, spirea and wax myrtle are light and open. A few compact Japanese hollies might be used to balance the loose form of a taller dogwood. Line patterning of branches varies form upright to spreading. Deciduous materials should be selected for their form during the growing season as well as for the interesting line patterns they create when they are dormant. When considering the form of a plant for a specific situation, one should consider the mature form of the plant as well as the immature form. Form as a positive element is closely related to space.

Space, or volume, is the negative element in design, the area in between; because of this it is usually difficult to comprehend. Space achieves form, volume, and scale when defined by tangible visual elements form the surrounding landscape. A landscape is three-dimensional: It has height, width, and length. The three-dimensionality of landscaping is an art, an art to be walked through and experienced from a variety of angles; the fact that it is to be absorbed points to the importance of the concept of space. A landscape is composed of several spaces (much like the rooms of a house): the ground, the ground fixtures, and the ceiling or sky. Each has a specific purpose, but each is also a part of a whole.

Before surfaces are applied to the earth, the natural ground forms need to be considered. A common practice of developers is to level hills and fill valleys, producing monotony. The designer should strive to accentuate the highs and lows of the terrain, e.g., building homes and planting trees on high points and creating pools in low spots. Verticals determine to a great extent the emotional quality of space. A vast space without verticals tends to frighten and humble an individual; yet, at the opposite extreme, too many verticals tend to excite and confuse. Although the sky is the obvious ceiling to the outside space, it becomes an element in design when viewed through a canopy of leaves or a latticed roof.

Principles of landscape composition

Unity means "oneness". It is the fitting together of parts that have a relationship to one another. When one of these parts is overly strong or weak, the unity is disrupted. Parts are unified by an overriding concept or idea. If successful, the unity presents one image from several angles. Unity is a achieved by using similar plant textures, forms, or colors, by planning noticeable repetition and transition from one group to another, by enclosing areas which set the scheme apart, or by developing patterns.

While unity is essential, variety humanizes a design and saves it from monotony. Too much unity can lead to sterility, whereas too much variety can lead to confusion. Variety can be tempered by dominance and subordination. To reduce monotony, different textures, shapes, heights, or colors of plants may be employed as accents. Not only must this occur on a small scale, it must also occur on a large scale. One feature should become a focal point.

In selecting plants for an environmental design, one must coordinate and anticipate problems. Cultural and ecological conditions must be considered. When plants are planted in an unsuitable environment, additional maintenance will be necessary. Rate of growth must be a factor in choosing a plant for a specific purpose. At times, rapidly growing plants are needed to fill a space quickly, but most can be used only temporarily or in a protected location. Therefore, the designer must be familiar with the growth habits of plants as well as design principles and techniques.

Glossary

1. unity   *n.* 统一性，一致性，个体，统一体
2. focalization   *n.* 焦点
3. balance   *n.* 平衡
4. scale   *n.* 比例，比例尺
5. proportion   *n.* 比例
6. rhythm   *n.* 节奏，韵律
7. canvas   *n.* 帆布
8. sculptor   *n.* 雕刻家
9. texture   *n.* 组织，结构，特征
10. form   *n.* 形状，形式，形态
11. space   *n.* 空间，位置，距离
12. static   *n.* 静态，静止；*adj.* 静态的
13. harmonize   *v.* 协调
14. azalea   *n.* 杜鹃花
15. analogy   *n.* 相似，类似
16. sasanqua   *n.* 油茶
17. cleyera   *n.* 红淡比属植物
18. loquat   *n.* 枇杷
19. aucuba   *n.* 桃叶珊瑚，桃叶珊瑚属植物
20. evergreen   *adj.* 常绿的，常青的；*n.* 常绿植物
21. hemlock   *n.* 铁杉，铁杉属植物
22. podocarpus   *n.* 罗汉松，罗汉松属植物

23. *Rhododendron*　*n.* 杜鹃属，杜鹃属植物
24. *Loropetalum*　*n.* 檵木属（金缕梅科）
25. spirea　*n.* 绣线菊，绣线菊类的植物
26. wax myrtle　杨梅，杨梅属之植物
27. three-dimensional　*adj.* 三维的，立体的
28. monotony　*n.* 单调

Exercises

A. Please answer the following questions in English.
1. What are the elements of landscape composition?
2. What principles we should comply with in landscape composition?
3. How to understand the principle of *unity* in landscape composition?
4. Please design a home yard using the principles of landscaping.
5. When you choose plants in landscape, what factors you take into account?

B. Please translate the following paragraph into Chinese.

The key goals of landscaping design may be summed up into two—function and aesthetics. Horticulture is both a science and an art. Landscaping may be likened to using plants to paint a picture, with the open space as the canvas. One key difference is that unlike painting on canvas, the subjects in the picture are not static but change with time. The changes may be in form, size, and age. It takes time to stabilize plant characteristics, which can be controlled only with good maintenance.

C. Please translate the following sentences into English.

1. 园林景观设计是在传统园林理论的基础上，具有建筑、植物、美学、文学等相关专业知识的人士对自然环境进行有意识改造的思维过程和筹划策略。具体讲，就是在一定的地域范围内，运用园林艺术和工程技术手段，通过改造地形、种植植物、营造建筑和布置园路等途径创造美的自然环境和生活、游憩境域的过程。

2. 通过景观设计，可以使环境具有美学欣赏价值、日常使用功能，并能保证生态可持续发展。在一定程度上，体现了当时人类文明的发展程度和价值取向及设计者个人的审美观念。

Part B　Goals and Principles of Landscaping

Selected and rewritten from *Introductory Horticulture*, by H. Edward Reiley & Corroll L. Shry, Jr., and *Horticulture: principles and practices*, by George Acquaah.

Landscaping is the developing of the outdoors to serve the needs and desires of people. Some view landscaping as an art, others see it as a craft. It may correctly be regarded as both an art and a craft.

The art of landscaping is centered within the career field known as landscape design or landscape architecture. It is in the mind's eye of the landscape designer or architect that the landscape first takes shape. The successful designer must be able to look at undeveloped, scarred, and ugly land, and recognize its potential for becoming more attractive and/or functional for human use.

Goals of landscaping

In fulfilling aesthetic and functional purposes, landscaping may be specifically used to accomplish the following:

1. Enhance the aesthetic appeal of an area. Home and business environments can be beautified to make them more attractive and nurturing to the human spirit.

2. Enhance the neighborhood and increase property value. Homes with curb appeal have higher property values on the real estate market.

3. Blend concrete and architectural creations into the natural scenery. Buildings tend to have sharp geometric edges that can be softened with plants. Brick and mortar in a city can be overwhelming and excessively artificial. Plants can be used to introduce life into the area.

4. Provide privacy by shielding the general public from selected areas such as the backyards of homes, utility substations, and patios.

5. Control vehicular and pedestrian traffic. Just as pavements indicate where people should walk, trees, flower beds, and other feature can be used to discourage people from making undesirable shortcuts across lawns. Trees and other plants on a median in the street prevent from driving over the structure.

6. Hide unsightly conditions in the area. Plants can be used to create a wall around, for example, junkyards and storage areas.

7. Modify environmental factors. Trees can be planted to serve as windbreaks to reduce wind speeds, for example. Similarly, plants can be located to provide shade, block undesirable light, and modify local temperature.

8. Create recreational grounds to provide places for relaxation and community interaction.

9. Provide hobby activities for home owners. People can care for their gardens, water plants, and partakers in other activities for exercise and enjoyment.

10. Improve and conserve natural resources by reducing soil erosion, for example.

11. Provide therapeutic relief. Enjoying the landscape can be relaxing.

12. Reduce noise and environmental pollution.

Principles of Landscaping

There are five basic principles which guide the landscape architect or designer in planning the landscape's outdoor rooms. These principles are:

1. Simplicity
2. Balance

3. Focalization of interest
4. Rhythm and line
5. Scale and proportion

The principle of simplicity is very important to the overall unity of the design. When this principle is correctly applied, the landscape is understood and appreciated by the viewer. The principle of simplicity is accomplished by repeating specific plants throughout the design, and by massing plant types or colors into groups rather than spacing them so that each plant or color is seen separately. The fewer different objects there are for the eye to focus upon, the more simple the design will seem. Finally, straight-lined or gently curving bedlines around shrub plantings, rather than fussy, scalloped bedlines, add to the design's simplicity (Fig. 24-1).

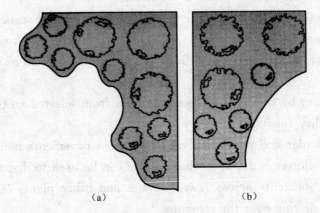

Fig. 24-1 A fussy bedline (a) and a simple bedline (b), (b) is easier to maintain

The principle of balance is applied by imagining the area of landscape placed on a seesaw. If properly balanced, the left side of the landscape should have no more visual weight than the right side. Balance may be either symmetrical or asymmetrical. Symmetrical balance is attained when one side of the landscape is an exact duplicate of the other side (Fig. 24-2). This is a form of balance common in formal designs. It is sometimes applied to modern residential design, but more frequently asymmetrical balance is used. With asymmetrical balance, one side of the landscape has the same visual weight as the other side, but they are not duplicates (Fig. 24-3).

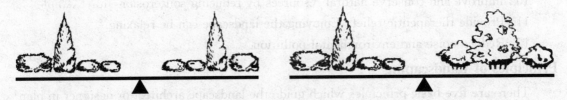

Fig. 24-2 Symmetrical balance   Fig. 24-3 Asymmetrical balance

The principle of focalization of interest recognizes that the viewer's eye wants to see only one feature as being most important within any given view. All other elements complement that important feature (the focal point) but do not compete with it for attention. When looking at a house from the street, the viewer's eye should go quickly to the front door. When sitting on the patio looking out across the backyard, the viewer may have no focal point at which to look unless one is created by the designer. Focal points may be created using especially attractive plants (specimen plants), statues, fountains, pools, and flower masses. Once created, all bedlines and plant arrangements should be designed to lead the eye of the viewer to the focal point (Fig. 24-4).

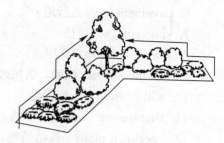

Fig. 24-4 Focal point design

The principle of rhythm and line also contributes to the overall unity of the landscape design. This principle is responsible for the sense of continuity between different areas of the landscape. One way in which this continuity can be developed is by extending planting beds from one area to another. For example, shrub beds developed around the entrance to the house can be continued around the sides and into the backyard. Such an arrangement helps to tie the front and rear areas of the property together. Another means by which rhythm is given to a design is to repeat shapes, angles, or lines between various areas and elements of the design.

The principle of scale and proportion helps to keep all elements of the landscape in the correct size relationship with not tower over the building when fully grown (Fig. 24-5). Plants selected for the landscape should add to human comfort in the setting. For example, plants and other materials used around a children's play area should be small so that the children can relate to them. In a world of giant adults, it is nice to feel as "tall as a tree", even when children and trees are only 3 1/2 feet (1foot=30.48 cm) tall.

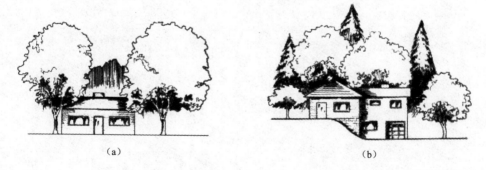

Fig. 24-5 Design (b) is better in proportion

Glossary

1. craft   *n.* 工艺，技能
2. landscape architecture   园林建筑
3. aesthetic   *n.* 审美；*adj.* 美学的

4. backyard n. 后院，后庭
5. pedestrian n. 行人；adj. 徒步的
6. pavement n. 人行道
7. shortcut n. 捷径
8. lawn n. 草地，草坪
9. windbreak n. 风障，防风带，防风林
10. soil erosion 土壤侵蚀
11. therapeutic adj. 治疗的，疗法的
12. specimen plant 孤植植物，标本植物，园景植物
13. statue n. 塑像，雕像
14. fountain n. 喷泉，源泉
15. continuity n. 连续性，连贯性

Questions

1. What are the goals of landscaping?
2. In order to achieve the goal of simplicity in landscape, what should a landscape designer do?
3. How to use the principle of focalization in landscape designing?

Lesson 25

Part A Establish New Lawns

Selected and rewritten from *Introductory Horticulture*, by H. Edward Reiley & Corroll L. Shry, Jr.

Lawns are a major part of most home landscapes. Basically, lawns are established for three reasons.

1. They add beauty to the landscape. A well-kept lawn is very appealing and inviting.
2. They are used as play areas for sports such as baseball, football, basketball, or lacrosse. Since these types of sports are tough on lawns, it is important to select a lawn grass that can take wear.
3. They provide an excellent cover to help control soil erosion while allowing the movement of air and water to roots of trees and shrubs in the soil below.

Soil and Grading

The first thing to consider in establishing a new lawn is the present condition of the soil. Is this an area in which the builder has graded off all the topsoil? Is the slope too steep to establish a lawn and mow it safely? Is the drainage adequate? These are all questions that must be answered before establishing a lawn.

The builder usually establishes the rough grade. The lot is graded so that the land slopes away from the foundation of the house, to help prevent any water from entering the basement. After the rough grade is established, topsoil which the builder has set aside may be spread over the subsoil which was kept in the rough grading. 6 inches (1inch=2.5 cm) of topsoil should be spread evenly over the surface and tilled to loosen and break up clods.

The general slope for the lawn after the topsoil is spread should not exceed 15 percent; that is, no more than a 15-foot (1foot=30.48 cm) drop for every 100 feet of lawn area. Slopes greater than 15 percent are unsafe to mow. If a slope steeper than 15 percent cannot be avoided, it should be covered with plants that do not require mowing.

Drainage

Good drainage ensures a balance between the air and water in the soil. This, in turn, encourages proper root growth. Grasses can endure relatively wet soil, but not bog or swamp conditions. There are two ways of establishing proper drainage in lawns. One method is to install drainage tile about 3 feet below the surface of the soil to drain the subsoil. Another method is to make use of the slope of the land to drain surface water away.

Preparation of Soil

As mentioned earlier, 6 inches of topsoil should be spread over the rough graded subsoil. A good garden loam is the best medium for most grasses. If quality topsoil is not available, the organic matter content of the soil should be increased by adding well-rotted sawdust, weed-free, well-rotted manure, or commercial peat moss at the rate of 6 cubic feet per thousand square feet of land. Work the material well into the soil with a rototiller. It may be necessary to remove stones or dirt clods. A good seedbed should have a firm and smooth, but not powder fine, surface texture.

Fertilizer

A complete fertilizer with high phosphorus content is recommended for use in establishing new lawns. Some companies manufacture a special fertilizer known as a *starter fertilizer* which is especially high in phosphorus.

Before applying fertilizer, the soil should be tested to determine the correct amount of fertilizer and lime to add. This can be done in one of two ways: with a special portable soil test kit, or by sending a sample of the soil away to a land grant university for testing. When test results are returned from these schools, they also contain a recommendation regarding the amount and analysis of fertilizer to apply.

Most lawn grasses grow best in a well-limed soil with a pH level from 6.0 to 6.5. If the soil test calls for lime, add the recommended amount evenly over the entire soil surface. Work it into the ground 4 to 6 inches before seeding.

Fertilizer should be spread in two different directions on new lawns. Spread one-half the recommended amount in a north-south direction and the rest in an east-west direction. This gives a better distribution of the fertilizer. Fertilizers are usually applied most efficiently by use of a spreader. It is important that the fertilizer be applied uniformly.

Starting the Lawn

Lawns are started in one of three ways: seeding, sodding, or plug/strip planting.

Seeding

It is very important to purchase the best lawn seed. All lawn grass seed is required by law to have a label with name, purity, percent of germination, company, etc.

Sowing Seed Seed may be planted by hand or with a mechanical seeder. To obtain uniform distribution, the seed is mixed with small amounts of a carrier, such as sand. The mixed material is divided into two equal parts: one part is sown in one direction, and the other part crosswise to the first sowing.

Covering the Seed The seed is lightly covered by hand raking. Large seeds are covered with 1/4 to 3/8 inch of soil and small seeds with 1/8 to 1/4 inch of soil. It is important that all seed is covered by and in close contact with the soil.

Mulching Mulching with a light covering of weed-free straw or hay helps to hold moisture and prevent the seed from washing away during watering or rainfall. Straw also helps to hide the seed from birds. Mulches applied evenly and lightly may be left in place and the grass is allowed to grow through. Peat moss or other fine material does not make satisfactory mulch. These materials become packed too tightly, resulting in the seed being planted too deep.

Firming the Seed The seeded area is firmed by rolling it with a light roller or cultipacker.

Watering New seedlings should be kept moist until they are well established. Once seeds have begun to germinate, they must not be allowed to dry out, or they will die. Avoid saturating the soil, however; excessive moisture is favorable for the development of damping off, a fungus disease.

Vegetative Planting

There are some grasses for which seed is not available, or the seed that is available does not produce plants that are true to type. These grasses must be planted by one of several vegetative methods, such as spot or plug sodding, strip sodding, sprigging, or stolonizing. Grasses planted by vegetative methods include zoysia, improved strains of Bermuda grass, St. Augustine grass, centipede grass, creeping bentgrass, and velvet bentgrass.

Whether plugged, strip sodded, sprigged, or stolonized, the planted material must be kept moist until well established. During the first year, light applications of a nitrogenous fertilizer every two to four weeks during the growing season helps speed the spread of the grass.

Glossary

1. mow   *vt. & vi.* 刈，割，修剪
2. clod   *n.* 块，（尤指）土块，泥块
3. loam   *n.* （含有黏土、沙以及有机物质的）肥土
4. peat moss   泥炭藓（泥煤的主成分）
5. rototiller   *n.* 旋转式耕耘机，旋转碎土器
6. phosphorus   *n.* 磷
7. hay   *n.* 干草
8. firm   *vt. & vi.* （使）坚硬（稳固）
9. cultipacker   *n.* 碎土镇压器
10. true to type   典型的，纯种的
11. spot sodding   点铺草坪法
12. strip sodding   成带铺草坪法
13. sprig   *n.* 分枝
14. stolonizing   *n.* 葡枝繁殖
15. zoysia   *n.* 结缕草

Exercises

A. Please answer the following questions in English.

1. Why do people establish many lawns everywhere?

2. How to improve soil conditions before starting a lawn?

3. How many vegetative planting methods for those grasses without seed or with seed unable to produce plants?

B. Please translate the following paragraph into Chinese.

Lawns are a standard feature of ornamental private and public gardens and landscapes in much of the world today. Lawns are created for aesthetic use in gardens, and for recreational use, including sports. They are typically planted near homes, often as part of gardens, and are also used in other ornamental landscapes and gardens. They are frequently a feature of public parks and other spaces. They form the playing surface for many outdoor sports, reducing erosion and dust as well as providing a cushion for players in sports such as rugby, football, cricket, baseball, golf, tennis, bocce and stake.

C. Please translate the following sentences into English.

1. 选择草种时，根据当地已有种植且表现良好的草坪种类来选择类似的种植品种，或根据现有品种的不足来挑选能克服现有缺陷的品种或种植方式，也可以提供当地条件，根据品种介绍由专家来指导选择适合的草种和种植方式。

2. 叶面喷水是草坪建植养护过程中的重要环节。草坪叶面喷水后，可以降低草坪地面和草坪植物组织的温度，减少蒸发；补充草坪植物体内水分的亏缺；同时还可以从叶片上洗掉有害物质。对新建植的草坪包括草皮、种子等喷水，可以避免脱水，保持湿润，促进根系下扎。对病虫危害的草坪喷水，可促进新根系的生长，增强其吸水能力，迅速恢复其活力。

Part B Maintaining the Lawn

Selected and rewritten from *Introductory Horticulture*, by H. Edward Reiley & Corroll L. Shry, Jr.

After the lawn has been seeded or planted vegetatively, care must be taken to keep it healthy. Proper lawn maintenance is dependent upon five factors.

1. Applying fertilizer and lime at the proper time and in the proper form and amount.

2. Mowing to the proper height at the correct time.

3. Watering properly.

4. Using chemicals for weed, insect, and disease control if necessary.

5. Using the lawn in such a way that the traffic is not too heavy.

Applying Fertilizer

If a healthy lawn is to be maintained, annual applications of a nitrogen fertilizer are needed. Nitrogen is leached from soil and must be replaced regularly.

Lawns require a fertilizer high in nitrogen. Many turf fertilizers supply nitrogen in an organic form. This form of nitrogen is released slowly and thus does not burn the grass. It also supplies nutrients over a longer period of time. The urea form of nitrogen is often used as a slow-release fertilizer for turf grasses. If an inorganic form of nitrogen which is released rapidly (such as nitrate of soda) is used, it must not be applied to wet, actively growing grass. Such an application would burn the grass badly.

Mowing the Lawn

There are two types of mowers used for mowing lawns, the reel mower and the rotary mower. The type of mower that is used generally depends upon individual preference; either does a good job. Close mowing of 1/2 to 1 inch (1inch=2.54 cm) is done most efficiently with a reel mower.

Most lawns are cut too short because the homeowner believes that the grass looks better when short. A very short cutting reduces the leaf area of the grass to such an extent that it cannot manufacture enough food. Also, grasses that are cut too short encourage weed growth since the grass plants cannot kill weed seeds by "shading them out". Cool-season grasses should not be cut shorter than 2 to 3 inches. Warm-season grasses are cut shorter, from 1/2 to 1 1/4 inches, depending upon the grass variety. Since warm-season grasses grow rapidly during warm weather, they are better able to compete with weeds growing during the same season. Bermuda grass should be clipped to 1/2 to 1 inch and zoysia 3/4 to 1 1/4 inches.

Lawns should be mowed often enough so that no more than one-third of the top, or 1 inch of growth, is cut off in any one mowing. For example, if grass is kept at a height of 2 or 3 inches, only 1 inch should be cut off. This means that when the grass reaches 3 or 4 inches in height, it is time to mow again.

Watering the Lawn

A great deal of water is required to give lawns the moisture they need. Unless an adequate supply is available, the lawn should not be watered at all. Shallow watering does more harm than good. This is because shallow watering causes the grass roots to move to the surface to absorb water. Here, they are more easily dried out and require still more frequent watering. Surface roots are more easily torn loose from the soil during winter freezing and thawing. Frequent watering also encourages the growth of fungus disease on the grass blades.

At least 1 inch of water should be applied at each application. An amount less than this does not penetrate the soil deeply enough. To determine when 1 inch has been applied by a sprinkler, set a rain gauge or any container with straight sides on the lawn on the area to be watered. When the container has 1 inch of water in it, 1 inch has been applied to the lawn.

Solving Problems in the Lawn

Controlling Weeds

If a lawn is heavily infested with weeds, chemicals should be used to eliminate the problem. However, development of a thick healthy turf is the best way to guard against serious weed problem.

Weeds in a lawn are usually an indication of an unhealthy lawn caused by poor maintenance practices. When weeds are spotted, first check maintenance practices and correct them if necessary. If weeds are still a problem, consider chemical control.

Two types of chemical weed killers are used on lawns. One is a preemergence weed killer, which kills germinating seeds and very tiny weed seedlings before the weeds become established. This is the type of weed killer which is applied in the spring to cool-season grasses for the control of crabgrass. It is often mixed with a fertilizer before application. Since crabgrass is a grass, the mature plant cannot be controlled without killing the lawn grass. However, the tender seedlings can be killed with small amounts of weed killer which are not strong enough to kill the lawn grass.

Disease Prevention

The best control measure for fungus disease is prevention. To reduce the chance of attack by fungus spores on lawns, you should do as follows:

1. Do not overuse nitrogen fertilizer.
2. Add lime as needed to maintain a pH of 6.0 to 6.5. (This helps to control thatch buildup.)
3. Avoid thatch buildup by collecting clippings or by raking and removing thatch.
4. Water only when necessary, and then water deeply. Do not repeat watering for one week.
5. Mow frequently, and remove only one-third of the top growth at any one mowing. Cut grass to the proper height and keep it within 1 inch of that height throughout the entire growing season.

Glossary

1. leach   vi. （将化学品、矿物质等）过滤；vt. （液体）过滤，滤去
2. urea   n. 尿素
3. rain gauge   雨量测量器
4. preemergence   adj. （植物种子）出土前的，出土前施用的
5. thatch   n. （作物下地面上的）杂草

Questions

1. To maintain your lawn, what steps you should take care?
2. What should you do to reduce the chance of attack by fungus spores on lawns?

Lesson 26

Part A Types of Greenhouses and Characteristics of Greenhouse-Related Equipment and Covering Materials

Selected and rewritten from Type and Structure of Greenhouses and Characteristics of Greenhouse-Related Equipment and Covering Materials, by Toru Maruo.

Type of Protected Cultivation Facilities

About 50 years have passed since plastic houses appeared and a traditional term "glasshouse cultivation" was replaced by a new concept of protected cultivation. At present, a broad variety of protected cultivation facilities coexist in Japan.

In general, the facilities included in the category of protected cultivation are considered to be glasshouses, plastic greenhouses, rain shelter greenhouses and tunnels in descending order of construction costs. But the definition of protected cultivation facilities is still expending, and in some cases includes plant factories as high-level ones and row covering as a low-level one.

Glasshouses and plastic greenhouses are usually called "greenhouses" collectively, but the general trend is that the ratio of glasshouses remains low and plastic greenhouses, especially simple pipe-framework greenhouses, have a high ratio. While most greenhouses are relatively small scales, larger facilities have gradually been increasing in recent years. In addition, the utilization of greenhouses is inefficient in summer because of unfavorable high temperature.

Structure of Protected Cultivation Facilities

As stated above, a variety of facilities for protected cultivation coexist in Japan, and these can be classified into many kinds of structures according to shape, structural materials, covering materials and so on. Recently, imported facilities from abroad, including the Netherlands, South Korea and China, as well as those with high roofs and low cost ones have come into use, too. Since Japan has typhoons, snowfalls, and earthquakes frequently, regional difference in the type of greenhouse is characterized in this country to escape from these natural disasters.

Plant Factories/Closed-Type Seedling Raising Facilities Fully controlled plant factories using high-pressure sodium lamps were put to practical use in Japan in the 1990s.

Recently, closed-type transplant production facilities equipped with highly efficient fluorescent lamps have reached the stage of practical application, and the programmed production and supply of high quality transplants have been started in these facilities.

Glasshouses   Greenhouses in Japan are now almost all the plastic greenhouses covered with flexible films, and glasshouses account for only 2.8 percent. But the ratio of large-scale glasshouses is a little rising recently. Glasshouses are used more for the cultivation of ornamental plants than that of vegetables. Their most common structure is the gable-roof one, but there are also the three-quarter roof type used for musk melons and the Venlo type glasshouses mainly for large-scale facilities. In particular, Venlo glasshouses, including important ones, tend to increase in recent years.

Plastic Greenhouses   Greenhouses in Japan are characterized by a high percentage of plastic greenhouses. Those with the largest total acreage across the country are pipe-frame greenhouse with no foundation covered with PVC films. Other types of plastic greenhouses include steel-reinforced pipe-frame houses. Because the long-life types of covering materials have been developed recently, these steel-frame and steel frame-reinforced houses are on the increase. Low-cost, weatherproof greenhouses, which were developed recently, are the combination of steel frames and pipes; the high-roof type of these houses was invented, too, which can provide an environment inside the facility close to that of glasshouses.

Rain Shelter Greenhouses   These are the structures aiming mainly at quality improvement, with only the roof covered with PVC films, etc. to avoid crops from exposed to rainwater. These shelters are used in summer in a considerably large area, mainly in cool districts.

Tunnels   The term "tunnel" is row covering referring to protective facilities too small for the grower to enter.

Direct Covering   "Direct covering" means the method of covering crops and the soil with unwoven fabric or other materials having a high light permeability and ventilation either directly or on the support poles. The purposes include heat insulation, frost protection, insect control, shading, prevention of damage from birds and wind protection. Direct covering is widely used from the south to the north.

Other Facilities   A variety of greenhouse with fully openable roofs has been developed and is expected to be introduced in the summer season (Fig. 26-1).

Fig. 26-1 Fully-opened vent greenhouse

The biggest advantage for this kind greenhouse is to well solve the problem of low light-transmission and light wave filtering, in the fine season, it may make plant absorb natural light full-wave radiation completely and touch directly with outer air, so the crops will have high-quality performance and no longer fragile. Large angle open on the roof, inside and outside completely communicates, good ventilation effect, the efficiency is almost 100%, comparing with tradition greenhouse, and it reduces the operation cost of lowering the temperature greatly. In the daytime when temperature rises on the high side, the vent opens together with inside shading net and side vent, then it change into a shading shed and gains effective temperature-lowering. In the nighttime, the temperature drops on the low side, the vent closes together with the other two systems, and then it again gains good warm-keeping performance of advanced greenhouse.

Type and Characteristics of Greenhouse-Related Equipment

A variety of greenhouses-related equipment has been developed, and some of them are those which have the characteristics adaptable to the special situation in Japan where the scale of greenhouses is relatively small.

Heating System   The ratio of the facilities having heating system is 42.9 percent of all the greenhouses in Japan. Main characteristics are the fact that the warm air heating system using plastic ducts amounts to as high as about 90 percent and that the petroleum-powered system has an extremely high ratio of 96 percent. The use of gas and other fuels is relatively little. There are many facilities equipped with no heaters, and in most cases, these facilities use heat insulation only for crop cultivation by multiple covering, such as triple and quadruple layer coverings.

Ventilation System   In addition to common roof and side ventilations, an automatic or manual ventilation device, that rolls up the covering films from eaves to ridge side and on the side window, highly developed partly because pipe-frame houses were mostly covered with flexible plastic films. Also, as the scale of greenhouses is growing larger, ventilation and circulation fans have been changed into large ones.

Heat Insulation and Shading Equipment   In Japan, heat insulation curtains came into wide use in relatively early days. Automatic two-shaft, double-layer curtains and shading curtains developed well, and are used all the year round in recent years.

Other Environment-Controlling Equipment   Other types of equipment for controlling the greenhouse environment include fine mist sprayers and other coolers, carbon dioxide generating system and supplement lighting device. But due to high humidity, the introduction of fine mist cooling, pad and fan coolers and other cooling system is limited.

Plant Management Equipment   Besides the equipment for controlling the greenhouse environment, various types of devices for sprinkling, solution application (fertigation), insect control, harvesting and transportation have been developed and using.

Hydroponics Equipment   Hydroponic equipment is widely used for the purpose of avoiding crop failure due to successive planting in the same greenhouse and of saving the labor of cultivation work. Also in recent years, the use of fertigation system, whose installation is less expensive, has increased.

Collection/Shipment Equipment   In Japan, because farm scales are small, farmers use joint and large collection/shipment and grading facilities in most cases. These facilities have many kinds of automatic grading machines and refrigerating equipment originally developed in Japan, such as non-destructive quality evaluation devices and refrigerating equipment, in order to adjust the diverse needs for shipment standards.

Other Equipment   Other greenhouse-related equipment includes various elevated and movable benches, insect trap devices and transplant production equipment.

Type and Characteristics of Covering Materials

One of the characteristics of horticultural covering materials in Japan is that besides glass, a variety of plastic materials have been developed and put to practical use, which reflects the fact that the chemical industry has highly developed. These plastic materials are very diverse according to use, including flexible and rigid films, unwoven fabric, cheesecloth and nets. New and higher-performance materials are also at stage of development.

Out Covering Materials   In Japan, the use of flexible PVC films is remarkably great, accounting for 74.5 percent. Recently, the application of longer-life film materials is increasing, mostly rigid polyethylene terephthalate (PETP) and fluorine (ETFE: ethylene-tetrafluoroethylene elastomer) films and soft polyolefin-based (PO) films, whereas that of polyethylene (PE) films is smaller compared with other countries. Behind the increasing use of longer-life films is a shortage of labor for re-covering, in addition to the fact that the strength of greenhouses has been improved. Also, the covering materials and liniment chemicals for those materials having good optical properties (e.g., ultraviolet ray permeability) and defogging/ anti-cloudiness/waterdrop control properties have been developed.

Inner Covering Materials   To cope with high energy costs, inner curtains were used early on in Japan mainly for thermal insulation purposes. The materials used for these curtains are mainly PVC, agricultural PE and PO, and unwoven fabric and other airpermeable materials are also employed for such purpose as shading, thermal insulation and dehumidification. Inner covering materials should have sticking and anti-cloudiness properties and should be light in weight, too.

Shading Materials   Unwoven fabric and nets used for shading purposes. Higher performance materials made of aluminum layered, etc. are also widely introduced.

Tunnel Materials   PVC, PE and PO are the main materials of tunnel covers for thermal insulation. Unwoven fabric and cheesecloth are also used for insect pest control.

Mulch Materials   Very thin PE films 0.02 mm thick or less are mostly used for mulches. Mulches have many types; they have different colors and reflectances, and include pored and biodegradable types.

Direct Covering Materials   The direct covering materials developed in Japan include those made of long-fiber unwoven fabric, sprit-fabric unwoven and cheesecloth. The main row covering materials are polypropylene (PP), polyester, polyvinyl alcohol and vinylon. Direct covering materials are used in the field but are more employed in greenhouses and tunnels; because of this, light permeability, ventilation, insect-control property and opening size of strands are important factors to these materials.

Glossary

1. rain shelter （避）防雨棚
2. plant factory 植物工厂
3. pipe-framework 管架结构；steel-frame greenhouse 钢骨架温室
4. closed-type seedling raising facility 闭锁型育苗设施
5. high-pressure sodium lamp 高压气体钠灯
6. highly efficient fluorescent lamp 高效荧光灯
7. gable-roof 人字（三角）屋顶
8. musk melon 甜瓜，哈密瓜
9. Venlo type glasshouse 芬洛型玻璃温室
10. weatherproof greenhouse 耐候温室
11. heating system 加热系统
12. multiple covering 多重覆盖
13. triple and quadruple layer covering 三、四层覆盖
14. ventilation system 通风系统
15. heat insulation and shading equipment 隔热遮阳设备
16. fertigation system 灌溉施肥系统
17. grading facility 分级设施
18. non-destructive quality evaluation device 无损型质量评价装置
19. refrigerating equipment 冷藏设备，制冷设备
20. unwoven fabric 无纺布
21. cheesecloth *n.* 薄纱棉布，纱布
22. polyethylene terephthalate (PETP) 聚对苯二甲酸乙二酯(醇)，俗称聚酯
23. fluorine *n.* 氟；ETFE 聚氟乙烯，乙烯-四氟乙烯塑料，四氟乙烯共聚物
24. polyolefin-based (PO) film 聚烯烃膜
25. polyethylene (PE) *n.* 聚乙烯
26. ultraviolet ray permeability 紫外线透过性
27. defogging *n.* 驱雾，除雾
28. dehumidification *v.* 除湿，减湿，去湿；*n.* 除湿干燥，降低湿度
29. polypropylene (PP) *n.* 聚丙烯
30. polyester *n.* 聚酯，聚酯纤维
31. polyvinyl alcohol 聚乙烯醇
32. vinylon *n.* 维尼纶（聚乙烯醇纤维）

Exercises

A. **Please answer the following questions in English.**
  1. Please list the main types of greenhouses in Japan.
  2. How to use the heat insulation and shading equipment in summer cultivation?

3. What covering materials are used in tropical region in summer?
4. Please talk about the development of greenhouse cultivation in China.
5. Please list some protected facilities which distribute in the tropical region.

B. Please translate the following paragraph into Chinese.

Ecotype restaurant is based on advanced greenhouse engineering technology, combined with landscaping technology, biology technology. Ecotype restaurant construct embodies talent-oriented and special sculpt and fine light transmission, which keeps the stable humidity and temperature and makes the evergreen natural environment. So it makes people feel naturalness and comfortable, softly, happy and high-spirit.

C. Please translate the following sentences into English.

1. 设施园艺栽培是在不适宜露地栽培园艺植物的季节或地区，利用特定的保护设施创造良好的小气候条件，以获得优质高产的栽培方法。

2. 我国热带、亚热带地区，夏季田间的强辐射、高温、台风、暴雨和病虫多发等灾害性气候，造成夏季蔬菜的生长障碍而出现夏秋缺菜，近年由于采用遮阳网、避雨棚和防虫网覆盖栽培和开放型大棚和温室，有效地缓解了南方夏秋淡季的蔬菜供应。

Part B Innovative Plant Factories

Selected and rewritten from *Innovative Plant Factories*, by Mike Nichols and Bruce Christie.

Early in 2006 we were invited to present a paper on "Organic Hydroponics" at the SHITA Conference in Tokyo, Japan. While in Japan we took the opportunity to visit some of the developments which were occurring in intensive horticulture in the Tokyo area. We have already reported on our greenhouse experiences in the previous issue, and this report concerns plant factories of which Japan is probably the world leader. We were hosted by Professor Shinohara from Chiba University and his colleagues, who arranged all our visits.

The plant factories in Japan that produce crops under controlled environmental conditions and optimized for the particular crop. These production units were designed to produce high-quality food in all seasons with minimal pesticide usage, and very efficient use of water.

Plant factories can be classified as semi-closed where some natural light is used in plant production to offset some of the lighting costs, or as a totally enclosed facility where all the light is provided artificially and the environment is totally controlled for maximum plant productivity.

A number of totally enclosed plant factories were established in the United States, such as Phytofarms in Illinois and Geniponics in New York, and Alaska where the outdoor environment precludes all-year-round plant production. A number of these facilities developed special innovations to cope with the excess heat produced by the high intensity discharge lamps and the challenge of optimizing plant spacing. These factories ultimately proved to be uneconomic and not commercially viable by the early 1990s in the United States. In Japan, however, they built on the ideas used by the Americans to develop plant factories, and many have been economically sustainable so far over a period of about 30 years. It has been suggested the high value of land and other inputs, plus some genuine innovation, has been the reason plant factories have survived and in the main appear to be going from strength to strength.

To be economically viable, plant factories must convert as much of the energy input from electricity into light and then marketable plant material. The majority of the plant factories utilize fluorescent lights, which are very efficient at converting electricity into light. They also have the advantage of producing relatively little heat from the tube producing the light, so they can be placed close to plant leaves with little risk of damage.

Currently, there are about 40 plant factories operating in Japan, with prototypes being tested in China as proof of concept before going into large scale production in regions of the world where the climate is hostile for reliable food plant production.

In 1990, the Cosmo Plant Company, led by Hisakazu Uchiyama, developed an innovative approach to lighting using light emitting diodes (LEDs), which held considerable promise due to their long life and increasing efficiency at energy conversion to specific wavelengths close to the action spectra of many crop plants. We now know that LEDs use about 2% of the power required by standard incandescent bulbs and will last about 10 times longer than a fluorescent tube and more than a hundred times the life of an incandescent bulb. Some of the durability comes about because LEDs do not have a filament that can be broken during handling.

In recent years, significant advances have been made in the manufacturing of LED bulbs. Once used only as power indicators on appliances, LEDs can now de used to light a room or in powerful flashlights. It is generally considered that LEDs will provide the next generation of lighting for plant factories, if only because they are able to produce radiation (light) of specific wavelength.

Plant Factory Visits

Green Labor Shop　At the Green Labor Shop (Fig. 26-2) with a floor area of 60 m^2 they produce 300 lettuces per day to supply six shops. The light are between 220 mm and 250 mm from the plants and the shelves are seven high, giving a productive area of 168 m^2 About 600, 32W fluorescent lamps are operated on a 16-hour photoperiod. The operator uses ozone to clean the nutrient solution, and only replace the solution twice a year.

Urban Farm　The Urban Farm crop range includes basil, chervil, and several different types of lettuce. Daily production, if devoted solely to lettuce, would be 1500 plants per day. Only half of the fluorescent lights have been replaced in the last seven years and electricity is approximately 25% of the operating costs at the Urban Farm. Vegetable products

Fig. 26-2　Green labor shop

are promoted as pesticide-free and free of soil. The farm has a uniform supply with a fixed-price throughout the year. In addition, vegetable products contain higher levels of vitamin A and sugar than those produced outdoors.

Cosmo Plant Factories The Cosmo Plant Factories opened the world's first commercial plant factory growing plants using light emitting diodes in the year 2000. The Cosmo Plant Farm uses mainly red (660 nm) and some blue LEDs. Until recently, most Cosmo Plant Factories were producing up to 7,000 lettuces per day when the company got into financial difficulties. Uchiyama is credited with most of the experimentation and technical innovation behind the Cosmo Plant production units.

The Future

There is little doubt in our minds that plant factories will be the way of the future, but in the short term the use of plant factories for propagating young vegetable seedlings would appear to have the greatest merit.

Consumers, whether they are the final consumer or the supermarkets/shops, require two things from vegetables-continuity of supply and quality.

Growing vegetables in the field (or even in a greenhouse) is weather dependant, and by growing the seedlings for a significant part of the life cycle in a totally controlled environment means the variations in maturity time can be significantly reduced, raising the possibility of producing two crops in the time when one would normally be grown.

One interesting factor to appear is that the leaf growth in a plant factory is different from that in a greenhouse.

Plant factories would appear to be the way of the future, perhaps not today, or even tomorrow, but with their greatly enhanced water efficiency, it will only be a short time before improved lighting systems will permit high value crops to be grown anywhere on the globe for local consumption.

In the short term, plant factories are already capable of providing an enhanced environment for producing high quality vegetables seedlings for industry.

Glossary

1. organic hydroponics 有机水培
2. fluorescent light 荧光灯，荧光
3. prototype *n.* 原型，原型系统
4. light emitting diode 发光二极管
5. incandescent bulb 白炽灯泡

Questions

1. Please define and evaluate the ***plant factory***.
2. Please classify the plant factory according to the information in this text.
3. Which kinds of light are used in the plant factory?

Lesson 27

Part A Greenhouse Construction

Selected and rewritten from *Greenhouse Management*, by J. J. Hanan • W. D. Holley & K. L. Goldsberry, and *The Solar Greenhouse Book*, by James C. McCullagh.

It is assumed the greenhouse operator has already evaluated the market potential that would be related to a new greenhouse business or expansion of present facilities. In either case, it is important that plans for all phases of greenhouse construction be developed and a tentative budget formulated. Such a procedure is part of good management. The plans will be required by the local building authority and complete plans, budget and projected income solicited by all potential financial lending agencies.

Basic Considerations

Location

"The location of a range of glass for commercial purposes, where the elements of expense and profit are to have first consideration, is of great importance." These words by Liberty Hyde Bailey are just as important today as they were then. Bailey went on to point out that the desirability of a location is also based on the adaptability and value of the land, cost of fuel delivered, ample and inexpensive water and the proximity to market.

Utilities

One of the major considerations for a greenhouse complex is utilities. Compromises in marketing potential and geographical location may have to be considered when utilities, especially fuel, are sought. The energy crisis of the 1970s curtailed greenhouse construction and prudent planning will be required to meet the utility needs of the operator in the future.

Climate

Another factor involved in location planning is weather conditions. What is the yearly available solar energy? How much moisture falls, summer and winter? What are the maximum and minimum temperatures and their duration? What are the hail and wind belts? Is air pollution a potential problem? Information on all of the foregoing questions allows the greenhouse operator to determine the degree to which he can maintain near optimum environmental conditions for plant growth. In some areas of the world, the availability of light is paramount, but where solar energy is abundant, other climatological factors take precedence. Information on climatic conditions can be obtained from government climatological reports, local weather stations and, if one has enough interest, much can be learned through communications with some of the "old-timers" in a community.

Topography

Another important consideration is the topography and soil type of the proposed building site. A building site of uniform grade, with a slight slope is most desirable. If ground beds are to be considered using the existing soil, little or no grading should be accomplished unless there is assurance the remaining soil will be reasonably consistent in texture, structure and depth. Water drainage in the subsoil horizons is also very important. Many greenhouses have been built on land where poor drainage exists and there are continuous nutrient, disease, and water problems.

Basic Layout

One of the merits of being able to build a new greenhouse facility is the opportunity to provide adequate growing, work, shipping, and storage space. Not all greenhouse complexes need the same type of facilities, but all need to be planned and laid out so expansion can occur easily and material handling systems employed.

The impact of the bedding plant business in the United States has contributed more to the planning of industry related facilities, than all the recommendations from extension personnel or professors for the past 50 years. Growers switching from other floricultural crops to bedding plants have found they need to modify their present facilities to meet the needs of handling a different crop.

The Greenhouse Orientation

The orientation of a proposed greenhouse structure should be included in the "layout" plans. By combining the climatological data available, one should be able to locate growing facilities for minimum effects of adverse winds and maximum available solar energy.

Wind Effects

Most geographical areas have at least one prevailing wind and many have two; one during summer months and another during the winter. Greenhouses with double top ventilators are adaptable to such conditions because a leeward vent can always be opened if needed.

The direction of the prevailing wind does not always indicate the direction of the higher velocity winds. On days when exhaust fans are operating and high winds keep the louvers closed, greenhouse temperatures can climb. Many greenhouse exhaust fans are the non-loading types and cannot function against winds approaching 20 mph(1mph=0.44704 m/s).

Damaging winds are generally associated with storms and there were no way to predict how they will affect the greenhouse structure. Only sound craftsmanship will sustain the majority of storms.

Wind can be modified by constructing fences of varying heights or growing trees and shrubs for windbreaks. Information that is available indicates a solid windbreak, which creates turbulence, is much less effective than one which allows a small amount of wind to pass through; windbreaks open in the lower portion allow the wind to push through the openings and shoot upward on the leeward side.

Greenhouse operators should consult wind experts before constructing a windbreak as some designs could cause turbulence over a greenhouse range and property damage.

Shading Effects

Shading by surrounding terrain, buildings and plant materials can affect plant growth and perhaps cost the grower money (Fig. 27-1).

Solar Energy Effects

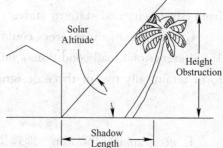

Fig. 27-1 Ratio of shadow length and obstruction height for selected solar

Through the years there has been much concern over the proper orientation of greenhouse structures in relation to the compass rose. Lawrence (1963) demonstrated that an E-W oriented glasshouse received more solar radiation than did N-S structures in Bayfordbury, England. Harnett (1974) reported that studies by L. G. Morris, at the National Institute of Agricultural Engineering, verified the work by Lawrence and showed further that insolation received in an E-W multispan house was greater than an N-S oriented greenhouse. Manbeck and Aldrich (1967) found that an east-west oriented house is preferable in northern latitudes above 40°~45°in the winter, but at other times of the year and at lower latitudes the N-S orientation is preferred.

Hainan (1970) compared the total shortwave radiation received in an N-S oriented FRP covered house to an E-W glasshouse and found that little difference occurred. He concluded that as far as solar transmittance is concerned, at latitudes approximately 42°N, there was little advantage of an E-W oriented house over an N-S house whether glass or FRP was used.

Standards for Construction

Few architects or engineers have a background in greenhouse construction and design. Consequently, many cities, counties, and states have based design requirements on the Uniform Building Code standards. In short, greenhouses in most areas of the world must conform to the same standards of design and construction as those used for homes and other small buildings.

During the past quarter century, greenhouses have been redesigned by growers, amateur engineers, and architects and plant enthusiasts. Configurations have been numerous and superstructure materials unbelievable. Oil well sucker rod, electrical conduit, plastic pipe, rolled metal and fiberglass reinforced plastic have been used for greenhouse framework, along with the standard materials of steel pipe, angle iron, wood, and aluminum.

Little, if any, attention has been given to the structural strengths of construction materials, especially by neophytes in the greenhouse business. Some greenhouse manufacturers have also overlooked structural needs in order to provide a more competitive product.

It is apparent that the geographical location has a definite bearing on structural needs and possibly greenhouse design. Structures in Wisconsin must consider ice and snow loads, those in Colorado are concerned with wind factors, while those in southern California are primarily interested in keeping rain and potential frost off plants. Fire codes will also vary from city to city and state to state.

Greenhouse manufacturers could conceivably manufacture greenhouse designs for 10~15 different total load conditions, but they cannot afford to customize each job and, therefore, retain only two or three designs, based on load factor needs.

Glossary

1. geographical location　地理位置
2. wind belts　风带
3. uniform grade　均匀坡度
4. water drainage　排水
5. poor drainage　排水不良
6. basic layout　基本布局
7. material handling systems　物料处理系统
8. greenhouse orientation　温室放线、定位
9. climatological data　气象资料
10. prevailing wind　主导风，盛行风
11. ventilator　n. 通风设备，通风装置
12. exhaust fan　排气扇，风机
13. louver　n. 百叶窗
14. greenhouse structure　温室结构
15. turbulence　n. 紊流，湍流
16. solar altitude　太阳高度角
17. E-W oriented house　东西走向温室
18. N-S oriented house　南北走向温室
19. multispan　adj. 连栋，连跨
20. latitude　n. 纬度
21. FRP（fiber reinforced plastic）玻璃钢
22. solar transmittance　太阳能透射率
23. Uniform Building Code standards　统一的建筑规范标准
24. electrical conduit　电缆
25. greenhouse framework　温室骨架
26. angle iron　角钢
27. aluminum　n. 铝型材
28. load　n. 荷载

Exercises

A. Please answer the following questions in English.

1. What kinds of factors need to be considered of greenhouse construction?
2. What kinds of elements need to be considered of greenhouse basic layout?
3. From what aspects can the wind influence the direction of greenhouse?
4. What are the relationships between the solar radiation and greenhouse direction?
5. How to solve the problem that there are no Uniform Building Code standards of greenhouse construction?

B. Please translate the following paragraph into Chinese.

The major vertical support of greenhouses is provided by rafters placed on two to four foot centers, depending on the strength needed. Depending on the width of the structure, truss or curved arch type rafters are used. Purlins are arranged horizontally and connect the rafters. Four to eight foot spacings are used depending on the size of the greenhouse. Cross ties are also used in certain houses. In areas where high winds occur, purlins are important in maintaining structural integrity of the greenhouse.

C. Please translate the following sentences into English.

1. 温室要与其南侧（向阳方）的建筑物、树木之间留出足够的距离，以保证温室的采光。东西两侧也要注意障碍物的遮光。温室北侧要便于通风、安装和维修。

2. 温室的朝向，指的是温室屋脊的走向。温室的朝向应结合当地纬度及主风向综合考虑。一般来说，我国大部分纬度范围内，温室的朝向宜取南北走向，使温室内各部位的采光比较均匀。若限于条件，必须取东西走向，应妥善布置室内走廊和栽培床，或适当采取局部人工补光措施，使作物栽培区得到足够的光照。

Part B Greenhouse Design

Selected and rewritten from *Greenhouse Management*, by J. J. Hanan • W. D. Holley &K. L. Goldsberry, and *The Solar Greenhouse Book*, by James C. McCullagh.

The glass covered structures have been limited in style. Many greenhouse structures classed as "lean-to or shed roof", even and uneven span, and "hillside" houses are still found throughout the world (Fig. 27-2). Some of these types are economically impractical and would not meet today's requirements of controlled environment. The sawtooth styles, however, have been instrumental in the development of the floriculture industry in Central America as well as other countries and are being considered in the US.

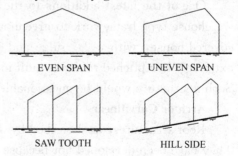

Fig. 27-2 Greenhouse styles still in use around the world

Until recent years, the pitch of the glasshouse roof has been of paramount importance. Based on physical phenomena related to the interception of the sun's "rays", designers found that a roof pitch of 35° was most satisfactory and less than 26° deterred snow removal and increased the possibility of "drip" due to condensation on the underside of the glass.

The twentieth century has provided the greenhouse industry with numerous roof pitches, shapes and designs. Researchers in Europe and other northern latitude countries have been concerned with greenhouse designs because of minimum light energy conditions.

Lawrence discussed the merits of four basic greenhouse shapes. The structure providing the maximum light transmission is the curved or semicircular roof. Since it is almost impossible to use glass on such a structure, the British designed a house with sloping side walls, which provides more light transmission efficiency than the conventional peak design. Thus, the Mansard design, which allows solar energy to be transmitted at an angle of incidence never greater than 40°, is recommended for the British greenhouse growers.

The introductions of plastic coverings and modern cooling techniques have allowed several modifications in greenhouse design in the past twenty years.

Free Standing Structures

Most greenhouses manufactured in the United States are patterned after the standard peak or arc type structures (Fig. 27-3).

Peak Roof

Structures are generally designed to be covered with glass or FRP panels. Some growers are covering "peak" structures with double layer film materials for air inflated purposes; in many instances, as an interim structure until they are financially able to install permanent coverings.

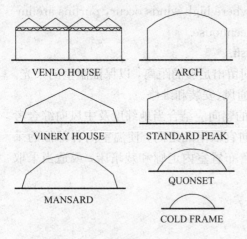

Fig. 27-3 Basic greenhouse structures common in the United States

One of the latest additions to the free standing design is the adaptation of industrial warehouse type framework to greenhouse needs. A 125×500′, 4 oz (1oz=28.35g) FRP covered house, with a 24′ ridge and 10′ eave was completed in 25 working days. The extremely low pitched roof was built in Waco, Texas, where snow is practically unknown. Such a structure would be questionable further north in some geographical locations.

Arch or Curvilinear

Roof structures, as described by Taft, have become the leading design of the 1970s. They have been developed not because of the light transmission considerations. But due to economic factors; they can be constructed for approximately 25% less cost than a peak roof structure. The curved or arched roof is also easily adaptable to both rigid and film coverings.

The arch type structure has been modified into several designs. Hardly a year goes by, when one of the greenhouse manufacturers or greenhouse operators introduces a "new and better" structure.

The quonset style structure can be designed low to the ground and used as temporary cold frames or placed on columns of any height to meet the crop requirements. The value of the arch or curved roof greenhouse is outstanding.

The Air-Inflated System

The greatest boon to the United States greenhouse industry in the last half century has been the air-inflated system of greenhouse construction. Dr. William Roberts (1968) an Agricultural Engineer at Rutgers University was instrumental in introducing the concept.

Air-inflated structures have a double layer plastic film cover that is kept relatively rigid and in place pneumatically. The double film, perferably 6 mil is pulled snugly over the superstructure and seal fastened to the structure at all outer edges.

Inflation is accomplished by using a small, approximately 1/70 hp, squirrelcage blower to pump air between the layers. It is recommended that the makeup air be taken from outside the greenhouse, because it is usually dryer and helps prevent condensate between the layers.

A maximum static pressure between the two film layers should range from 0.2 (6 mm) to 0.5 (12 mm) inches of water, depending on external wind pressures. A pressure of 0.2 in. is sufficient in 20~25 mph (1mph=0.44704 m/s) winds. In January, 1971, a Colorado State University Monsanto 602 (Trade Name) covered, air-inflated quonset ($20 \times 50'$) withstood winds of 30~70 mph over a 24-h period that contained a peak gust of 110 mph. The damper on the blower was completely open during this period of time.

The static pressure between the film layers can be measured with a simple manometer as described by Sheldrake: "One end of a piece of 0.25 in. (6mm) clear plastic tubing can be pushed through a small hole in the inside film layer. The tube remaining in the greenhouse should be bent to form a 10~12 in. (25~30 cm) U-tube and attached to the greenhouse superstructure with a small ruler positioned behind it. After 6~8 in. (15~20 cm) of water is poured into the U-tube, the water-column pressure can be measured by observing the difference between the levels of the water on both sides of the U. A difference of 0.25 in. (6 mm) is adequate (0.2 in. water column is approximately one pound per ft^2) (1 pound=0.45 kg, $1ft^2$=0.09 m^2)."

A recent innovation of the air-inflated system involves a flat roof superstructure of steel, wood, or cable. Scientific Farms of San Antonio, Texas, has a channel iron-frame air-inflated structure that is used for tomato production. Roberts described research conducted on an air-inflated cable supported greenhouse. The structure has potential in many areas of the world and could be easily modified to a cloth type house for summer use.

The air inflated system has been adapted to both peaked roof (Sheldrake, 1971) and arch greenhouse superstructures which in turn have been developed as facilities ranging from animal shelters to swimming pools.

Ridge and Furrow Configurations

The basic configuration for commercial greenhouse structures in the United States is the ridge and furrow house. They are least expensive to build, conserve ground area and require less fuel for heating than the free standing types. Such structures are generally used for production of a single plant species such as carnations, roses, pot mums or crops that can tolerate comparable environmental conditions.

The greenhouse of the 1970s combines the free standing peak or arch structures to form a ridge and furrow facility that can be readily covered with greenhouse grade plastic materials and even include the air inflated system.

The only limitation on the area covered by a ridge and furrow structure is the distance between the fan and cooling pad area. This should be limited to approximately 200 ft (1ft =30.48 cm), but will be discussed in more detail in the chapter on temperature.

There are some disadvantages to the ridge and furrow structures, namely reduced light due to shadows from the eaves and other superstructure, and the possibility of snow accumulation over the eaves. The plastic covers on arched ridge and furrow houses are less likely to present light problems than standard glasshouses, especially in "high light" areas. Snow load over the eaves is still a potential problem. Several greenhouses are underdesigned for weather conditions that only exist once in 25 years. Others are underdesigned for any snow load, especially at the eaves. Ridge and furrow houses must be designed and constructed to withstand all the load factors or they could fall like dominoes.

Glossary

1. shed roof　单坡屋顶
2. even span　等坡（屋顶）
3. roof pitch　屋面坡度
4. light transmission　透光率
5. free standing structure　落地式结构
6. peak roof　尖屋顶
7. low pitched roof　缓坡屋顶
8. quonset style structure　拱圆式结构
9. ridge and furrow house　有屋脊和天沟的温室（连栋式温室）
10. underdesigned　*adj.* 设计安全系数不足的

Questions

1. What kinds of greenhouse styles are still used in the world?
2. What are the basic roof structures of greenhouse in America?
3. Briefly state the advantages and disadvantages of multispan greenhouse.

Lesson 28

Part A Environmental Control of Protected Cultivation

Selected and rewritten from *Environmental Control of Protected Cultivation*, by Dr. Satoru Tsykagoshi.

The environmental control of greenhouses aims at artificially creating the conditions suited to the plant, and covers such factors as light, temperature, humidity, CO_2 concentration, air flow, soil, temperature and soft moisture. The accessing point for control is clearly defined for each of these factors, and a variety of controlling devices have been developed. However, the greenhouse environment is affected by the outside environment, and each environmental factor is under the influence of two or more other environmental factors.

Light Control

The light that reaches the greenhouse is partly blocked by covering materials, frameworks and other obstacles, and only 60 to 70 percent of it can enter the facility. One of the methods for increasing the amount of light inside the greenhouse is supplemental lighting. While it is technically possible to supplement light of tens of kilolux, the use of supplemental lighting is limited because of very high equipment and energy costs.

In summer, shading the light is widely carried out to reduce the excessive sunlight and to prevent excessive high temperature in the greenhouse. Cheesecloth is a main material used to protect the plants. Meshed plastic sheets such as PE and PVA are also widely used. Aluminum layered films is effectively used as heat insulation curtains.

The artificial lighting is used for photoperiodic treatment with illuminating light of several lux to tens of lux to extend the daylength. A good example was chrysanthemum culture from early on, and artificial lighting is now employed for the cultivation of strawberries, perillas and some other crops. In the case of strawberries, incandescent lamp are installed in the facility at a height of 120 to 150 cm above the plants and at a rate of 3.5 to 4 W/m^2; and the artificial illumination is started in mid-November to mid-December. To shorten the daylength, soft polyvinyl chloride (PVC) films are mainly used as covering materials.

Temperature Control

When the temperature in the greenhouse rises too high in the daytime, the heat is discharged into outside by ventilation, and at night when the thermometer fails, the room temperature is kept at optimum for plant growth by heat insulation and heating. The most popular heating method in Japan is warm air heating, which is adopted by about 88% of the facilities equipped with heating devices. The length and layout of warm air ducts should be properly adjusted to realize a uniform temperature distribution in the greenhouse. Warm water heating follows, accounting for about 8%. Recently, thermal insulating screen in terms of water curtain, by groundwater is sprinkled over the curtains in the facility, is increasing.

To control these excessive high temperatures, fine mist cooling, which utilizes the heat of vaporization of water, has recently been introduced; the total area where fine mist cooling is used is estimated at about 1,000 ha at present. Pad and fan cooling is employed at some propagation greenhouses and potted plant cultivation. Since cooling is needed only for about two months in summer and does not always lead to advantages in farm management, the use of cooling systems has not increased quickly.

CO_2 Control

The introduction of CO_2 application in Japan was started around 1965, and by about 1975, many kinds of CO_2 generating systems were available on the market. But some generators did not come into wide use because proper directions were not understood, resulting in unstable effects, and also because their combustion units were of poor quality and generated toxic gases. As a result of subsequent studies and experiments, lowered prices of CO_2 concentration sensors and control equipment, and improvement in the control accuracy, the acreage where CO_2 generating systems are introduced is on the increase since 1991. CO_2 generating systems are divided into two types: the liquid CO_2 gas devises and the generator of LP gas or kerosene. The former is suited for automatic control by a sensor. Although different according to the crop, the CO_2 concentration is considered to be kept at 5×10^{-4} to 6×10^{-4} on a cloudy day and at 1×10^{-3} to 1.2×10^{-3} on a fine day.

Humidity Control

In general protected cultivation, the effect of irrigation, temperature and ventilation on the humidity in the facility is intricate. The accuracy of the humidity sensor becomes poor when the humidity goes up to 90 percent or more, and once dew is formed on the surface of the sensor, the sensor cannot accurately indicate the humidity for a long time thereafter. Because of this, neither strict humidity control nor automatic control is carried out at present. Commonly used methods for humidity control include humidification by sprinkling over the passage in the greenhouse or by a misting device, humidity control by the mulching of rows and passages, and discharging of water condensing on the covering material into the outside.

Air flow Control

The rate of air flows in the greenhouse is influenced by the outside wind velocity, ventilation rate, convection caused by temperature differences, and the shape of the greenhouse. To increase the air flow rate positively, an air circulating fan is used. Elevating the air flow rate not merely helps to make the greenhouse environment uniform but also contributes to activating plant photosynthesis and to the prevention of diseases.

Soil Temperature Control

In hydroponics, it is a general practice to install warm and cold water pipes for the purpose of controlling the temperature of the growing media and nutrient solution. But in soil culture, the cooling of the underground part has little been introduced except in part of flowering plant cultivation. For soil heating, electric cables are used in propagation facilities and in small facilities in some cases, but in general protected cultivation, mulching is widely used and more positive soil heating systems are not adopted.

Recently, a deep-layer soil heating system, by which plastic tubes are buried in the ground about 60 cm deep is available on the market. By heating antifreeze, instead of water, with a boiler, this system can keep the soil temperature about 20 cm in depth at 20°C or so. If the system is used together with solar heat soil disinfection in summer, the temperature of the soil 60 cm deep or more can be raised to 50°C or more, and so soil disinfection can be carried out more effectively.

Soil Moisture Control

There are many kinds of watering methods in the commercial greenhouse. Overhead sprinkling is the system by which sprinkling is made by an appliance mounted on the upper part of the facility, and can sprinkle water over a wide area in a relatively short period of time. In soil surface sprinkling, water is sprinkled from a device placed on the ground, and this method is used most widely in protected cultivation. Underground sprinkling is the method of sprinkling water from the tube buried in the ground over a long period of time; this system is not widely used in protected cultivation mainly because the sprinkling work cannot be monitored from above the ground and so it is difficult to control the amount of water.

Micro-sprinklers are the small-size versions of ordinary sprinklers used in the open field, and are employed for overhead and soil surface sprinkling. Small nozzles can be fixed to PVC pipes at regular intervals and jet out water. Multi-pore pipes are the pipes or soft tubes with pores at regular intervals, and are widely used in open field cultivation, too. The use of drip watering appliances is increasing as the acreage of soil culture fertilized with nutrient solution is expanding. Porous tubes are made from rubber or ceramics, and the water oozing out of them is provided to the plant. These tubes are mainly used for underground sprinkling.

Multiple Environment Control

The multiple management and control of the environmental factors in the greenhouse enable the production of high-level and high-quality crops.

Based on such data as temperature, light intensity, precipitation, CO_2 concentration, the aperture of ridge and side vents, wind velocity and wind direction, the computer for multiple environment control coordinates individual control devices so that the greenhouse environment is able to become a better one for the plant. The computer can also take emergency steps: to shut the windward ventilation windows when strong winds begin to blow, to close the ridge vents when rain begins to fall, etc. Troubles of the control equipment or sensors and warnings on abnormal states are reported to the farmer concerned by mobile phone or by other means. The computer also has the function of a data logger and analyzer of environmental data and is linked to the cultivation support center by the Internet; therefore, the users are able to quickly contact the center and to receive aid from it based on the analyzed data.

Glossary

1. air flow　气流
2. light control　光量控制
3. supplemental lighting　补光
4. kilolux　*n.* 千勒克司
5. aluminum layered film　缀铝膜
6. photoperiodic　*adj.* 光周期的
7. illuminating light　补光灯
8. artificial illumination　人工光源
9. daylength　*n.* 日照时间
10. warm air heating　热风供暖
11. uniform temperature　恒温
12. water curtain　水幕
13. mist cooling　喷雾降温
14. pad and fan cooling　风机湿垫降温
15. CO_2 generating system　CO_2发生系统
16. combustion unit　点火设备
17. CO_2 concentration sensor　CO_2浓度传感器
18. LP gas　液化石油气
19. humidity control　湿度调节
20. humidity sensor　湿度传感器
21. misting device　喷雾器
22. discharging of water　排水量
23. air flow control　气流控制
24. wind velocity　风速，风力
25. ventilation rate　换气次数
26. air circulating fan　循环风扇

27. deep-layer soil heating system　深层土壤加热系统
28. individual control device　分级控制装置
29. data logger　数据记录器

Exercises

A. Please answer the following questions in English.

1. What are the factors of Environmental Control of Protected Cultivation?
2. What are the measures of greenhouse light controlling?
3. What are the main methods of greenhouse cooling?
4. Why some parts of CO_2 generating system can not be popularized?
5. What kinds of project measures of soil moisture control can be commonly seen?

B. Please translate the following paragraph into Chinese.

The primary form of insulation for a greenhouse is the double layer of plastic on the top, side walls, and end walls. However, the north wall can be insulated more thoroughly than with double poly (on a north-south oriented greenhouse). Not enough light enters the greenhouse through the north end wall to supplement light from the other walls and top. Therefore, construct a solid wall. This can be insulated with polystyrene boards, fiberglass batting, or any other means. The wall can be finished with plywood or with any other suitable material.

C. Please translate the following sentences into English.

1. 为了减少进入温室内的热量，需控制日射与增加防热功能，并促进通风。由于本地区温室有许多为开放或半开放式建筑，所以在建设地的选择与结构设计上应以增加通风为着眼点。若仍不满足降温需求，可再配合风机强制通风或采用蒸发冷却方式等来缓和暑热。

2. 自然通风在冬天效果最好，因为室内外空气的温差最大。由于空气温差，可使屋顶排气孔成为绝佳的出气口，侧面排气孔大则成为绝佳的进气口；当天气很热时，内外的空气温差就很小，甚至不存在，自然通风效果不明显。

Part B　Cooling Greenhouse

Selected and rewritten from *Greenhouse Management*, by J. J. Hanan · W. D. Holley & K. L. Goldsberry.

Air Cooling Systems

Evaporative Pads

The pad and fan method of cooling greenhouses revolutionized the industry. Prior to its use, many growers left their greenhouses vacant in the summer because of excessive temperatures. If plants were grown, the greenhouses had to be heavily shaded in order to achieve good quality and production and provide decent working conditions for employees.

Evaporative pad cooling is one of the most inexpensive methods of lowering the temperature inside any building. It does, however, increase the humidity which is often undesirable. It is very impractical to consider cooling greenhouses with refrigeration systems as it will require approximately two tons of refrigeration per 750 ft^3 (1ft^3 = 0.028 m^3) of greenhouse to maintain desirable growing temperatures. Such a system of cooling would require the total volume of air to be cooled and not just the area immediately surrounding the plants.

Aspen excelsior pads have been the primary material for evaporative cooling systems. The excelsior is made by shredding *Populus tremuloides*, which is made into mats by enclosing it in a cloth netting. The mats are then replaced in a framework forming a solid pad area.

The cooling efficiency of aspen pads is dependent on several variables including density, thickness, salt accumulation, dirt and age. Studies have found that pad thickness was important and that a 1.5-in. (1in. = 2.54 cm) thickness was superior to a 2-in. heavier material for cooling efficiency. The thinner pad has been unacceptable, however, because of thin spots. In 1960, Holley and Manring observed the cooling efficiency of new and one year old aspen pads. New pads lowered the air temperature 3.9~4.4℃.

Other cooling pad materials include impregnated paper, "hog hair" and aluminized paper. Where neoprene covered hog's hair has been used, some growers have reported good results with pads up to two years, provided that excessive salts do not accumulate.

The latest addition to the selection of cooling pads is the impregnated rigid paper material (Fig. 28-1). It is self-supporting and requires only a superstructure with anti-rot salts, wetting agents and fungicides impregnated in a cross fluted paper material.

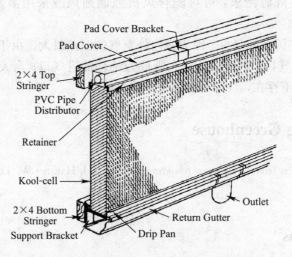

Fig. 28-1　Installation material for Kool-cell

Cooling Pad Design

The cooling pad system needs to be properly designed in order to cool a house to within 3～4℃ of the outside wet bulb temperature. The size of the pad system is determined by the total cubic feet per minute of air flow required for forced ventilation. The most uniform distribution of air coming through a cooling pad is accomplished with an installation the full width of the greenhouse.

Most pad systems should be designed to provide at least 0.5 gal. (1 gal. =3.8 L) water per min. per linear foot (1 foot=30.48 cm) of the pad system length. This amount not only provides enough water for wetting the pad, but also provides more than that evaporated.

Conventionally, water for pads is applied through a pipe at the top of the pads (Fig. 28-2). Some greenhouse operators have also used low pressure mist nozzles with relatively good results.

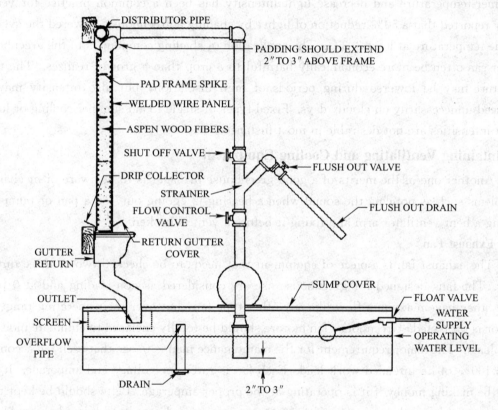

Fig. 28-2 Typical evaporative cooling pad system

Mist Cooling

Some greenhouse environments are more conducive to mist cooling than others. In 1957, Holley found that some rose varieties performed better under mist than when cooled with a fan and pad system. The rose house with top ventilators fully opened, shaded roof and a high pressure mist system in operation, maintained temperatures 4.4℃ above those achieved in a second fan and pad cooled house. Carpenter and Willis observed growth responses of chrysanthemums, snapdragons, and carnations when cooled by mist, fog and fan and pad systems. The fan and pad cooled house provided the best environment for the growth of all plants. When mist is applied in a greenhouse, the air circulation must be such that it flows from the mist nozzles to the plant growing area.

It is possible that growers converting to foliage plant crops should consider mist cooling instead of a fan and pad system. Some foliage plans do not perform well in temperatures normally produced by fan and pad systems. Many species of foliage plants are burned when they are exposed to temperatures above the air stream created by the fans, and a mist cooling should provide a better environment.

Cooling by Shading

The application of a shading compound to the outside of a greenhouse to help control summer temperature and decrease light intensity has been a common practice for years. Gray reported that a 50% reduction of light, by shading a greenhouse, lowered the average inside temperature at least 3.3℃. The application of shading compounds to the greenhouse cover can often be more economically harmful to a crop than a grower realizes. The temperature may be lowered during periods of high insolation, but also intensity may be reduced unnecessarily on cloudy days. Fixed types of shade to aid summer cooling or lower light intensities are not desirable in most instances.

Maintaining Ventilating and Cooling Equipment

Another one of the merits of a good greenhouse manager is to be aware of mechanical problems such as noticing the sound when a bearing is "going out" on a pan or pump or, seeing a bent ventilator arm and fixing it before a vent is broken.

Exhaust Fan

The exhaust fan is a piece of equipment that needs to be checked two or three times a year. The fans designed for greenhouse use are considered as non-loading and at 0 pressure, they have maximum flow like any other type fan, but over their operating range the motor is protected. Greenhouse fan motors should be totally enclosed to eliminate moisture problems. The major requirement for the maintenance man is to see that each fan accomplishes 100% of its intended work load. Each fan is rated for voltage and amperage. It will only be making money if it is operating at the proper amperage. Belts should be kept tight and changed when they start to wear. A temperature rise due to one broken belt could lead to a disaster.

Pad Systems

The evaporative cooling pad also requires maintenance. The aspen pads tend to sag if not installed properly and if the proper weight material is not used. They can also have thin sections that are relatively inefficient.

The accumulation of salts and algae is more of a problem in some areas than others. Algaecides may need to be added periodically where pads are not allowed to dry out before the exhaust fans are de-energized.

The water supply for evaporative cooling pads should be as salt free as possible. If possible, do not use nutrient treated water which has been used for watering plants. Excessive salt build up can be partially removed by periodically "hosing" the pads with a medium pressure nozzle.

Other Equipment

Plastic tubes, louvers, and ventilators all require some attention periodically. When plastic tubes are dirty, they obstruct light transmission, and if they are in a cultured plant house, dust could carry diseases. Louvers on exhaust fans tend to get bent and worn. A louver that does not close in winter could cause some frozen plants. The ventilator on the cooling pad system may not close tightly on a cold fall evening and the water supply pipes could freeze. Maintenance is an important concern of a manager.

Glossary

1. evaporative pad cooling　湿垫蒸发降温
2. refrigeration system　制冷系统
3. cooling efficiency　冷却效率
4. impregnated paper　浸油纸
5. cross fluted　交叉凹槽状
6. mist cooling　喷雾降温
7. exhaust fan　排气扇

Questions

1. Please briefly present the main component elements of pad and fan cooling system.
2. Please briefly present the key points of Cooling Pad Design.
3. Please concisely state the leading measure of temperature cooling.

Lesson 29

Part A Hydroponics

Selected and rewritten from *Hydroponic*, by Yuji Udagawa., *Hydroponic Food Production*, 2nd Edition, by Howard M. Resh, Ph. D., and *Soilless Culture*, by Chen Jingfen.

Introduction

Actually, hydroponics is only one form of soilless culture. It refers to a technique in which plant roots are suspended in either a static, continuously aerated nutrient solution or a continuous flow or mist of nutrient solution. The growing of plants in an inorganic substance (such as sand, gravel, perlite, rock wool) or in an organic material (such as sphagnum peat moss, pine bark, or coconut fiber) and periodically watered with a nutrient solution should be referred to as soilless culture but not necessarily hydroponics. Some may argue with these definitions, as the common conception of hydroponics is that plants are grown without soil, with 16 of the 19 required essential elements provided by means of a nutrient solution that periodically bathes the roots.

Of all the soilless methods, water culture, by definition, is truly hydroponics. Water culture includes aeroponics. In aeroponic systems plant roots are suspended into a closed dark chamber in which jets of nutrient solution are periodically sprayed over them to maintain 100 percent relative humidity.

For successful operation a number of plant requirements must be met.

Root Aeration

This may be achieved in one of two ways. First, forced aeration (by a pump or compressor) is used to bubble air into the nutrient solution through a perforated pipe placed at the bottom of the bed or container. Second, the nutrient solution is circulated with a pump through the beds and back to a reservoir. A series of baffles placed at the end of the beds will aerate the water as it returns to the reservoir. A rate of about one to two complete changes per hour is required for a bed 100 feet (1foot=30.48 cm) long containing from 4 to 6 inches (1inch=2.54 cm) of nutrient solution. Best results can be achieved in a system in which the nutrient solution is pumped into the beds and allowed to flow past the plant roots continuously. In this way freshly aerated solution will be in constant contact with the plant roots.

Root Darkness

Plants can function normally with their roots exposed to light during the daytime, provided they are always at 100 percent relative humidity. However, light will promote the growth of algae, which interferes with plant growth by competing for nutrients, reducing solution acidity, creating odors, competing for oxygen from the nutrient solution at night, and producing toxic products through its decomposition which could interfere with plant growth. To eliminate algae growth construct beds of or cover containers with opaque materials.

Plant Support

Plants may be supported by the use of a litter tray which sits above the nutrient solution as part of the bed.

Advantages and Disadvantages of Hydroponics

Advantages

1. Crops can be grown where no suitable soil exists or where the soil is contaminated with disease. Soilborne plant diseases are more readily eradicated in closed systems, which can be totally flooded with an eradicant.

2. Labor for tilling, cultivating, fumigating, watering, and other traditional practices is largely eliminated.

3. Maximum yields are possible, making the system economically feasible in highdensity and expensive land areas.

4. Conservation of water and nutrients is a feature of all systems. This can lead to a reduction in pollution of land and streams because valuable chemicals need not be lost.

5. A hydroponic system can be clean, lightweight, and mechanized. More complete control of the environment is generally a feature of the system, root environment, timely nutrient feeding or irrigation, and in greenhouse-type operations, the light, temperature, humidity, and composition of the air can be manipulated.

6. Water carrying high soluble salts may be used if done with extreme care. If the soluble salt concentrations in the water supply are over 5×10^{-4}, an open system of hydroponics may be used if care is given to frequent leaching of the growing medium to reduce the salt accumulations.

Disadvantages

1. The original construction cost per square meter is expensive.

2. Trained personnel must direct the growing operation. Knowledge of how plants grow and of the principles of nutrition is important.

3. Introduced soil-borne diseases and nematodes may be spread quickly to all beds on the same nutrient tank of a closed system.

4. Most available plant varieties adapted to controlled growing conditions will require research and development.

5. The reaction of the plant to good or poor nutrition is unbelievably fast. The grower must observe the plants every day.

Main Systems of Hydroponics

Nutrient Film Technique (NFT) This is a hydroponics method by while the nutrient solution is made to flow down in a sate of thin films 1‰. This method can be introduced with a small-sized reservoir, and is characterized by small consumption of nutrient solution and light-weight growing beds. Because of these features, it is easy to establish high bench systems. This system is mostly applied to tomatoes, strawberries, butter-head lettuce and spinach.

NFT growing systems consist of a series of narrow channels through which nutrient solution is re-circulated from supply tank. A plumbing system of plastic tubing and a submersible pump in the tank are the basic components. The channels are generally constructed of opaque plastic film or plastic pipe, asphalt-coated wood and fiberglass also have been used. The basic characteristic of all NFT system is the shallow depth of solution that is maintained in the channels. Flow is usually continuous, but sometimes systems are operated intermittently by supplying solution a few minutes per hour. The purpose of intermittent flow is to assure adequate aeration of the root system. This also reduces the energy required, but under rapid growth conditions, plants could experience water stress if the flow period is too short or infrequent. Therefore, intermittent flow management seems better adapted to mild temperature periods or to plantings during the early stage of development. Capillary matting is sometimes used in the side-to-side meandering of the solution stream around young root systems. But it also acts as a reservoir by retaining nutrients and water during periods when flow ceases.

Fig. 29-1 Tube culture

Tube Culture Tube culture (Fig. 29-1) is a modification of the NFT and water culture. The principles are the same. The nutrient solution is pumped through 4-inch polyvinyl chloride (PVC) drain pipes covered with black polyethylene film. The PVC pipe is cut in half and black polyethylene placed over the top of it to prevent light from entering. Holes are cut in the top of the polyethylene through which seedlings grown in cubes are set into the nutrient solution flowing along the bottom of the PVC pipes. During crop changeover the polyethylene cover and plants are removed, the tube washed with a bleach sterilizing agent and a new polyethylene cover replaced ready for new seedlings.

Deep Flow Technique (DFT) This is one of hydroponics systems in which all or part of the roots is submerged in the nutrient solution. According to the method of oxygen supply to the roots, it is classified into the following four types: (1) air supply method: air is supplied to the nutrient solution to enrich the dissolved oxygen; (2) circulation method: the nutrient solution is caused to circulate to facilitate dissolved oxygen; (3) ebb and flow method: the level of the nutrient solution is varied as ebb and flow; (4) flow-down method: the nutrient solution is caused to flow down to enrich the dissolved oxygen. DFT hydroponics is mainly used for the cultivation of leaf vegetables.

Dynamic Root Floating Hydroponics (DRF)　　High temperature is known to be the limiting factor of growing vegetables during the summer season in tropical region. In order to solve this problem, much research work was done on nutrient culture technique so that to produce the pesticide free and high quality vegetables under the subtropical and tropical condition.

After a series of experiment of various nutrient culture systems, we found that the high temperature coupled with the shortage of dissolved oxygen (DO) in the nutrient are the main reasons why the yield of vegetables is so low in the conventional type of soilless culture under the subtropical and tropical condition.

The designs for various nutrient flow systems had been made to overcome these difficulties. A new system called dynamic root floating (DRF) hydroponics system which had been proven to be ideal to grow various kinds of vegetables not only during the hot summer season but even better in the rest of seasons of a year.

Fig. 29-2　DRF hydroponics system

The DRF hydroponics system (Fig. 29-2) was designed to compose with aero-root type culture unit, aspirator, water level adjuster, the typhoon-proof low-height plastic house and nutrient concentration gradient controller. The controller was designed to keep air space $0 \sim 4$ cm in depth between water level and panel of culture bed. The sufficient oxygen supply is attained through up and down movement ($4 \sim 8$ cm) of water flow with the help of specially designed air aspirator and water level adjuster. Because of ample oxygen supply and keeping root alternatively in wet and semi-dry conditions, the roots grow vigorously all the time, resulted in a high productivity of vegetables even under the high temperature condition.

The DRF system can be installed either in small scale for home garden or extended to be a big commercial production scale. DRF is operated by the automatic system therefore much labor can be saved. This system can withstand against heavy rainfall and free from insect and disease damages if it is properly managed.

Aeroponics　　Aeroponics is the growing of plants in an opaque trough or supporting container in which their roots are suspended and bathed in a nutrient mist rather than a nutrient solution. This culture is widely used in laboratory studies in plant physiology but not as commonly used as other methods on a commercial scale. Several Italian companies are, however, using aeroponics in the growing of numerous vegetable crops such as lettuce, cucumbers, melons and tomatoes.

Media Culture Soilless culture in bags, pots, or troughs with a light-weight medium is the simplest, most economical and easiest to manage of all soilless systems. The most common media used in containerized systems of soilless culture are peat-litter or a mixture of bark and wood chips. Container types range from long wooden troughs in which one or two rows of plants are grown, to polyethylene bags or rigid plastic pots containing one to three plants.

Rock-Wool Culture (Fig. 29-3) Rock-wool is a fibrous material manufactured from diabase and limestone by a special procedure at very high temperature, resulting in a product with very high porosity (3%~5% dry matter). The rock-wool slabs have a stable structure, are homogeneous, sterile and chemically inert. The use of rock-wool as a growth substrate has grown at a very fast rate during the last decade. The main vegetables grown in the system are tomatoes, strawberries and fruit vegetables.

Fig. 29-3 Rock-wool culture

Glossary

1. hydroponic　　*n.* 水培；*adj.* 营养液栽培的
2. inorganic substance　　无机物质
3. gravel　　*n.* 砂砾，砾石
4. perlite　　*n.* 珍珠岩
5. rockwool　　*n.* 岩棉，岩棉纤维
6. sphagnum peat moss　　泥炭藓
7. pine bark　　松树皮
8. coconut fiber　　椰子纤维
9. aeroponic　　*n.* 气培法
10. chamber　　*n.* 腔，室；*adj.* 室内的
11. compressor　　*n.* 压气机，压缩机
12. reservoir　　*n.* 贮液池，水库，蓄水池
13. decomposition　　*n.* 分解，腐烂，分解作用
14. fumigate　　*v.* 用烟熏，熏蒸消毒；fumigant　*n.* 薰剂
15. salt accumulation　　盐分积累，盐累积
16. nematode　　*n.* 线虫，线虫病
17. nutrient film technique(NFT)　　营养液膜技术
18. intermittent flow　　间歇性流动
19. capillary matting　　具毛管作用的垫子
20. tube culture　　管道栽培，管道水培
21. deep flow technique(DFT)　　深液流水培技术

22. dynamic root floating hydroponic (DRF) 动态浮根水培
23. polyvinyl chloride (PVC) 聚氯乙烯
24. diabase n. 辉绿岩
25. limestone n. 石灰岩，石灰石
26. porosity n. 多孔性，有孔性，孔隙度，疏松

Exercises

A. Please answer the following questions in English.
1. What are the requirements for most plants to grow in successful hydroponics?
2. What are the advantages and disadvantages of hydroponics?
3. Please evaluate the main hydroponics systems.
4. How to supply oxygen to the roots in the DFT system?
5. What is the working theory of the DRF system?

B. Please translate the following paragraph into Chinese.

A hydroponic system was developed in the greenhouses in order to evaluate the Deep Flow Technique (DFT) and the Dynamic Root Floating Technique (DRF) for their use in the humid tropics. Using pak-choi plants, an experimental cycle of 23 days was carried out, in which intrinsic parameters of the system were measured, such as pH, electrical conductivity, dissolved oxygen, and chemical composition of the nutrient solution. Temperature conditions in the greenhouse were also registered during the experimental cycle. In four treatments of 30 plants of pak-choi each, the two techniques were evaluated, one treatment with a constant solution level (DFT) and the other with a reduced solution level (DRF). Pak-choi plants grown using the DRF technique produced a higher total fresh weight, foliar, and radical biomass than those under the DFT technique.

C. Please translate the following sentences into English.

1. 无土栽培是指不用天然土壤栽培作物，而将作物栽培在营养液或固体基质中，来代替天然土壤向作物提供水分、养分、氧气和温度，使作物能够正常生长并完成其整个生命周期。

2. 岩棉块有稳定的结构、匀质性好、无毒、化学性稳定，所以在过去的十几年间发展速度很快，容器培或袋培中经常使用岩棉块和其他轻量基质来作为无土栽培中的固体栽培基质。

Part B Type and Management of Nutrient Solution

Selected and rewritten from *Hydroponic*, by Yuji Udagawa.

Nutrient Solution

Characteristics of Nutrient Solution

In hydroponics, all the necessary nutrients are given to the plants in the form of nutrient solution. Of these nutrients, nitrogen, phosphorus, potassium, calcium, magnesium and sulfur are required in large quantities (macronutrients); the absorption ratio of these nutrients differs according to the kind of vegetables, and so the proper composition of nutrient solution is determined for each vegetable. Iron, boron, manganese, zinc, copper and molybdenum are the important nutrients essential for the plant growth although they are needed only in a small quantity (micronutrients).

The nitrogen sources absorbed by vegetables have two types: nitrate nitrogen and ammonium nitrogen. No microbial activities can be expected in hydroponics, and so no ammonium nitrogen can be converted into nitrate nitrogen. When they take in nitrate nitrogen, vegetables can temporarily store the nitrate nitrogen in their leaves if the temperature is too low or the sunshine is insufficient. But because they can store no ammonium nitrogen and the ammonium nitrogen is consumed for the synthesis of amino acids, so-called carbon-nitrogen ratios (C/N) lower and damage from excessive nitrogen is caused. Moreover, if ammonium nitrogen is accumulated in large quantities, plant injuries occur. The ratio of nitrate nitrogen and ammonium nitrogen in the nutrient solution should be adjusted to a proper level.

Water Used for Nutrient Solution

Well water, tap water and rainwater are the main water sources used for dissolving minerals. The quality of well water and tap water greatly varies according to the area and location. For example, the water in the area near the coast and in the site that used to be marshland often has a high content of sodium, chlorine or calcium. Thus the water quality should be inspected in advance. If the water with 5×10^{-5} or more bicarbonate content is used, it becomes difficult to adjust the pH of the nutrient solution; so such water is used after it has been neutralized to less than 5×10^{-5} with phosphoric acids or nitric acids. Rainwater often has a too low content of bicarbonates, and so in this case potassium bicarbonate is added so that its content rises to 3×10^{-5} or more.

How to Make Nutrient Solution

To make nutrient solution, macronutrients are prepared using such mineral salts as potassium nitrate, calcium nitrate, magnesium sulfate, ammonium phosphate and potassium phosphate, whereas chelated iron, boric acids, manganese sulfate and the like are used to make micronutrients. The appropriate composition and concentration of macronutrients differ from plants.

Electric Conductivity (EC) Control

Because the absorption of water and nutrients differs with vegetables and each vegetable has a suitable concentration level of its own, the nutrient solution should be adjusted to the appropriate level. On the other hand, when the concentration of the nutrient solution is increased, the intake of nutrients becomes greater up to a certain level of concentration but the osmotic pressure of the solution rises, which restricts the absorption of water. To control the plant growth utilizing this characteristic, management of the concentration are often used. The control of the concentration is made on the basis of the value of the concentration (in dS/m) of all the nutrients in the nutrient solution measured by EC meter.

pH Control

The pH of the nutrient solution affects the absorption of each nutrient in the solution, while too high or two low pH values cause direct damage to the plant. If the plant absorbs a relatively large quantity of cations, the pH value lowers, and if its anion absorption is relatively great, the pH value increases. For most vegetables, the suitable pH values are 5.5 to 6.5. The pH of the nutrient solution is adjusted in advance using diluted sulfuric acid or potassium hydroxide. Because the roots of vegetables are vulnerable to a sudden pH change, the extent of each pH adjustment is restricted to 0.2 to 0.3.

Solution Temperature Control

While the water absorption of the plant increases with temperature rises, the temperature suited to its nutrient intake is different from vegetable to vegetable. The nutrient absorption is greatly influenced by light and ambient air temperatures. It sometimes becomes necessary to warm the nutrient solution and the growing bed in the cold season and to cool them in the hot season to secure the suitable root temperature, which varies according to the kind of vegetables.

Disease Control Methods

Hydroponics has few risks of soil-borne diseases. But once the nutrient solution and the growing bed are infected with a pathogen, the pathogen quickly increases because no antagonism micro-organisms exist there, causing serious damage to the crop. Thus it is very important to prevent seeds or seedlings from carrying any pathogen into the solution or the growing bed and to avoid the invasion of pathogens into the solution. When a pathogen intrudes into the hydroponics system, the entire system and the solution should be sterilized immediately.

Growing Techniques of Main Vegetables in Hydroponics

Tomato

Sowing and Seedling Culture

Using granulated rock wool, etc., as the growing media, tomato seeds are sown as drill seedling at inter-row spacing of 10 cm and at seed intervals of 1 cm. After germination, the nutrient solution (EC: 2.4 dS/m) is applied in a way that the seedling bed does not dry up. Just before transplanting, the temperature of the seedling bed is kept at a little lower level. Transplanting is conducted at the two true leaves stage. Just after the transplanting, the growing bed and air temperatures are kept at slightly higher levels, and the nutrient solution is applied as needed. When planting is near at hand, the bed and air temperatures are lowered a little again.

Planting

Seedlings are planted at the leaf stages of 5 to 6.

Nutrient Solution Control

Yamazaki's nutrient solution formula for tomato is recommended. In the hot season, to minimize the concentration of ammonium nitrogen as much as possible for preventing blossom-end rot, potassium phosphate is applied instead of ammonium phosphate. Set at 1.2 dS/m at transplanting, the EC is then gradually increased to 2.0 to 2.4 dS/m by the third flower cluster blooming. The nutrient solution is kept at 21°C to 24°C.

Control of the Aerial Environment

The temperature in the greenhouse is maintained at 13°C to 28 °C. The humidity is made higher at night and lower in the day. CO_2 is applied from one month after planting at a concentration of 1×10^{-3}.

Harvesting and Preparation

"First-type" tomatoes are required to be harvested when the coloring has reached about 70 percent, whereas fully-matured varieties and "cherry tomatoes" are harvested after the fruit has totally been colored.

Butter-head Lettuce

Sowing and Seedling Culture

Lettuce seeds are sown on the urethane mat. The humidity is kept at a proper level by piling up sowing boxes or by covering the boxes with plastic films. When radicles appear, the boxes are moved to a greenhouse environment and are greened. The nutrient solution is applied after greening.

Transplanting and Spacing

When the number of true leaves reaches three or so, lettuce seedling are transplanted in foaming polystyrene planting boards 0.6 m × 0.9 m at a rate of 128 plants a board. When true leaves increase to about 7, spacing is made so that each board has 32 plants.

Nutrient Solution Control

Yamazaki's formula for lettuce is recommended. During the hot season, ammonium nitrogen is removed to prevent tip burn and to promote growth, and in the cold season, growth is promoted by increasing the ratio of ammonium nitrogen to over 20 percent of the total nitrogen. In particular, when the nutrient solution is warmed, ammonium nitrogen restricts the succulent growth. The concentration of the nutrient solution is changed according to the cultivars and the light intensity in the growth period, but is about EC 2.4 dS/m in general. The proper temperature of the solution is 20°C in the cold season and 25°C in the hot season.

Control of the Aerial Environment

The higher light intensities are available, the better growth is promoted and better quality is expected. The air temperature is set at 12°C or more in the day and at least at 8°C at night during the winter season. Also, growth is promoted and tip burn is checked by increasing ventilation rates to decrease humidity in the day and by keeping humidity at 95% or more at night. CO_2 is applied at a rate of 8×10^{-4} or 9×10^{-4}.

Harvesting and Preparation

The price of butter-head lettuce is determined according to the number of leaves having a leaf blade width of 11 cm or more, supposing it weighs 80 to 120 g.

Glossary

1. nitrogen   *n.* [化]氮
2. phosphorus   *n.* [化]磷,磷肥
3. potassium   *n.* [化]钾
4. calcium   *n.* [化]钙
5. magnesium   *n.* [化]镁
6. sulfur   *n.* 硫,硫磺
7. macronutrient   *n.* 大量元素,常量营养元素
8. iron   *n.* 铁
9. boron   *n.* 硼
10. manganese   *n.* 锰
11. zinc   *n.* 锌
12. copper   *n.* 铜
13. molybdenum   *n.* 钼
14. micronutrient   *n.* 微量营养素
15. nitrate nitrogen   硝态氮
16. ammonium nitrogen   铵态氮
17. well water   井水
18. tap water   自来水
19. rain water   雨水
20. nitric acid   硝酸
21. bicarbonate   *n.* 碳酸氢,碳酸氢盐
22. potassium nitrate   硝酸钾
23. potassium phosphate   磷酸钾
24. sodium   *n.* 钠
25. chlorine   *n.* 氯
26. calcium nitrate   硝酸钙
27. magnesium sulfate   硫酸镁
28. ammonium phosphate   磷酸铵
29. chelated iron   络合铁
30. boric acid   硼酸
31. manganese sulfate   硫酸锰
32. EC meter   EC 计
33. cation   *n.* 阳离子,正离子
34. diluted sulfuric acid   稀硫酸
35. potassium hydroxide   氢氧化钾
36. pathogen   *n.* 病原菌,病原,病原学

37. antagonism micro-organism　拮抗性微生物
38. granulated rock wool　颗粒状的岩棉，粒化岩棉
39. germination　*n.* 萌发，发芽
40. transplant　*v.* 移植，移栽
41. Yamazaki's nutrient solution formula　山崎营养液配方
42. blossom-end rot　脐腐病
43. urethane mat　聚氨酯垫
44. radicle　*n.* 胚根，幼根，根状部
45. foaming polystyrene　泡沫聚苯乙烯，聚苯乙烯泡沫

Questions

1. What are the characteristics of nutrient solution?
2. How to control the EC and pH of the nutrient solution in hydroponics?
3. How to lower the solution temperature in hydroponics in summer?

Lesson 30

Part A Writing a Research Paper

Selected and rewritten from *Whitesides Group: Writing a Paper*, by George M. Whitesides, and *Writing Research Papers*, by David R. Caprette.

What is a Scientific Paper?

A paper is an organized description of hypotheses, data and conclusions, intended to instruct the reader. Papers are a central part of research. If your research does not generate papers, it might just as well not have been done. "Interesting and unpublished" is equivalent to "non-existent".

Realize that your objective in research is to formulate and test hypotheses, to draw conclusions from these tests, and to teach these conclusions to others. Your objective is not to "collect data".

Outlines

An outline is a written plan of the organization of a paper, including the data on which it rests. You should, in fact, think of an outline as a carefully organized and presented set of data, with attendant objectives, hypotheses and conclusions, rather than an outline of text. It can be relatively efficient to go through several (even many) cycles of an outline before beginning to write text.

The classical approach is to start with a blank piece of paper, and write down, in any order, all important ideas that occur to you concerning the paper. Ask yourself the obvious questions: " Why did I do this work?" "What does it mean?" "What hypothesis did I mean to test?" "What ones did I actually test?" "What were the results?" "Did the work yield a new method? What?" "What measurements did I make?" Sketches possible are figures and schemes. It is essential to try to get the major ideas written down. If you start the research to test one hypothesis, and decide, when you see what you have, that the data really seem to test some other hypothesis better, don't worry, write them both down, and pick the best combinations of hypotheses, objectives and data. Often the objectives of a paper when it is finished are different from those used to justify starting the work.

When you have written down what you can, start with another piece of paper and try to organize the jumble of the first one. Sort all of your ideas into three major heaps (1~3).

1. Introduction

Why did I do the work? What were the central motivations and hypotheses?

2. Results and Discussion

What were the results?

3. Conclusions

What does it all mean? What hypotheses were proved or disproved? What did I learn? Why does it make a difference?

Next, take each of these sections, and organize it on yet finer scale. Concentrate on organizing the data. Construct figures, tables, and schemes to present the data as clearly and compactly as possible. This process can be slow——I may sketch a figure 5～10 times in different ways, trying to decide how it is most clear (and looks best aesthetically).

Finally, put everything—outline of sections, tables, sketches of figures——in good order.

You can then start writing, with some assurance that much of your prose will be used.

What Should a Paper Contain?

1. Title page
2. Abstract
3. Introduction
4. Materials and methods
5. Results
6. Discussion
7. Conclusions
8. References

Title Page

Select an informative title as illustrated in the examples in your writing portfolio example package. Include the name(s) and address(es) of all authors, and date submitted. "Biology lab #1" would not be an informative title, for example.

Abstract

An abstract is a concise single paragraph summary of completed work or work in progress. In a minute or less a reader can learn the rationale behind the study, general approach to the problem, pertinent results, and important conclusions or new questions.

There are three examples as follows.

1) Twenty Years of Transgenic Plants Resistant to Cucumber Mosaic Virus

Morroni M, Thompson JR, Tepfer M.

Plant Virology Group, ICGEB Biosafety Outstation, Via Piovega 23, 31056 Ca' Tron di Roncade, Italy.

ABSTRACT Plant genetic engineering has promised researchers improved speed and flexibility with regard to the introduction of new traits into cultivated crops. A variety of approaches have been applied to produce virus-resistant transgenic plants, some of which have proven to be remarkably successful. Studies on transgenic resistance to Cucumber mosaic virus probably have been the most intense of any plant virus. Several effective strategies based on pathogen-derived resistance have been identified; namely, resistance mediated by the viral coat protein, the viral replicase, and post-transcriptional gene silencing. Techniques using non-pathogen-derived resistance strategies, some of which could offer broader resistance, generally have proven to be much less effective. Not only do the results obtained so far provide a useful guide to help focus on future strategies, but they also suggest that there are a number of possible mechanisms involved in conferring these resistances. Further detailed studies on the interplay between viral transgene-derived molecules and their host are needed in order to elucidate the mechanisms of resistance and pathogenicity.

2) Impact of Wheat Cultivation on Microbial Communities from Replant Soils and Apple Growth in Greenhouse Trials

Mazzola M, Gu YH.

USDA Agricultural Research Service, Tree Fruit Research Laboratory, 1104 N. Western Avenue, Wenatchee, WA 98801

ABSTRACT Studies were conducted to assess the impact of short-term rotations of wheat on microbial community composition and growth of apple in soils from replant orchard sites. Soils from two orchards were cultivated with three successive 28-day growth cycles of "Eltan", "Penewawa", or "Rely" wheat in the greenhouse and subsequently planted to "Gala" apple seedlings. Cultivation of orchard replant soils with any of the three wheat cultivars enhanced growth of apple relative to that achieved in untreated soils. Improved growth was associated with a marked reduction in apple root infection by species of *Rhizoctonia* and *Pythium*. Populations of plant-parasitic nematodes were below damage threshold levels in these orchard soils; however, apple seedlings grown in wheat-cultivated soils had significantly lower root populations of *Pratylenchus* spp. than did seedlings grown in untreated soils. Growth of apple in "Penewawa"-cultivated soils often was superior to that observed in soils planted with "Eltan" or "Rely". In untreated orchard soils, fluorescent pseudomonad populations isolated from soil and the apple rhizosphere were dominated by *Pseudomonas fluorescens* biotype C and *Pseudomonas syringae*. Cultivation of replant soils with wheat induced a characteristic transformation of the fluorescent pseudomonad population, and *Pseudomonas putida* dominated the population of this bacterial group recovered from wheat-cultivated replant orchard soils. Results from this study suggest that use of short-term wheat cropping sequences during orchard renovation could be useful in management of replant disease and that this disease-control option may operate, in part, through modification of the fluorescent pseudomonad community.

3) Influence of Gamma-Radiation on the Nutritional and Functional Qualities of Lotus Seed Flour

Bhat R, Sridhar KR, Karim AA, Young CC, Arun AB.

Food Technology Division, School of Industrial Technology, Universiti Sains Malaysia, Penang 11800, Malaysia.

ABSTRACT In the present study, we investigated the physicochemical and functional properties of lotus seed flour exposed to low and high doses of gamma-radiation (0~30 kGy; the dose recommended for quarantine and hygienic purposes). The results indicated raw seed flour to be rich in nutrients with minimal quantities of antinutritional factors. Irradiation resulted in a dose-dependent increase in some of the proximal constituents. The raw and gamma-irradiated seeds meet the Food and Agricultural Organization World Health Organization recommended pattern of essential amino acids. Some of the antinutritional factors (phytic acid, total phenolics, and tannins) were lowered with gamma-irradiation, while the seed flours were devoid of lectins, 1-3, 4-dihydroxyphenylalanine, and polonium-210. The functional properties of the seed flour were significantly improved with gamma-radiation. Gamma-radiation selectively preserved or improved the desired nutritional and functional traits of lotus seeds, thus ensuring a safe production of appropriate nutraceutically valued products.

Introduction

The introductions should not exceed two pages. The purpose of an introduction is to acquaint the reader with the rationale behind the work, with the intention of defending it. It places your work in a theoretical context, and enables the reader to understand and appreciate your objectives.

Materials and Methods

There is no specific page limit, but a key concept is to keep this section as concise as you possibly can. This should be the easiest section to write, but many students misunderstand the purpose. The objective is to document all specialized materials and general procedures, so that another individual may use some or all of the methods in another study or judge the scientific merit of your work. It is not to be a step by step description of everything you did, nor is a methods section a set of instructions. In particular, it is not supposed to tell a story. By the way, your notebook should contain all of the information that you need for this section.

Results

The page length of this section is set by the amount and types of data to be reported. Continue to be concise, using figures and tables, if appropriate, to present results most effectively. The purpose of a results section is to present and illustrate your findings. Make this section a completely objective report of the results, and save all interpretation for the discussion.

Discussion

The objective here is to provide an interpretation of your results and support for all of your conclusions, using evidence from your experiment and generally accepted knowledge, if appropriate. The significance of findings should be clearly described.

Interpret your data in the discussion in appropriate depth. This means that when you explain a phenomenon you must describe mechanisms that may account for the observation. If your results differ from your expectations, explain why that may have happened. If your results agree, then describe the theory that the evidence supported. It is never appropriate to simply state that the data agreed with expectations, and let it drop at that.

References

List all literature cited in your paper, in alphabetical order, by first author. In a proper research paper, only primary literature is used (original research articles authored by the original investigators). Be cautious about using web sites as references——anyone can put just about anything on a web site, and you have no sure way of knowing if it is truth or fiction. If you are citing an on line journal, use the journal citation (name, volume, year, page numbers). Some of your papers may not require references, and if that is the case simply state that "no references were consulted."

Glossary

1. jumble   *n.* 混杂，混乱
2. rationale   *n.* 理由，逻辑依据，基本原理
3. flexibility   *n.* 机动性，灵活性
4. transgenic   *adj.* 基因改造的，转基因的
5. replicase   *n.* 复制酶
6. post-transcriptional   *adj.* 转录后的
7. pathogenicity   *n.* 病原性，致病性
8. *Rhizoctonia*   *n.* 丝核菌属
9. *Pythium*   *n.* 腐霉属
10. nematode   *n.* 线虫类
11. *Pratylenchus*   *n.* 短体线虫
12. rhizosphere   *n.* 根围（指围绕植物根系在土壤中的一个区域）
13. *Pseudomonas fluorescens*   荧光假单胞菌
14. *Pseudomonas syringae*   丁香假单胞菌
15. physicochemical   *adj.* 物理化学的
16. hygienic   *adj.* 卫生的，清洁的
17. nutraceutically   *adj.* 营养食品的，保健食品的

Exercises

A. Please answer the following questions in English.

1. What is a scientific paper?
2. What are the elements of a research paper? Please describe the necessary parts of a research report.
3. Why do we make an outline before beginning to write text?

4. Which is more important in a research paper, the discussion part or the conclusion part? Why?

B. Please translate the following paragraph into Chinese.

The objective here is to provide an interpretation of your results and support for all of your conclusions, using evidence from your experiment and generally accepted knowledge, if appropriate. The significance of findings should be clearly described.

Interpret your data in the discussion in appropriate depth. This means that when you explain a phenomenon you must describe mechanisms that may account for the observation. If your results differ from your expectations, explain why that may have happened. If your results agree, then describe the theory that the evidence supported. It is never appropriate to simply state that the data agreed with expectations, and let it drop at that.

C. Please translate the following sentences into English.

找一页空白的纸，以任何顺序，写下与这篇文章有关的所有重要观点，自问一些显而易见的问题。如果你研究的开始是为证实一个假设，然而当你发现你有的数据仿佛真的可以更好地验证其他的假设时，你也不必担心。把它们两者都写出来，去选择假设、目的和数据的最佳组合。

Part B Common Errors in Student Research Papers

This is not an exhaustive list. With every new lab protocol, you folks come up with the darnedest ways of messing up a perfectly good paper. However, if you heed the comments here your reports stand a much better chance of being mistaken for professionally written research papers.

Verb Tense

Use of the wrong verb tense, at best, is irritating to read and reflects poorly on the student's writing skills. At worst, the reader can be confused as to what facts are already known and what was newly discovered in the actual study that is the subject of the paper. As a rule, use past tense to describe events that have happened. Such events include procedures that you have conducted and results that you observed. Use present tense to describe generally accepted facts.

Mixing tenses is even worse——this sort of thing hurts my ears. Unfortunately, the people who read the news in television and radio broadcasts are frequently unaware of verb tense at all.

Proofread

Incomplete sentences, redundant phrases, obvious misspellings, and other symptoms of a hurriedly-written paper can cost you. Please start your work early enough so that you can proofread it. Check spelling of scientific names, names of people, names of compounds, etc. Spelling and grammatical errors can be embarrassing. Since many very different terms have similar names, a spelling error can result in a completely incorrect statement.

When you print off your paper, please make sure that tables are not split over more than one page, that headings are not "orphaned", pages submitted out of sequence, etc. Remember, someone has to read this thing! If the reader is an editor or reviewer, you might get a rejection notice because you were too sloppy.

Irrelevant Information

Anecdotal Information

Sometimes you may feel the need to justify a statement or procedure by stating "the instructor told us to do this instead of that". You might think it appropriate to write "we used Microsoft Excel to produce a graph of x versus y". Such information is anecdotal and is considered to be superfluous. In some cases omission of anecdotal information is unfortunate. Papers in the older literature tend to be a lot more exciting and often more informative for those not "in the know", because the researcher could report how a conclusion was reached, including the reasoning and various sidetracks that led him/her to conclusions. The writer could actually tell the story of the investigation process. Modern papers omit such information because the volume of literature is so great, most of us doing a search don't have time to wade through more material than we need. Publication costs are too high to permit printing of superfluous information.

A research paper summarizes a study. It does not identify who did what. Reference to instructors, fellow students, teams, partners, etc. are not appropriate, nor is it appropriate to refer to "the lab".

Unnecessary Background

If you state facts or describe mechanisms, do so in order to make a point or to help interpret results, and do refer to the present study. If you find yourself writing everything you know about the subject, you are wasting your time (and that of your reader). Stick to the appropriate point, and include a reference to your source of background information if you feel that it is important.

Material That is Inappropriate for the Readership

It isn't necessary to tell fellow scientists that your study is pertinent to the field of biochemistry. Your readers can figure out to what field(s) your work applies. You need not define terms that are well known to the intended readership. For example, do you really think it is necessary to define systolic blood pressure if your readership consists of physicians or cardiovascular physiologists?

Subjectivity and Use of Superlatives

Subjectivity refers to feelings, opinions, etc. For example, in your discussion you might write, "We felt that the fixative was bad, because we had difficulty finding flagella on our *Chlamydomonas*." Another researcher is unlikely to risk time and resources on the basis of your "feeling". On the other hand, you might write, "The percentage of cells with flagella was inversely proportional to the time they spent in fixative, suggesting that the fixative was causing cells to shed flagella." This is information that another scientist can use.

Proof

The requirements for scientific proof are extremely rigorous. It is highly doubtful that any single experiment can be so well controlled that its conclusions can be regarded as proof. In fact, for any result to be accepted it must be confirmed independently. In fact, we can never know if a model as we describe it presents an accurate picture of any natural process. We can never look at the original blueprint to check our conclusions. So your data may strongly support a position, or they may allow you to reject a hypothesis, but they aren't likely to provide anything close to proof.

Grammar and Spelling

Please avoid obvious grammatical errors. Granted, you aren't writing an English paper (heck, an English teacher would tear my own writing style to shreds). However, clear written communication requires proper sentence structure and use of words. Make sure that your sentences are complete, that they make sense when you proofread, and that you have verb/subject agreement.

Spelling errors in a paper make you look amateurish. For example, *absorbance* is read from a *spectrophotometer*. You don't read *absorbency* from a *spectrometer*. Worse, they can change the entire meaning of your writing. One letter changes the chemical compound you describe. I know the action of *cycloheximide* in eukaryotic cells, but I do not know the action of *cyclohexamide*.

Inaccurate Word or Phrase

E. g., changing temperature had the following *affect* on the subject.

"Affect" is a verb. "Effect" is a noun. What happened to the subject was an effect. The temperature change affected the subject. Please learn the difference.

E. g., the data lead to the *assumption* that x has no relationship to y.

If you base a conclusion on data, then your conclusion is a deduction, not an assumption. In fact, in experimental science assumptions are usually avoided. A purpose of controls is to eliminate the need to assume anything.

E. g., our inability to ensure that all cells in the population were in the same stage of development *skewed* our data.

This statement doesn't reveal very much. The writer intended to say that the data points were more scattered, that is, the non-uniformity of the population resulted in unacceptably high experimental error. The word "skew" means "having an oblique position, turned or twisted to one side, slanting, sloping". It can be used as an adverb or noun as well. In statistics, the word refers to an asymmetric distribution of data. Nowhere in the definition is there any reference to the state of being incorrect or more scattered. Thus, not only is the word overused, but also is misused.

Oversimplification

E. g., we used a spectrophotometer to determine protein concentrations for each of our samples. We used an oscilloscope to measure resting potentials in crayfish muscle.

The spectrophotometer or oscilloscope may be a novel, mysterious, and versatile device to you, but I suspect that even an expert biochemist would have a hard time finding a protein concentration using only a spectrophotometer. The first statement leaves out the dye reagent, standards, pipettors, etc. that are required to perform the assay. The second statement omits any reference to the micropipets or the specialized electronic instrumentation that is required in order to measure transmembrane potentials.

What information did you intend to convey? If you intend to describe the methodology, then write a complete description. If you intend only to summarize the procedures then you might seek a phrase that sums up what was done without oversimplifying. For example, "We used a colorimetric assay to determine protein concentrations in each of our samples."

Superficiality

The purpose of a discussion is to interpret the results, not to simply state them in a different way. In most cases a superficial discussion ignores mechanisms or fails to explain them completely. It should be clear to the reader why a specific result came to pass. The statement, "the result agreed with the known theoretical value", tells us nothing about the mechanism(s) behind the result. What is the basis for expecting a particular result? Explanations may not be easy and your explanation may not be correct, but you will get most or all of the available credit for posing a reasonable explanation, even if it is not quite right. Superficial statements, on the other hand, will waste your time.

Common Mistakes in Reporting Results

Converted data are data that have been analyzed, usually summarized, and presented in such a way that only the information pertinent to the objectives of the study is presented. *Raw data* refer to results of individual replicate trials, individual observations, chart records, and other information that comes directly from the laboratory.

Once you have presented converted data, do not present the same data in a different way. For example, if the data are plotted, then don't include a table of data as well. Present a figure (such as a graph) if appropriate. If the data are better represented by a table, then use a table. The caption with any figure or table should include all pertinent information. One should not have to go into the body of the paper to find out the results of statistical tests on the data, or the rationale behind a curve fit.

Raw data are not usually included in your results. Raw data include lists of observations, measurements taken in order to obtain a final result (e. g., absorbance, relative mobility, tick marks on a microscope reticule).

Use an appropriate number of decimal places (if you need decimal places at all) to report means and other measured or calculated values. The number of decimal places and/or significant figures must reflect the degree of precision of the original measurement. See our analytical resources for information on uncertain quantities and significant figures. Since the number of significant figures used reflects the level of precision of the measurement or calculation, there is never any need to qualify a measurement or calculation as "about" or "approximate".

Graphs and other pictures that represent data are called figures, and are numbered consecutively. Tables are distinguished from figures, and are numbered consecutively as well. For example, a paper with two graphs, a reproduction of a segment of chart record and two tables will have figures 1, 2, and 3, and tables 1 and 2. Do note that I distinguished graphs from chart records. Not everything with gridlines is a graph. Graphs are analytical tools. Chart records are raw data (which may be presented in results as an example, if appropriate).

Do not draw conclusions in the result section. Reserve the data interpretation for the discussion.

Glossary

1. poorly   adv. 拙劣地，蹩脚地
2. biochemistry   n. 生物化学
3. rigorous   adj. 严格的，严厉的
4. absorbance   n. 吸光率
5. spectrophotometer   n. 分光光度计
6. cycloheximide   n. 环己酰亚胺
7. eukaryotic   adj. 真核的
8. cyclohexamide   n. 环己酰胺

Questions

1. Which errors are commonly in student research papers?
2. Which errors are commonly in reporting results?
3. According to what you have learnt, please give several examples about inaccurate words or phrases.

References

Edited by Chen Yanli

[1] Adams C R, Bamford K M, Early M P. *Principles of Horticulture* [M]. Oxford: Butterworth-Heinemann, 2008.

[2] Agustin B, Molina Jr. *Tissue Culture in the Banana Industry in International training course of biotechnology for seed and seedling production* [OL]. http://musalit.inibap.org/pdf/IN040225.

[3] Agustin B, Molina Jr. *Tissue Culture in the Banana Industry* [M/OL]. Regional Coordinator INIBAP Asia Pacific, 2002. http://musalit.inibap.org/pdf/IN040225_en.pdf.

[4] Bhat R, Sridhar K R, Karim A A, Young C C, Arun A B. *Influence of γ-Radiation on the Nutritional and Functional Qualities of Lotus Seed Flour* [J]. J. Agric. Food Chem., 2009, 57(20): 9524-9531.

[5] Caprette David R. *Writing Research Papers*. Rice University, 2007.

[6] Dennis Gonsalves, Steve Ferreira, Richard Manshardt, et al. *Transgenic Virus Resistant Papaya: New Hope for Controlling Papaya Ringspot Virus in Hawaii* [OL]. http://www.plantmanagementnetwork.org/pub/php/review/papaya.

[7] Tsykagoshi Satoru. *Environmental Control of Protected Cultivation* [J]. Farming Japan, 2005, 39(1): 19-23.

[8] Coleman Eliot. *The New Organic Grower* [M]. Avon: Bath Press, 1990.

[9] Gallagher Eric, O'Hare Paul, Stephenson Russ, et al. *Macadamia Problem Solver & bug identifier* [R]. New South Wales: Department of Primary Industries, 2003.

[10] Mendoza Evelyn Mae Tecson, Laurena Antonio C., Botella J R. *Recent Advances in the Development of Transgenic Papaya* [J]. Biotechnology Annual Review, 2008, 14: 423-462.

[11] Peryea Frank J. *Associate Soil Scientist and Associate Horticulturist* [OL]. http://www.tfrec.wsu.edu/summary/FJP.html.

[12] Stanhill G., Enoch H. Zvi. *Greenhouse Ecosystems* [M]. New York: Elsevier Science, 1999.

[13] Fowler Gene. *Common Errors in Student Research Papers* [OL]. http://www.ruf.rice.edu/~bioslabs/tools/report/reportform.html.

[14] Fowler Gene. *Writing Research Papers* [OL]. http://www.ruf.rice.edu/~bioslabs/tools/report/reportform.html.

[15] Acquaah George. *Horticulture: principles and practices* [M]. 4th ed. New Jersey: PrenticeHall, 2008.

[16] Whitesides George M. *Writing a Paper*. Department of Chemistry and Chemical Biology, Harvard University, Cambridge, USA.

[17] Brown H D. *Vegetable Science* [M]. Philedelphia: J. B. lippincott Company, 1949.

[18] Reiley H Edward, Shry Jr. Carroll L. *Introductory Horticulture* [M]. [S. L.]: Litton Educational Publishing, 1979.

[19] Nakasone Henry Y, Paull Robert E. *Tropical Fruits* [M]. [S. L.]: CAB Internatinal, 1998.

[20] Resh Howard M. *Hydroponic Food Production* [M]. 2nd ed. Santa Barbara, Calif.: Woodbridge Press Publishing Company, 1983

[21] Edmond J B, Musser A M, Anderews F S. *Fundamental of Horticulture* [M]. New York: McGraw Hill, 1957.

[22] Berghoef J, Jeutscher K L, Pol P A van de. *Horticulture production systems* [M]. [S. L.]: MSc Course Hortonomy, 1995.

[23] Berghoef J, Jeutscher K L, Pol P A van de. *Protected Cultivation of Ornamental Crops* [M]. [S. L.]: MSc Course Hortonomy, 1995.

[24] Hanan J J, Holley W D, Goldsberry K L. *Greenhouse Management* [M]. [S. L.]: Springer-Verlag, 1978.

[25] Teixeira da Silva Jaime A. Rashid Zinia. Nhut Duong Tan, et al. *Papaya (Carica papaya L.) Biology and Biotechnology* [J]. Tree and Forestry Science and Biotechnology, 2007,1(1): 48-66.

[26] McCullagh James C. *The Solar Greenhouse Book* [M]. Emmaus, PA: Rodale Press, 1989.

[27] Lester James D. *Writing Research Papers: A Complete Guide Writing Research Papers* [M]. 8th ed. [S. L.]: Harpercollins College Div, 1996.

[28] Douglas James Sholto. *Advanced Guide to Hydroponics* [M]. [S. L.]: Pelham Books, 1976.

[29] Douglas James Sholto. *Beginner's Guide to Hydroponics* [M]. [S. L.]: Pelham Books, 1978.

[30] Wales Jimmy. *Bonsai: Wikipedia, the free encyclopedia* [OL]. http://en.wikipedia.org/wiki/Bonsai.

[31] Mastalerz John W. *The Greenhouse Environment* [M]. [S. L.]: John Wiley & Sons, 1986.

[32] Lenteren van Joop C. *A greenhouse without pesticides: fact or fantasy?* [J]. Crop Protection, 2000, 19(6): 375-384.

[33] Li Yaling. *Special English for Horticulture* [M]. Beijing: China Agriculture Press, 2002.

[34] McMullen Marcia P, Lamey H Arthur. *Seed Treatment for Disease Control*. North Dakota State University, 2000.

[35] Mazzola M, Gu Y H. *Impact of wheat cultivation on microbial communities from replant soils and apple growth in greenhouse trials* [J]. Phytopathology, 2000, 90(2):114-119.

[36] Nichols Mike, Christie Bruce. *Innovative Plant Factories* [J]. Practical Hydroponics & Greenhouse, 2008, 99:44-46.

[37] Papademetrious Minas K, Dent Frank J. *Lychee Production in the Asia-Pacific Region*[R]. Bangkok, Thailand: Food and Agriculture Organization of the United Nations Regional Office for Asia and the Pacific, 2002.

[38] West-wood M N. *Temperate-zone Pomology* [M]. 3rd ed. Portland: Timber Press,1993.

[39] Morroni M, Thompson J R, Tepfer M. *Twenty years of transgenic plants resistant to Cucumber mosaic virus* [J]. Mol Plant Microbe Interact, 2008, 21(6): 675-684.

[40] Paper Net. *Type of Tropical Flowers* [OL]. http://www.tropicalflower.org/.

[41] Lampkin Nicolas. *Organic Farming* [M]. [S. L.]: Farming Press, 1990.

[42] O'Hare Paul, Stephenson Russ, Quinlan Kevin, et al. *Macadamia Grower's handbook* [M]. New South Wales:Department of Primary Industries and Fisheries, 2004.

[43] Halface R Gordon, Barden John A. *Horticulture* [M]. New York: Mcgraw Hill, 1979.

[44] Rai Rhitu. *Genetics and Plant Breeding* [OL], 2007. http://nsdl.niscair.res.in/bitstream/123456789/668/1.

[45] Litz Richard E. *The mango: Botany, Production and uses* [M]. [S. L.]: CAB Internatinal, 2009.

[46] Atkinson Robert E. *Orchids … in your home* [M/OL]. [S. L.]: T. F. H. Publications, 1961.

http://www.foru2know.com.

[47] Baudendistel Robert F. *Horticulture: A Basic Awareness* [M]. [S. L.]: Reston Publishing, 1979.

[48] Morgan Ron. *Flower Arranging: Basic Flower Arrangements* [OL]. http://www.save-on-crafts.com/eigbasflowar.html.

[49] Rudner Lawrence M, Schafer William D. *How to write a scholarly research report* [J]. Practical Assessment, Research & Evaluation, 1999, 6(13).

[50] Mitra S K. *Postharvest Physiology and Storage of Tropical and Subtropical Fruits* [M]. [S. L.]: CAB International, 1997.

[51] Thompson H C, Kelly W C. *Vegetable Crops* [M]. 5th ed. New York: McGraw Hill, 1957.

[52] Maruo Toru. *Type and Structure of Greenhouses and Characteristics of Greenhouse-related Equipment and covering Materials* [J]. Farming Japan, 2005, 39(1).

[53] Hutton Wendy, Cassio Alberto. *Tropical Fruits of Thailand & SE Asia* [M]. Bangkok: Asia Books, 2000.

[54] Chandler William Henry. *Evergreen Orchards* [M]. Philadelphia: LEA & Febiger, 1950.

[55] Warren William, Tettoni Luca Invernizzi. *Tropical Plants for Home and Garden* [M]. [S. L.]: Thames & Hudson, 2006.

[56] Udagawa Yuji. *Hydroponic* [J]. Farming Japan, 2005, 39(1).

Appendix I List of Subtropical and Tropical Fruit Tree Species in Chinese, Latin and English
附录 I 热带亚热带果树中文、拉丁文和英文名录

(Edited by Feng Suping and Chen Yanli)

Table I -1

中文名	拉丁学名	英文名
阿月浑子	*Pistacia vera* L.	pistachio
澳洲坚果(夏威夷果、昆士兰果、澳洲胡桃)	*Macadamia integrifolia* Maiden & Betche(光壳种); *M. tetraphylla* S. Johnson(粗壳种)	macadamia nut, hawaii nut, queensland nut
巴西坚果	*Bertholletia excelsa* H. B. K.	Brazil nut
板栗	*Castanea mollissima* Bl.	chestnut
薜荔	*Ficus pumila* Linn.	climbing fig
槟榔	*Areca catechu* L.	areca
菠萝	*Ananas comosus* (L.) Merr.	pineapple
菠萝蜜(树菠萝)	*Artocarpus heterophyllus* Lam.	jackfruit
草莓	*Fragaria ananassa* Duch.	strawberry
草莓番石榴	*Psidium littorale* Raddi.	strawberry guava, Chinese guava
长山核桃	*Carya illinoinensis* K. Koch	pecan
刺葵	*Phoenix hanceana* Naud.	hance date
刺黄果	*Carissa carandas* Linn.	carissa, bengal currant
第伦桃	*Dillenia indica* Linn.	Indian dillenia
滇藏杜英	*Elaeocarpus braceanus* Watt ex C. B. Clarke	blueberry tree
蛋黄果	*Lucuma nervosa* A. DC	canistel, egg fruit
番荔枝	*Annona squamosa* L.	sugar apple
番木瓜	*Carica papaya* L.	papaya
番樱桃(红果仔)	*Eugenia uniflora* Linn.	pitanga, Surinam-cherry
番石榴(鸡矢果、拔子)	*Psidium guajava* L.	guava
费约果	*Feijoa sellowiana* Berg	feijoa
佛手柑	*Citrus medica* var. *sarcodactylis* Swingle.	fingered citron
橄榄	*Canarium* spp.	Chinese olive
白榄	*C. album* (Lour) Raeusch	Chinese white olive
乌榄	*C. pimela* Koening	Chinese black olive
橄仁树		
光果樱	*Malpighia glabra* L.	west Indies cherry
果桑	*Morus* spp.	mulberry

续表

中文名	拉丁学名	英文名
白桑	*M. alba* L.	white mulberry, Russian mulberry
黑桑	*M. rubra* L.	black mulberry
红桑	*M. rubra* L.	red mulberry
海枣	*Phoenix dactylifera* L.	date palm
红毛丹	*Nephelium lappaceum* L.	rambutan
红花南五味子	*Kadsura coccinea* (Lem.) A. C. Smith	scaslet kadsura
猴面包	*Adansonia digitata* L.	baobab
黄皮	*Clausena lansium* (Lour.) Skeels	wampee, wampi
火棘	*Pyracantha fortuneana* (Maxim) Li.	firethorn
火龙果	*Hylocerews* spp.	pitaya, dragen fruit
红肉火龙果	*H. polyrbizus* (weber.) Britt & Rose	pitaya, dragonfruit
白肉火龙果	*H. undatus* (Haw.) Britt & Rose	pitaya, dragonfruit
鸡蛋果（西番莲、百香果）	*Passiflora edulis* Sims（紫果种）；*P. edulis* Sims. f, *flavicarpa* Deg.（黄果种）	passionfruit, granadilla
加椰芒果	*Spondias cytherea* Sonn.	otaheite apple, ambarella
尖百达（小菠萝蜜）	*Artocarpus champeden* Spreng.	chempedak lemasa
金毛丹	*Nephelium mutabile* Bl.	pulasan
金星果	*Chrysophyllum cainito* L.	star apple, caimito
金樱子	*Rosa laevigata* Michx	Cherokee rose
桔柑	*Citrus tachibana* Tan.	tachibana, orange
咖啡	*Coffea* spp.	coffee
小粒种咖啡	*Coffea arabica* L.	arabica coffee
中粒种咖啡	*Coffea canephora pierre* Froehn	robusta coffee
大粒种咖啡	*Coffea liberica* Hiern	liberican coffee
可可	*Theobroma cacao* L.	cacao
腊肠树	*Cassia fistula* L.	sausage tree
莱檬（青柠）	*Citrus aurantifolia* Blanco	lime
榄仁树	*Terminalia caappa* L.	tropical-almond
岭南酸枣	*Allospondias lakonensis* (Pierre) Stapf.	Canton mombin
梨	*Pyrus* species	pear
白梨	*P. bretschneideri* Rehd.	Snow pear
西洋梨	*P. communis* L.	European pear
砂梨	*P. pyrifolia* Nakai	Asian pear
龙荔	*Dimocarpus confines* H. S. Lo	confined dimocarpus
李	*Prunus* species	plum
湄洲李	*P. americana* Marsh.	American plum
欧洲李	*P. domestica* L.	European plum
加拿大李	*P. nigra* Ait.	Canadian plum
中国李	*P. salicina* Lindl	Chinese plum
馒头果（大果榕）	*Ficus auriculata* Lour.	eared strangler fig
毛叶枣（印度枣）	*Ziziphus mauritiana* Lam.	ber, Indian jujube, cottony jujube

续表

中文名	拉丁学名	英文名
荔枝	*Litchi chinensis* Sonn.	lychee, litchi
莲雾(洋蒲桃)	*Syzygium samarangense* Merr. Et Perry	wax jambu, wax apple
榴莲	*Durio zibethinus* Murr.	durian
龙眼	*Dimocarpus longan* Lour.	longan, dragon's eye
露兜树	*Pandanus tectorius* Sol.	pandan, screwpine
洛神葵(玫瑰茄)	*Hibiscus sabdariffa* L.	roselle
买麻藤	*Gnetum montanum* Markgr.	sweetberry, jointfir
马拉巴粟(瓜栗、中美木棉)	*Pachira macrocarpa* (Cham. et Schl.) Schl. ex Bailey	Malabar chestnut, cayenne nut
芒果	*Mangifera indica* L.	mango
梅	*Prunus mume* Sieb. et Zucc.	mume, plum, Japanese apricot
猕猴桃	*Actinidia* species	kiwifruit
美味猕猴桃	*A. deliciosa* Liang et Ferguson	kiwifruit
中华猕猴桃	*A. chinensis* Planch.	Chinese gooseberry
木菠萝(菠萝蜜、包蜜)	*Artocarpus heterophyllus* Lam. [*A. integra* (Thunb.) Merr.]	jackfruit
木奶果	*Baccaurea ramiflora* Lour.	burmese grape
面包果	*Artocarpus altilis* Fosberg	breadfruit
南酸枣	*Choerospondias axillaris* (Roxb) Burtt & Hill	axillary mombin
柠檬	*Citrus limon* (L.) Burm. f.	lemon
牛心番荔枝(牛心梨)	*Annona reticulata* L.	bullock's heart, custard apple
椪柑	*Citrus poonensis* Hort. ex Tanaka.	ponkan
枇杷	*Eriobotrya japonica* Lindl.	loquat
苹婆(凤眼果)	*Sterculia nobilis* Smith	pimpon, pimpu
葡萄	*Vitis* species	grape
美洲葡萄	*V. labrusca* L.	fox grape, eastern grape
欧洲葡萄	*V. vinifera* L.	grape
葡萄柚	*Citrus paradisi* Macf.	grapefruit
蒲桃	*Syzygium jambos* Alston	rose apple
仁面子	*Dracontomelon dao* (Bl) Merr. et R.	dao dragonplum
人心果	*Achras sapota* L.	sapodilla, chiku
三叶木桔	*Aegle marmelos* (L.) Corr.	bael
山核桃	*Carya cathayensis* Sargent	Chinese hickory
山楂	*Crataegus pinnatifida* Bge	hawthorn
山竹子	*Garcinia mangostana* L.	mangosteen, mangis
蛇皮果(沙拉克椰子)	*Zalacca edulis* Wall.	salak, salak palm
神秘果	*Synsepalum dulcificum* Denill	miracle fruit
石榴	*Punica granatum* L.	pomegranate
柿	*Diospyros kaki* L. f.	persimmon
四季橘	*Citrus microcarpa* Bunge	calamondin
酸橙	*Citrus aurantium* L.	sour orange

续表

中文名	拉丁学名	英文名
酸橘	*Citrus sunki* Hot.	sour mandarin
酸藤果	*Embelia laeta* (Linn) Mez.	joyful embelia
树番茄	*Cyphomandra betacea* Stndt	tree tomato
桃金娘	*Rhodomyrtus tomentosa* (Ait) Hassk	downy rose mystle
台湾林檎	*Malus formosana* Kawak. et Koidz	Taiwan crab apple
甜瓜	*Cucumis melo* L.	melon, muskmelon
树莓	*Rubus* species	raspberry
红树莓	*R. indaeus* L.	European raspberry
黑树莓	*R. occidentalis* L.	American raspberry
黑莓	*R. allegheninsis* Porter	blackberry
酸豆(罗望子,酸角)	*Tamarindus indica* L.	tamarind, tamarindo, Indian date
沙梨	*Pyrus pyrifolia* (Burm.) Nakai	sand pear
糖椰子	*Borassus flabellifer* L.	sugar palm
桃	*Prunus persica* (L.) Batsch.	peach
甜橙	*Citrus sinensis* (L.) Osbeck	sweet orange
榅桲	*Cydonia oblonga* L.	quince
文丁果(牙买加樱桃)	*Muntingia calabura* L.	Jamaica cherry, ceri kampung
五月茶	*Antidesma bunius* (L.) Spreng	bignay, buni
乌饭树	*Vaccinium bracteatum* Thunb	oriental blueberry
无花果	*Ficus carica* L.	fig
锡兰橄榄	*Elaeocarpus serratus* L.	Ceylon olive
仙人掌	*Opuntia dillenii* (Ker.) Haw	prickly pear
西瓜	*Citrullus vulgaris* Schrad	watermelon
香肉果	*Casimiroa edulis* Llave ex Lex.	white sapote
香瓜茄(人参果)	*Solanum muricatum* Ait.	pepino, melon pear
香榧	*Torreya grandis* Fort.	Chinese torreya
香蕉	*Musa* spp.	banana, plantain
杏	*Prunus armeniaca* L.	apricot
羊奶果	*Elaeagnus conferta* Roxb.	denseflower elaeagnus
杨梅	*Myrica rubra* Sieb. et Zucc	strawberry tree, red bayberry
阳桃(杨桃、羊桃、五敛子)	*Averrhoa carambola* L.	carambola, starfruit
腰果	*Anacardium occidentale* L.	cashew
野山楂	*Crataegus cuneata* Sieb. et Zucc	nippon hawthorn
野木瓜	*Stauntonia chinensis* DC	Chinese stauntonvine
椰子	*Cocos nucifera* L.	coconut
银杏(白果)	*Ginkgo biloba* L.	maidenhair tree, ginkgo
樱桃	*Prunus* species	cherry
欧洲甜樱桃	*P. avium* L.	sweet cherry
欧洲酸樱桃	*P. cerasus* L.	sour cherry
中国樱桃	*P. pseudocerasus* Lindl.	early Chinese cherry

续表

中文名	拉丁学名	英文名
油橄榄	*Olea europaea* L.	olive
油梨	*Persea americana* Mill	avocado
油桃	*Prunus persica var. nectarina* Maxim	nectarine
柚	*Citrus grandis* (L.) Osbeck	pummelo
余甘子	*Phyllanthus emblica* L.	emblic myrobalan, aonla
云母树	*Dendrobenthamia capitata* (Wall.) Hutch.	evergreen dogwood
云南核桃	*Juglans sigillata* Dode	Yunnan walnut
越橘	*Vaccinium* species	blueberry
狭叶越橘（矮）	*V. angustifolium* Ait.	lowbush blueberry
伞房花越橘（高）	*V. corymbosum* L.	highbush blueberry
大果蔓越橘	*V. macrocarpon* Ait.	cranberry
枣	*Zizyphus jujuba* Mill.	jujube, common jujube, Chinese jujube
枣椰子	*Phoenix dactylifera* L.	edible date
榛	*Corylus* species	filbert, hazelnut
美洲榛	*C. americana* L.	American filbert
欧洲榛	*C. avellana* L.	European filbert
华榛	*C. chinensis* Fr.	Chinese filbert

Appendix Ⅱ List of Subtropical and Tropical Vegetable Species in Chinese, Latin and English

附录Ⅱ 热带亚热带蔬菜中文、拉丁文和英文名录

(Edited by Feng Suping and Chen Yanli)

Table Ⅱ-1

中文名	拉丁学名	英文名
百合	*Lilium* sp.	goldband lily
爆粒玉米	*Zea mays* L.	popcorn
荸荠	*Eleocharis tuberosa* (Roxb.) Roem. et Schult	water-chestnut
扁豆	*Dolichos lablab* L.	lablab, hyacinth bean
菠菜	*Spinacia oleracea* L.	spinach
薄荷	*Mentha arvensis* L.	field mint
菜豆	*Phaseolus vulgaris* L.	common bean, kidney bean, snap bean, shell bean, garden bean, green bean
菜瓜	*Cucumis melo* L. var. *flexuosus* Naud.	snake melon
菜薹(菜心)	*Brassica campestris* L. ssp. chinensis var. *utilis* Tsen et Lee	flowering Chinese cabbage
菜用大豆(毛豆)	*Glycine max* (L.) Merr.	soybean, edible soybean
蚕豆	*Vicia faba* L.	broad bean, fava bean, windsor bean, horsebean
糙皮甜瓜(网纹甜瓜、哈密瓜)	*Cucumis melo* L. var. *reticulates* Naud.	cantaloupe, netted melon
草菇	*Volvariella volvacea* (Bull. ex Fr.) Sing.	straw mushroom
草石蚕	*Stachys sieboldii* Miq.	Chinese artichoke
朝鲜蓟	*Cynara scolymus* L.	globe artichoke
车前草	*Plantago major* L. var. *asiatica* Decne.	plantain
慈姑	*Sagittaria sagittifolia* L.	Chinese arrowhead
大白菜	*Brassica campestris* L. ssp. *pekinensis* (Lour) Lsson	Chinese cabbage
大葱	*Allium fistulosum* L. var. *giganteum* Makino	welsh onion, spanish onion, Japanese leek, Japanese bunching onion
大肥菇(双环蘑菇)	*Agaricus bitorquis* (Quei.) Sacc.	spring mushroom
大黄(食用)	*Rheum officinale* Baill.	rhubarb, pie plant, garden rhubarb, wine plant
大蒜	*Allium sativum* L.	garlic
刀豆	*Canavalia gladiata* DC.	sword bean, jackbean
冬瓜	*Benincasa hispida* Cogn.	wax gourd, winter melon, white pumpkin, chinese squash, chinese waxgourd
豆薯(凉薯)	*Pachyrrhizus erosus* (L.) Urban	yam bean

续表

中文名	拉丁学名	英文名
番茄	*Lycopersicon esculentum* Miller	tomato, love apple (France), golden apple (Italy)
樱桃番茄	*L. esculentum var. cerasiforme* Alef.	cherry tomato, salsd tomato
番杏(夏菠菜)	*Tetagonia expansa* Murray	New Zealand spinach
佛手瓜	*Sechium edule* Swartz	chayote, vegetable pear
茯苓	*Poria coccos* (Schw.) Wolf.	tuckahoe
甘薯(地瓜)	*Ipomoea batatas* Lam.	sweet potato, southern yam
根芥菜(大头菜)	*Brassica juncea Coss.* var. *megarrhiza* Tsen et lee (syn. napiformis Pall et Bols)	root mustard
枸杞	*Lycium Chinese* Miller	Chinese wolfberry
海带	*Laminaria japonica* Aresch	sea tangle
黑籽南瓜	*Cucurbita ficifolia* Bouch	fig-leaf gourd
红花菜豆	*Phaseolus coccineus* L., P. multiflorus Willd.	scarlet runner bean
猴头	*Hericium erinaceus* (Bull.)	bear's head, medusa fungi, hedgehog hydnum
胡萝卜	*Daucus carota* L. var. *sativa* DC.	carrot
葫芦	*Lagenaria vulgaris* Ser. var. *gourda* Makino	cuban pumpkin
瓠瓜	*Lagenaria vulgaris* Ser.	calabash gourd, bottle gourd
花生	*Arachis hypogaea* L.	peanut, earth nut, groundnut, goober (pea)
滑菇	*Pholiota nameko* Ito ex Imai.	nameko
黄豆芽	*Glycine max* (L.) Merr.	soybean sprouts
黄瓜	*Cucumis sativus* L.	cucumber
黄花菜(金针菜)	*Hemerocallis* sp.	common yellow daylily
黄秋葵	*Hibiscus esculentus* L.	okra, gumbo
茴香	*Foeniculum vulgare* Mill.	fennel
蕺菜(鱼腥草)	*Houttuynia cordata* Thunb.	heartleaf, houttuynia
姜	*Zingiber officinale* Ros.	ginger
豇豆	*Vigna unguiculata* W. ssp. *sesquipedalis* (L.) Verd	cowpea, yard-long bean, asparagus bean
茭白	*Zizania caduciflora* Hand-Mazz.	wild rice, water bamboo
结球甘蓝	*Brassica oleracea* L. var. *capitata* L.	cabbage, green cabbage
紫甘蓝	*Brassica oleracea* L. var. *capitata*	purple cabbage
花椰菜(菜花)	*Brassica oleracea* L. var. *botrytis* DC.	cauliflower, heading broccoli
木立花椰菜(绿菜花)	*Brassica oleracea* L. var. *ital-ica* Plenck.	broccoli, calabrese, Italian broccoli, green sprouting broccoli
球茎甘蓝(大头菜)	*Brassica oleracea* L. var. *caulorapa* DC.	kohlrabi
羽衣甘蓝(散叶甘蓝)	*Brassica oleracea* L. var. *acephala* DC.	collard, kale, borecole
芥菜	*Capsella bursa-pastoris* L.	shepherd's purse
芥兰	*Brassica alboglabra* Bailey	Chinese kale, kailan
金针菇	*Flammulina velutipes* (Curt. Ex Fr.) Sing.	winter mushroom
茎芥菜(榨菜)	*Brassica juncea* Cosson var. *tumida* Tsen et Lee	stem mustard, preseved mustard, zha-tsai

中文名	拉丁学名	英文名
韭菜	*Allium tuberosum* Rottl. ex Spr.	Chinese chives, garlic chive, oriental chive
韭葱	*Allium porrum* L.	leek
菊芋(鬼子姜)	*Helianthus tuberosus* L.	jerusalem artichoke, sunchoke, girasole
蕨菜	*Pteridium aguilinum* (L.) Kohn. var. *latiusculum* (Desv.) Underw.	wild brake
口蘑	*Tricholoma mongolicum* Imai.	saint George's mushroom, Mongolian mushroom
苦瓜	*Momordica charantia* L.	bitter gourd, bitter melon, balsam pear (apple), alligator pear, bitter cucumber
苦苣	*Cichorium endivia* L.	common sowthistle
块菌	*Tuber melanosporum* Vitt.	truffle
款冬	*Petasites* (*Tussilago*) *japonicus* Miq.	coltsfoot
辣根	*Cochlearia armoracia* L.	horse-radish
辣椒(属)	*Capsicum frutescens* L., *C. annuum* L.	pepper, pimiento
甜椒	*Capsicum frutescens* L., *C. annuum* L. var. *grossum* Bailey	sweet pepper
五色椒	*Capsicum annuum* var. *annuum/cerasiforme* group	cherry pepper
干辣椒	*Capsicum frutescens* L.	chili
朝天椒	*Capsicum annuum* L. var. *conoides* Bailey	celestial(pepper)
尖辣椒(牛角椒)	*Capsicum annuum* L. var. *longum* Bailey	cayenne, cayenne pepper
萝卜芽	*Raphanus sativus* L.	radish sprouts
落葵(木耳菜)	*Basella* sp.	Malabar spinach, white Malabar nightshade
马齿苋	*Portulaca oleracea* L.	purslane, pusley
马铃薯	*Solanum tuberosum* L.	potato, white potato, Irish potato
毛木耳	*Auricularia polytricha* (Mont) Sace.	villous Jew's-ear
美味牛肝菌	*Boletus edulis* Bull. ex Fr.	cep
蜜环菌(榛菌)	*Armillaria mellea* (Vahl. Ex Fr.) Karst.	honey mushroom, honey agaric
魔芋	*Amorphophallus* ssp.	elephant-foot yam, elephant taro
木耳	*Auricularia auricula* (L. ex Hook) Underw.	jew's-ear
木薯	*Manihot esculenta* Crantz, *M. utilissima*	cassava
南瓜	*Cucurbita moschata* Duch.	pumpkin
牛蒡	*Arctium lappa* L.	gobo, edible burdock, domestic burdock
平菇	*Pleurotus ostreatus* (Jacq. Ex Fr.) Quel.	oyster cap fungus
婆罗门参	*Tragopogon porrifolius* L.	salsify, oyster plant (USA)
茄子	*Solanum melongena* L.	eggplant, aubergine
芹菜	*Apium graveolens* L.	celery
山药	*Dioscorea batatas* Decne	yam
蛇瓜	*Trichosanthes anguina* L.	serpent gourd
石刁柏(芦笋)	*Asparagus officinalis* L.	asparagus
莳菜(土茴香)	*Anethum graveolens* L.	dill
双孢蘑菇	*Agaricus bisporus* (Lange) Imbach	white mushroom
水芹	*Oenanthe stolonifera* DC.	water dropwort

中文名	拉丁学名	英文名
丝瓜	*Luffa cylindrica* Roemer.	luffa, sponge gourd, vegetable sponge, dishrag gourd, dishcloth gourd
四棱豆	*Psophocarpus tetragonolobus* D.C	asparagus pea
松口蘑(松蘑)	*Tricholoma matsutake* (Ito et Imai) Sing.	Japanese pineal fungus, matsutake
松乳菇	*Lactarius deliciosus* (L. ex Fr.) Gray	saffron milk-cap
酸浆	*Physalis pubescens* L.	husk tomato
笋瓜	*Cucurbita maxima* Duch. exlam.	winter squash
薹菜	*Brassica campestris* L. ssp. *chinensis* var. *tai-tsai* Hort.	rape
甜菜	*Beta vulgaris* L. var. *rapacea* Koch	table beet, garden beet
甜瓜	*Cucumis melo* L.	melon, muskmelon
甜玉米	*Zea mays* L. var. *rugosa* Bonaf	sweet corn
茼蒿	*Chrysanthemum coronarium* L. var. *spatisum* Bailey	garland chrysanthemum, crown daisy, chop suey green
豌豆	*Pisum sativum* L.	garden pea, vegetable pea
食荚豌豆(甜豌豆)	*Pisum sativum* var. macrocarpon	edible-podded pea
皱粒豌豆	*Pisum sativum* var. *plicalum* AL.	English pea
薇菜(扫帚菜)	*Vicia sativa* L.	vetch
蕹菜(空心菜)	*Ipomoea aquatica* Forsk.	water spinach, swamp cabbage
莴苣	*Lactuca sativa* L.	lettuce
直立莴苣(长叶莴苣)	*Lactuca sativa* L. var. *romana* Gars.	cos lettuce, romaine lettuce
莴笋	*Lactuca sativa* L. var. *angustana* Irish.	asparagus lettuce
散叶莴苣	*Lactuca sativa* var. *intybacea* Hort.	leaf lettuce, loose-leaf lettuce, loose-head lettuce
皱叶莴苣	*Lactuca sativa* L. var. *crispa* L.	crisphead, iceberg
芜菁	*Brassica campestris* L. ssp. *rapifera* Matzg	turnip
芜菁甘蓝	*Brassica napobrassica* DC.	swede
西瓜	*Citrullus lanatus* (Thunb) Mansfeld, *C. vulgaris* Schard.	watermelon
西葫芦	*Cucurbita pepo* L.	summer squash
细香葱	*Allium schoenoprasum* L.	chives
苋菜	*Amaranthus mangostanus* L.	amaranth, edible amaranth
香椿	*Toona sinensis* Roem.	Chinese toona
香菇	*Lentinus edodes* (Berk.) Sing.	pasania fungus, straw mushroom
香瓜(光皮)	*Cucumis melo* var. *inodorus* Naudin.	casaba melon, honeydew melon
香芹菜	*Petroselinum hortense* Hoffm.	parsley
小白菜(油菜)	*Brassica campestris* L. ssp. chinensis(L.)	Chinese cabbage
雪豆(白扁豆、棉豆)	*Phaseolus lunatus* L.	lima bean
芫荽(香菜)	*Coriandrum sativum* L.	coriander, Chinese parsley
羊肚菌	*Morchella esculenta* (L.) Pers.	morel
洋葱	*Allium cepa* L.	onion
叶芥菜(青菜)	*Brassica juncea* Cosson. var. *foliosa* Bailey	leaf mustard

续表

中文名	拉丁学名	英文名
叶用甜菜（牛皮菜）	*Beta vulgaris* L. var. *cicla* Koch	chard, Swiss chard, leaf beet
银耳	*Tremella fuciformis* Berk.	white fungus, jelly fungi
芋头	*Colocasia esculenta* (L.) Schott.	taro, dasheen
竹荪	*Dictyophora indusiata* (Vent. Ex Pers.) Fischer	verled lady
竹笋	*Phyllostachys* sp.	bamboo shoot
籽芥菜	*Brassica juncea* Coss. var. *gracilis* Tsen et Lee	seedy mustard
紫背天葵	*Gynura bicolor* DC.	suizen jina
紫菜	*Porphyra* sp. C. Ag.	laver
紫苏	*Perilla nankinensis* Denc.	perilla

267

Appendix Ⅲ List of Subtropical and Tropical Flower Species in Chinese, Latin and English
附录Ⅲ 热带亚热带花卉中文、拉丁文和英文名录

(Edited by Feng Suping and Chen Yanli)

Table Ⅲ-1

中文名	拉丁学名	英文名
矮牵牛	*Petunia hybrida* Vilm.	common garden petunia
霸王鞭	*Euphorbia royleana* Boiss.	epiphyllum hybridusleafy cactus
白芨	*Bletilla striata* Rchb. f.	hyacinth bletilla
百合	*Lilium brownii var. viridulum* Baker	lily
百日草	*Zinnia elegans* Jacq.	common zinnia
百子莲	*Agapanthus africanus* Hoffmg.	African lily
半枝莲	*Portulaca grandiflora* Hook.	rose-moss
贝叶棕	*Corypha umbraculifera* Linn.	talipot palm
变叶木	*Codiaeum variegatum* BL. var. *pictum* Muell.	garden croton
波斯菊	*Cosmos bipinnatus* Cav.	common cosmos
长春花	*Catharanthus roseus* (L.) G. Don	Madagascar periwinkle
常春藤	*Hedera helix* L.	ivy
雏菊	*Bellis perennis* L.	English daisy
垂叶榕	*Ficus benjamina* L.	willow fig tree
慈姑	*Sagittaria sagittifolia* L.	Chinese arrowhead
刺桐	*Erythrina indica* Lam.	erythrina
葱兰	*Zephyranthes candida* Herb.	white zephyranthes
翠菊	*Callistephus chinensis* (L.) Nees	China-aster
大丽花	*Dahlia pinnata* Cav.	garden dahlia
大岩桐	*Sinningia speciosa* Benth. Et Hook	gloxinia
倒挂金钟	*Fuchsia hybrida* Voss.	lady's-eardrops
吊兰	*Chlorophytum comosum* Baker	spider ivy
吊竹兰	*Zebrina pendula* Sch.	inch plant
短穗鱼尾葵	*Caryota mitis* Lour	tufted fishtail palm
番红花	*Crocus sativus* L.	saffron
飞燕草	*Consolida ajacis* (L.) Schur	rocket larkspur
非洲菊	*Gerbera jamesonii* Bolus	flame-ray gerbera
非洲紫罗兰	*Saintpaulia ionantha* H. Wendl.	African violet
风铃草	*Campanula medium* L.	canterbury bells
风信子	*Hyacinthus orientalis* L.	hyacinth
凤凰木	*Delonix regia* (Boj.) Raf.	royal poinciana

续表

中文名	拉丁学名	英文名
凤仙花	*Impatiens balsamina* L.	garden balsam
福禄考	*Phlox drummondii* Hook.	phlox
高山罂粟	*Papaver alpinum* L.	Alpine poppy
瓜叶菊	*Senecio cruentus* DC.	florists cineraria
旱金莲	*Tropaeolum majus* L.	common nasturtium
荷花	*Nelumbo nucifera* Gaertn.	lotus
合欢	*Albizzia julibrissin* Durazz	silktree siris
黄槐	*Cassia surattensis* Burm. F.	scrambled eggs tree
红秋葵	*Hibiscus coccineus* Walt.	scarlet rose mallow
虎尾兰	*Sansevieria zeylanica* Willd.	snake plant
虎眼万年青	*Ornithogalum caudatum* Ait.	whiplash star of bethlehem
花毛茛	*Ranunculus asiaticus* L.	Persian buttercup
花叶万年青	*Dieffenbachia picta* Schott	spotted dieffenbachia
红豆	*Semen adenanthera* Pavonia	sandal beadtree
红掌	*Anthurium andreanum* Lindl.	flamingo lily
黄菖蒲	*Iris pseudacorus* L.	yellow flag iris
黄蜀葵	*Abelmoschus manihot* Medic	sunset hibiscus
火炬花	*Kniphofia uvaria* Hook.	torch lily
藿香蓟	*Ageratum conyzoides* L.	tropic ageratum
鸡蛋花	*Flos seu* Cortex Plumeriae	frangipani
鸡冠花	*Celosia argentea* L. var. *cristata* Kuntze	cockscomb
夹竹桃	*Nerium indicum* Mill	oleander
金丝桃	*Hypericum chinense* L.	St. John's wort
金银花	*Lonicera japonica* Thunb	honeysuckle flower
金鱼草	*Antirrhinum majus* L.	common snapdragon
金鱼藻	*Ceratophyllum demersum* L.	horn wort
金盏菊	*Calendula officinalis* L.	pot marigold
锦葵	*Malva sylvestris* L.	mallow
桔梗	*Platycodon grandiflorus* A. DC.	balloon flower
菊花	*Chrysanthemum morifolium* Ramat.	florists chrysanthemum
君子兰	*Clivia miniata* Regel	scarlet kafirlily
卡特兰	*Cattleya labiata* Lindl.	autumn cattleya
连翘	*Forsythia suspensa*（Thunb.）Vahl.	weeping forsythia
铃兰	*Convallaria majalis* L.	lily of the valley
旅人蕉	*Ravenala madagascariensis* Adans.	traveller's-tree
龙血树	*Dracaena angustifolia* Roxb.	dragon dracaena
耧斗菜	*Aquilegia vulgaris* L.	European crowfoot
马蹄莲	*Zantedeschia aethiopica* Spreng.	commom callalily
麦冬	*Liriope platyphylla* Wang et Tang	big blue liriope
麦秆菊	*Helichrysum bracteatum* Andr.	strawflower
毛地黄	*Digitalis purpurea* L.	foxglove

中文名	拉丁学名	英文名
美女樱	*Verbena hybmida* Voss	common garden verbena
美人蕉	*Canna variabilis* Willd.	India canna
木棉树	*Bombax ceiba* Linn.	commen bomhax flower
欧洲报春	*Primula vulgaris* Huds.	English primrose
蓬莱蕉	*Monstera deliciosa* Liebm.	monstera
蒲包花	*Calceolaria herbeohybrida* Voss.	calceolaria, slipperwort
蒲草	*Typha angustata* Bory et Chaub.	cattail
蒲葵	*Livistona chinensis* (Jacq.) R. Br.	Chinese fan palm
千屈菜	*Lythrum salicaria* L.	purple lythrum
千日红	*Gomphrena globosa* L.	common globe-amaranth
牵牛花	*Pharbitis nil* Choisy, *Ipomoea nil* Roth	white edge morning glory
秋海棠	*Begonia semperflorens* Link et Otto	begonia
日本鸢尾	*Iris japonica* Thunb.	butterfly flower
榕树	*Ficus microcarpa* L.	smallfruit fig
三角梅	*Bougainvillea spectabilis* Willd	bougainvillea
三色堇	*Viola tricolor* L.	wild pansy
散尾葵	*Chrysalidocarpus lutescens* H. Wendl.	butterfly palm
扫帚草	*Kochia scoparia* Schrad.	summer cypress, belvedere
山茶	*Camellia japonica* L.	common camellia
山梗菜	*Lobelia erinus* L.	edging lobelia
芍药	*Paeonia lactiflora* Pall.	Chinese peony
蛇目菊	*Coreopsis tinctoria* Nutt.	calliopsis
石蒜	*Lycoris radiata* Herb.	red spider lily
矢车菊	*Centaurea cyanus* L.	cornflower
蜀葵	*Althaea rosea* Cav.	hollyhock
水葱	*Scirpus tabernaemontani* Gmel.	softstem bulrush
睡莲	*Nymphaea tetragona* Georgi	water lily
四季报春	*Primula obconica* Hance	top primrose
宿根福禄考	*Phlox paniculata* L.	perennial phlox
唐菖蒲	*Gladiolus hybridus* Hort.	garden gladiolus
铁线莲	*Clematis florida* Thunb.	cream clematis
晚香玉	*Polianthes tuberosa* L.	tuberose
王莲	*Victoria amazornica* Sowerby	royal water platter
王棕	*Roystonea regia* (HBK.)O. F. Cook	royal palm
文殊兰	*Crinum asiaticum* L. var. *sinicum* Baker	grand crinum
文竹	*Asparagus plumosus* Baker	asparagus fern
五彩石竹	*Dianthus barbatus* L.	London tuft, sweet william
乌头	*Aconitum chinense* Sieb.	common monkshood
五色椒	*Capsicum frutescens* L. var. *cerasiforme* Bailey	cherry redpepper
仙人掌	*Opuntia stricta* (Haw.) Haw. var. *dillenii* (Ker-Gawl.) Benson	cactus
香龙血树	*Dracaena fragrans* Ker-Gawl.	fragrant dracaena

续表

中文名	拉丁学名	英文名
香石竹	*Dianthus caryophyllus* L.	carnation, clove pink
香豌豆	*Lathyrus odoratus* L.	sweet pea
相思子	*Abrus precatorius* Linn.	coralhead plant seed
向日葵	*Helianthus Giganteus* L.	sunflower
小苍兰	*Freesia refracta* Klatt	freesia
萱草（黄花菜）	*Hemerocallis fulva* L.	orange daylily
鸭舌草	*Monochoria vaginalis* Presl ex Kunth	duck tongue weed
沿街草（麦冬草）	*Ophiopogon japonicus* L. f. Ker-Gawl.	dwarf lily turf
一串红	*Salvia splendens* Ker-Gawl.	scarlet sage
一品红	*Euphorbia pulcherrima* Willd.	poinsettia
一叶兰	*Aspidistra elatior* Blume	common aspidistra
罂粟秋牡丹	*Anemone coronaria* L.	poppy anemone
虞美人	*Papaver rhoeas* L.	corn poppy
羽扇豆	*Lupinus polyphyllus* Lidl.	Washington lupine
玉簪	*Hosta plantaginea* Aschers.	fragrant plantain lily
郁金香	*Tulipa gesneriana* L.	tulip
月见草	*Oenothera biennis* L.	common evening primrose
中国水仙	*Narcissus tazetta* var. *chinensis* Roem.	Chinese sacred lily
朱顶红	*Hippeastrum vittatum* Herb.	amaryllis, barackslily
朱槿	*Hibiscus rosa-sinensis* L.	rose of China
竹芋	*Maranta arundinacea* L.	arrowroot, Bermuda arrowroot
紫荆	*Cercis chinensis* Bunge	China Redbud
紫罗兰	*Matthiola incana* R. Br.	stock, gilli-flower
紫茉莉	*Mirabilis jalapa* L.	common four-o'clock
紫玉簪	*Hosta ventricosa* (Salisb.) Stearn	blue plantain lily flower
棕榈	*Trachycarpus fortunei* (Hook.) H. Wendl.	fortunes windmill palm

Appendix IV Glossary

(Edited by Chen Yanli and Feng Suping)

A

1-aminocyclopropane-1- carboxylic acid 1-氨基环丙烷-1-羧酸
abiotic stress 非生物胁迫
abortion *n.* 败育
abscission *n.* 脱落,脱离
abscission zone 离区
absorbance *n.* 吸光率
Acer *n.* 槭属
acetosyringone *n.* 乙酰丁香酮
achene *n.* 瘦果
Achillea *n.* 蓍属,蓍草属
acidity *n.* 酸度,酸性
acoustical *adj.* 听觉的
adnate *adj.* 贴生的,联生的,并生的
adventitious *adj.* 偶然的,偶发的
adventitious root 不定根
adverse condition 不利条件,逆境条件
aeroponic *n.* 气培法
aesthetic *n.* 审美; *adj.* 美学的
African violet *n.* 非洲紫罗兰
Ageratum *n.* 霍香,胜红蓟属,藿香蓟属
aggregate fruit 聚合果,聚心皮果
agronomy *n.* 农艺学,农学
air circulating fan 环流风扇
air flow 气流
alcohols *n.* 醇类
Alfisol *n.* 淋溶土,淀积土
algae *n.* 藻,藻类植物,水藻,海藻
alkalinity *n.* 碱度,碱性
alkaloid *n.* 生物碱
alkyl ester 烷基酯
alluvial deposit 冲击物
alluvial flood plains 冲积平原
almond *n.* [植物] 杏仁,扁桃树,巴旦杏树
aloe vera [植物] 芦荟(芦荟属植物)
alternate bearing 大小年结果
aluminum *n.* 铝
aluminum layered film 缀铝膜
aluminum wire 铝丝,铝线
ambient temperature 环境温度
amino acid *n.* 氨基酸
ammonium nitrogen 铵态氮
ammonium phosphate 磷酸铵
analogous colors 类似色
analogy *n.* 相似,类似
anatomy *n.* 解剖学,解剖
anchor pin 锚定销,连接销
anchorage *n.* 锚位,锚地,(砧木)固着土地,扎根,固定
angiosperm *n.* 被子植物
angle iron 角钢
Animal Plant Health Inspection Service (APHIS) (动植物卫生检验局),是美国农业部(USDA)的一个下属机构。
annual *adj.* 一年生的; *n.* 一年生植物
antagonism microorganism 拮抗性微生物
anthocyanin *n.* 花青素,花色苷
anthracnose *n.* 炭疽病
Anthurium *n.* 花烛属植物
antibiotic *n.* 抗生素,抗菌素; *adj.* 抗菌的
antiseptic *adj.* 防腐的,杀毒的,无菌的; *n.* 防腐剂,杀毒剂
aphid *n.* 蚜虫
apical meristem 顶端分生组织,茎尖分生组织
apricot *n.* 杏,杏树
arboriculture *n.* 树木栽培学,树艺学

architecture　n. 建筑学，建筑
Aridisol　n. 旱成土
aridity　n. 荒芜，干旱，干燥(旱)度
Artemisia　n. 蒿属，蒿，沙蒿，青蒿
artichoke　n. 朝鲜蓟
artificial illuminatio　人工光源
Ascochyta　n .［真菌］壳二孢属，囊二孢
asexual reproduction　无性生殖
asexually propagated crop　无性繁殖作物
asparagus　n. 芦笋，石刁柏
aster　n. 紫菀属植物，紫菀
aster yellow　紫菀黄化病
astringency　n. 涩味
atmospheric　adj. 大气的，大气层(压)的
Aucuba　n. 桃叶珊瑚，桃叶珊瑚属
auxin　n. 植物生长激素
avocado　n. 鳄梨，油梨
azalea　n. 杜鹃花，杜鹃花属植物

B

backyard　n. 后院，后庭
bacteria　n. 细菌
bacteriology　n. 细菌学
balance　n. 平衡
banana bunchy top virus（BBTV）　香蕉束顶病病毒
barbecue pit　n. 烧烤炉
bark　n. 树皮，茎皮
basic layout　基本布局
bedding plant　花坛植物
beet　n. 甜菜
Begonia　n. 秋海棠，秋海棠属
berry　n 浆果
bicarbonate　碳酸氢，碳酸氢盐
biennial　adj. 二年生的； n. 二年生植物
bilateral symmetry　两侧对称，左右对称
binary plasmid　二元质粒
binominal system　二名制
biochemistry　n. 生物化学
blackberry　n. 黑莓
blade　n. 叶片
blight　n. 枯萎病
blossom-end rot　n. 脐腐病

blueberry　n. 越橘，蓝莓
bog　n. 沼泽，沼泽地
bonsai　n. 盆栽，盆景
bonsai training　盆景整形，盆栽整枝
boric acid　硼酸
boron　n. 硼
botanist　n. 植物学家，植物工作者
botany　n. 植物学
botrytis blight　灰霉病
Botrytis cinerea　灰葡萄孢菌
bougainvillea　n. 叶子花
box elder　梣叶槭
bract　n. 苞片，托叶
Brassaia　n. 澳洲鸭脚木
Brassavola nodosa　拉索兰
breadfruit　n. 面包果
breeder　n. 育种工作者
broccoli　n. 花椰菜，花茎甘蓝，西兰花
Bromeliaceae　凤梨科，凤梨属植物
browning　n. 褐变
bud union　芽接口，愈合处
Buddleja　n. 醉鱼草属
buffer capacity　缓冲能力
bulb　n. 鳞茎，球茎，种球
bulbil　n. 鳞芽，球芽
bumblebee　n. 大黄蜂，雄蜂
Burkina-Faso　布基纳法索(非洲国家)
burlap　n. 粗麻布，粗麻袋，打包麻布
bush　n. 灌木，灌木丛

C

cabbage　n. 卷心菜
cactus　n. 仙人掌
Caladium　n.［植］贝母，彩叶芋属
calanthe　n. 脊兰
calcium　n.［化］钙
calcium nitrate　硝酸钙
Calendula　n. 金盏菊属，金盏菊，金盏草
callus tissue　愈伤组织
calyx　n. 花萼
camellia　n. 山茶
canker　n. 溃疡，(树的)癌肿病； v. 患溃疡，腐蚀，溃烂

cantaloupe n. 罗马甜瓜，香瓜，哈密瓜
canvas n. 帆布
capacitance probe 电容探测器，电容探头
capillary matting 具毛管作用的垫子
capsule n. 蒴果，孢蒴
captan n. 克菌丹（一种用硫醇制的杀真菌剂和杀虫剂）
carambola n. 杨桃
carbohydrate n. 碳水化合物，碳水化物
carbon dioxide 二氧化碳
carnation n. 石竹，康乃馨
carotinoid n. 类胡萝卜素，胡萝卜素
carpel n. ［植］心皮
carpet grass n. 地毯草
carrot n. 胡萝卜
catering n. 饮食界，提供餐饮服务
cation n. 阳离子，正离子
cation exchange capacity 阳离子交换能力
cattleya n. 洋兰
cavity n. 腔，洞
cefotaxime n. 氨噻肟头孢菌素
celery n. 芹菜
cell division 细胞分裂
cell sap 细胞液
cellulose n. 纤维素，纤维素酶
central-leader training 中心领导枝树形，中轴式整枝
cereal n. 谷类植物，谷物；adj. 谷类（的），谷物（的）
cessation n. 停止，中止
chamber n. 腔，室；adj. 室内的
cheesecloth n. 薄纱棉布，纱布
chelated iron 络合铁
chemical pinching 化学摘心
chemical pruning agent 化学修剪剂
cherimoya n. 番荔枝
cherry n. 樱桃
chestnut n. 栗子，板栗，栗树
chicken wire 铁丝织网
chiku n. 人心果，即 sapodilla，一种热带水果，泰国称作 Lamoot，印度尼西亚称作 Chiku，我国台湾称为吴凤柿
chilling injury 寒害，冷害

chive n. 细香葱
chlorine n. 氯
chloroneb n. 地茂散（杀真菌剂）
chlorophyll n. 叶绿素
chloroplast n. 叶绿体
chlorotic adj. 萎黄病的，变色病的
Chrysanthemum n. 菊花，菊，菊属
chrysanthemum stunt viroid 菊花矮化类病毒
CITES 濒危野生动植物种国际贸易公约（Convention on International Trade in Endangered Species of Wild Fauna and Flora）的简称
Citrus n. 柑橘属果树
Cladosporium 分子孢子菌属
clay fraction 粘粒
Cleyera n. 红淡比属
climacteric fruit 呼吸跃变型果实
climatological data 气象资料
clinometer n. 测斜仪，倾斜仪，量坡仪，倾斜计
clod n. 块，（尤指）土块，泥块
clonal adj. ［生］无性（繁殖）系的
closed-type seedling raising facility 闭锁型育苗设施
cloud-free adj. 无云的
cloudiness n. 云量，多云状态，（混）浊度
CO_2 concentration sensors CO_2 浓度传感器
CO_2 generating systems CO_2 发生系统
coalesce v. 联合，合并
coconut fiber 椰子纤维
cold storage 冷藏
colloidal adj. 胶状的，胶质的
colloidal material 胶体物质
combustion units 点火设备
commercial horticulture 商品园艺学，市场化园艺
commodity n. 商品
compatibility adj. 亲和的
Compositae n. 菊科植物，菊科
compost n. 混合肥料，堆肥
compressor n. 压气机，压缩机
coniferous adj. 松类的，结球果的
connotation n. 内涵，含义
continuity n. 连续性，连贯性
contour n. 等高线，外形，轮廓线，轮廓
controlled pollination 人工授粉

controlled-atmosphere (CA) storage　气调贮藏
conveyor　*n.* 输送机，输送设备，搬运者
cooling efficiency　冷却效率
copper　*n.* 铜
corky cell　木栓细胞
corm　*n.* 球茎，球鳞盘
corolla　*n.* 花冠
corollatube　*n.* 冠筒，花冠筒
corsage　*n.* 装饰的花束
cosmetic　*n.* 化妆品，装饰品；　*adj.* 化妆用的，化妆品的
cottonwood　*n.* 杨木
cotyledon　*n.* 子叶，绒毛叶
craft　*n.* 工艺，技能
cranberry　*n.* 蔓越橘
crate　*n.* 板条箱，篓子
crescent　*n.* 新月，新月形之物；　*adj.* 新月形的
cross-breed　*n.* 杂种
crossfluted　*adj.* 交叉凹槽状
cross-pollination　*n.* 异花授粉，杂交授粉
crotch　*n.* 分叉处，叉柱
croton　*n.* 巴豆
crown　*n.* 树冠，根颈
Cruciferae　*n.* ［植］十字花科，十字花科植物
Cucumber mosaic virus (CMV)　黄瓜花叶病毒
cucurbit　*n.* 葫芦科植物，瓜类
Cucurbitaceae　*n.* 葫芦科
cultipacker　*n.* 碎土镇压器
cultivar　*n.* 品种
cut flower　切花，鲜切花
cuticle　*n.* 角质层，表皮层
cutin　*n.* 表皮素，蜡状质
Cyclamen　*n.* 仙客来，仙客来属
cycloheximide　*n.* 环己酰亚胺
cyclone　*n.* 旋风，飓风
cycocel　*n.* 矮壮素
cymbidium　*n.* ［植］兰，兰花，兰属（*Cymbidium*）植物
cymose inflorescence　聚伞状花序
cysticerci　*n.* 囊状虫，幼虫
cytogenesis　*n.* 细胞发生
cytokinin　*n.* 细胞激动素，细胞分裂素
cytoplasm　*n.* 细胞质，胞浆，胞质

D

daffodil　*n.* 黄水仙，水仙
daminozide　*n.* 丁酰肼
damping-off　*n.* 猝倒病
dark reaction　暗反应
data logger　数据记录器
date　*n.* 椰枣，枣椰子
daylength　日照时间
deciduous　*adj.* 落叶的
deciduous tree　落叶树，落叶树种
decomposition　*n.* 分解，腐烂，分解作用
deep flow technique　深液流水培技术
deep-layer soil heating system　深层土壤加热系统
deficiency symptom　缺素症，营养缺乏症状
defogging　*n.* 驱雾
deformation　*n.* 变形，畸形，损形
dehumidification　*n.* 除湿干燥，降低湿度
dehydrate　*v.* 脱水，失水，干燥
dehydrated scale　脱水鳞片
delayed light emission　延迟发光
demand fluctuation　需求波动
Dendrobium　石斛，石斛属植物
deposition　*n.* 沉积
desiccation　*n.* 干燥，除湿，脱水
dessert　*n.* 甜食
deterioration　*n.* 恶化，降低，退化，腐烂
detrimental　*adj.* 有害的，不利的
d-fructose　*n.* d-果糖
d-glucose　*n.* d-葡萄糖
diabase　*n.* 辉绿岩
Dianthus　*n.* 香石竹，石竹属，石竹类属植物
dibasic acid　二元酸，二碱价酸
dichogamous　*adj.* ［植］雌雄（蕊）异熟的
dicotyledon　*n.* 双子叶植物，双子叶
Dieffenbachia　*n.* 花叶万年青属植物
differentiation　分化
diluted sulfuric acid　稀硫酸
dioecious　*adj.* 雌雄异体的，雌雄异株的
dioecism　*n.* 雌雄异株
discharging of water　排水量
discoloration　*n.* 变色，褪色
disease incidence　发病率

disinfestation n. 灭虫，灭昆虫法
disintegrate v. 分裂，解体，分解
dissect v. 解剖，切细，仔细分析
distal adj. 末梢的
distribution center 配送中心
diurnal temperature 昼夜温度
divergent evolution 趋异进化，分裂演进
dormant pruning 冬季修剪，休眠期修剪
Dracaena n. [植]龙血树属植物
dragon's eye fruit 龙眼
dressings n. 敷料剂
drippers or trickle tape 滴灌带
drive n. 快车道
drupe n. 核果
duration n. 持续，持久
durian n. 榴莲
dutch iris 鸢尾
dwarfing adj. 矮化的
dynamic root floating hydroponic 动态浮根水培

E

Easter lily 复活节百合
EC meter EC 计
ecology n. 生态学
ecosystematic adj. 生态系统的
egg n. 卵
electrical conduit 电缆
elevation n. 海拔，高程，升高，标高
elite n. 良种，原种
emasculate v. 阉割，使柔弱，删削，使无力； adj. 阉割了的，柔弱的
emasculation n. 去雄
embryo n. 胚，胚胎，胚芽（期），萌芽期；
embryo sac 胚囊
embryogenic culture 胚发生培养
embryological adj. 胚胎学的
embryology n. 胚胎学
embryonic leaf 胚芽，胚叶
endosperm n. 胚乳
entomology n. 昆虫学
environment variable 环境因子，环境变量
Environmental Protection Agency (EPA) （美国）环境保护局

epidemic adj. 传染性的，流行性的，n. 传染病，流行病
epidermi n. 表皮
epiphyte 附生菌，附生植物
Epipremnum n. 拎树藤属
equilibrium n. 平衡，平静，均衡，保持平衡的能力
equinoxes n. 二分点（春分点与秋分点）
erosion n. 侵蚀
espalier training 篱形整枝，树墙式整枝
ETFE 聚氟乙烯
ethephon n. 乙烯利，乙烯
eucalyptus n. 桉树
eukaryotic adj. 真核的
Euphorbia n. 大戟属植物
Euphorbiaceaec n. 大戟科
evaporative pad cooling 湿垫(帘)蒸发降温
evapotranspiration n. 耗水量，蒸(散)发量，蒸发蒸腾量
even span 等坡（屋顶）
evergreen adj. 常绿的，常青的；n. 常绿植物
evergreen plant 常绿植物
E-W oriented house 东西走向温室
exhaust fan 排气扇，风机
exotic adj. 外来的，非本地的，引进种
explant n. 外植体；v. 移植，外植
extrapolate v. 推断，推知，预测，推测

F

farmers market 农贸市场，农夫市集
farmstead n. 农庄
fatty acid 脂肪酸
feed additive 饲料添加剂
felted coccid 毡蚧
female flower 雌花
female gamete 雌配子
fern n. 蕨类植物，蕨类，真蕨纲
ferric oxide n. 氧化铁，三氧化二铁
fertigation n. 肥灌
fertigation system 施肥灌溉系统
fertile adj. 肥沃的，能繁殖的；n. 多产，肥沃
fertilization n. 受精，施肥
fertilized egg 受精卵

fibrous　adj. 含纤维的，纤维状的
ficus　n. 榕树
Ficus benjamina　垂叶榕
field heat　田间热，场热
filbert　n. 榛，榛属(Cory lus)
fir　n. 枞，冷杉
firm　vt. & vi. (使)坚硬[稳固]
firmness　n. 硬度
flamingo flower　彩斑芋
flavor　n. 风味，气味
flexibility　n. 机动性，灵活性
floral anatomy　花部解剖
floribunda roses　丰花月季
floricultural product　花卉园艺产品
floriculture　n. 花卉，花卉栽培
florist　n. 花匠，花商，花卉研究者
flower arrangement　插花
flower induction　成花诱导
flowering pot plant　盆栽观花植物
fludioxonil　n. 咯菌腈，勿落菌恶(由瑞士诺华公司开发)
fluorescent light　荧光灯，荧光，日光灯
fluorine　n. 氟
foaming polystyrene　发泡聚苯乙烯
focalization　n. 焦点
foliage plant　观叶植物
follicle　n. 小囊，滤泡，卵泡
Food and Drug Administration (FDA)　(美国)食品和药物管理局
forage　n. 粮草，食料，刍草，粮秣
forcing vegetables　促成栽培的蔬菜
forest tree　林木
forestry　n. 林业，林学，森林学
forked　adj. 叉状的，有叉的
form　n. 形状，形式，形态
fountain　n. 喷泉，源泉
Fragaria　n. 草莓属
free standing structures　落地式结构
freezing point　冰点
frost damage　霜冻害
FRP (fiber reinforced plastic)　玻璃钢
fructose　n. 果糖
fruit cracking　果实开裂，果实裂缝

fruit set　坐果
fruit thinning　疏果
fruit-bearing plant　结实植物，观果植物
Fuchsias　倒挂金钟属植物
fumigant　薰剂
fumigate　v. 熏蒸，熏蒸消毒
fumigation　n. 熏蒸
fungal　adj. 真菌的
fungi　n. 真菌，真菌科，真菌类
fungicide　n. 杀菌剂
fungus　n. 菌，霉菌，真菌
furrow irrigation　沟灌，畦灌
Fusarium　n. 镰刀霉，镰刀菌属
Fusarium wilt　镰刀霉枯萎病，凋萎病，干腐病

G

gable roof　人字(三角)屋顶
gamete　n. 配子
garden cress　独行菜，水芹(藜菜属，十字花科)
garden perennials　多年生园艺植物
gardenia　n. 栀子
gelatinous　adj. 胶状的
generic name　属名
genetic　adj. 遗传的，起源的
genetic engineering　遗传工程
genetic background　遗传背景，遗传基础
genetic engineer　基因工程
genetic incompatibility　遗传不亲和
genetic information　遗传信息，基因信息
genetic mutation　基因突变，遗传变异
genetic variation　遗传变异
genotype　n. 基因型，遗传型
genetic　adj. 遗传的，基因的
genus　n. 属，种，类
geographical location　地理位置
Geranium　n. 天竺葵，老鹳草属植物
Gerberas　n. 大丁草，大丁草属，非洲菊
germination　n. 萌发，发芽
germplasm　n. 种质资源
glaciation　n. 冰河作用
Gladioli　n. 唐菖蒲，唐菖蒲属
gladiolus　n. 剑兰
glandular hair　n. 腺毛，汗毛

glass marble 玻璃球
glasshouse n. 玻璃暖房，温室
glucose n. 葡萄糖
glue n. 胶，各种胶合物
glyphosate n. 草甘膦
gooseberry n. 醋栗，醋栗树
gourd n. 葫芦，瓜类
grading facility 分级设施
grading line 分级生产线
Graminae n. 禾本科植物，禾本科
granular adj. 颗粒状的
granulated rock wool 颗粒状的岩棉，粒化岩棉
grape n. 葡萄
grapefruit n. 葡萄柚
grapevines n. 葡萄藤，葡萄树
gravel n. 沙砾，砾石
greenhouse framework 温室骨架
greenhouse orientation 温室放线、定位
greenhouse plant 温室植物
greenhouse structure 温室结构
green-manure crop 绿肥作物
grocer n. 杂货商，食品商
growing point 生长点
growth regulators 生长调节剂
growth retardant 生长抑制剂
guava n. 番石榴
gymnosperm n. 裸子植物，裸子植物门
gynoecious n. 纯雌植物，雌株
gynostemium n. 合蕊冠，合蕊柱

H

hail n. 雹，冰雹
hand detasseling 人工去雄
hand pinching 手动摘心
hare n. 野兔
harmonize v. 协调
harvest maturity 采收成熟度，可采成熟度
hay n. 干草
heading-back 截短
heat insulation and shading equipment 隔热遮阳设备
heat stress 热胁迫
heating system 加热系统

heatproof foam 隔热泡沫
hectare n. 公顷
Hedera helix n. 常春藤
hedge n. 树篱
hedgerow n. 灌木树篱，栅栏，隔板
Helianthus n. 向日葵，向日葵属
Heliconias n. 蝎尾蕉，蝎尾蕉属植物
Hemlock n. 铁杉属
hepatitis B surface gen（HBsAg） 乙肝表面抗原
herb n. 草本，草本植物，药草
herbaceous perennial 多年生草本植物
herbaceous plant 草本植物
herbicide n. 除草剂
hereditary character 遗传特性
hermaphroditic adj. 两性的，雌雄同体的
hermaphroditic flower 两性花
heterozygous genotype 杂合基因型
hexose sugar 己糖
hibiscus n. 芙蓉，木槿
highly efficient fluorescent lamp 高效荧光灯
high-pressure sodium lamp 高压气体钠灯
histochemical adj. 组织化学的
hollyhock n. 蜀葵
homozygous adj. [生]同型结合的，纯合子的
honeydew n. 甘汁，蜜露
horizon n. 土层，层位
hormone n. 荷尔蒙，激素
horticulture n. 园艺，园艺学
host plant 寄主植物
hot glue gun 热熔胶枪
hoya n. [植]球兰
humidity n. 湿度
humidity control 湿度调节
humidity sensor 湿度传感器
hummingbird n. 蜂鸟
humus n. 腐殖质
hurricane n. 飓风
hybrid n. 杂交种
hybrid seed 杂种种子
hybrid tea 杂种香水月季
Hydrangea n. 八仙花属，绣球，绣球属
hydrazine sulfate 硫酸肼
hydrocooling n. 水冷却，水冷，凉水冷却

hydrolysis n. 水解
hydroponic n. 水培；adj. 营养液栽培的
hygiene n. 卫生学，保健法
hygienic adj. 卫生的，清洁的
hymexazol n. 恶霉灵
hypobaric storage 减压储藏

I

ideotype n. 理想株型
illuminating light 补光灯
imaginary line 假想线，假设线，虚线
Impatiens n. [植]凤仙花属植物
impregnated paper 浸油纸
improvement n. 改进，改良，改善，改正
in embryo 初期的，萌芽时期的
in response to 响应，适应
in vitro culture 离体培养，体外培养
incandescent bulb 白炽灯泡
indices index 的复数
individual control device 分级控制装置
infectious adj. 侵染性的，易传播的
infestation n. 侵扰，侵袭，侵染，蔓延
inflorescence n. 花序
ingenuity n. 智巧，创造力，精巧的设计
ingredient n. 成分，因素
inocula n. 接种物
inorganic substance 无机物质
insecticide n. 杀虫剂
insectivorous plant 食虫植物
insoluble adj. 不溶性的
integrated pest management 害虫综合防治
intercropping n. 间作，套种，间混作，间套作
interference RNA RNA 干扰
intermittent flow 间歇性流动
International Code of Botanical Nomenclature 国际植物命名法规
internode n. 节间
interplant n. 套种，间作，间种物
in-vitro 体外的
Iris n. 鸢尾属植物
iron n. 铁
irradiance level 辐照度
isotherm n. 等温线

J

jasmine n. 茉莉花
jumble n. 混杂，混乱
jumbo size 大尺寸
Juniper n. 刺柏，刺柏属，杜松，杜松属
juvenile period 童期

K

Kalanchoe blossfeldiana 落地生根，长寿花
kanamycin n. 卡那霉素
kangaroo/wallaby n. 袋鼠/小袋鼠
kelp n. 巨藻，大型海藻，海草灰
Kenya n. 肯尼亚
kikuyu grass 隐花狼尾草
killing temperature 致死温度
kilolux n. 千勒克司

L

labour-intensive production process 劳动密集型生产加工
Lacanobia oleracea 西红柿夜蛾
ladybug n. 瓢虫
landscape n. 园林，景观
landscape architecture 园林建筑
landscape design 景观设计，园林设计
latania scale 拉塔尼亚芭蕉蚧
latitude n. 纬度
lawn n. 草坪，草地
layering n. 压条法
leach v. 过滤，萃取，水浸；n. 过滤，过滤器，滤灰槽
leaf cutting 叶插
leaf miner (*Liriomyza* spp.) 斑潜蝇
leaf mold 腐殖土
leaf sheath 叶鞘
leaf-bud cutting 叶芽插
leafhopper n. 叶蝉
leaflet n. 小叶
legume n. 豆科，豆科植物
leguminous crop 豆类作物，豆科作物
lemon n. 柠檬
lenticel n. 皮孔

lentil n. 扁豆
lesion n. 损害，损伤
lettuce n. 生菜
leucoplast n. 白色体
lichen n. 地衣，苔藓，青苔
light control 光量控制
light emitting diode 发光二极管
light penetration 透光度
light reaction 光反应
light transmission 透光率
ligneous adj. 木质的，木头的
lignin n. 木质素
Liliaceae n. 百合科
lily n. 百合花
lily pond 睡莲池塘，莲花池
lime n. 来檬
limestone n. 石灰岩
lipid n. 脂质，油脂
liquefied petroleum gas（LPG） 液化石油气
load n. 荷载
loam n.（含有黏土、沙以及有机物质的）肥土
logarithmic phase 对数期，对数生长期
looper n. 尺蠖
lopper n. 修枝剪
loquat n. 枇杷
Loropetalum n. 檵木属
louver n. 百叶窗
low pitched roof 缓坡屋顶
lycopersicin n. 番茄素

M

Macadamia n. 澳洲坚果，澳洲坚果属
macronutrient n. 大量元素，常量营养素
macroscopic adj. 肉眼可见的，宏观的
maggot n. 五谷虫
magnesium n. ［化］镁
magnesium sulfate 硫酸镁
male gamete 雄配子
male sterile 雄性不育
Malus n. 苹果属
manganese n. 锰
manganese sulfate 硫酸锰
mango n. 芒果

manifest n. 表现，征候，显示； adj. 显然的；
  v. 表明，显示，表露
maranta n. ［植］竹竿
Marantaceae n. 竹芋科
marigold n. 金盏草，万寿菊
marinade n. 腌泡汁
marker assisted selection（MAS） 标记辅助育种
mass effect 质量效应
material handling system 物料处理系统
meat tenderizer 嫩肉粉
medium n. 培养基
mefenoxam n.（精）甲霜灵
megaspore n. 大孢子
meiosis n. 减数分裂
mellow adj. 熟透的，黄熟的，松软的； v.（使）
  成熟
meristem n. 分生组织，分裂组织
meristematic cell 分生细胞
metalaxyl n. 甲霜林
metallic adj. 金属的，金属般的
meteorology n. 气象学，气象
methodology n. 方法学，方法论
methyl bromide 溴甲烷
methyl caproate 己酸甲酯
methyl caprylate 辛酸甲酯
methyl laurate 月桂酸甲酯
methyl stearate 硬脂酸甲酯
mica-type 云母型
micronutrient n. 微量营养素
microorganism n. 微生物
micro-propagation n. 微繁，微体快繁
micropyle n. 珠孔
microscopic adj. 微小的，细微的，用显微镜可
  看见的
microspore n. 小（型分生）孢子
midlatitudes n. 中间纬度
midrib n. 中脉，中脊
mid-to late-season cultivar 中长季节品种，中晚
  熟品种
Mimulus n. 沟酸浆属植物
mineral substance 矿物质
minisprinkler n. 微喷灌装置
mist cooling 喷雾降温

misting device 喷雾器
mite n. 螨
mitosis n. 有丝分裂
modified leader training 改良闭心式整枝
molybdenum n. 钼
monoembryony n. 单胚
monoaxial adj. 单轴
monocotyledon n. 单子叶植物，单子叶
monoecious adj. 雄雌同株的，雌雄同体的
monopodial adj. [植]单轴的
monotony n. 单调
monsoon n. 季风，季风期
Monstera n. [植]蓬莱蕉
montmorillonite n. 蒙脱石，蒙脱土
morphological adj. 形态学的
moss n. 苔藓，泥沼
mother plant 母株
mow vt. & vi 刈，割，修剪
multiple covering 多重覆盖
multispan adj. 连栋，连跨
musk melon 甜瓜，哈密瓜
mycelium n. 菌丝(体)

N

naphthalene acetic acid 萘乙酸
narcissus 水仙
natural selection 自然选择
necrosis n. 枯斑，坏死，坏疽
nematode n. 线虫，线虫病；adj. 线虫类的
neutral adj. 中立的，中性的
Nicotiana n. 烟草，烟草属
nitrate nitrogen 硝态氮
nitrate n. 硝酸盐
nitric acid 硝酸
nitrogen n. [化]氮
nomenclature n. 系统命名法，(某一学科的)术语，专门名称
non-climacteric fruit 非呼吸跃变型果实
non-destructive quality evaluation device 无损伤质量评价装置
noninjurious adj. 无害的
N-S oriented house 南北走向温室
nucleoprotein n. 核蛋白质

nursery crop 苗圃作物
nursery stock 定植苗，出圃苗，苗木
nutraceutically adj 营养食品的，保健食品的
nutrient film technique 营养液膜技术

O

odor n. 香味
off-year n. 小年
olericulture n. 蔬菜栽培，蔬菜学
onion n. 洋葱
open-center system 开心式系统
optimum storage conditions 最佳贮藏条件
orange n. 橘子
orchard n. 果园
Orchidaceae n. 兰科
Orchids n. 兰科植物，兰花，兰属植物
organic hydroponics 有机水培
organism n. 生物，(尤指)微生物，有机组织
oriental poppy 东方罂粟
ornamental plant 观赏植物
ornamental shrub 观赏灌木
osmosis n. 渗透，渗透性
osmosis pressure 渗透压
Osmunda 紫萁属
oval n. 椭圆形 adj. 卵形的，椭圆形的
overplanting n. 移植
overripening n. 过熟
ovule n. 胚珠
Oxisol n. 氧化土
oxygen n. 氧气

P

pack n. 包装，包裹；v. 包装，包裹
packaging n. 包装，装封
packhouse n. 货仓
packing house 包装工厂，包装车间
pad and fan cooling 风机湿帘降温
palatability n. 适口性，风味，口感
paleobotany n. 古植物学
palm n. 棕榈树，棕榈科植物
Papaver n. 罂粟，罂粟属
Papaveraceae n. 罂粟科，罂粟科植物
papaya n. 番木瓜

281

papaya ringspot virus（PRSV） 番木瓜环斑花叶病
parasitic *adj.* 寄生的，寄生虫的
parasitize *v.* 寄生，寄生于
parenchyma tissue 薄壁组织
parent plants 亲本
parsley *n.* 欧芹，洋芫荽，洋香菜
parthenocarpically *adv.* 单性结实地
parthenocarpy *n.* [植]单性结实
part-time farmer 兼营农场主
passionfruit 鸡蛋果，又名百香果
pathogen *n.* 病菌，病原体
pathogenicity *n.* 病原性，致病性
pavement *n.* 人行道
（Polymerase Chain Reaction）聚合酶链式反应简称PCR，是一种分子生物学技术，用于放大特定的DNA片段的拷贝，是一种在生物体外复制DNA的技术
peak roof 尖屋顶
peat moss 泥炭沼，泥炭藓
pecan *n.* 美洲山核桃
pectic substance 果胶质，果胶物质
pectin *n.* 胶质
pedestrian *n.* 行人； *adj.* 徒步的
pedicel *n.* [植]花梗
peduncle *n.* 花梗，梗
Pelargonium *n.* 天竺葵属植物
pendulous *adj.* 悬垂的，下垂的
Peperomia *n.* 豆瓣绿属植物
per capita consumption 按人口平均计算的消费量
perception *n.* 感受
perennial *adj.* 多年生的； *n.* 多年生植物
perennial ornamental 多年生的观赏植物
perianth *n.* 花被
perimeter *n.* 周界
perishability 易腐性
perishable *adj.* 容易腐烂的
perlite *n.* 珍珠岩
permeability *n.* 透性，透水性，通透性
perpendicular *adj.* （与……）垂直（正交）的； *n.* 垂线，垂直面
pesticide *n.* 农药，杀虫剂
petal *n.* 花瓣

petiole *n.* 叶柄，柄，柄部
Phaius *n.* 鹤顶兰属植物
phalaenopsis *n.* 蝴蝶兰
pharmaceutical crop 药用植物
phenol *n.* 苯酚； *adj.* 苯酚的
phenology *n.* 物候，物候学，生物气候学
phenotype *n.* 表（现）型，外貌同型（生物）
phenotypic *adj.* 表型的
Philadelphus *n.* 山梅花属
Philippines *n.* 菲律宾
Philodendron *n.* 喜林芋，喜林芋属
phloem *n.* 韧皮部，韧皮
Phlox *n.* 草夹竹桃属植物，草夹竹桃
phosphatide *n.* 磷脂
phosphon *n.* 氯化磷
phosphorous acid 亚磷酸
phosphorus *n.* [化]磷，磷肥
photochemical *adj.* 光化作用的，光化学的
photoperiod *n.* 光（周）期，光照期
photoperiodism *n.* 光周期性，光周期现象
photosynthesis *n.* 光合作用
photosynthesize *v.* 光合作用
phylogenetic *adj.* 系统发育的 系统发生的
physicochemical *adj.* 物理化学的
physiology *n.* 生理学
Phytophthora *n.* 疫霉属
phytotoxic *adj.* 植物性毒素的
pickle *vt.* 腌渍(泡菜等)；腌菜
pick-your-own *adj.* 由顾客自摘自采的（水果、蔬菜等）
pick-your-own marketing 自选市场
picnic facility 野餐设施
pigment *n.* 色素
Pilea *n.* 冷水花属
pinching *v.* 摘心，打顶
pine *n.* 松树
pine bark 松树皮
pineapple *n.* 菠萝，凤梨
pinnate *adj.* 羽状的
Pinus *n.* 松属
pipe framework 管架结构
pistil *n.* [植]雌蕊
pistillate *adj.* 雌蕊的，有雌蕊的

plankton n. 浮游生物
plant factory 植物工厂
plant nursery 植物苗圃
plant patent 植物专利
plant pathology 植物病理学
plant tissue analysis 植物组织分析，植物组织分析法
plantain n. 大蕉
plasma membrane 质膜
plasmolyzing adj. 质壁分离的，胞质皱缩的
plasticity n. 可塑性，塑性，适应性
plastid n. 质体，色素体，成形原体
plough v. 翻地，犁耕，耕
plum n. 李子
podocarpus n. 罗汉松
poinsettia n. 一品红，猩猩木
poisonous adj. 有毒的
Polar region 南北极地区
pollen n. 花粉
pollen anatomy 花粉解剖学
pollen grain 花粉粒
polyaxial adj. 多轴
polyembryony n. 多胚性，多胚现象
polyester n. 聚酯，涤纶，聚酯纤维
polyethylene (PE) n. 聚乙烯
polyethylene bag 聚乙烯袋
polyethylene terephthalate (PETP) 聚对苯二甲酸乙二酯，俗称聚酯
polyolefin-based (PO) film 聚烯烃膜
polypropylene (PP) n. 聚丙烯
polyvinyl alcohol 聚乙烯醇
polyvinyl chloride (PVC) 聚氯乙烯
pome n. 仁果，梨果
pomology n. 果树学，果树栽培学
pompon n. 球型大丽花；彩球
ponderosa n. 美国黄松
poor drainage 排水不良
poorly adv. 拙劣地，蹩脚地
poorly-aerated soil 通气性不良的土壤
pork tapeworm 猪肉绦虫
porosity n. 多孔性，有孔性，孔隙度
positioner n. 定位器
postharvest n. 采后

postharvest handling 采后处理
post-harvest loss 采后损失，采后耗损
post-transcriptional adj. 转录后的
pot plant 盆栽植物，盆栽花卉
potassium n. [化]钾
potassium aluminum sulfate 硫酸铝钾
potassium hydroxide 氢氧化钾
potassium nitrate 硝酸钾
potassium phosphate 磷酸钾
powdery mildew 白粉病，白粉菌
pratylenchus n. 短体线虫
praying mantis 螳螂
precipitation n. 降水量，降水；降落，落下；沉淀（作用）
precursor n. 前体，先质
predation n. 捕食，捕食现象，掠食
preemergence adj. （植物种子）出土前的，出土前施用的
pregermination n. 发芽处理，催芽
premature n. 早熟
prepackage n. 事先做好的包装，出售前预先包装
preservation n. 保存，保藏，储藏，保持
presizing n. 预先筛分，填孔处理
presorting n. 预先分类，发货前清点
prevailing wind 主风，盛行风
profile n. 断面，剖面
progenitor n. 祖，祖先
proliferate v. 增生，增殖
propagation n. 繁殖；[物]传播
propagule n. 繁殖体
propensity n. 嗜好，习性
proportion n. 比例
protein molecule 蛋白质分子
protopectin n. 原果胶
protoplasm n. 原生质，原浆
prototype n. 原型，原型系统
pruner n. 修枝(根)剪
Prunus n. 李属
Pseudomonas fluorescens 荧光假单胞菌
Pseudomonas syringae 丁香假单胞菌
pseudostem n. 假茎（由叶鞘组成的茎）
psylla n. 木虱

pteridophyte　*n.* 蕨类植物，羊齿植物
pulverize　*vt.* 粉碎，研磨
pumpkin　*n.* 南瓜
purplish　*adj.* 略带紫色的
pustule　*n.* 脓疱
Pythium　*n.* [真菌]腐霉属

Q

quarantine　*n.* 检疫，隔离（期），检疫所；　*vt.* 对……进行检疫；对……进行隔离
quince　*n.* 榅桲，榅桲属(*Cydonia*)
quonset style structure　拱圆式结构

R

radicle　*n.* 胚根，幼根，根状部
railcar　*n.* 轨道车，动车，滑轨车
rain gauge　雨量测量器
rain shelter　（避）防雨棚
rainfall　*n.* 降雨，降雨量
rainwater　雨水
rambutan　*n.* 红毛丹
raspberry　*n.* 悬钩子(树)，木莓(树)，树莓
rationale　*n.* 基本原理
ratoon　*n.* 块茎芽，根蘖，宿根
ravage　*n.* 破坏，蹂躏；　*v.* 毁坏，破坏，掠夺
red spider mite　红蜘蛛，螨
red shouldered leaf beetle　花生红肩叶甲
redundant　*adj.* 多余的
reflection　*n.* 反射
refrigerating equipment　冷藏设备
refrigeration system　制冷系统
rehabilitate　*v.* 使复原，恢复，康复
rejuvenate　*v.* 复壮，使年轻，使恢复
relative humidity　相对湿度
replicase　*n.* 复制酶
reservoir　*n.* 贮液池，蓄水池
residual soil　残积土
respiration　*n.* 呼吸，呼吸作用，呼吸强度
respiration rate　呼吸速率
retail seller　零售商
reverse transcription PCR　反转录 RCR
rex begonia　*n.* 毛叶秋海棠
Rhizoctonia　*n.* [微]丝核菌属

rhizome　*n.* [植]根茎，根状茎，地下茎
rhizosphere　*n.* 根围，根际
Rhododendron　*n.* 杜鹃属
rhubarb　*n.* 大黄(蓼科)，食用大黄
rhythm　*n.* 节奏，韵律
ridge and furrow house　脊沟连跨的温室
rigorous　*adj.* 严格的，严厉的
ringing　*n.* 环剥，环割
RNAi (RNA interference)　RNA 干扰
roadside marketing　路边市场
rock garden　岩石庭院，假山花园
rockwool　*n.* 岩棉，岩棉纤维
roof pitch　屋面坡度
root cellar　地窖，储藏根用蔬菜的地窖
root cutting　根插
root pruning　剪根，切根修剪
root-knot nematodes　根结线虫
root-rot-susceptible　易感根腐病的
rootstock　*n.* 砧木
Rosaceae　*n.* 蔷薇科
rose apple　蒲桃
rotenone　*n.* 鱼藤酮[杀虫药]
rototiller　*n.* 旋转式耕耘机，旋转碎土器
Rubus　*n.* 悬钩子属，悬钩子
rust　*n.* 锈病

S

S-adenosyl methionine　腺苷蛋氨酸
salt accumulation　盐分积累，盐累积
salt-sensitive plant　盐度敏感植物
samara　*n.* 翅果，翼果
sanitation　*n.* 环境卫生
Sansevieria　*n.* [植]虎尾兰属
sap concentration　汁液浓缩，汁液浓度
sapote　*n.* 山榄果，白柿，白人心果、香肉果
sasanqua　*n.* 油茶
sawdust　*n.* 木屑
saxifraga　*n.* 虎耳草
scale　*n.* 比例，比例尺
scale insect　*n.* [昆]介壳虫
scaly skin　鳞状表皮
scientific name　学名
scion　*n.* 接穗

scion cultivar　嫁接品种，嫁接栽培品种
sculptor　n. 雕刻家
secondary forest　次生林
Sedum　n. 景天属植物
seed tapes and pelleting　种子包衣和丸粒化
seedless　adj. 无核的
seed-propagated　adj. 种子繁殖的，实生繁殖的
seed-reproduced plant　种子繁殖性植物
self-fertilization　n. 自体受精
self-incompatible　adj. 自交不亲和的，自交不孕的
self-pollinate　v. [植]自花传粉
semi-permeable membrane　半透膜
semi-woody plant　半木本植物
Senecio　n. 千里光属，千里光，狗舌草，瓜叶菊
senile　adj. 衰老的，高龄的
sensitive plant　[植]含羞草
sesquioxide　n. 倍半氧化物
sessile　adj. 固有的，固着的，无柄的
sexual reproduction　有性繁殖
shallow container　浅容器
shed roof　单坡屋顶，单面倾斜的屋顶
shelf-life　n. 货架期，货架寿命
short haul　短途运输
shortcut　n. 捷径
shrink film　收缩薄膜
shrub　n. 灌木，灌丛
side effect　副作用
simple layering　普通压条，单枝压条
sizing　n. 分级（根据大小）
slasher　n. 切碎器，茎秆剁碎机，锯木机
slice　vt. 把……切成薄片；n. 切开[下]片，薄片，切片
slimy　adj. 似黏液的，黏滑的
slip　n. 根出条，萌蘖枝，接枝，插枝；v. 分蘖
slug　n. 蛞蝓，鼻涕虫
smallholder　n. 小农，小农地主
smother grass　窒息草
snapdragon　n. 金鱼草
sodium　n. 钠
sodium hypochlorite　次氯酸钠
soft maple　糖槭，银槭
soil analysis　土壤分析

soil erosion　土壤侵蚀
soil fumigation　土壤熏蒸
soil-borne　adj. 土壤带有的；土壤传播的
soil-borne disease　土传病害
Solanaceae　n. 茄科
solar altitude　太阳高度角
solar radiation　太阳辐射，日射
solar transmittance　太阳能透射率
somaclonal variation　体细胞克隆变异，体细胞无性系变异
somatic cell　体细胞
sorting　n. 分等
soursop　n. 刺果酸荔枝
southern hybridization　南方氏杂交法，南方杂交分析
space　n. 空间，间隔
specific name　种名
specimen　n. 样本，标本
specimen plant　标本植物，园景植物，孤植植物
spectrophotometer　n. 分光光度计
sphagnum　n. 冰苔，水藓
sphagnum peat moss　泥炭藓
spider plant　[植]吊兰
spiny adj. 长满刺的；多刺的，带刺的
spiral　n. 旋涡，螺旋形之物　adj. 螺旋形的，盘旋的
spirea　n. 绣线菊，绣线菊类的植物
spoilage　n. 变质，酸败，腐败
spore　n. （细菌、苔藓、蕨类植物）孢子
sportak　n. 一种新型咪唑类广谱杀菌剂
spot or plug sodding　斑点，斑块
sprig　n. 小枝，繁殖段
spruce　n. 云杉
spurge　n. 大戟
squash　n. 南瓜，倭瓜，笋瓜，西葫芦
stamen　n. 雄蕊
staminate　adj. 雄蕊的，有雄蕊的，只有雄蕊的
star apple　金星果，星苹果
starch　n. 淀粉；v. 给……上浆
static　n. 静态，静止；adj. 静态的
Statice　n. [植]匙叶草属植物
statue　n. 塑像，雕像
steel-frame greenhouse　钢骨架温室

stem cutting 枝插
sterilisation *n.* 消毒
sterility *n.* 不育
sterilize *v.* 杀菌
stigma *n.* 柱头
stimulant *n.* 刺激物，激励物
stipule *n.* 托叶
stock *n.* 砧木
stolon *n.* 匍匐枝，芽茎走根
stomata *n.* 气孔
stone fruit ［植］核果类果树，核果类
stored carbohydrate 贮藏的碳水化合物
strawflower *n.* 麦秆菊，蜡菊，贝细工
strawberry *n.* 草莓
streaky *adj.* 有斑点的，有条纹的
strip sodding 条状草地，带状草地
styrofoam *n.* 泡沫，聚苯乙烯
subculture *n.* 继代培养；次培养基；次培养菌；
　　　　v. 次培养的
suberin *n.* ［生化］软木脂
subordinate *n.* 隶属，下属；*adj.* 下级的
subtropical fruit 亚热带果树
succulent *n.* 肉质植物
sucker *n.* （植物的）吸芽，根蘖，根出条
sucrose *n.* 蔗糖
sugarbeet *n.* 糖用甜菜
sulfur *n.* 硫磺，硫
summer pruning 夏剪
sunburn *n.* 日伤，晒斑，晒伤
supplemental lighting 补光
surinam cherry 苏里南樱桃，毕当茄，红果仔
susceptible *adj.* 易受影响的，过敏的，易感染的
suspension culture 悬浮培养
sweet corn 甜玉米
sweet pea ［植］香豌豆，麝香豌豆花
sweet william ［植］美洲石竹，美人草，须苞石竹
symbiotic *adj.* 共生的
sympodial *adj.* ［植］合轴的
synchronize *v.* 同步，同时发生

T

Tachigaren *n.* 土菌消
Taenia solium 猪肉绦虫（学名）

tangerine *n.* 柑橘，橘子
tannin compound 单宁类化合物
tap water 自来水
taproot *n.* （植物的）主根，直根
taxonomist *n.* 分类学家
taxonomy *n.* 分类，分类学，分类法
TBZ {N/2}-特-丁基-{N/4}-乙基-6-甲硫基-1,3,
　　5-三嗪-2,4 二胺
temperate fruit 温带水果
tendril *n.* 卷须，蔓
tensiometer *n.* 张力计,（流体）压强计
tephritid fruit fly 实蝇科
terminology *n.* 术语，专用术语，术语学
terpene *n.* 萜烯，萜(烃)，松烯
terrace *n.* 梯田
terrestrial plant 陆生植物
texture *n.* 组织，结构，肌理，特征
texture triangle 土壤结构三角图
thallophyte *n.* 原植体植物，叶状体植物，菌藻
　　　植物
thatch *n.* （作物下地面上的）杂草，茅草
the Uniform Building Code standards 统一的建筑
　　　规范标准
therapeutic *adj.* 治疗的
thiabendazole *n.* 涕必灵，噻苯咪唑
thinning *n.* 疏剪，间苗，疏苗
thinning-out 疏剪
thiram *n.* ［药］二硫四甲秋兰姆，福美双，双硫胺
　　　甲酰(杀菌药)
thorn *n.* 带刺小灌木，荆棘
three-dimensional *adj.* 三维的，立体的
threshold value 极限值，域值
thrip *n.* 蓟马
thrips *n.* 牧草虫
thrive *vi.* 兴盛，兴隆
thunderstorm *n.* 雷暴
tilth *n.* 耕种，耕作(深度)，翻耕
tinned fruit 水果罐头
tip layering 顶压条，先端压条开沟压条
tissue culture 组织培养，组培
tobacco *n.* 烟草
tomato mosaic virus 番茄花叶病毒
topography *n.* 地形(势)，地形学，地形测量学

top-root ratio 根冠比
topsoil structure 表层土壤结构
totipotency n. (细胞的)全能性
toxic adj. 有毒的
tracheid n. 管胞(木材学词汇),木材的管胞
tractor-trailer 拖拉机挂车
trailer n. 挂车,拖车
transgenic adj. 转基因的,基因改造的
translucent adj. 半透明的
transpiration n. 蒸腾,蒸腾速率
transplant v. 移植,移栽
tree architecture 树形
trellis training 棚架式整枝
trench layering 沟槽式压条,开沟压条法
trim n. 整齐,装饰,修剪; adj. 整齐的; v. 整理,修剪
triple and quadruple layer covering 三、四层覆盖
Tropic of Cancer 北回归线
Tropic of Capricorn 南回归线
true to type 典型的,纯种的
tube culture 管道栽培
tuber n. 块茎
tulip n. 郁金香
tunic n. 鳞茎皮,膜皮
turbulence n. 紊流,湍流
turgidity n. 膨胀
turpentine n. 松节油
twig girdler 环蛀蝙蛾(旋皮虫)
typhoon n. 台风

U

Ultisol n. 老成土(在美国土壤分类学中的,是高度风化和淋溶的一种黄色至红色的土壤)
ultraviolet ray permeability 紫外线透过性
Umbelliferae n. 伞形科,伞形花序植物
unconsolidated adj. 松散的
undercooled adj. 过冷却的
underdesigned adj. 设计安全系数不足的
uniform grade 均匀坡度
uniform temperature 恒温
unity n. 统一性,一致性,统一体
unwoven fabric 无纺布
urea n. 尿素

urethane mat 聚氨酯垫
USDA 美国农业部

V

vaccine n. 疫苗
vacuum cooling 真空冷却,真空预冷,真空制冷
vacuum pack 真空包装(品)
vanda n. 万代兰
Vapam n. 威百亩(杀菌,杀线虫剂)
variability n. 变异性,变异,变异度
vascular n. 导管
vascular system 维管系统
vegetative growth 营养生长
vegetative propagation 无性繁殖,营养繁殖
Venlo type glasshouse 芬洛型温室
ventilation n. 通风
ventilation system 通风系统
ventilator n. 通风设备,通风装置
vermiculite n. 蛭石
vertical adj. 垂直的; n. 垂直线
Verticillium n. 轮枝孢属,轮生菌属
Vertisol n. (土壤学用语)变性土,转化土
Viburnum n. 荚蒾属植物
vine n. 攀爬植物,藤,蔓
vinylon n. 维尼纶(聚乙烯醇纤维)
viroid n. 类病毒
volcanic lava 熔岩,火山岩

W

walnut n. 胡桃
warm air heating 热风供暖
water conduction 水分传导,水分输导,导水
water curtain 水幕
water deficit 水分亏缺
water drainage 排水
water stress 水分胁迫
water table 地下水位
water-logged adj. 浸透水的,半淹没的,沼泽化的
waterproof adj. 不透水的,防水的; v. 使防水
wax myrtle 杨梅,杨梅属的植物
waxing n. 涂蜡,打蜡
weatherproof greenhouse 耐候温室

weevil n. （香蕉）假茎象甲
well water 井水
well-adapted seed 适应性强的种子
wholesaler n. 批发商
wind belt 风带
wind velocity 风速，风力
windbreak n. 防风林带，防风障
winter injury 冻害
wireworm n. 线虫
woody perennials 木本多年生植物
woody plant 木本植物

X

xylem n. 木质部

Y

Yamazaki's nutrient solution formula 山崎营养液配方

Z

Zimbabwe n. 津巴布韦，津巴布韦人
zinc n. 锌
zonal adj. 带状的
Zoysia n. 结缕草属
Zygocactus n. [植]蟹爪兰属
zygote n. 合子，受精卵

β-glucuronidase n. 葡萄糖醛酸苷酶